SHAKESPEARIAN AND OTHER ESSAYS

SHAKESPEARIAN AND OTHER ESSAYS

JAMES SMITH

Emeritus Professor of English Language and Literature
University of Fribourg, Switzerland

CAMBRIDGE UNIVERSITY PRESS

Published by the Syndics of the Cambridge University Press
Bentley House, 200 Euston Road, London NW1 2DB
American Branch: 32 East 57th Street, New York, N.Y. 10022

© Cambridge University Press 1974

Library of Congress Catalogue Card Number: 73–83110

ISBN: 0 521 20373 2

First published 1974

Printed in Great Britain
at the University Printing House, Cambridge
(Brooke Crutchley, University Printer)

CONTENTS

PREFATORY NOTE

This book contains a selection of James Smith's published essays, together with such additional studies of Shakespeare's comedies as were to be found after his death. The published essays from *Scrutiny* and the review from *The Criterion* of Professor William Empson's first book are reprinted with very few corrections. The unpublished studies required a considerable labour of collation and of deciphering; for the most part they consisted of carbon copies, copiously emended in long hand and occasionally by handwritten inserted leaves that were very difficult to read. Where I have felt uncertain of my interpretations I have enclosed doubtful words and phrases in square brackets. Some evidence about the dates of composition of the unprinted essays will be found in the memoir of James Smith at the end of the book. The footnotes added by me are initialled E. M. W.; the others are Smith's own.

I must thank Sir Geoffrey Keynes and Dr Philip McNair for their kindness in helping me to check one quotation from Donne and two from *Il Paradiso*. I must also thank Mr Michael Black for his support, encouragement and criticism in a task perhaps too rashly undertaken.   EDWARD M. WILSON

1

AS YOU LIKE IT[1]

It is a commonplace that Jaques and Hamlet are akin. But it is also a commonplace that Jaques is an intruder into *As You Like It,* so that in spite of the kinship the plays are not usually held to have much connection. I have begun to doubt whether not only *As You Like It* and *Hamlet,* but almost all the comedies and the tragedies as a whole are not closely connected, and in a way which may be quite important.

Recent criticism of Shakespeare has directed itself with profit upon the tragedies, the 'problem plays' and certain of the histories. The early comedies, on the other hand, have either been disparaged or entirely overlooked. Yet the same criticism owes part of its success to a notion of what it calls Shakespeare's 'integrity'; his manifold interests, it has maintained, being co-ordinated so as rarely to thwart, regularly to strengthen, one another. Hence he was alert and active as few have been, while his writing commanded not part but the whole of his resources.

Such a notion seems sound and proves useful. Belief in an author's integrity, however, ought to forbid the dismissal of any part of his work, at least its hasty dismissal. The comedies, to which he gave a number of years of his life, are no insignificant part of Shakespeare's. If it is true that they shed no light on the tragedies nor the tragedies on them, it would seem he deserves credit for a unique dissipation rather than concentration of his powers.

It is of course comprehensible that the comedies should be shunned. To some readers they are less inviting than the tragedies, to all they are more wearisome when their study is begun. Not only are the texts in a state of comparative impurity, the form itself is impure. Being less serious than tragedy – this I am aware is disputed, but would suggest that the word has a number of meanings – being less serious than tragedy, comedy admits of interludes and sideshows; further, the material for the sideshows is not infrequently such that it might be

[1] The substance of a paper read to the Cambridge English Club.

material for the comedy itself. Decision is important but not always easy whether or not it should be disregarded.

The desultory nature of the following notes may, I hope, be forgiven, partly because of complications such as these, partly because of contemporary distractions which leave no time for elaboration. I start with Jaques's melancholy, in respect of which alone he has been likened to Hamlet.

It is, I think, most accessible to study in his encounter with Rosalind at the beginning of Act IV. Having abundant leisure he needs a companion to while it away. 'I prethee, pretty youth', he says, 'let me be better acquainted with thee.' But Rosalind, who has heard unfavourable reports, is by no means eager to comply: 'They say you are a melancholy fellow.' As for that, replies Jaques, his melancholy is at least sincere, for it is as pleasing to him as jollity to other men: 'I doe love it better then laughing.' But sincerity is irrelevant unless to deepen his offence. As there is an excess of laughter so there is of sadness which should not be pleasing to anybody:

Those that are in extremity of either, are abhominable fellowes, and betray themselves to every moderne censure, worse then drunkards.

The rebuke is no more than a rebuke of common sense. Your melancholy, objects Rosalind, is not justifiable merely because it is your melancholy, for it may be one of the things which, though they exist, ought not to do so. But the rebuke is none the less pertinent, common sense implying a minimum of alertness and Jaques being afflicted with languor. Either as cause or as consequence of his state he is blind and fails to see, or is stupid and fails to ponder obvious truths.

The force of the rebuke is to be noticed. From Shakespeare, mediaeval rather than modern in this as other matters, drunkards receive no more than temporary tolerance: Falstaff is in the end cast off, Sir Toby beat about the coxcomb. And the respect which they receive is not even temporary. Wine and wassail make

> Memorie, the Warder of the Braine
> . . . a Fume, and the Receit of Reason
> A Lymbeck only;

the sleep they produce is 'swinish', by them nature is 'drenched'. A drunkard as such forfeits not only his manhood but his humanity. Nor does Rosalind's 'modern' mean what the word does now, 'modish' or what has been invented of late. Rather it is that which has always been the mode, and which stands plain to reason so that there never was need to invent it. In this play for example the justice is described as

Full of wise sawes and moderne instances

– of instances which belong to proverbial wisdom, apt and sound so that they have become trite. What Rosalind is saying is that Jaques by his melancholy is turned into a beast, and that an old woman would be less ignorant, less pitiable than he.

Taken aback, for the moment he can think of nothing but to reaffirm his liking: 'Why, 'tis good to be sad and say nothing.' Crudely however, so that he lays himself open to the crude retort: 'Why then, 'tis good to be a poste.' And it would seem to be this which finally rouses him to a defence.

His melancholy, he begins, is not like others Rosalind has heard of:

I have neither the Schollers melancholy, which is emulation: nor the Musitians, which is fantasticall; nor the Courtiers, which is proud; nor the Souldiers, which is ambitious...

and so on. Jaques's melancholy has its source not in private hopes, anxieties and disappointments but in what is of wider importance as it is in the world outside. 'It is a melancholy', he continues, 'of mine owne' – one that is which he is the first to discover – 'compounded of many simples, extracted from many objects.' Or in other words it is 'the sundrie contemplation of my travells, in which (m)y often rumination wraps me in a most humorous sadnesse'.

Jaques's meaning may not be quite clear, and I do not think it is or can be, but his intention would seem to be so. By boasting of originality, breadth and freshness of information he hopes to impress, perhaps to intimidate, the youthful Rosalind. But she mistakes, and I suspect purposely, his drift: as she is intelligent enough to distrust originality, she is subtle enough to challenge it in this way. Seizing on the word 'travels' she exclaims:

A traveller: by my faith you have great reason to be sad; I feare you have sold your owne lands, to see other mens; then to have seene much, and to have nothing, is to have rich eyes and poore hands.

She ventures after all, that is, to assimilate his melancholy to other people's, suggesting that it may be due to poverty, which is a private anxiety. But Jaques rejects with scorn the notion that his travels have on a balance brought him anything but profit: 'I have gain'd', he insists, 'my experience.' Once more he is implying that something, because it exists, has a title to do so; that his experience, as it has been gained, was necessarily worth the gaining. Once more therefore, and if possible more vigorously this time, she appeals to common sense for his condemnation. Whatever profit he imagines he has brought back from his travels, there is something which the merest stay-at-home could tell him is a loss:

Jaques. I have gain'd my experience.
Rosalind. And your experience makes you sad: I had rather have a foole to make me merrie, then experience to make me sad, and to travaile for it too.

Whether or not Rosalind is aware of it, this second rebuke is of peculiar force as addressed to Jaques. Of all the characters it is he alone who, in previous scenes, has expressed complete satisfaction in the company of Touchstone, the fool. He has gone even further, and claimed that nowhere but in folly ought satisfaction to be found:

> Oh noble foole,
> A worthy foole: Motley's the onely weare...
> ...O that I were a foole,
> I am ambitious for a motley coat.

Yet now he has to be reminded that there is an office which fools can perform. About his conduct it seems there is a grave inconsistency, for at one time he countenances factitious gaiety, at another equally factitious gloom.

If it stood alone, such an inconsistency might be puzzling; but it has a companion, which also serves to explain it. In claiming in his interchange with Rosalind that all experience is worth while, Jaques is claiming in effect that no experience is worth anything at all. In asserting that, in the present, there are no reasons why he should do one thing rather than another – why, for example, he should be merry rather than mope – he is shutting his eyes to reasons why, in the future, one thing rather than another should be done. In other words he is posing as a sceptic, and scepticism is an inconsistent doctrine. Though a belief itself, it denies the possibility of belief; it denies to man the possibility of action, though by his nature he cannot refrain from acting. And it is because Jaques, in his more alert moments, is aware of this second inconsistency that he commits the first. He seeks shelter in the motley to persuade himself that though he acts and cannot help doing so, he nevertheless does nothing. For if his actions are mere folly they are of no account, and as good as nothing at all.

It is however only at rare moments, as for example when stirred by a first meeting with Touchstone, that Jaques is alert. For the greater part of his time he is characterized by the languor already referred to: which keeps him from making sustained efforts, even that which (as he is not wholly unintelligent) being a fool requires. Instead of concerning himself to justify his scepticism, he quietly submits to it; and his submission is his melancholy, his 'sadness.' A man in whose eyes the world contains nothing of value, cannot be spurred to action either by the sight of objects he wishes to obtain, or by the thought of ideals he hopes to realize. The only action open to him – and as he is human, he cannot remain wholly inert – no more than half deserves the name, for in it he is as much passive as active. He needs, so to speak, to be betrayed into action – to be propelled into it from behind, by agencies of which he is not completely aware. Such agencies are the mechanism of habit, or a conspiracy of circumstance. In comedy where characters are not relentlessly harassed by circumstance, they are able continually to yield to habit.

The travels to which Jaques refers the origin of his scepticism are equally likely to have been its consequence, for travel and exploration degenerate into habit. When the senses are dazzled by a ceaseless and rapid change of objects, the intellect has no time to discriminate between them, the will no occasion for choice, so that in the end a man becomes capable of neither. The habit is then a necessity to life, which at the same time and to the same extent has slackened, become languid. It concerns itself only with the surface of objects while their substance is neglected. Jaques's decision in Act V proceeds from a habit of this kind:

> The Duke hath put on a Religious life...
> To him will I.

His pretext is that

> out of these convertites
> There is much matter to be heard, and learn'd.

But his reason, rather than to learn, is to avoid learning. He quits the court for the monastery much as amateur students, threatened with the labour of mastering a subject, abandon it for the preliminaries of another – usually as different as possible. If during the course of the play Jaques does not engage on travel, it should be remembered that he frequently changes, not his surroundings, but his interlocutor. He indulges the habit of gossip, which is that of a traveller immobilized. That he has abundant leisure for gossip is only natural: time hangs heavy on a sceptic's hands, for whom the world contains nothing that can take it off.

It hangs heavy on Hamlet's, and this is the most obvious point of resemblance between him and Jaques. 'I have of late', Hamlet complains, 'lost all my mirth, forgone all custome of exercise'; and he goes on to give general reasons. They imply scepticism of a kind: the earth and sky, he says, seem but a 'foule and pestilent congregation of vapours', such as do not encourage enterprise: man himself has come to appear but the 'Quintessence of dust', with whom he would not willingly have commerce. In the same way, to refer to another tragedy, time hangs heavy on Macbeth's hands, at least as he draws near his end. Neither sight nor sound can rouse his interest, nor could it be roused by any conceivable sight or sound. He finds himself incapable of believing in the reality even of his wife's death: the report of it, he suggests, should be kept from him until tomorrow. But at the same time he knows that tomorrow will find him as insensible, as incredulous as today.

Scepticism of a kind: but it is immediately obvious that Hamlet speaks with a disgust or an impatience, Macbeth with a weariness, which to Jaques are unknown. Even in this matter in which alone they are similar, their dissimilarity is yet greater. Anticipating a little, it might be said that Macbeth and Hamlet lead a fuller, a more complete life than Jaques; they are, that is, more conscious of themselves, and rather than languid are continuously, perhaps, feverishly alert.

One consequence is that they cannot easily be betrayed into action. Whereas Jaques looks back without regret, even with complacency on his travels, it is only with reluctance that Macbeth lapses into the habit of fighting for fighting's sake:

> Why should I play the Roman Foole, and dye
> On mine owne sword? whiles I see lives, the gashes
> Do better upon them.

Sentiment and rhythm are flat to extinction, Macbeth is speaking sullenly. What he is about to do may be better than nothing, it is all he can do; nevertheless it is no more than might be done by a common bully, by an animal. For them it might be a full life; for himself, Macbeth admits, it can be no more than the slackened half-life of habit. Similarly the 'custome of exercise' and all customs have lost their hold on Hamlet; for him to act he needs to be surprised by extraordinary circumstance.

Nevertheless, as has been said, neither he nor Macbeth is idle. The energy which their state of mind forbids they should employ on the world, they employ on the state of mind itself; so that not only the inconsistency, the evil (what Rosalind meant by the 'beastliness') of scepticism is continually before them. They see it is not the solution to a problem, but rather a problem which presses to be solved; not the tempering of feeling and the invigoration of thought, but the denial of both. They not only reject Jaques's flight into folly, which was to preserve scepticism; they agonize over the sort of reflections with which, in both languid and alert moments, Jaques is lulled. 'And all our yesterdayes', exclaims Macbeth in despair at what forces itself upon him as the nothingness of man,

> And all our yesterdayes have lighted Fooles
> The way to dusty death;

''tis but an hour agoe', observes Jaques with satisfaction,

> 'Tis but an hour agoe, since it was nine,
> And after one houre more, 'twill be eleven,
> And so from houre to houre, we ripe, and ripe,
> And then from houre to houre, we rot, and rot...

or rather Touchstone observes this, from whom Jaques is quoting. Touchstone is by profession and conviction a fool, the seriousness of whose statements will come up for consideration later; Jaques is as little serious as, in a quotation, it is possible to be. He is echoing more sound than sense; the latter he has not plumbed (the movement, the rhythm show it), and the statement he has made no more than half his own – fitting accompaniment and expression of a half-life of habit. Elsewhere he compares human life to a theatrical performance as though, in harmony with his scepticism, to stress its unreality; but very soon, in harmony with his languor, the theatre begins to appear a substantial, for all he cares a permanent, structure. Performances in it last a long time, so that it is possible to make a full display of talent:

> one man in his time playes many parts,
> His Acts being seven ages.

And then Jaques recites the ages, diverting himself with objects separated on this occasion not in space but in time. When the same comparison occurs to Macbeth he is so overwhelmed with the notion of unreality that he does not allow even the actor to act: the latter 'struts and frets...upon the Stage', struts and frets not for a full performance but only for 'his houre...and then is heard no more.' In Macbeth's verse the comparison flares up and extinguishes itself in indignation at what it implies of man's lot:

> It is a Tale
> Told by an Ideot, full of sound and fury
> Signifying nothing.

That of Jaques continues to demean itself elegantly even when describing in detail man's end

> Sans teeth, sans eyes, sans taste, sans everything.

Once again the rhythm and the movement show that Jaques is meaning little of what he says; that a true traveller once more, he is occupied with the surface only, not the substance of objects before him.

If I may look aside or ahead for a moment, I would venture to suggest that the essential difference between comedy and tragedy may perhaps be this sort of difference: not one of kind, I mean, but of degree. As far as I can see it is possible and even probable that tragedy and comedy – Shakespearian comedy at any rate – treat of the same problems, comedy doing so (to repeat the word) less seriously. And by 'less seriously', I may now explain, I mean that the problems are not forced to an issue: a lucky happening, a lucky trait of character (or what for the purposes of the play appears lucky) allowing them to be evaded. As, for example, conditions in Arden and conditions of his own temper preserve Jaques from fully realizing the nature and consequences of his scepticism: to Rosalind, to the reader, it is obvious that his interests are restricted, his vigour lessened, but he is never put to the test. Hamlet, on the other hand, in a similar spiritual state, is called upon to avenge a father, foil an uncle and govern a kingdom. And when at last chance forces him into action it is not only that he may slaughter but also that he may be slaughtered: in other words, not that in spite of his disability he may achieve his end, but that because of it he may fail. In *Othello* hardly an accident happens which does not lend plausibility to Iago's deceit, so that the problem posed by human malice on the one hand, human ignorance on the other, cannot but be faced; in *Much Ado* there is a final accident – and a very obvious one, for its name is Dogberry – which unmasks Don John. In *Lear* accident of the wildest form unites with malice and with the elements to convince a human being of his imbecility; in *The Winter's Tale* accident equally wild serves to hide that imbecility, if not from Leontes (who is however encouraged to forget it) at least from Florizel. In comedy the materials for tragedy are procured, in some cases heaped up; but they are not, so to speak, attended to, certainly not closely examined. And so what might have caused grief causes only a smile, or at worst a grimace.

I apologize for speculations of this kind, which can only remain gratuitous until it is known more exactly what comedy, more especially what *As You Like It*, is about. At least one other resemblance, possibly an important one, between it and the tragedies, calls, I think, for attention. As Hamlet's melancholy is caused by the sin of others and Macbeth's by sin of his own, so Jaques – if the Duke is to be trusted – has not only travelled but been

> a Libertine,
> As sensuall as the brutish sting itself.

And the cure for all three, according to each of the three plays, is very much the same. Fortinbras reproaches Hamlet, and Hamlet reproaches himself, with lacking a 'hue of resolution' which, as it is 'native', it is a defect he should not possess; Macbeth contrasts the division of counsels within him, suspending activity, with the strong monarchy or 'single state' enjoyed in the healthy man by the reason. Similarly Rosalind confronts Jaques with the desirability of what she calls merriment or mirth: from her remark already quoted it is obvious she does not mean laughter, not at any rate laughter without measure, and therefore not laughter in the first place. For the confusion of Jaques it is necessary she should speak emphatically; in a conversation which irks her she is to be excused if she is brief. Were the occasion other, or were she given to reflection, she might perhaps describe this 'mirth' more closely – as something similar to her own 'alertness' which has already drawn attention: the prerequisite of common sense, and what in more recent times, according to the sympathies and perspicacity of the speaker, has been known either as 'vitality' or 'faith'. The meaning of 'mirth' in fifteenth- and sixteenth-century devotional books should be borne in mind, and its meaning on the lips of, say, St Thomas More. Hamlet, it will be remembered, noted as first among his distressing symptoms that he had 'lost all his mirth'.

This scene at the beginning of Act IV sheds light, I do not think it would be too much to claim, on all that Jaques says or does. If so it is important to a not inconsiderable part of the play, and in that at least Jaques cannot be an intruder. For his quips and monologues, however loose in their immediate context, have a dependence on this dialogue to which he is indispensable. He is so not only by what he says, but also by what he causes to be said to him. I am going to suggest that, in spite of the familiar verdict, he is no more of an intruder anywhere. For the rest of the play consists largely of situations which, if he is taken as primary melancholic, might be described as modelled on that in which he finds himself with Rosalind. Either she or a temporary ally or deputy of hers – frequently Corin the Old Shepherd – faces and condemns a succession of characters who, like Jaques, are incapable of or indisposed to action. Silvius, Touchstone, Orlando, the Duke, each has a melancholy of his own; and so too has Rosalind, in so far as she is in love with Orlando. But not even that escapes her judgment, since she can judge it disguised as someone other than herself. Add that the minor characters occasionally condemn or at least reprove one another, and it is possible to gain some notion of the pattern which Shakespeare seems to have intended for *As You Like It*. A single *motif* is repeated, giving unity to the whole; but at the same time it varies continually, so that the whole is complex.

Such I think was Shakespeare's intended pattern: unfortunately it has been either obscured by revision, or incomplete revision has failed to impress it clearly on the play. The theory of the New Cambridge editors must no doubt be accepted, that there are at least two strata of text, an early and a late. This is a difficulty of the kind referred to, that a student must expect from textual impurities in a comedy. But certain portions of the pattern are sufficiently clear to give, to a careful reader, some idea of the whole.

Take for example the relations obtaining between the Old Shepherd on the one hand, and Jaques and Touchstone on the other. The latter has been much sentimentalized, partly because of his wit, partly because of a supposed loyalty to Celia. But his wit has been treated as though it were a mere interlude, a diversion for the reader as well as for the Duke; whereas little else would seem more closely knit into the play. And as will be suggested, this is the reverse of sentimental. As for Touchstone's loyalty, it would seem to be mentioned only in Celia's line,

> He'll go along o'er the wide world with mee.

It may have had importance in an earlier version, but in that which has survived Shakespeare is no more concerned with how the characters arrive in Arden – whether under Touchstone's convoy or not – than how they are extricated from it. Touchstone's loyalty is about as interesting to him, and should be as interesting to the reader, as Oliver's green and gold snake.

What is interesting is a disingenuous reply which Touchstone gives to the question: 'And how like you this shepherds life?' He pretends to make distinctions where it is impossible there should be any:

Truely...in respect of it selfe, it is a good life; but in respect that it is a shepheards life, it is naught. In respect that it is solitary, I like it verie well: but in respect that it is private, it is a very vile life.

A shepherd's life, no more than other things, can be distinguished from itself, nor can what is solitary be other than private. What Touchstone is saying is that he neither likes nor dislikes the shepherd's life, while at the same time he does both; or in other words, that towards the shepherd's life he has no feelings whatever. And in truth towards all things if not quite all, Touchstone is as apathetic as Jaques. He too has his melancholy,

11

as has been said: and naturally resembling Jaques more than Hamlet or Macbeth, he too accepts distraction from a habit. It is not the ceaseless search for novelty or gossip, but what he calls 'philosophy' or the barren intercourse of a mind with itself. He multiplies distinctions like the above, or pursues similarities based solely on sound or letter, neglecting the meaning of a word. The result is scepticism in a very practical sense, such as unchecked would destroy language and all possibility of thought. Even the old Shepherd is not slow to realize this, for his sole reply to the blunt question, 'Has't any Philosophie in thee?' is to recite a number of obvious truths:

I know the more one sickens, the worse at ease he is: and that hee that wants money, meanes, and content, is without three good friends. That the propertie of raine is to wet, and fire to burne

and so on. However obvious, they are at least truths, at least significant; and he concludes:

hee that hath learned no wit by Nature, nor Art, may complaine of dull breeding, or comes of a very dull kindred.

In other words: he who cannot behave in a more responsible way than Touchstone is an idiot. But 'idiot is what I mean by a philosopher' –

Such a one is a naturall philosopher

rejoins Touchstone, indifferent enough to his diversion not to claim that it is more than it is.

He proceeds to indulge in it at length. The Shepherd he says is damned because he has not been to Court, Court manners being good and what is not good being wicked. Too patiently the Shepherd replies with a distinction which, as it is he and not Touchstone makes it, is of primary importance:

those that are good manners at the Court, are as ridiculous in the Countrey, as the behaviour of the Countrie is most mockeable at the Court.

But this is brushed aside, and Touchstone emphasizes his perversity by changing the order in which court and country are ranked. Henceforward, he decrees, they shall be on a level, or rather the court shall be the more wicked. In despair the Shepherd retires from a conversation in which words, as they have so variable a meaning, have as good as no meaning at all:

You have too Courtly a wit, for mee, Ile rest.

Had he said 'too philosophical a wit' his point might have been more immediately clear; but for him no doubt as for Touchstone, court and 'philosophy' are closely allied.

To justify himself he adds the following description:

Sir, I am a true Labourer, I earne that I eate: get that I weare: owe no man hate, envie no mans happinesse; glad of other mens good (,) content with my harme: and the greatest of my pride, is to see my Ewes graze, and my Lambes sucke.

Of himself, that is, he claims to go about his own affairs, and to go about them with the mirth or minimum of serenity demanded by Rosalind. He has no need of 'incision' – whatever that may mean – or of any other remedy to conduct himself like an adult being; whereas Touchstone who suggests the remedy has at the moment no affairs, appears to be able to conceive of no affairs to go about at all.

For Shepherd and audience the conversation is over. To them it seems that Touchstone is defeated beyond recovery; not how-ever to Touchstone himself. He insists on adding a last word, and in doing so hints at one of the things to which he is not yet wholly indifferent, in respect of which therefore he parts com-pany with Jaques. Mention of ewes and sucking lambs spurs him on to the following:

That is another simple sinne in you, to bring the Ewes and the Rammes together, and to offer to get your living by the copulation of Cattle, to be bawd to a Belwether, and to betray a shee-Lambe of a twelvemonth to a crooked-pated olde Cuckoldly Ramme, out of all reasonable match. If thou bee'st not damn'd for this, the divell himselfe will have no shepherds, I cannot see how else thou shouldst escape.

About this there are two things to be noticed: first that it is nasty, and secondly that it is the nastier because it falls outside the conversation. Touchstone is no longer endeavouring to prove anything about country and court, whether sound or fantastic: he assimilates the sexual life of men to that of beasts solely because it seems of itself worth while to do so. Yet this should not cause surprise: if in this passage he appears to exalt the latter, elsewhere in deeds as well as words he is diligent to degrade the former.

Upon their first arrival in Arden, when he and Rosalind over-hear Silvius's complaint, Rosalind sighs:

> *Jove, Jove,* this Shepherds passion
> Is much upon my fashion.

'And mine', exclaims Touchstone, adding however immediately, 'but it growes something stale with mee.' That is, he is impatient of the elaborations and accretions received by the sexual desire, when a persistent subject in an otherwise healthy mind. His next appearance is as the wooer of Audrey, a country wench who thanks the gods that she is 'foul', and whom no elaborations have been necessary to win. Her desire to be a 'woman of the world', in other words a married woman, is ingenuous and no more a secret from Touchstone than from anyone else.

It is by no means to her discredit, nor would it be to Touchstone's if gratifying her desire, he thereby eased his own and was thankful. But the opposite is true. He is neither eased, nor does he spare an occasion, public or private, of pouring ridicule on the ingenuousness of which he has taken advantage. It is as though, aware that he can no longer hope for desire to be restrained, he sought to humiliate it with the least attractive object; then proceeded to revenge himself upon the object for his own lack of restraint. Audrey protests that she is 'honest' or chaste; but that, he answers, has had no share in drawing his attentions:

Audrey. Would you not have me honest?
Touchstone. No truly, unless thou wert hard favour'd...
Audrey. Well, I am not faire, and therefore I pray the Gods make me honest.
Touchestone. Truly, and to cast away honesty upon a foule slut, were to put good meate in an uncleane dish...But be it, as it may bee, I wil marrie thee.

To a large extent this conversation, like most of Touchstone's, is mere playing with words; but in so far as it has any meaning, it is that the word 'honesty' deserves only to be played with. And when at last he brings himself to mention honesty with an air of seriousness, it is not that she but that he himself may be praised:

a poore virgin sir, an il-favor'd thing sir, but mine owne, a poore humour of mine sir, to take that that no man else will: rich honestie dwels like a miser sir, in a poore house, as your Pearle in your foule oyster.

He is presenting her to the Duke as his intended; and since her exterior has nothing to explain his choice, hints that an explanation is to be found within. That is, he is claiming for himself the credit due to perspicacity.

Unfortunately he puts forward at the same time a claim to modesty, thus showing with how little seriousness he is continuing to speak. Did he value honesty at all, he would not represent the choice of it as a sacrifice: nor would he describe Audrey its exemplar as a 'poor thing'. His modesty, it should further be noticed, itself suggests confusion or deceit, for not only does it permit of advertisement, it is advertised not at Touchstone's expense but at someone else's. He does not in one respect decry himself so that he may be exalted in another; rather in order to exalt himself he decries his future wife. The first would in any case be tiresome, as is all inverted vanity; but the second, as a hypocritical form of selfishness, is contemptible.

Given that Touchstone is a man of sense, a performance like this can be due only to his attempting two things at once, and two things not very compatible one with another. As usual he is seeking to ridicule Audrey; but at the same time, I think, to recommend himself to the Duke. While sharing all Jaques's objections to purposeful activity he is without Jaques's income: he must provide himself with a living or must starve. And scepticism and melancholy being essentially unnatural, no one starves for their sake. At Touchstone's entry on the stage it was hinted that the Duke might be willing to appoint a jester:

Good my Lord, bid him welcome: This is the Motley-minded Gentleman, that I have so often met in the Forrest: he hath bin a Courtier he sweares ...Good my Lord, like this fellow.

And the Duke is well known to be, in Jaques's word, 'disputatious'. It is solely to please him that Touchstone, among his other preoccupations, does what he can to handle the notions 'honesty' and 'modesty'; were he speaking to a crony or to himself they would not enter his head, no more than the Euphuistic apologue about oysters with which he ends.

A similar reason is to be advanced for his string of Court witticisms which follow, about the causes of a quarrel and the degrees of a lie. So long as to be tiresome, the modern reader is tempted to dismiss it as an interlude; it is not however wholly without dramatic excuse. At the stage reached by his candidature, Touchstone thinks it proper to give an exhibition of professional skill. And that too he makes subserve his sexual passion: having drawn all eyes to himself, for a moment he directs them to Audrey:

Upon a lye, seven times removed: (beare your bodie more seeming Audrey)...

and so she is ridiculed once more.

It seems likely he obtains his appointment: at any rate he makes the impression he desires. 'He is very swift and sententious', say the Duke.

he uses his folly like a stalking-horse, and under the presentation of that he shoots his wit.

Which of course is just what the real Touchstone never does, in spite of what the critics say. The judgment of the Old Shepherd is sounder, that Touchstone's folly has no purpose at all, or if any, only that of discrediting and ruining purpose. And so is Jaques sounder, when he recognizes in Touchstone's folly the cover for his scepticism.

It is interesting, and significant of the subtle pattern which Shakespeare intends to weave – a pattern not only of intrigue but of ideas – that the Duke, who is thus easily gulled when Touchstone assumes a virtue, protests immediately when required to accept as a virtue Touchstone's vice. Jaques describes to him, and asks for himself, the liberty of railing which Touchstone enjoys:

> weed your better judgements
> Of all opinion that grows ranke in them,
> That I am wise. I must have liberty
> Withall, as large a Charter as the winde,
> To blow on whom I please, for so fooles have...
> Invest me in my motley: Give me leave
> To speake my mind.

Such impunity, the Duke sees, can have no results of the kind Jaques promises:

> I will through and through
> Cleanse the foule bodie of th' infected world...

but only evil for himself and others:

> Fie on thee. I can tell what thou wouldst do...
> Most mischeevous foule sin.

16

And he proceeds to diagnose it correctly. Only a man ruined by evil, he suggests, confines himself to the correction of evil; for this implies not that evil finds him peculiarly sensitive, but that he is insensitive both to evil and to good. To good because he neglects and therefore runs the risk of destroying it; to evil because he seeks no relief from what should stifle and nauseate. Brutalized to this degree, Jaques can see no reason why others should not be brutalized too:

> all th' imbossed sores, and headed evils,
> That thou with license of free foot hast caught,
> Would'st thou disgorge into the generall world.

The portrait is drawn in high colours, but Hamlet would recognize it. Jaques presumably does not, being as has been said less alert, and therefore less perspicacious; but here unfortunately there is a cut in the text of *As You Like It*.

Further instances of this Shakespearian subtlety are two scenes in which Jaques and Touchstone, usually allies, are brought if not into conflict, into contrast. As Touchstone is as acutely sensitive to the brutish sting as ever Jaques may have been in the past, in the present he can on occasion be resolute as Jaques is not. In response to the sting he can make conquest of Audrey, browbeat William for her possession:

Abandon the society of this Female, or Clowne thou perishest. . . I will kill thee a hundred and fifty wayes, therefore tremble and depart.

William obediently trembles. But it is Jaques of all characters whom Shakespeare chooses to administer a rebuke to Touchstone for this; as though to make it clear that if he condemns inertia he does not, with a crudeness familiar in more recent times, advocate precipitancy; if he deplores apathy, he does not commend brute appetite. When Touchstone contemplates a hedge-marriage so that he might have 'a good excuse hereafter' to leave his wife, it is Jaques prevents him:

And will you (being a man of your breeding) be married under a bush like a beggar? Get you to church.

And at the final leave-taking it is Jaques who foretells to Touchstone a future of wrangling, a 'loving voyage. . . but for two moneths victuall'd'.

At the opposite pole to the characters hitherto considered, tolerating no elaboration in love, stand Silvius and Phebe who seek to conform their lives to the pastoral convention, one of the fullest elaborations known. The scenes in which they appear are perhaps too short to have the effect intended, now that the convention, if not forgotten, is no longer familiar. But to an Elizabethan the sentiments and the verse – the former largely echoes, external as well as internal to the play: the latter easy yet mannered – would suffice to evoke a wealthy tradition. A modern judges of this perhaps most readily by the apostrophe to Marlowe:

> Dead Shepheard, now I (f)ind thy saw of might,
> Who ever lov'd, that lov'd not at first sight?

No incongruity is intended or feared from his introduction with fleece and crook: the tradition being rich enough to absorb him, vigorous enough to assert even beside him its actuality.

And also the apostrophe may serve to dispel some of the mist which has hung about pastoral in England since the seventeenth century, and notably since the attack of Johnson. Though actual, pastoral need not be realistic; and to apply to it realistic canons as he did is to misconceive it entirely. It is not an attempt to portray a shepherd's life: but in its purity – though frequently of course it is impure – to portray a life in which physical misery is reduced to a minimum or has disappeared. Traditionally such a life is called a shepherd's: in which therefore man is held to enjoy every happiness, if only his desires will let him. But as becomes clear with the progress of the pastoral, his desires will not. Removed from the danger of physical pain those of the intellect and the imagination become the acuter; in particular the passion of love, with neither social pressure nor economic necessity inclining it in any direction, becomes incalculable in its vagaries. It remains an ever-open source of calamity. A tragic note or undertone is thus inseparable from pastoral, and if subdued is only the more insistent. It is in permanent contrast with the composure or gaiety of the rest of the score.

By their share in a tradition of this kind, the Silvius and Phebe scenes have a claim to be effective out of all proportion to their length; and the effect they are intended to produce is in the first place a serious, not a comic one. That there is a close connection between Shakespearian tragedy and comedy, I have already stated, is one of my assumptions in this paper.

As the Old Shepherd is contrasted with Touchstone, so he is

18

with Silvius. When the latter pours out his complaints, Corin's attitude is far from one of incomprehension:

> Oh *Corin*, that thou knew'st how I do love her.
> – I partly guesse; for I have lov'd ere now.

Far also from impatience, for the complaints are not of the briefest; far however from approval. To put the matter at its crudest, Silvius is not prudent in his conduct:

> That is the way to make her scorne you still.

And however charitably Corin listens to the recital of another's extravagances, he has no regret that now he is rid of his own:

> How many actions most ridiculous
> Hast thou been drawne to by thy fantasie?
> – Into a thousand that I have forgotten.

His attitude seems to be that Silvius's extravagances will pass with time as his own have passed; meanwhile they may at least be tolerated, for they are decent.

Touchstone's reaction to the meeting with Silvius has already been noticed. Rosalind's is somewhat more complicated:

> Alas poor Shepheard searching of (thy wound),
> I have by hard adventure found my own.

She approves of the premises on which the pastoral convention is based, both that the wound of love is genuine, and that it is sharp and serious. But the assumption that therefore it is deserving of sole attention, or that by receiving such attention it can in any way be cured: she criticizes as does Corin, and less patiently. It conflicts with the common sense for which she is everywhere advocate, and which requires either as condition or as symptom of health a wide awareness of opportunity, a generous assumption of responsibility. By confining his attention to love Silvius is restricting both, frustrating his energies like the other melancholics. That Rosalind should be less patient than Corin is natural as she is younger: she cannot trust the action of time upon Silvius, when as yet she is not certain what it will be upon herself.

For she too is tempted by love, and in danger of the pastoral convention. Though she rebukes Silvius and Phebe from the outset, she does so in language more nearly approaching theirs than ever she approached Jaques's. But the luck of comedy which (it has been suggested) stifles problems is on her side, causing Phebe to fall in love with her. She needs only to reveal herself as a woman, and the folly of pastoralism – as a convention which allows freedom to fancy or desire – comes crashing to the ground. Taught by such an example and by it teaching others, she pronounces the judgment that if Silvius and Phebe persist in love yet would remain rational creatures, they must get married.

It is the same judgment she pronounces on all lovers in the play. Of the four who are left, two only call for separate consideration: herself and Orlando.

Orlando has achieved an extravagance but, unlike Silvius, not a decent one: his verse, even in Touchstone's ears, is the 'right Butter-womens ranke to Market'. As Touchstone is concerned only to destroy he finds criticism easy, but specimens of the verse prove he is not wholly unreliable. And therefore Rosalind chooses to deal with Orlando in prose:

These are all lies, men have died from time to time, and wormes have eaten them, but not for love.
– I would not have my right *Rosalind* of this mind, for I protest her frowne might kill me.
– By this hand, it will not kill a flie.

Her purpose once again is to disabuse her interlocutor about the supposed supreme importance of love. And to do so effectively she makes use at times of a coarseness almost rivalling Touchstone's:

What would you say to me now, and I were your verie, verie Rosalind?
– I would kisse before I spoke.
– Nay, you were better speak first, and when you were gravel'd, for lacke of matter, you might take occasion to kisse: verie good Orators when they are out, they will spit, and for lovers, lacking (God warne us) matter, the cleanliest shift is to kisse.

Not that she agrees with Touchstone, except materially. She may say very much the same as he says, but her purpose is different. It is not to deny that desire, no more than other things, has value; but to assess its proper value, by no means so high as Orlando thinks.

She can undertake to do so with some sureness, and command some confidence from the reader, because she herself has first-hand acquaintance with desire. All criticisms passed on others are also criticisms on herself, and she is aware of this (or if not, as on one occasion, Celia is at hand to remind her). The consequences for the play are manifold. First the criticisms, which as applying to other persons might seem scattered, are bound together as applying to her: over the pattern of the repeating *motif*, such as has been already described, she superimposes as it were another pattern, or encloses it in a frame. Then the final criticism, or judgment which resumes them all, is seen to issue from the body of the play itself, not to be imposed on it by author or authority from without. Finally a breadth and a sanity in the judgment are guaranteed. If Rosalind freely acknowledges in herself the absurdities she rebukes in others – 'Ile tell thee *Aliena*', she says, 'I cannot be out of sight of *Orlando*: Ile goe find a shadow, and sigh till he come' – in return she transfers to others her own seriousness and suffering:

O coz, coz, coz; my pretty little coz, that thou didst know how many fathom deepe I am in love: but it cannot bee sounded: my affection hath an unknowne bottome, like the Bay of Portugall.

Or in a phrase which has a foretaste or reminiscence of Donne:

One inch of delay more, is a South-sea of discoverie. I pre'thee tell me, who it is quickely, and speake apace.

The final judgment would seem to run somewhat as follows. As Rosalind says to Orlando at their first meeting: 'Love is purely a madnesse, and I tel you, deserves wel a darke house, and a whip, as madmen do'; it is however a madness which, owing to the number of victims, there are only two ways of controlling. One is to 'forsweare the ful stream of the world, and to live in a nooke merely Monasticke' – and this way does not generally recommend itself. The second then must be adopted, which is marriage. Above all, whines and cries such as combine to a chorus in Act V must be prevented:

Tell this youth what 'tis to love.
– It is to be all made of sighes and teares,
And so am I for *Phebe*.
– And I for *Ganimed*.
– And I for *Rosalind*.
– And I for no woman.
– It is to be all made of faith and service,
And so am I for Phebe...

da capo three times. Rosalind, though as lover she joined in, as critic and judge rejects it as 'the howling of Irish wolves against the Moone'. To it the alacrity of Oliver and Celia are to be preferred: 'They are in the verie wrath of love, and they will together. Clubbes cannot part them.'

If once again this seems reminiscent of Touchstone, and of Touchstone at his worst, the distinction already drawn should be remembered. The same words can mean different things on Touchstone's lips and on Rosalind's. She is not inciting her fellow characters to marriages which shall hold only until the 'blood breaks', but to 'high wedlock' which is 'great Juno's crown', and a 'blessed bond' – the masquing song, though possibly not by Shakespeare, aptly summarizes certain of the play's sentiments. Further, that Rosalind and Touchstone agree on a single topic, even a topic so important as the qualities of desire, does not mean that one of them is not superior to the other. Rosalind is very obviously the superior: not however in respect of the topic on which she and Touchstone agree. She is distinguished and privileged beyond him, not because she knows desire – rather that confounds both him and her – but because she is, whereas he is not, at the same time many things besides. She is not only a capable manager of her own life, but a powerful influence for good on the lives of others. And finally a word may be put in for Touchstone himself. If Shakespeare, as has been said, does not condemn apathy in order to commend lust, neither does he disapprove of lust in order to advocate Puritanism. Touchstone is on the way to tragedy because he has allowed desire to get out of control; had he controlled it, he would have built up a life more satisfactory than do those who, while living in the world, neglect desire altogether or overmuch. And therefore he remains a positive critic even in his failure, and to some extent because of it; it is proper not only that he himself should rebuke Orlando, but also that Rosalind, taking it would seem words from his lips, should rebuke large groups of people.

If *As You Like It* is planned at all in the way I have suggested, the least title it deserves is, I think, 'unsentimental'. But for common practice I would go further and call it 'unromantic'; and suggest that, to get the measure of its unromanticism, no more is necessary than to read it alongside its source, Lodge's *Rosalynde*. And the title 'unromantic' would possibly be confirmed by an investigation of the Duke's melancholy, which in this paper it has not been possible to investigate.

There is little time to return to the topic from which the paper started, the relation namely between the tragedies and the comedies. But perhaps it is obvious that, conceived as unromantic, the early comedies are a fitting preparation for the 'problem plays', while from these to the tragedies is but a step.

2

MUCH ADO ABOUT NOTHING

NOTES FROM A BOOK IN PREPARATION

It will be remembered that Coleridge chose *Much Ado* as an illustration of his famous 'fourth distinguishing characteristic' of Shakespeare, in accordance with which 'the interest in the plot' in the latter's plays 'is always in fact on account of the characters, not *vice-versa*...the plot is a mere canvass and no more'. And he went on to exemplify: 'Take away from *Much Ado*...all that which is not indispensable to the plot, either as having little to do with it, or, at best, like Dogberry and his comrades forced into the service, when any other less ingeniously absurd watchmen and night-constables would have answered the mere necessities of the action; – take away Benedick, Beatrice, Dogberry, and the reaction of the former on the character of Hero, – and what remains?' The implication is nothing, or almost nothing; so that the play as a whole has no purpose – that it has no unity and, failing to show even a thwarted striving towards unity, is most conveniently for the critic resolved into its elements.

As Coleridge's sharp distinction between plot and character would now no longer be accepted, it becomes at least possible that his judgment on *Much Ado* should be modified – perhaps, indeed, reversed. Antecedently, this would seem probable; for whatever they have said or written, post-Coleridgeans have not, perhaps, ceased to enjoy the play as a whole: at least they have not been reduced to reading it as some of Dickens's novels are read, with a methodical skipping of scenes or chapters. Are they not to be held more justified in their practice than in their theory? The best way to attack this problem is perhaps to consider one by one the elements which Coleridge claims to have isolated from the plot and from each other, asking whether in fact they can be so isolated: whether they or the plot do not succumb to the operation or, if they survive it, whether they are not maimed thereby.

And first of Dogberry: though with regard to him, it is indeed difficult to maintain the detachment desirable in an analysis. Let us begin however by noting that, though he and his fellows are at times styled malaprops, the term is not altogether happy. Mrs Malaprop is not a character who, on a second reading of *The Rivals*, gives any great if indeed any pleasure; for her pride in 'the derangement of epitaphs' is a foolish pride that the reader, for discretion's sake, prefers to ignore. Mrs Quickly of *The Merry Wives*, with her 'alligant' and 'alicholy', has perhaps something of the same pride – though having other things too, she does not prove quite so embarrassing on continued acquaintance; and in any case, rather than painfully aping, she is probably lazily echoing her superiors. As for the Mrs Quickly of the historical plays, she is another person: with her 'Arthur's bosom', she gives expression, as best she may, not to a selfish foolishness but to a charitable concern for souls – at least, for one soul; arriving in a moment of illumination, or perhaps at the end of a train of thought, at a striking conclusion about the state of the blessed.

Dogberry and his fellows, [if] from time to time the victims of syllables like Mrs Malaprop, are more frequently and more significantly, like the second Mrs Quickly, the victims of ideas. When Verges speaks of 'suffering salvation body and soul', and Dogberry of being 'condemned into everlasting redemption', it is impossible they are being deceived merely by similitude of sounds. Rather, they are being confounded by ideas with which, though unfitted to do so, they feel it incumbent upon themselves to cope. Such utterances are of a piece with Dogberry's method of counting; with his preposterous examination of Conrad and Borachio, in which condemnation precedes questioning; with his farewell of Leonato, to whom, in an endeavour to conserve both their dignities, he 'humbly gives leave to depart'; with his desire 'to be written down an ass', in which the same sense of his own dignity is in conflict with, among other things, a sense that it needs vindication. It is not Mrs Malaprop, but rather Bottom, who comes to mind here: Bottom who, like Dogberry, is torn between conflicting impulses – whether those of producing his interlude in as splendid a manner as possible, while at the same time showing as much deference as possible to the ladies; or of claiming as his own the 'most rare vision' which, as a vision, certainly had been his, while for its rarity it seemed such as could not rightly belong to any man.

In thus addressing themselves to intellectual or moral feats of which they are not capable, Bottom, Mrs Quickly and Dogberry do of course display a form of pride. Given his attitude towards Verges:

a good old man, sir, hee will be talking as they say, when the age is in, the wit is out, God helpe us, it is a world to see.

Dogberry's pride needs no stressing. It is however no longer a foolish pride; or if foolish, then not with the folly of Mrs Malaprop, but rather of all the protagonists of drama, comic or tragic, who measure themselves against tasks which ultimately prove too much for them. Perhaps with justice it is to be classified as a form of *hybris*, a comic *hybris*; and if so, then some kind of essential relation between the Dogberry scenes and the tragically inclined scenes of the main plot is immediately suggested.

The suggestion is strengthened, once Dogberry's strength rather than his weakness, his triumphs rather than his failures, are considered. For he has established himself as Constable of Messina, not only to the content of his subordinates, but with the tolerance of his superiors. In this respect he is no longer to be compared with Bottom – who, it is to be feared, would never gain a firm footing, however humble, at the court of Theseus – but with Falstaff, a character of greater importance. Unlike Bottom, Dogberry and his companions have taken fairly accurate measure both of themselves and of those who surround them; so that, if swayed by *hybris* in a certain degree, they take care that this degree shall fall short of destructive. For example, they are quite clear 'what belongs to a Watch': they will 'sleep rather than talk'; rather than bid a man stand against his will, they will let him go and thank God they are rid of a knave; rather than take a thief, they will 'let him shew himselfe for what he is', and steal out of their company. In short, they will exert themselves, or fight, no longer than they see reason: to adapt Poins's words. Indeed, in this matter they are more consistent than Falstaff, who, in dismissing Prince Henry as 'a Fellow that never had the Ache in his shoulders', is for once allowing himself to be puffed up by *hybris*. In his boasts to Shallow, Falstaff betrays not a little of a Bottom-like recklessness:

Master *Robert Shallow*, choose what Office thou wilt in the Land, 'tis thine...Boote, boote, Master *Shallow*, I know the young King is sick for mee.

And discomfiture of course follows. Whereas Dogberry has perfectly accommodated himself to those on whom he depends, making their ideals his own. His list of qualifications is revealing:

I am a wise fellow, and which is more, an officer, and which is more, a householder, and which is more, as pretty a peece of flesh as any in Messina, and one that knowes the Law, goe to, & a rich fellow enough, goe to, and a fellow that hath had losses, and one that hath two gownes, and everything handsome about him.

It needs little acquaintance with the Leonato circle to realize that for them too it is a principal concern that everything, as far as possible, shall remain 'handsome about them'.

The few adjectives we have had occasion to apply to Claudio – prim and shallow – suggest this; and so far, we have not studied Claudio with any closeness. Nor has the time yet come to do so; we can however note how everything about his wooing confirms the propriety of adjectives of this kind. His leaving, not only the wooing of Hero, but the falling in love with her until circumstances are convenient, and

> warre-thoughts
> Have left their places vacant;

his abandoning that love once it appears the Prince contemplates asserting an opposing claim; his preliminary enquiry

> Hath Leonato any sonne my Lord?
> – No childe but Hero, she's his onely heire,

and so on: his conduct is of a piece – is conduct, we may add, fitting for a 'Count Comfect', as Beatrice calls him: conduct directed in the first place to the setting up and the keeping up of appearances. Yet it is conduct that, recommending itself to Leonato, earns his emphatic approval. For though he arrogates to himself a merit for forgiving Claudio for an insult which, as yet, everyone assumes to have had fatal consequences, he is careful not to exaggerate this merit. In his eyes, it does not justify him in offering, as a pledge of forgiveness, the hand of a niece whom he has not previously declared to be, not only as beautiful, but as rich as Hero. Indeed, she is richer:

> My brother hath a daughter...
> And she alone is heire to both of us.

Marrying off the young before they have time to get into mischief, and so ruin appearances –

> Wisedome and bloud combating in so tender a body, we have ten proofes to one, that bloud hath the victory.

taking care to do so however in such a way that fortune shall not be impaired, social position shall be safeguarded; this would seem to be the prime occupation of society in Messina. Obviously, it is an important occupation; but equally obviously, it has no claims to be considered as unique. To fill up the gap, war is allowed of as a diversion for males and, for both the sexes, games and small talk. Thus, though not active about things of great importance nor, it would appear, importantly active about anything, society in Messina manages to keep up the appearance of great activity.

Such a society has the merit of being a society, that is, a more or less stable organization of human beings for common ends; and *ex hypothesi*, it is charming on the surface. For appearances lie on the surface. Yet for that reason they may be hollow; and there is a danger that faculties, exercised exclusively on appearances, may incapacitate themselves for dealing with, or even for recognizing, substance, when on occasion this presents itself. Something of the kind would seem to have happened to Pedro, Leonato, Claudio and their like; who when faced with the substance of Hero's grief, display an incompetence as great as that of any Dogberry; give rein to a *hybris* which is, perhaps, greater. For it is inconceivable that any but the most pampered and therefore the most spoilt members of a society should, in circumstances of such distress, show themselves as immune as they do from self-questioning, as free from misgiving. *Hybris* on this scale is of course tragic; but, it may be suggested, *hybris* on this scale is also ridiculous – indeed, unless the ridiculous aspect is first acknowledged, the tragic may escape acknowledgment altogether. For human vanity alone constitutes a strong temptation to discount it as preposterous. The figures of Dogberry and his kind are necessary in the background, to reduce the figures in the foreground to the required proportions – to the proportions of apes (as Isabella says, in *Measure for Measure*), apes for whom no tricks are too ferocious, too fantastic. Coleridge's isolation of Dogberry from the main plot is perhaps the effective reason for his dismissal of that plot as a 'mere canvass'; and if so, this of itself suggests that the isolation is not to be justified. But there is the further point: because of the same isolation, Coleridge dismisses Dogberry as 'ingeniously absurd'. Undoubtedly he is: but also, he is relevantly absurd – relevantly absurd to the main plot, and to life such as the main plot renders it. And finally, Dogberry is relevant not only for his absurdity, but for the limitations placed on this absurdity by his persistent if purblind prudence, [by] the steady if myopic eye which he keeps fixed on appearances – on his office as constable, on his comfort, on the main chance. This immediately establishes his commensurability with the figures of the main plot; who like him, take care not to prejudice what is comfort in their eyes.

Having perhaps established this point, we may allow ourselves to go even further than Coleridge in separating Dogberry and the rest from what he called the 'mere necessities of the action'. 'Any other watchmen', he says, 'would have served the latter equally well'; whereas now it would seem clear that, in all probability, they would have served it better. Few if any other watchmen would have taken stock of themselves as frankly as Dogberry; they would not therefore appear guilty of an inconsistency, as Dogberry's assistants seem to be, in arresting the swashbucklers Conrad and Borachio. For they have just declared an intention to attempt no such thing. Or perhaps this inconsistency is due, not to the watchmen, but to the swashbucklers; who indeed, from this point in the play onwards, show a remarkable meekness. But the matter is hardly worth discussing; nor, perhaps, whether the carelessness involved on the author's part is to be described as positive or negative.

We must pass on to a consideration of the scenes presenting Benedick and Beatrice. And these, I think we shall find, not only lose in significance in being separated from the rest of the play but, as a single element, dissolve. If relations can be established between some of these scenes and some of the rest, not all can be related to the same scenes; with the result that they cannot all be related amongst themselves. In other words, they would appear to be inconsistent with one another; and this is perhaps most readily evident in the most famous of them all, the eavesdropping scenes.

If, for example, we consider that in which Beatrice eavesdrops upon Hero and Ursula, we find her described as 'coy and wilde, As Haggerds of the rocke'; as 'so odde, and from all fashion' that she 'cannot be commendable'; as, in short, another Katharina from *The Taming of the Shrew*. Like Katharina, she is unscrupulous in the methods she adopts to keep the other sex at distance:

> I never yet saw man,
> How wise, how noble, yong, how rarely featur'd.
> But she would spell him backward...
> So turnes she every man the wrong side out,
> And never gives to Truth and Vertue, that
> Which simplenesse and merit purchaseth.

Lest it should be thought that Hero is knowingly giving a false report, seizing the opportunity, once she feels safe from her cousin's tongue, to return mock for mock – a proceeding which, however, would not be in accordance with Hero's submissive or (to repeat the adjective) shallow nature – Beatrice herself takes occasion to confirm it. Once the stage is empty, she steps forward and soliloquizes in verse flatter than any of Katharina's:

> What fire is in mine eares? can this be true?
> Stand I condemn'd for pride and scorne so much?
> Contempt, farewell, and maiden pride, adew,
> No glory lives behind the backe of such.
> And *Benedicke*, love on, I will requite thee,
> Taming my wilde heart to thy loving hand.

Beatrice, in other words, confesses she has hitherto been as savage as an Amazon; in future, she will be as patient as Grizzel.

Now whatever else she may be, Beatrice in other scenes is hardly as ingenuous as this; nor is she *farouche*. Rather than restive in society to which men as well as women are admitted, she shows herself mistress of its minor arts, and delighting in her mastery. Perhaps the best illustration is the scene in which the engagement of Claudio and Hero is announced. It is not Beatrice but Hero who, with her unnatural submissiveness, shows embarrassment; to relieve which Beatrice draws attention to herself, assuming the role conventionally assigned to spinsters on such occasions:

Good Lord for alliance: thus goes every one to the world but I, and I am sun-burn'd, I may sit in a corner and cry, heigh ho for a husband.

Taking his cue the Prince, who also is a master of the social arts, proposes himself as a husband, and the little comedy, thus started, is played out successfully to the end. Beatrice maintains a befittingly humorous tone; and lest she should have overstepped propriety in provoking, even in jest, an offer from the Prince, includes a gesture of respect towards him:

Will you have me? Lady.
– No, my Lord, unlesse I might have another for working daies, your Grace is too costly to weare every day: but I beseech your Grace pardon mee, I was borne to speake all mirth, and no matter.

Nevertheless, when the Prince addresses her too patronizingly, presuming on the intimacy which collaboration for social ends has temporarily established between them, without hesitation she administers a rebuke:

...out of question, you were borne in a merry houre.
– No sure my Lord, my Mother cried, but then there was a starre daunst, and under that I was borne: cosins God give you joy.

And so she withdraws, the honours going with her.

Almost immediately afterwards the Prince observes: 'She cannot indure to heare tell of a husband', and Leonato continues: 'O by no meanes, she mockes all her wooers out of suite.' Yet it should be noted that, in the play, we are not shown Beatrice as indiscriminately scolding males. That is what, according to Hero, she should do; but what in fact she does – leaving out of account for the moment her attitude towards Benedick – is to scold the male sex in general. And there is a difference between the two, for a general condemnation has none of the force of successive condemnations of individuals. In Beatrice's case indeed, the generalities would not seem to be intended as forceful but feigned, and to be taken as feigned:

Well neece, I hope to see you one day fitted with a husband.
– Not till God make men of some other metall than earth, would it not grieve a woman to be over-mastred with a peece of valiant dust? to make account of her life to a clod of waiward marle? no unckle ile none: *Adams* sonnes are my brethren, and truly I hold it a sinne to match in my kindred.

She alleges no private grievance, maintains no argument, but jumps from one commonplace to another – all of which many other persons have uttered many times before, and in similar contexts. Indeed, rather than expressing any feeling of her own,

Beatrice once more may be assuming a conventional role, such as is approved of and perhaps required by society in certain circumstances.

At this point a comparison with Benedick may be instructive. For as Beatrice of the male, so Benedick is a 'professed tyrant' of the female sex, and on grounds of a similar nature. He alleges the faithlessness and extravagance of women, which in society are commonplaces approved of for certain purposes. Benedick's in propounding them would seem to be sufficiently obvious. As has been noted, Messina is a match-making society; in which, if a bachelor is to preserve himself from troublesome pursuit, he is in need of a weapon. The weapon conventionally allowed him is an affected misogyny, or the prolongation, beyond the days of adolescence, of an adolescent cynicism with regard to women. This is the weapon wielded by Claudio – *teste* Benedick – before turning his thoughts to Hero; it is the one to which he returns as the most natural thing in the world, once it appears that Hero is not for him. The case of Beatrice, of course, is not exactly similar: for if, in the society of Messina, an unmarried young man is somewhat of a phenomenon, much more so is an unmarried young woman. Normally, young women need no weapons for their defence, being defended by those of their family, behind which they cower until summoned forth to accept the husband already provided for them – making curtsey, in Beatrice's words, and saying: 'as it please you, father'. Now for some reason or other – not difficult to divine, but it would hardly be in place to do so here – Beatrice is already 'out' in the world, without provision of a husband as yet. In the absence of feminine precedents, she could do not better than what she very sensibly does do: follow masculine example, and answer to their affected misogyny with the affectation of misandry.

Of which, of course, her attacks on Benedick are by no means to be taken as expressions. It would be as great a mistake to transfer to him Beatrice's amused if contemptuous toleration of the male sex as a whole –

away to S. *Peter*...hee shewes mee where the Batchellers sit, and there live wee as merry as the day is long

– as it is for Hero to transfer to the sex as a whole her *animus* against Benedick. For that there is such *animus* would seem to be clear. The blows dealt by Beatrice are as persistent and as heavy as those dealt by Katharina, though their instrument is the tongue rather than three-legged stools; though too they are not random blows. Beatrice is accurately aware which person she intends to hit, and of the weak points in that person's armour: her eye is sharp, her hand steady and her aim, therefore, sure. As a consequence, she rouses Benedick to a frenzy:

O she misusde me past the indurance of a block...she speakes poynyards, and every word stabbes: if her breath were as terrible as terminations, there were no living neere her, she would infect to the north starre... while she is heere, a man may live as quiet in hell, as in a sanctuary, and people sinne upon purpose, because they would goe thither, so indeed all disquiet, horror and perturbation followes her.

The taunt which appears to anger Benedick most is that he is the Prince's jester: not so much that he is a poor jester, 'duller than a great thaw', as that he is an official one. Among his duties are included that of jesting continually, whether by fair means or foul, and consequently that of accepting whatever reward the Prince and his friends think fit – be it applause, or be it a beating. The office is certainly not of the noblest; yet the very exaggeration of the charge, one would think, should prevent it from being taken seriously. Benedick, however, does so, finding it necessary to reassure himself: 'I am not so reputed.'

If we add to this, the fact that Benedick is, after all, taken as a kind of jester by his companions – the Prince and Claudio, for example, seek him out when they are 'high proofe melancholly, and would faine have it beaten away'; when we add too that Beatrice herself, the author of the charge, is in the Prince's eyes (though not, as we have noted, in her own) no more than a 'merry heart', we are faced with an interesting problem. Why are they, both of them, in a high degree susceptible about a practice in which they indulge persistently and, to all appearances, deliberately? How has one of them become so accurately aware of the susceptibility of the other?

At least part of the truth would seem to be that the affectations of misogyny and misandry, diligently maintained by Benedick and Beatrice for a single end, is approved for many other ends by the people among whom they move – if not, indeed, approved absolutely. Perhaps in no other way does the society of Messina define – and condemn – itself so clearly, as in the frank delight and relief it finds in retreating, as soon as possible, into the irresponsibilities of adolescence. Once the indispensable match is made, fortunes and position secured and the family perpetuated, the married state and the affections on which it is supposed to be based and which it fosters have little if any further interest for them. If they can, they would continue being 'March chicks' well into December. Now, if Benedick and Beatrice are not of this mind – and if this is not already apparent, let us assume for the moment that they are not – they may well feel themselves degraded in being compelled, for a purpose of their own, to appear to encourage it; and any mention of that encouragement will touch them on the raw.

Why then – the further question arises – does this purpose seem to them so immensely important as to justify the degradation? Why are they so intent, against the example of their fellows and the precept of nature, on remaining single? Of the many possible answers, it is necessary to take account only of that which they themselves suggest. They wish to preserve themselves free from entanglements so that, should the opportunity of marrying each other present itself, it may be seized; for according not only to their actions – which might be misinterpreted – but their express declarations, they are in love with each other. The relevant words of Benedick are, not so much his praise of Beatrice's beauty when Claudio would have him praise Hero, as his exclamation, in the very height of his frenzy against Beatrice, 'I would not marry her.' As yet, no one has suggested that he should; so that the suggestion is all his own. And to a quip of the Prince's, to the effect that she has 'lost the heart of Signior *Benedick*', Beatrice answers:

Indeed my Lorde, hee lent it me a while, and I gave him use for it, a double heart for a single one, marry once before he wonne it of mee, with false dice, therefore your Grace may well say I have lost it.

The reply has an unexpected seriousness, lost of course on the Prince. At some previous period, the two would seem to have arrived at an understanding – perhaps they were engaged, and if so, that would explain why Beatrice is 'out'. There was a rupture, due it would seem to Benedick; which neither however can bear to take as final. So Beatrice chooses to remain 'out', in order that all contact between them may not be lost. Yet what kind of contact can they have in Messina, where discussion of serious matters is taboo? To mark their preoccupation with each other, they can only impart an unusual violence to the vapid cynicisms in which, henceforward, they must converse. Unless indeed, and until, a gust of tragedy should blow through the air of Messina, dispelling vapidities for a while.

Yet their violence should confine itself within certain limits – the limits, for example, which decency imposes. These Beatrice seems to overstep in reproaching Benedick for humiliating himself to a jester: it is a humiliation he endures, which she knows he endures, and which he knows she knows he endures, for her sake. To him she appears to touch the depth of ingratitude; and therefore, 'though bitter', he cries, she is also 'base'.

The examination of this part of the play is dragging somewhat; though perhaps this may be justified, at least in part, by its obscurity. In any case, before taking a further step forward we should perhaps take one backward, and note how all said above of the inconsistency between the Beatrice of the eavesdropping and of the other scenes is to be repeated, almost *totidem verbis*, of the Benedick. To return for a moment to bibliography, this is the more interesting in that the conversation overheard by Benedick is in prose. Further, it is more carefully written than that overheard by Beatrice, and richer in content: the Prince, unlike Hero, seizes the occasion to twit his eavesdropper; and some attempt is made to hide the ingenuousness of the latter. The excuses proffered by Benedick for walking into the trap – 'the world must be peopled', and so on – do, however humorous, make it appear that he is aware of the trap: that he is walking into it with his eyes wide, or at any rate half, open. Yet this is not so; or if so, then his eyes, opened for a moment, are immediately and tightly sealed. Out of Beatrice's plain and forbidding words, 'Against my will I am sent to bid you come in to dinner', he spells a welcome and a self-surrender as painfully, with as little plausibility, as ever Malvolio did out of MOAI.

What then is to be thought of the eavesdropping scenes? To ask whether the events on which they are based are probable or possible might lead to endless argument, and it will perhaps be sufficient to ask whether they are necessary. Two people torn apart by a misunderstanding which has begun to appear progressively less important, while the consequences it has already brought and still threatens come to appear very important indeed; two people kept apart by conventions, or a respect for appearances, which forbid the misunderstanding being discussed or even mentioned, other than allusively: what further can be needed to bring these people together, than that the conventions should reveal themselves, glaringly and publicly, for what they are? – for conventions, that is, which if they may procure human happiness up to a certain point, once that point is passed may not only cease to procure, but effectively prevent it. The conventions do so, of course, in the scene in which Hero is repudiated: Hero of all persons, who more than any has bowed to conventions, yet who on that account is treated only with the greater cruelty. Discussion of her supposed offence is even less to be permitted, than was a discussion of Benedick's; and unlike Benedick – she is the weaker, but also, it is to be presumed, the blow which she receives is the heavier – she has no defence, and crumples. What more probable, natural, and in accord with the whole purpose of the play – if we are not mistaken in our reading of this – than that the apparently lifeless body of Hero should rouse Benedick and Beatrice to the courage of the conviction which has formed within them, that life has something to offer, too valuable for its seizure to be delayed on pretexts of doubtful moment? And the observance of the conventions, which hitherto has been their pretext, has shown itself to be of less moment than ever they suspected or feared.

A reconciliation following directly upon, and proceeding solely from, the spectacle of Hero is, it may be suggested, more likely than the primitive engineering of Prince Pedro to establish those relations existing between Benedick and Beatrice in the closing scenes of the play. The moment of stress once past, they return, not indeed to their former violence of expression, but to an irony which, while not unresponsive to their affection, decently veils it. They do not parade their feelings, nor do they renounce their self-respect, as the eavesdroppers would seem to do.

Between the early scenes of sparring and that of the reconciliation lie two acts, across which, inevitably, the reconciliation appears somewhat abrupt. By bridging the gap, Shakespeare might no doubt have removed this effect. But he did not choose to do so, and it is useless to speculate what he might have done.

Instead, he chose to stop the gap – a more respectful verb

would hardly be in place – with the eavesdroppings. If the question 'Why?' is raised, perhaps the only way to answer is to fall back on the theory of diversions in comedy, and suggest they were intended as such – diversions for the spectator, not for the reader, for the scenes are said to be successful on the stage. If so, however, Shakespeare has laid himself open to a charge of gross carelessness – carelessness, too, of the most positive kind: for he has included in his comedy diversions which are neither obviously irrelevant to the main action nor illustrative of it, so to speak, from the outside (for a diversion need not be wholly alien to this, though lying apart from it); but rather obscure the main action by getting between it and the reader. Such irresponsibility may cause the latter to stare and gasp; he should, however, reflect that it is of a piece with the mismanagement of eavesdropping in the earlier part of the play, and with the inconsequential treatment of Prince Pedro.

So far from lending themselves to separation from the main plot, therefore, the Benedick and Beatrice scenes, or such among them as are of serious significance, lead up to it and find in it their conclusion; while apart from it, the serious are confounded with the trivial. Further, the main plot is as dependent on them as they on it; and through the main plot, they are related to the Dogberry scenes. For as these light up the ridiculous, so Benedick and Beatrice, it might be suggested, light up the shallow and superficial aspect of Messina society: long intimate with an ache of their own, they are the only ones – apart from the priest – to show charity and reasonableness in the presence of the aches of others. This goes very well, it might be observed, with the role of jesters which they have assumed: for these are traditionally the deformed or maimed, and therefore suffering, members of any group.

Thus the tragic scenes of the repudiation of Hero and its immediate consequences would seem to be the centre of unity in *Much Ado*. Other sections of the play look to them for completion; themselves, they draw strength and significance from the other sections. In its closing pages, this article may perhaps attempt to indicate the extent to which they do so.

First however a warning: in these scenes the inequalities resulting from the employment of fragments of differing dates of composition are perhaps more striking than elsewhere. The reader must prepare for the not unexacting task of adapting himself, now to circumspect and transparent verse, now to rapid and more concentrated prose – tuning and re-tuning his ear, hastening or retarding his intelligence as may, at any moment, be appropriate. But if he will undertake the task, he will perhaps find it not unrewarding.

The first characteristic of the scenes to call the attention is, as has been hinted, the complete lack of consideration shown for Hero. Claudio sets about his hangman's task with all the primness he has displayed on other occasions: with regard for the conventional decorum of the office or, to adapt one of his own words, the 'comeliness'. He is aware of nothing but of what is due to himself and to society from him, and of that he is fully aware, so that he is hampered by no human weakness:

> There *Leonato*, take her backe againe,
> Give not this rotten Orenge to your friend.

And the Prince speaks in exactly the same tone:

> I stand dishonour'd that have gone about
> To linke my deare friend to a common stale.

'Friend', 'friend' – the echo is revealing. For Leonato is the only person to whom the Prince and Claudio show the slightest tenderness – '*Leonato*, I am sorry you must heare', says the Prince – proving thereby that they recognize in him one of themselves. On his side, Leonato proves himself worthy of the recognition. Until Benedick and Beatrice have set him an example, and until the priest has remonstrated with him, neither does he show any tenderness except to himself:

> Do not live *Hero*...
> Thought I thy spirits were stronger than thy shames
> Myself would on the re[ar]ward of reproaches
> Strike at thy life. Griev'd I, I had but one?...
> O one too much by thee: why had I one?

and so on, rising to a fine point of self-pity:

> Why had I not with charitable hand
> Tooke up a beggars issue at my gates,
> Who smeered thus, and mir'd with infamie,
> I might have said, no part of it is mine:
> This shame derives itself from unknowne loines,
> But mine, and mine I lov'd, and mine I prais'd,

> And mine that I was proud on mine so much,
> That I my selfe, was to my selfe not mine:
> Valewing of her, why she, O she is falne
> Into a pit of Inke.

Indeed, the only member of the group of 'friends' to make the slightest gesture towards Hero is Don John: a fact which is not insignificant and which should be remembered in any consideration of the latter. 'Pretty lady', he says,

> I am sorry for thy much misgovernment.

In doing so, of course, his motives are mixed; but at any rate he shows himself aware of human factors in the situation before him – whatever use he make of them – to which even the lady's father is, for the moment, blind.

For time, given the opportunity – procured, as has been said, by the example of Benedick and Beatrice, the wisdom of the priest – does not fail to work on Leonato, so that, by the beginning of Act V, not only does his soul tell him 'Hero is belied', but also, he begins to speak of her as one he loves, not only because she is his (compare the emphasis on the word 'mine', in the passage just quoted), but for her own sake. It is perhaps not fanciful to see the emergence of generous feeling in the following verses:

> Bring me a father that so lov'd his childe,
> Whose joy of her is over-whelmed like mine,
> And bid him speake of patience,
> Measure his woe the length and breadth of mine,
> And let it answer every straine for straine,
> As thus for thus, and such a griefe for such,
> In every lineament, branch, shape, and forme:
> If such a one will smile and stroke his beard,
> And sorrow, wagge,[1] crie hem, when he should grone
> Patch griefe with proverbs, make misfortune drunke,
> With candle-wasters: bring him yet to me,
> And I of him will gather patience:
> But there is no such man.

Leonato is still primarily occupied with his own grief, but this he now considers not merely as his own, but as directed to an object outside of himself. Whatever the softening that has taken place in him, however, nothing similar has happened to the

---

[1] Amended by the New Cambridge editors to 'sorry wag'.

Prince and Claudio. Time has not been able to effect it; nor does the sight of Leonato and Antonio, no longer 'friends' to established conventions and keeping up appearances as such, but raving at what they feel an injustice. Laying 'reverence' by, and forgetting 'grey heaires and bruise of many daies', they endeavour to provoke the young men to a duel. The latter will not, of course, allow themselves to be drawn:

> Marry beshrew my hand,
> If it should give your age such cause of feare

but what they do is something worse, for they remain impassive. 'Gentlemen both', says the Prince, with an urbanity which, however deferent to Beatrice in the drawing-room, is here an insult both to Leonato and to the Prince himself:

> we will not wake your patience.
> My heart is sorry for your daughters death:
> But on my honour she was charg'd with nothing
> But what was true, and very full of proofe.

Two old dogs mouthing a bone, on which not only for their lack of teeth but for its own hardness, they make no impression.

Perhaps in this part of the opening scene of Act V the transcription from experience is too immediate, so that what force it possesses is overlaid for the reader by a repulsion which it inspires. If so, the defect is in harmony with the early date, and still somewhat primitive texture; and in any case it is removed, once the old men, retiring from the stage, yield their place to Benedick. This is the new Benedick, roused as has been said to the courage of a conviction that all does not happen always for the best in Messina. Towards Leonato, he has assumed a certain responsibility for Hero's future; and he has further been commissioned by Beatrice to kill, or rather, as it would appear, to assassinate Claudio. For this impetuous lady demands that Benedick shall proceed as unscrupulously towards Claudio as she, in the matter of jesters, had proceeded towards Benedick.

A duel in form is the only possible solution. That is not refused by Claudio, for no gentleman could do such a thing. But as for convincing his prospective anatagonist that anything serious lies behind his challenge, Benedick no more than Leonato and Antonio succeeds in making the slightest impression. Claudio and the Prince are back again to their old ways and to their old conversation; seriousness is taboo – and here, it must be admitted, Shakespeare makes good use of reference to the eavesdropping scenes. Benedick the gull, whom alone the Prince and Claudio choose to recognize in the man before them, forms too striking a contrast to be neglected with Benedick the married man: they use the term in jest, but need not be followed in this. When at length Benedick withdraws, their comment is illuminating:

Prince. He is in earnest.
Claudio. In most profound earnest, and Ile warrant you, for the love of Beatrice.
Prince. And hath challeng'd thee.
Claudio. Most sincerely.
Prince. What a prettie thing a man is, when he goes in his doublet and hose, and leaves off his wit.

Because he no longer consents to be frivolous with the frivolous, Benedick, who alone among the men has shown signs of awakening to wisdom, is dismissed as a greater fool than ever.

Perhaps it is this short interchange, rather than the famous 'Kill Claudio!' which, as Q put it, 'serves to nail the play'. The utter bewilderment of the Prince's 'He is in earnest', indicates the impossibility of his or Claudio's ever awakening to anything which lies beneath appearances, which stretches beyond conventions. Should events take their course, the duel is inevitable.

But naturally, as the play is a comedy, they do not. The genius of comedy brings the watchmen on the stage, with their chance discovery which has escaped the collective wisdoms of the city. The Prince and Claudio emerge unscathed – but also, it is to be feared, uninstructed – from the dangers which involve them, and in which they have involved others; Leonato, relieved, can be his old self again; as for Benedick and Beatrice, they of course are changed, but hold it prudent, now that over-riding necessity no longer bids otherwise, to keep the change to themselves. Messina can return to its former gaieties, all joining in a dance which, if the Dogberries are not invited to it, they would have at any rate appreciated, and which they would hardly have disgraced.

All, that is, except one; and as the last word of the play is for Don John, perhaps he may have the last word here. This 'tart' personage, who halts even Beatrice, seems to have had little justice shown him by commentators. Coleridge's 'he is merely shown and then withdrawn', is for example not true – we have just had evidence to the contrary; while if it were, with what skill and what clarity is he shown! The Prince has professed to be reconciled with him, but all that follows is that he is 'trusted with a mussell, and enfranchis'd with a clog' – the Prince, we see once more, has little delicacy in dealing with the unfortunate. Neither crumpling under this treatment like Hero, nor exercising the 'patient sufferance' of Benedick and Beatrice – Don John will neither 'claw no man in his humour', nor 'fashion a carriage to rob love from any' – he reacts violently, blindly: threatening more than his enemy with destruction.

It would seem difficult to resist the conclusion that, as Dogberry illustrates the ridiculous, and Benedick and Beatrice the shallow aspect of Messina society, so Don John is sketched in to suggest – in a comedy no more than a suggestion would be fitting – the tragedy it involves. Even the soundest and justest of societies rests ultimately on the exclusion, and if necessary the elimination, of those who refuse to conform; Messina's, if we are right, is none of the most comprehensive. Perhaps therefore it is not altogether inappropriate that *Much Ado* should end with talk – even on Benedick's lips – of 'brave punishments' for Don John.

3

THE MERCHANT OF VENICE

The *Merchant of Venice* is a fairy-tale, says Mr Granville-Barker, but certain of the characters attain to lifelikeness and reality. Though it is not immediately obvious how both these statements can be true, at least they make, or seem to make, an approach to the truth, each from its own side. In what way and to what extent they do so suggests a problem into which it is interesting, and maybe important, to inquire. A solution, it might seem, could be provided by an element which fairy-tale and reality possessed in common; and in virtue of which reality, without sacrificing opacity and hardness, occasionally acquired pliancy to human wishes, occasionally a fairy-tale's limpidity. Luck perhaps is capable of discharging such a part.

In the *Merchant of Venice*, at any rate, its function is extensive. Some of the characters enjoy a run of it so unbroken that they mistake its very nature: they count on it as a matter of course. The inconstancy of luck, it is true, furnishes Solanio and Salerio with a theme to descant upon, but only for them to display, along with the zest and agility, the incomprehension of choir-boys. They are moved to laughter, as by an absurdity, when luck forsakes an enemy; nor do they find it easy to refrain from laughter, even when a friend is forsaken. The same theme is so difficult or so impossible for Jessica and Lorenzo to grasp that, though shorn of income, they squander all the capital they have had the luck to lay hands on. And if these characters seem too episodic to be of primary importance, or too peripheral to be of any, one at least of their kind, from the beginning to the end of the play, remains close to its centre. That is Bassanio.

Though deep in debt, Bassanio begs as a favour that he may sink deeper. For, he argues, if supplied with the large retinue, the fine clothes, the splendid gifts that befit the suitor to an heiress, he will 'questionless be fortunate' in his suit to Portia; and even among heiresses less notable for riches, as well as for beauty and for virtue. Presumably the adverb 'questionless' must be discounted, for though a charmer certified by experience of the power of his charms, Bassanio can scarcely be so fatuous as to believe them invincible. Presumably too he would have grounds, if not for the certainty, at least for a hope of success, if Portia were to be wooed in a normal manner; for mouths other than his own report that his charms have not left her indifferent. Even so, his project smacks of an optimism, a presumption, a recklessness, a levity – for the moment, call it what you will – inconceivable unless fortified by ignorance: either of itself, or of other things, or of both together. For the only manner of wooing Portia is so remote from the normal as hardly to deserve the name. So far from deciding the choice which is to be made of her husband, fine clothes and the like cannot even influence it. At the most, they may secure admission to a lottery on which the choice depends.

The lottery furthermore is ruinous, since it contains no blanks. All who miss the prize incur a penalty no less severe than lifelong celibacy. Portia accordingly commends as 'reasonable' a number of lords who hasten to withdraw their suit. The charmer Bassanio might be expected to do the like, since the penalty would considerably cut down his operations. It is however the opposite which happens: he is 'on the rack' until he has tried his luck.

'But', a number of critics might at this point interrupt, 'he is on the rack for quite a different reason. What you have baptized a lottery is not a lottery at all, but a test on which Bassanio may rely to establish his title to Portia.' The answer is perhaps inadequate that the name 'lottery' is Portia's own. Deeply vexed that she is not allowed to choose a husband for herself, she may find relief for her vexation in slandering the mechanism to which the choice has been entrusted. But discussion is superfluous, since the problem goes as near as makes no difference to being solved, once a contrast is drawn between an early version of the casket story and the version which Shakespeare elaborated – or which, if he found it elaborated by a predecessor unknown to us, he deliberately preferred to use.

In the *Gesta Romanorum*, a maiden is required to choose between three caskets, one of gold, one of silver and one of lead. She rejects the golden casket because it is inscribed, 'Who so chooseth me shall find that he deserveth', and because this inscription conveys, as she complains, nothing certain to her mind. The casket of silver is rejected for an opposite reason, its inscription, 'Who so chooseth me shall find that his nature desireth', filling her with too grim a certainty. 'My nature desireth the lust of the flesh', she confesses, and turns therefore to the leaden casket, on which she reads: 'Who so chooseth me shall find that God hath disposed.' This fixes her choice since, as she reflects, God never disposed harm to anybody. When the leaden casket is opened, it is seen to be filled with jewels: not only does God dispose no harm but, to those content to wait upon His mercy, He disposes the greatest good. Those who presume on their own deserts, on the other hand, must be content with what they themselves can dispose; and since they have renounced God's mercy, this can only be a death. Accordingly, the golden casket is packed with dead men's bones; and that of silver, while overflowing with the earth from which flesh is made, swarms also with the worms to which it falls a prey. All three caskets fit to form a scheme or diagram of the human lot: the contents representing its remuneratory and punitive sanctions; the materials, the temptations by which these sanctions are hidden; and the inscriptions, the intimations by which they are revealed. Neither blinded by avarice nor weakened by lust, the maiden is able to recognize the inscriptions for what they are and to make a bid for remuneration. She shows both wisdom and virtue. Therefore the emperor of Rome bestows upon her the hand of his eldest son.

Of all the innovations made by the *Merchant of Venice*, the most central would seem to be its refusal to allow room or function to a character who might correspond to the emperor. In one of the caskets with which Portia's wooers are confronted, Portia herself is contained; or at least her portrait is contained, and the portrait does duty for her person. So that no one who happens upon the right casket stands in need of having her bestowed upon him. However blindly he has chosen, however tightly he has closed both bodily eyes and those of his reason, he holds her already in his hand: even though he has given no proof of wisdom or of virtue or of anything; even though he has been no more than lucky in a game of 'find the lady' – a game, that is, of chance.

Nor would this seem to be an exceptional but a typical, or

indeed the only possible, case. No straining of nerves or wits to scrutinize the outsides of the caskets could lead, but only mislead, an inquirer into their contents. Out of abundant caution, an attempt will be made to verify this statement; but it has long appeared sufficiently plausible for exploitation. It has for example been adduced as evidence that Shakespeare's caskets, like those of the *Gesta Romanorum*, provide a test; they are so devised, critics have contended, as to reject all wooers foolish enough to follow false appearances, to promote none but the wooer who, by flouting such appearances, gives proof of strength or depth of mind. The zeal of these critics outruns their logic. Because they themselves, with their detailed knowledge of the insides of the caskets, are justified in denouncing the outsides as false, they require the wooers to do the same. Yet the wooers know no more than that Portia hides within some casket or other; and relying on knowledge so scanty neither strength nor depth of mind, but only folly or worse, could venture to denounce anything. Recourse has therefore been had to a supposed doctrine of contemporary Platonism, according to which outsides are false always and everywhere. It would be difficult to imagine anything more fantastic. If the Platonism of the Renaissance attributed the highest value to an inner and concealed aspect of things, it by no means disdained their visible exterior: rather, it taught that, as the one increased in value, so did the other. For seeking Portia within the least prepossessing of covers, Bassanio has been lauded as a loyal follower of Castiglione: but Castiglione himself looked for inward goodness beneath, not outward ugliness, but outward beauty. And if he had not done so, we go on to ask – or rather, we remove the discussion from the narrow ground of Platonism, and ask: if outward beauty might not be a sign of inward goodness, what must be the sad position in which Portia finds herself – the Portia not of the portrait, but of flesh and blood? In body she is admirable: must she then be contemptible in soul? Her material wealth is so vast as to win her the name of the golden fleece: spiritually therefore is she of no account? These questions require no answer. Obviously they are based on sophisms of the kind that Marocco finds entered upon his scroll. 'Gilded tombs[1] do worms enfold' – of course they do, but only because they are

---

[1] I take *tombs* for Q, F *timber* to be *emendatio certissima*.

tombs; 'All that glisters is not gold' – no more it is, but gold continues to glister, nevertheless.

Nor do the inscriptions on the caskets help an inquirer any more than their materials. 'Who chooseth me shall gain what many men desire' – this indicates the quality or substance of what is offered for choice about as precisely as the proverbial piece of string might indicate its length. And even so, any precision that is attained is patently false. What is as long as a piece of string has at least some length; what many men desire should under some conditions be desirable: but no man of sound mind and body ever desired what the golden casket contains, a death's head. Except of course in the sense in which all men desire it: the sense, namely, in which they are identical with what the inscription in the *Gesta Romanorum* called their 'nature'. But Shakespeare employs no term of the kind; nor can his phrase, 'what many men desire', be stretched so as to cover all men. In common usage, whatever may be the usage of logicians, it implies the opposite: 'what some men do not desire'. Therefore it turns the mind away from philosophic and ultimate considerations on to those which are historical and immediate. If for the former man is always and everywhere the same, for the latter man does not exist, but only men. Men may be and are different from one another, and from themselves at different times. But no one ever differed to such an extent as to desire a death.

It is to historical and immediate considerations that Arragon allows his mind to turn when choosing the silver casket. This promises 'as much as he deserves', and a casket in the *Gesta Romanorum*, it will be remembered, made a similar promise. It will also be remembered that, according to the *Gesta Romanorum*, a man who presumes on his deserts gains nothing but a death. That holds however only when a man sets himself up against God: by setting himself up against his fellows, on the other hand, it may be not only possible but proper for him to gain a variety of agreeable things. To deny or to overlook this fact would be a sign, not of genuine humility, but of inverted pride; since humility requires a man to seek and occupy his proper place – if not a place higher than the proper, quite as certainly not a lower. Only in this way is hierarchy secured and order maintained, two notions which we know to have been dear to

Shakespeare. They would seem dear to Arragon: and his exclamation, 'I will assume desert', may be taken to mean, 'I will put my desert to the test – only if I deserve Portia will I marry her, and if not, not.' The sentiment is admirable, and to say that it is inadequately rewarded by what Arragon finds in his casket – 'the portrait of a blinking idiot' – would be to abuse language. The lottery distributes trash and treasure as is the wont of lotteries, without pretence of reward.

So we arrive at Bassanio and the leaden casket which warn him that he 'must give and hazard all he hath'. In neglecting this warning, it has been held, he displays the spirit of resignation and self-sacrifice proper to a bridegroom. But such an opinion, surely, is unnecessarily disobliging both to Portia in particular and to brides in general. Even Dr Johnson, who allowed that marriage has many pains, insisted that it is not barren of pleasures. Or, continue the critics, by his choice Bassanio manifests a willingness to 'give and hazard all' for the sake of Portia. Once again, they make the mistake of assimilating a wooer's knowledge to their own. Unless he acts blindly, Bassanio can choose only on the ground of differences which are obvious at the moment of choice; and these cannot comprise Portia, whose whereabouts have yet to be discovered. Until the lottery is drawn nothing is known for certain save that she may lurk within one casket or the other; so that with respect to her they are not at all different, but exactly alike. In Bassanio's eyes, they can vary only in inscription and material. Either therefore he gives and hazards for the sake of doing so; or he gives and hazards for lead. In any context but the play, he would long ago have been condemned as perverse.

And that he may in a measure choose perversely would seem to follow from his preliminary soliloquy. This does no more than amplify sophistic maxims of the kind we have already met with: 'Gilded tombs do worms enfold', and so on. Since these are the fruit of worldly wisdom, and profitable as such to be held at the back of the mind when dealing with the world, it may appear harsh to qualify them as 'sophistic'. But as worldly prudence, when regarded as the sole and sufficient form of prudence, converts to diabolic, so these maxims, when advanced to the front from the back of the mind, exchange their profit for a poison. To refer to them more than is necessary is a sign of illiberality; to refer exclusively to them a sign of cynicism. Considerations such as these may perhaps shed light on Antonio when he turns the maxims against Shylock; probably they correct any over-favourable estimate we might otherwise form of Arragon; certainly they get rid of a problem by which Q confessed himself puzzled, and which has puzzled many who have not confessed. What had altered Bassanio, Q enquired, that he of all men, when faced with the caskets, should suddenly indulge in 'sanctimonious talk'? If the talk cannot be sanctimonious but prudent at the most in a worldly sense, the problem vanishes.

It does so of course only to be replaced by another problem, if worldly prudence is the base and burthen of the talk. What has altered Bassanio, it then becomes our duty to ask, that he of all men should vex, or at any rate divert, himself with cynicism? But this time a solution would not seem far to seek. Cynicism was recognized by the Elizabethans as rooted in melancholy; and Bassanio's fear of false hair, however wilful or jaunty, more than faintly recalls Hamlet's fear of false complexions, however frantic and fierce. Nor is it in the least unlikely that the good things of this world, which Bassanio has hitherto enjoyed to the full, should momentarily distaste or disgust him. It might be a fine stroke to make them do so at the moment which is to decide whether or not he is to enjoy Portia, who has come to appear especially good. A persuasion that 'crisped, snaky, golden locks' are rarely if ever worth possessing will serve as comfort should the 'golden mesh' of Portia be withheld. Or if this harvesting of sour grapes against a possible future is considered too 'deep' a process for a Shakespearian character to engage on – though there is little reason why: the adjective 'deep' applying rather to a modern theory than to an age-old human habit – mere surface observation suffices to establish that, at moments of crisis, the most heedless of men may be shaken by the wildest fears, as by a qualm.

Or again, if the surface presented by Bassanio is considered to show no sign of shaking, it remains perfectly possible that his talk is neither sanctimonious nor cynical, but something between the two – more or less idle talk, as we might say. Heedless as he is, he may yield to the whim or, as Americans might say, he may have the 'hunch' to repeat, without much caring to approve or to disapprove, fallacies that he has often heard repeated in a similar fashion. And certainly, a preference for the paleness or plainness of lead looks very like a hunch on the part of one who, before addressing the golden Portia, insisted on being himself equipped with gold. But hunches and whims are the offspring of chance: so that neither upon this interpretation does the choice reflect credit upon Bassanio.

He wins Portia, not because of any merit which the caskets prove him to possess, but because he is favoured by luck. As was suggested at the beginning of this contrast between the *Merchant of Venice* and the *Gesta Romanorum*, and as may now perhaps be affirmed with comparative certainty, it is impossible for Portia to be won in any other way. If in the *Gesta* the caskets fit together to form something, in the *Merchant* they form nothing because they cannot fit: they are too disparate. One of them bears an inscription couched in the imperative mood, two in the indicative; two inscriptions concern themselves with one man or all men, a third restricts its concern to the many. Nor do the contents of a casket fit the inscription which it bears, so that the confusions of the crossword puzzle are multiplied by those of the brantub. The caskets furnish, not a test but, as Marocco complained, a game of dice at which Hercules might be beaten by a weakling page; or at which, as Arragon might have complained, Nestor might be beaten by a page who is empty-headed.

To make this assertion is not of course to assert that Bassanio is empty-headed or a weakling; still less is it to assert that, if he were, he must cease to be interesting or attractive or even lovable. Rather because than in spite of a momentary melancholy, he might remain the recognizable study of a human being. And if he does so, he provides the first piece of evidence we have come across that the *Merchant of Venice*, however large the part it allows to luck, preserves a significantly close contact with reality. In a fairy-tale the characters are recognizable only as ninepins, since they are set up or thrown down by the sole *fiat* of luck; nor does it render them a whit more real that they should be described as good or evil, since the good always end by being up and the evil by being down – if not synonymous, the terms are convertible. Human beings on the other hand are required to do what they can to set themselves up, although they often fail or succeed only in the opposite: on account either of inadequate forces at their command, or of a mismanagement of these forces, or of a thwarting by forces that are commanded by other people. If unintentional, such a thwarting can be ascribed to no sublunary agency except luck, which thus retains, in reality as in a fairy-tale, an opportunity of humiliating humanity. And there are other opportunities which it retains: even to be helped by luck is a humiliation to a creature which is offered, and has accepted, autonomy as an ideal.

Human beings may succeed, and yet be evil; they may be good, and yet fail; but most often they neither succeed nor fail completely, and they are good and evil at the same time. The extent to which they are the one and the other can be determined, if at all, only by a prolonged observation of their doings, and of the doings of all with whom they come into contact, whether enemies or friends. In this way it may be feasible to discriminate, however tentatively, between intentions and performances; to press forward, however slightly, into the secret of a man's thoughts and feelings – a secret by which, since it is a secret, we are exasperated; but which also exacts reverence, since it is the sole breeding-ground, the proper forcing-house, of acts that belong to a man. As each such house sets a stamp upon the acts which are its products, the factors within it, however numerous, must be assumed to work in unison; but the factors are also various, so that the products, when distributed over space and time, set up not a unison but a harmony. And at times the harmony is so strange as, upon first hearing, to crash like a discord. For a due appreciation, it needs to be attended to with the patience of which affection alone is capable: the affection demanded by anything that is human. If a momentary melancholy sounds discordant in Bassanio – and it probably does – the reason largely is that he has hardly appeared a candidate for such affection: so far we have considered him, not so much as a human being, but rather as a fairy-tale character – a passive, or at any rate a contented, client upon luck. We have also considered him in isolation, though friends throng about him; and though the friend who, like himself, yearns for the closest intimacy strives to maintain the greatest possible independence of luck. That is Portia.

Early scenes in the play hint that she is not without a liking for Bassanio. The scene in which they are first presented together makes it clear that the liking has blossomed into desire. Up to this point, she has impressed as her own mistress: one who sets herself a purpose in all that she does, and who pursues that purpose with diligence and common sense. Threatened by the melancholy by which purpose is lamed – 'By my troth', she complains to Nerissa, 'my little body is aweary of this great world' – she devotes herself immediately to gossip and to sentence-chopping; since common sense informs her that, for all who lie under such a threat, the most trivial occupation is better than none. Marocco and Arragon she receives with dignity and courtesy: neither taking advantage of the feelings of complacency which they may exhibit before the choice, or of despite after; nor giving advantage by exhibiting feelings of her own, whether apprehension or relief. But now her feelings show through and between almost all the words she utters: and if previously perhaps she had reminded us of Elizabeth Bennet, now we might for a moment imagine ourselves eavesdropping upon overtures made by Elizabeth's sister Lydia. Desire, it would seem, has weakened not only Portia's capacity for self-control, but her notion of it. One thing however it has not been able to weaken in the slightest: her resolution, namely, to abide by the terms of her father's will. Caught between dutifulness and desire, it is inevitable that she should find support in hope, and in a hope the more intense, the more shrewdly she discerns its insecurity. Or in other words, it is inevitable that, however much the practice repugns, she should in a measure rely upon luck.

Rather, say the critics for whom the lottery is not a lottery, she relies upon the certainty of being provided with the fittest and worthiest husband. These critics quote the assurance with which she dismisses Bassanio to the caskets –

> If you do love me, you will find me out – (III. ii. 41)

and there is a similar assurance of Nerissa's which they may also quote. Words from Nerissa are however of no great weight; and as for Portia's words, very few lines pass before they are exposed as hollow – as noises emitted, not to register fact, but to keep the spirits up. 'Let music sound', she commands,

> Then if he lose he makes a swan-like end. (*ibid*. 44)

Thus she both envisages the possibility of his failing to find her, and prepares what consolation she can for the distress with which failure may fill him. She would hardly take this trouble if, as her words imply, failure denoted a lack of love.

Nor would she compare herself to Hesione, Bassanio to Alcides, and their attendants to the Dardanian wives. By doing so, she projects a transaction of the here and now on to a distant time and country; with the intention that, should the need arise, the distance may soften the blow which she too will receive from a failure.

The need does not arise, and it is the blow of success which finds Portia defenceless. If the neglect of adequate precautions against such an agreeable possibility suggests the insecurity of her hope, its intensity is movingly exemplified when, ceasing to express herself rationally like Elizabeth Bennet or even to babble like Lydia, she begins to rave like the mother of these young ladies.

You remember the incontinence of language into which Mrs Bennet collapses when she hears of Elizabeth's engagement. It ends: 'A house in town! Everything that is charming! Ten thousand a year! O Lord, what will become of me. I shall go distracted.' If Portia does not admit to distraction, she speaks distractedly; if not ravished at the thought of wealth to be received, she is depressed at the thought of wealth beyond even her powers to give; and for the sake of the penniless Bassanio, wishes herself not only 'ten thousand times more fair', but 'ten thousand times More rich'. The last two words are thrown to the beginning of a line – or, in most modern texts, set in a line by themselves – as though to point the comedy of the passage; and when Portia, whom neither Marocco nor Arragon could daunt, finds Bassanio dwarf her down to an 'unlettered school-girl', the comedy borders upon broad, even painful farce. Yet as has been said, the passage is at the same time moving. Shakespeare is aware of the mysterious harmonies of humanity not only more than a fairy-tale, but more than Miss Austen; or at any rate, he succeeds better in capturing them. In the *Merchant of Venice* the degree of his success may be due to his having exercised himself in previous plays in blending the fear and the fun aroused by the 'almighty, dreadful, little might' of desire in the casket scenes. The blend has developed a peculiar richness: desire ruthlessly destroys the dignity of Portia before the song has had time to fade which disparages desire –

Tell me where is fancy bred?...
It is engendered in the eyes;
With gazing fed; and fancy dies
In the cradle where it lies.   (III. ii. 63f)

The question whether Portia's fancy faces a similar doom is
not so much premature as it is crude, since there are many things
into which fancy may die. At no time was she likely to be impressed by the revelation that Bassanio not only lacks money,
as he avowed, but owes it; least of all at the present time. The
further revelation that, because the money has not been repaid,
a friend stands in danger of death – a danger vividly set forth by
Bassanio – does no more than provide her, now that she is free
from an impotent attendance upon luck, with a new and a
momentous purpose to pursue. She despatches Bassanio to
Venice with twenty times the amount of the debt. It is however
noteworthy that, before many hours have elapsed, she decides
to go to Venice herself. If not disillusioned in the sense of disappointed, she would no longer seem to lie under the illusion
that, by setting herself at the side of Bassanio, she must show as
an 'unlettered schoolgirl'. It is yet more noteworthy that she
goes to Venice in the guise of a man: as though already overcome
by disappointment of a kind, as though in a measure doubtful of
Bassanio's ability, when left to himself, to play a manly part.
Perhaps the doubt has spread to a society as yet hardly known
to her: to the friends who have formed Bassanio and whom he
himself has helped to form; more especially to the friend who, in
so curious a manner, has contrived to put himself in the way of
death.

If so, she is right; for as we know, though she cannot, the
friend has for some time been mutilated by melancholy. That
this affliction of Antonio's should be thrust before the reader at
length and at the very opening of the play has often been a matter
for wonderment: but at least one reason would seem tolerably
clear – that of explaining why Antonio stands in an abject need
of help. Almost equally clearly, a second reason is to contrast
Antonio with Portia, by whom an efficient help is extended. Of
her own accord, Portia takes steps to master melancholy; in
spite of the exhortations of his friends, Antonio either fails to do
so or never makes the attempt. And yet a third reason may be
suggested which, if sound, must be acknowledged as all-

important: the melancholy binds the play together. Announced at the opening, it prepares for a denouement the life of which, so to speak, may be the opposition between Portia and a Shylock as purposeful and almost as clear-sighted as herself; but the indispensable skeleton of which, the background by which the life is deepened and defined – this is an opposition between Portia and Shylock taken together, and a baffled, an apathetic Antonio.

This second opposition and the melancholy spring from a single source: the recklessness with which Antonio and the young men about him have been accustomed to comport themselves. Hitherto we have learnt of the recklessness only from the reliance upon luck which is its consequence, and as has been noted, this tends to make fairy-tale characters of the young men. In order to know them better, an endeavour must be made to seize the recklessness in its cause. This would appear to be the abundance of good things with which the young men are surrounded, and for which Antonio is responsible in the case of at least one of them, possibly in the case of all; for he is, as all agree,

> the kindest man,
> The best-conditioned and unwearied spirit
> In doing courtesies. (III. ii. 293)

By this abundance, they have been shielded from the more obvious and more brutal incitements to activity which are employed by the outside world. Either negligent of external incitements at once more recondite and more subtle, or insensitive to these, they are saved from idleness only by incitements which they discover within themselves – by their passions, namely, or their whims. The second word may seem the more appropriate, since the worst of the young men is not destitute of refinement: and this makes their recklessness an initially pleasing spectacle – far more pleasing, certainly, than if they did nothing at all. Closer examination, however, emphasizes the truth that, for the refining and ordering of the passions, the only efficient agent is the outside world upon which they are intended to operate. Exercised for the sake of the exercise alone, and with a minimum regard to the outside changes they produce, they fare as do animals removed from the fields and woods into cages: they grow clumsy because obese, and either they avoid contact or they fall in one another's way. For example, the expedition to Belmont – reckless as we have seen because it threatened a dangerous consequence; reckless we may now add because prompted by an inadequate cause, since Antonio's purse, as long as he had a purse, was little likely to be closed to Bassanio – this expedition cannot be accomplished if Gratiano continues with his 'infinite deal of nonsense': with his speaking recklessly, that is, and to no purpose save to ease an itch for speaking. Therefore Bassanio, with a foresight exceptional among the young men, insists upon discretion as long as the expedition lasts. But this same Bassanio not only permits, but requires Gratiano to 'put on his wildest suit of mirth' on other occasions – and it needs no apostolic distrust of the tongue for a shudder to descend the spine at the thought of the 'merriment' which ensues. On the other hand, an invincible deafness and blindness is imperative not to observe that the love of Bassanio and Gratiano for their wives, however sincere, consistently and conveniently 'keeps quarter'. No infusion of it mellows Gratiano's announcement of the material gains which the expedition has brought: 'We are the Jasons', he whoops, 'we have won the fleece.' No memory of it restrains either Gratiano or Bassanio, when their friend is being tried, from striking an attitude that involves the sacrifice of their wives. These are 'fopperies' which not only a rigorist such as Shylock is compelled to condemn. Nor is it only over-sensitive ears that wince at a prospect of prolonged, purposeless guffawing such as is opened by Bassanio's welcome to Solanio and Salerio:

> Good signiors both, when shall we laugh? say when!   (I. i. 66)

But it is useless to labour a point which the sole figure of a Lancelot suffices to make: attracted to Bassanio by rich liveries and good food, he finds among Bassanio's associates, one of them a woman, a willing audience for clumsy and worse than clumsy jokes.

Appropriately, it is none of the young men but their manager or leader who commits the most reckless act of all. Since he keeps others besides himself in luxuries, Antonio's estate must needs be vast; yet he ventures the whole of this estate

> Upon the fortunes of this present year.   (I. i. 44)

It is the throw of a voluptuary or a madman, of which Antonio himself, by the opening of the play, has grown ashamed. In public he denies it, and the denial necessarily casts doubt on the other denials by which it is accompanied – as that he has no positive knowledge of the origin of his melancholy or that, negatively, the melancholy has nothing to do with his merchandizing. Yet these contentions need not be wholly false; nor indeed is it possible that the second should be so, in view of the readiness with which Antonio signs the bond for Shylock. Other forces are at work than the alarm caused by a stray or unwontedly perceptive glance cast upon the outside world – at its 'waters, winds and rocks'; and these forces may at least in part be concealed from Antonio. The coarse and chaotic delights of recklessness cannot satisfy a mind which, however late in life, draws towards maturity. On the other hand, the delights proper to the mature are not to be enjoyed without a discharge of corresponding duties; and for this Antonio has not so much trained as disabled himself. Recondite and subtle incitements to activity are no longer easy to descry, once the custom has developed of ignoring them; it is still less easy to persist in a single activity, once the custom has developed of zigzagging after whim. The more Antonio feels the weight of this handicap, the more he may fear failure in his efforts to change his mode of behaviour. Pride may therefore put a stop to them; and if at the same time pride forbids a return to the earlier mode, Antonio is sooner or later doomed to stagnation. Stagnation is less a cessation of activities than their mutual throttling, so that it spells melancholy: in the best of cases a deadlock, in the worst a death.

But whatever the stringency with which Antonio has managed to tie his own hands, he does not thereby rid himself of responsibilities incurred when his hands were free. Almost inevitably, these responsibilities are many and dangerous: for the reckless, who pay a minimum regard to the outside changes they produce, with difficulty avoid giving offence. With equal difficulty, those who take offence refrain from punitive measures – unless indeed they are cowardly; and if selfish and resolute, they may refuse to stop short of measures that are vindictive. Shylock is eminently both. In response to acts of Antonio's that, however oppressive when taken together, are trivial in themselves, he lays murderous plans. Naturally he clamours for the execution of these plans, once his household has been disrupted and his coffers plundered; since these outrages, though perpetrated by the young men, may plausibly be charged against Antonio, whom everyone acknowledges as their leader. Thus the main conflict in the play approaches its sharpest point; and the nearer the approach, the more human the conflict appears – natural as has been said, in that it bears the stamp of both Shylock and Antonio, but at the same time mysterious. We are increasingly aware that we have no more than a vague knowledge of the forces of good and evil that are engaged on either side. However vehement our indignation at Shylock's selfishness, the obvious injustices he has suffered require our sympathies; and our sympathies for the victim of selfishness, however strong, are restrained by the obvious follies of Antonio, and the worse than follies of his friends. If under any circumstances a resolution such as Shylock's must earn our respect, as contrasted with Antonio's lethargy it goes near to commanding admiration; but it commands detestation as well, since it is an unnecessarily violent and therefore cruel weapon to be employed upon a lethargy. We cannot foretell the skill, or lack of skill, with which the forces of good and evil will be managed; it is impossible to divine whether luck will intervene, and if so, on whose behalf. The conflict is in short obscured in its origins, its course and its conclusion; it is all the more natural and human, so that we follow it with the greater suspense.

Precisely this conflict however has been claimed by recent critics as the clearest of all the parts of the play. Reacting against the Victorian sentimentalizing of Shylock, they refuse him the slightest scrap of sympathy: he is, they say, as barefaced an ogre as ever rampaged through a fairy-tale, and they have therefore no hesitation in prophesying for him an ogre's end. In so far as they speak from impression, they can be answered only by the remark that other impressions are possible, and perhaps inevitable if the play is considered in all its parts. But when they descend to argument, they may perhaps be more efficaciously dealt with. Noting, for example, that in a number of Elizabethan and Jacobean plays besides the *Merchant of Venice* a daughter rebels against a usurious father; and that in all these plays sympathy is required for the daughter alone: Shakespeare, they conclude, cannot possibly have required anything different or anything further. It is however exceedingly hazardous to assume that, because plays are alike in a single detail, they must be alike in another; and the widest difference of opinion is possible whether details are alike or not. Not all would agree that to rebel against a father is the same as to rob him; and a majority would strenuously deny that to rob him out of sheer covetousness is at all comparable with doing so on behalf of a lover whom the father, in the exercise of his usurer's profession, is supposed to have already robbed. Jessica alone commits the former crime; all other predatory daughters may flatter themselves that they are no more culpably, no less laudably engaged than in restoring property to its rightful owner. And one[1] of them even so – Rebecca in *The Hog hath lost his Pearl* – has the grace to regret that it should be her father whom she must rob; rather than compunction, Jessica shows complacency, or at least nonchalance, in her robbing. Nor is any elopement other than Jessica's introduced by a comment as sinister as Gratiano's: that though a lover enters with 'unbated fire' upon his amorous enterprise, he emerges from it 'lean, rent and beggared' as by a strumpet. Nowhere else is wild gaiety on the lover's part contrasted with, on the part of the father, not merely sharp greed but disciplined sobriety. The complaints of no father but Shylock are shot through and through with pain. When the usurer Mammon in *Jack Drum's Entertainment* cries after his obligations and his bonds, his bonds and his obligations, he laments merely the simultaneous loss of two things that are dear to him; nor does Gripe in *Wily Beguiled* do more, though his cry, 'My daughter! my money! what shall I do?' is more closely copied from Shylock's. For in *Wily Beguiled* the daughter, though eloping, is ignorant of the robbery made upon her father; while in the *Merchant of Venice* she is responsible for it. Shylock laments the loss of one dear thing, his money, which he suffers because of another dear thing, his daughter, to whom the money had been confided. Therefore he feels himself wounded, not only in his purse, not only in the parental affection which he might share with an animal, but in the trust which none but a human being might invite or repose. However remotely, his distress resembles Othello's, when persuaded that Desdemona has violated, not only the loyalty which she owes him with her body, but loyalties of a wider,

---

[1] In the *Match at Midnight*, Moll Bloodhound shows a reluctance that needs to be overcome by a sophism.

deeper, nobler kind. And as Othello proceeds to the murder of Desdemona and her supposed accomplice, so Shylock prays that Jessica might be 'dead at (his) feet and the jewels in her ear!... hearsed at (his) foot and the ducats in her coffin'. To respond to this prayer as to an outburst of ogreish cruelty, even to begin to compare Shylock with grotesques such as Gripe and Mammon – this surely is to have ears as dull and understandings as limited as those of Solanio and Salerio, when they echo the guttersnipes of Venice.

But, continue the critics, a Jew on the Elizabethan stage cannot have appeared other than grotesque, since he was played with a snout large enough to shadow Paul's, and red enough to serve as lanthorn and candlelight. If so, at least one Jew, Gerontus in the *Three Ladies of London*, must be allowed to have overcome his physical disabilities, since he is held up not merely for sympathy but for imitation; and if one Jew, why not two? On the subject of Jewry, at any rate, Shylock is more eloquent than Gerontus. But we have no time, even if there were need, to quote the relevant passages, since the critics in question are far too dangerous to be brushed aside on the plea of a single character in a single play – who may, after all, have constituted an exception. If possible, the critics need to be despatched; for they imply the doctrine that a popular playwright necessarily restricts his interests to those of the greater, that is the least intelligent, part of his audience. Such a doctrine threatens our understanding, not only of Shakespeare, but of any playwright who attains to both popularity and distinction. If it is sound, Marlowe for example must no longer be held to have woven a contempt and hatred of Christianity into the texture of his *Tamburlaine* and *Jew of Malta*; since the mob, had they suspected anything of the kind, would have wrecked the stage.

The conclusion is absurd, and absurd to such a degree as to encourage the suggestion that Shakespeare intended to rouse sympathy – the sympathy of an intelligent reader, that is – for Shylock not only as a human being, not only as a Jew, but also as a usurer. Certainly usurers enjoyed little favour in Elizabethan times, and least of all amongst the Puritan preachers. But it would not seem inevitable that, on this point alone, Shakespeare should have joined forces with the Puritans. And though considerably broader speculators upon human affairs, such as

Bacon and Ben Johnson, continued as late as 1625 to cherish the notion that usury impeded trade, it would not seem impossible for Shakespeare, at an earlier date, to have shown himself broader still. His mind was after all more mobile than Jonson's; and unlike Bacon, he had mixed intimately with the world of trade which, by its practice at least, had long acknowledged the benefits of usury. If so, he may very well, for the delectation of the populace, have arrayed Shylock in some of the comic habits traditional to the usurer – in the habit, for example, of starving his servants, while boasting that they gormandize; and in that of wasting a borrower's purse by procuring him an unprofitable servant, or by feasting at his expense; for the discharge of a conscience in part consonant with that of the populace, Shakespeare may very well have allowed credit to Antonio for rescuing those who 'made moan' of foreclosures which were threatened by Shylock; while at the same time, and for the complete discharge of a conscience peculiarly sensitive, Shakespeare awarded blame rather than credit for the practice of lending money gratis, and so bringing down 'the rate of usance...in Venice'. By removing an efficient check upon reckless deals, such open-handedness is as likely to disorder trade as it disorders the lives of the young men. As has been noted, the discipline which enables Shylock to accumulate ducats contrasts favourably with the levity which allows Lorenzo to welcome as though they fell from heaven accumulations falling from other people's balconies. For a similar reason, Antonio's custom of railing,

> Even there where merchants most do congregate,   (I. iii. 46)

upon Shylock's 'bargains and (his) well-won thrift' makes the opposite of a pretty picture. Subsidized and arbitrary squeamishness, it appears, reads dogged and painful industry a lecture upon deportment.

But whatever the exact proportions of good and evil that assist Shylock, up to the crisis of the trial he so skilfully manages both of them as, though a private person, to overawe the public powers of Venice. However grudgingly, they hold themselves ready to his nod. Other private persons therefore, unless clever enough to disconcert Shylock's managements, have no hope save of their curses frightening him from giving the nod, or of their prayers dissuading him. Such is the case of Antonio's friends. But Shylock's resolution renders him impervious to fright; and as he retorts, prayers to be effective need to be turned with more wit than at least the 'good youth' Gratiano is endowed with. As for Bassanio, he cuts a pitiable enough figure without the aid of any retort. Recklessly yielding to the impulse to strike an attitude, he blusters:

> Good cheer, Antonio! what man, courage yet;
> The Jew shall have my flesh, blood, bones and all
> Ere thou shalt lose for me one drop of blood. (IV. i. 111f)

Thereby, as Professor Coghill has remarked, he shows himself a liar; but also, he shows himself a Bottom who, having blundered out of comic into tragic surroundings, provokes not so much amusement as contempt. Cast for the part of spectator at Antonio's martyrdom, he covets the part of martyr as well; while remaining a spectator, he would seize for himself a share of whatever limelight falls upon Antonio.

Not that Antonio is likely to mind. Within three acts he has taken leave of Bassanio on as many as three occasions, and on one of them in terms little less than insulting. Such conduct implies not so much a reluctance as a readiness to part with his friend: a readiness to be expected from the melancholic who, in intention at least, has already parted with the world. With relief it would seem as well as with resignation, Antonio contemplates himself as a 'tainted wether', a rotten fruit.

The result is that, when Portia plunges into the conflict as Antonio's champion, she finds herself fighting not only single-handed but empty-handed. No weapons are in sight save those that Shylock wields. Therefore the sole policy for her to pursue is to induce him to turn the weapons upon himself: to disconcert him in their management, as was suggested a moment ago. For success, she will require a modicum of luck: Shylock must give the answers that she counts on to the questions that she poses. But the skill with which the questions are chosen so as to permit of the intervention of luck, the alertness with which luck is exploited once it has intervened: these impart to the trial scene the life for which it is justly famous.

By her mercy-speech, Portia provides Shylock with the opportunity to repeat the cry of the Jews at the crucifixion: 'My deeds upon my head!' Thereby he swells, by once more exercis-

ing, a Luciferian self-confidence. She proceeds to swell it yet
further: the law, she assures him, is wholly at his back, and that
anything should prevail against the law is unthinkable. Rewarded
by the cry

> A Daniel come to judgment, yea a Daniel!
> O wise young judge, how I do honour thee,   (IV. i. 220)

she goes on to lull whatever suspicions of her benignancy it is
still possible for him to entertain. Conscientiously examining
the bond, she confirms that it has fallen due. She busies herself
about the conditions necessary for the execution of the bond.

> Are there balance here to weigh
> The flesh?   (*ibid.* 252)

'I have them ready', comes the answer. Then

> Have by some surgeon, Shylock, on your charge,
> To stop his wounds, lest he do bleed to death.

He takes the suggestion to be as charitable as it appears; though
a moment's reflection would suffice to convince him that, were it
so in fact, it would have been addressed, or would in any case be
repeated, to persons other than himself. Since Bassanio has
offered to pay three thousand, six thousand, thirty thousand
ducats, it is known to everyone in the court that he carries
money enough to fee all the surgeons in Venice. But what by
now has come to seem a certain victory excites Shylock too
violently for him to reflect. The crisis has arrived at which his
previously clear sight begins to dim, at which the point of his
weapon, hitherto unerringly directed upon his enemy, wavers
and begins to seek out himself. Seizing back the bond, he triumphantly points out that it makes no mention of a surgeon. After
Antonio's supposedly last words, which provide a further
illustration of his inertia; after a further illustration of the ranting
ineptitude of the young men, provided by their regrets at not
being allowed to make a holocaust of themselves, their families
and 'all the world': Portia needs no more than herself to take
back the bond and to point out that, if it makes no mention of
a surgeon, neither does it of blood – that Shylock is not permitted to shed the blood which he has refused to staunch.
Diamond has cut diamond, or rather, diamond has cut himself.
The equity of preparing the way for him to do so if he wishes,

and of standing aside while he carries out the wish: this is so evident that for the moment all memory of law and justice goes by the board. It is a moment at which reality assumes the limpidity of a fairy-tale. By failing to plead the griefs he labours under as human being, as Jew, or even as usurer; by proceeding on the sole ground of a 'lodged hate and...loathing' which he bears Antonio; by insisting on the sight and sound of streaming blood as necessary and sufficient for the glutting of his hate: Shylock succeeds in harrowing like the ogre which he is not. Against his present blackness, everything else shows as white. Even the 'wild, rude and bold' voice of Gratiano takes on a seraphic tone as he trumpets

A second Daniel, a Daniel, Jew!   (*ibid.* 329)

It is a view-halloo in which all, including the reader, exultantly join. And the more adequately to deride what at the moment seems the futility of the law, this is enriched by a new chapter – new at any rate according to Professor Charlton; and if not new, it has curiously avoided Portia's and everybody's notice hitherto – according to which, and *ex post facto*, Shylock is himself amenable to the penalties he has sought to inflict. No justice for the ogre: a contemptuous mercy may be shown, but justice is as little the medium where he may be coped with as a bird in water or a fish in air.

Thus the trial-scene ends amidst a general jubilation, an all-but universal ebriety; but the play cannot end in such a manner, on pain of a complete divorce from the real. Hence the fifth act, opened by that precious pair Jessica and Lorenzo. They prelude of music and moonlight, but also of stealing: of a stealing of love, of stealing away to a lover, and of stealing both oneself and other things from a father. Few but Shakespeare could have conceived of such a harmony, and still fewer have ventured upon its execution: but not only its authenticity, its relevance becomes apparent when, the moon having withdrawn and Portia having put a stop to the music, there develops the wrangle about the rings. Husbands are to be taught that, though the memory of justice may for a moment be obliterated, inexorably it re-asserts itself; and for the first time in their lives, the two husbands under instruction are to be submitted to the yoke of justice. Adversaries are rarely obliging enough, as was Shylock, to entrench themselves within their wrongdoings: whatever wrongs they conceive or commit – and, from the point of view of the husbands, the women's disguising of themselves may be regarded as a wrong – they insist tenaciously on such rights as they possess. These rights are to be accommodated, not at a blow and in a blaze as Shylock was dealt with, but by an adjustment so irksome as to resemble a fumbling in the dark. The details of the adjustment are at any rate liable to be so fine that, if they are to be at all scrupulously observed, the eyes must wander from them no further than they can see in the dark. Recklessness of any kind must therefore be abandoned: and in particular the striking of attitudes which, however soothing to the person who strikes them, risk throwing others, and ultimately himself, into confusion. Inevitably the husbands yield, since the women who finished Shylock with a ruthless expedition are the last to be suspected of exaggerated or ill-timed respect for detail. Antonio alone proves recalcitrant: awaking from his apathy to find himself still alive, he takes the unexpected result of the trial, not as a reproof, but as a vindication of recklessness. He casts aside the intolerable burden of maturity: and having emerged unscathed from a wager which endangered his body, is eager to enter upon another which shall put his soul in peril. Portia's acceptance amounts to a nullification of the wager, since she and no longer Antonio is the leader of the young men: even the mercantile affairs of Antonio have come to repose in her competent hands.

It is tempting to seek Portia's considered judgment on what has happened in the *Merchant of Venice* – caskets, wedding, trial and all – in the verses which she exchanges with Nerissa on their return to Belmont. That the verses are enigmatic renders the search difficult, but hardly hopeless, since presumably they are intended to convey some meaning or other. And that the meaning is weighty is suggested, not only by their tone, but by their enigmatic quality itself.

> How far that little candle throws his beams!
> So shines a good deed in a naughty world, (V. i. 91)

reflects Portia, inclined apparently to plume herself on the rescue of Antonio in which she has just succeeded. If so, the flatness of Nerissa's reply –

> When the moon shone, we did not see the candle –

while thoroughly appropriate to Nerissa, is as thoroughly inappropriate to the context and incompatible with the respect she owes her mistress. Rather than rebuking Nerissa, however, Portia shows herself content to accept rebuke:

> So doth the greater glory dim the less,

she agrees; and goes on to give Nerissa's thought a majestic and melodious development –

> A substitute shines brightly as a king
> Until a king be by; and then his state
> Empties itself as does an inland brook
> Into the main of waters.   (*ibid.* 95)

Any inclination to plume herself, it now seems, has vanished: whatever her achievement, in her eyes it has now grown as 'indistinct As water is in water', absorbed into a whole which, whether or not better, is vaster than itself and at least on that account more glorious.

From what immediately follows it might appear that the whole cannot be better: for 'Nothing is good...without respect': without, that is, the operation of the reason, by which a thing is first abstracted from the whole and then related to other things which have been abstracted in like manner.

> The crow doth sing as sweetly as the lark
> When neither is attended –   (*ibid.* 103f)

apart from relationships of the kind 'the odds is gone, And there is nothing...remarkable'. On the other hand, an excess of relationships may undo the work of abstraction:

> The nightingale, if she should sing by day
> When every goose is cackling, would be thought
> No better a musician than the wren.

Goodness, that is, depends upon a mean: neither too many nor too few things must be considered at the same time, enterprises neither too narrow nor too wide in scope must be undertaken.

But whether too many or too few, too narrow or too wide cannot be decided by the reason alone: which, once embarked upon its proper task of abstracting and relating, asks for nothing more than to continue. Hence it may clutter with objects the eye that would see and the hand that would labour, and so undermine the confidence of their owner in the powers of each: as Troilus is to complain in a later play,

> reason and respect
> Make livers pale, and lustihood deject.
>> (*Troilus and Cressida*, II. ii. 49)

Reason needs to be halted in its task; and can be halted only by the owner of hand and eye. Presumably he does so when prompted, from without and from within, that he has before him objects of the number and the kind that he has both the desire and the capacity to deal with: when, in the words of Marston, 'time, place and blood' seem to 'strike music'; when, to use Portia's word, the 'season', the fitting, the propitious moment appears to have arrived. And if it has,

> How many things by season seasoned are
> To their right praise and true perfection!   (V. i. 108)

Since the fitness of the moment depends upon a subjective factor, it may differ from owner to owner and, for the same owner, from time to time. It would therefore seem possible to conceive of an owner of such extensive powers of hand and eye as to be able to dispense with abstraction: to deal with the whole rather than mere parts of it, and to relate that whole to himself. To such an Owner the whole will be not only 'glorious' but good, or rather, He will make no distinction between goodness and glory. Portia's thought, if it allows of completion in this way, purges itself of scepticism; and what at first sight appeared to be such is revealed as the unavoidable accompaniment, the familiar obverse of a mystical persuasion – or at any rate an actual faith.

Completing Portia's thought in another direction, it is possible to conceive of an owner of a humbler kind training himself and being trained so as to diminish the likelihood of his being deceived by promptings, and to increase the likelihood of his profiting from every 'season' that offers itself. In this matter however the greatest caution is necessary, and nothing more than a modest confidence can be hoped for; certainly nothing equal to an absolute security. The whole comprises so many and such strange things that it is impossible for all to fall within a limited experience; and for what has not been experienced, nothing can prepare. The blood for instance may prompt with unexpected and unprecedented violence, as perhaps it prompted Portia when first brought into more than occasional contact with Bassanio; and on doing so, it cannot wholly be disregarded even by those trained to an extreme of self-control. As Portia herself says, 'The brain may devise laws for the blood, but a hot temper leaps o'er a cold decree.' Of the promptings from without, those most likely to deceive are perhaps the sudden clearings amongst objects effected at least partly by luck: the comparative or absolute limpidities with which luck may, for a moment, endow the world. The danger is great of assuming that such limpidities will endure, and dangerous consequences may follow from the assumption. On the other hand, it may be foolhardy, or even fatal, not to take advantage of the limpidities. Had Portia scrupled to clamp about Shylock's neck the pillory into which he unguardedly stretched it, she must not only have witnessed, but part performed, the slaughter of Antonio; from the plight in which she was plunged by her father's will, there opened no avenue of escape save an unreserved yielding to fancy. 'God sort all!' as she exclaims when girding herself for the wrangle of the rings; as she might have exclaimed when girding herself for each of the crises in her life; and as she must exclaim when viewing these crises in retrospect. Though as yet they seem to have had happy issues, who can tell whether the issues will continue to seem happy when a year, a decade, a whole life-time has passed? Then and only then will it be known what Portia was 'doomed' to by the caskets: whether her fancy evaporated without leaving a trace, whether it rotted to her own distress and to that of all her intimates, or whether, to everyone's comfort and her own, it died into something deeper, wider, more august than its transitory self.

By his use of fairy-tale element, Shakespeare gives to his play the shape of a comedy; by the element of reality, he raises it to a level at which a term like comedy ceases to have a meaning. He makes of it a mirror of the human struggle with what is too opaque to allow a shape, or at times anything, to be seen; too hard to allow the imposition of a shape. The struggle is the more impressive.

4

ALL'S WELL THAT ENDS WELL

The scenes in which Parolles is baited contain some notable writing. There are for example the lines in verse with which Parolles concluded IV. iii; and in the same scene some remarks in prose exchanged by the Captains which of themselves, one could think, suffice to disprove the charge of horseplay. One of these is perhaps quoted as often as anything else in Shakespeare:

> The web of our life is of a mingled yarn, good and ill together; our virtues would be proud if our faults whipped them not, and our crimes would despair if they were not cherished by our virtues. (IV. iii. 319ff)

It may however be doubted whether these lines are as often understood in their context. Certainly Brigstocke, who was charged with the first Arden edition (1904) – the editor of the second (1959) makes no comment on these lines – failed to do so: for he glossed the Captain's last two phrases as meaning: 'we should despair on account of our crimes, had we not our virtues to console us' – whereas, according to the text, it is not we but our crimes which are liable to despair; whereas it is not we but they which our virtues are credited (or reproached) with cherishing. Evidently Brigstocke paid inadequate attention to the opening phrase in which the Captain deplores the 'mingled', not the web of the life as such, but the 'yarn' of which the 'web' is put together. The first of these figures, which is not Shakespeare's, would imply that in our life good and evil, like the strands in a web, are comparatively easy to distinguish; according to the second, each strand contains both good and evil in itself. In consequence good and evil cannot be separated by the eye or by the hand without the web of life dissolving into a heap of fibres, a heap which is shapeless because its elements bear no more than a local relation one to another; without, in other words, life itself collapsing.

In this speech of the Captain's Shakespeare is, I think, echoing a notion already suggested by the Countess at the opening of the play, that in some cases and on some occasions our 'virtuous qualities' are 'virtues and traitors too'. But neither can I cite this passage without discussion, for it contains implications not all of which, it would seem, have been realized. Let me therefore quote it in full. The Countess is endeavouring to explain to Lafeu the confidence she feels in Helen's future:

I have those hopes of her good that her education promises: her dispositions she inherits, which makes fair gifts fairer; for where an unclean mind carries virtuous qualities, there commendations go with pity, they are virtues and traitors too; in her they are better for their simpleness; she derives her honesty and achieves her goodness. (I. i. 36ff)

Faithful to a tradition, springing it seems from Warburton – no very creditable source by the way – the recent Arden editor nonchalantly takes the Countess's 'virtuous qualities', not as 'fine moral qualities', but 'the qualities of a virtuoso, skill, capacity, technical powers' (likewise the New Cambridge Shakespeare spoke of 'qualities of "virtu"', Brigstocke of *passione delle belle arti*). The recent editor, it is true, is able to quote in his support a phrase from *Il Cortegiano*, as translated by Sir Thomas Hoby in 1561, but – whatever his usual practice – in this place Hoby is Italianizing. For according to the *OED* 'virtuous', in the sense of 'belonging to the virtuosi' hardly became current in England before the second half of the seventeenth century, nor did the word 'virtuoso' itself and the related 'virtuosity' – the root word 'virtu' – delaying its entry until the eighteenth. Further, granting that the *OED*'s 'first quotations' are at times belated, can we assume that the 'education' provided by the Countess for Helen consisted in the hiring of schoolmasters 'cunning in Greek, Latin and other languages', or 'in music and mathematics', such as Baptista desired for his socially mature daughter Bianca (*The Taming of the Shrew*, II. i. 81ff) – and not rather in her 'bringing up', in the training for social maturity – which, in the sixteenth century, membership of a noble household was valued for supplying? Can we, above all, assume that the word 'goodness', with which the Countess triumphantly concludes her praise – she uses the word absolutely, be it noted, and without qualification of any kind – can we imagine that this implies no more than the ability to conjugate a foreign verb, or to proving a date? That seems to me quite impossible.

If so, the Countess is resolutely rejecting the possibility that

any 'fine moral quality' that Helen possesses should be put to
an evil use. Were this 'fine moral quality' perfect, the Countess
would be uttering a tautology, or rather nonsense; but in fact
[she] fills out and weights down her words, since such qualities
are never perfect in human beings as long as they remain on this
earth – unless they happen to be saints, and not always (it
might be added) even then. That persons whom common usage
compels us – at least in certain situations – to acknowledge as
'virtuous' to a degree: that such persons may be trying as
companions, on occasion even perilous – that in Helen's words
(I. i. 101) virtue as it is normally encountered may have
'steely bones' – is a matter of experience none the less bitter,
because daily. Since the saints are more or less secure of the use
to which their virtues will be put, we may feel secure to an equal
degree in the society of the saints. But we rarely meet with such,
nor are they dealt with in this comedy.

Nor is the comedy written for or about theologians or
philosophers, and it must be admitted that the Countess is far
from sound in expecting the perfection of virtue from below
and by way of natural disposition (or 'dispositions' – as will
perhaps become apparent in a moment – this plural has not been
idly chosen), rather than from above and by way of grace.
Nevertheless she is far from talking unintelligibly or even
unintelligently: there is no necessary opposition between nature
and grace, and for moral purpose to be achieved or even undertaken, the two not only can but must co-operate. A person may
be precipitated into vice with the help of a natural disposition,
say towards lust or avarice; but then, he may be hoisted into
virtue with the help of a disposition of an opposite kind – and
what is more, the same person [who] may be sometimes inclined towards lust may also be inclined towards generosity.
Then indeed his open-handedness will be carried by an unclean
mind, so that, though it must be admired, it also calls to be
pitied. No doubt the Countess is optimistic in her belief that, by
nature, Helen is wholly disposed to fulfil [her dispositions] by
the training she has received; before the scene is out proof is to
be provided that what appears her filial piety is so far from
'simple' as not to be filial piety at all. Nevertheless the Countess
should [?make] the Captain a formal notion of the 'mingled
yarn' out of which human life is woven.

And of this the Countess's son, Bertram, by now so well favoured in his dispositions, though as yet far short of her in experience of life – of this even Bertram is not without an inkling. He shows this when, Diana having refused his advances, he taunts her with being 'holy-cruel' (IV. ii. 32): that is, with employing holiness, which if she possesses it, counts among her virtues, for the purpose of giving him pain. If such were her intention, it would be criminal. The intention is by no means impossible, perhaps not even uncommon: though to Brigstocke it seemed so, for (in his notes, not in the text) he proposed the reading 'wholly cruel'. Such a proposal is hardly conceivable nowadays, largely perhaps because pious pornography has familiarized us with Bertram's invitation (he does not use the phrase, but it can be forged) that Diana show herself 'lustful-holy' – cultivate holiness that is with the co-operation of whatever lust is to be found amongst her dispositions.

The three interpretations of the text we have so far rejected have this in common, that they are commonplace, whereas they might have been subtle. The passages to which they refer come from different portions of the play, of which perhaps they may be taken as representative. As a whole, this would seem to remain in close contact with the commonplace so that, without an attention that is constantly alert, it can be taken as such; while to attention of the required kind, it reveals itself as of an impressive subtlety. And the subtlety would seem still the more impressive because it does not, so to speak, overlay the commonplace alongside and by means of which it is achieved; nor does it depress the commonplace by force of contrast but rather, by that of assimilation, ennoble it. So that the commonplace is felt to be at once present to the play and absent from it: as present conferring an immediate relevance to everyday actions and affairs, as absent investing these affairs with an appearance that is different and new. To distinguish for a moment between the poetic and dramatic aspects of *All's Well*, subtlety of this kind is I think to be traced both in the construction and the verse. The verse might perhaps be said to display a Wordsworthian character: a dependence on verbal qualities not felt in the words taken singly, which as such are commonplace; while in the lines built up of the words, and in the words as constituent of the lines, they are felt continuously throughout.

I am not of course suggesting that there is not a quantity of
bad verse in *All's Well* – not so much, I think, as is ordinarily
assumed; but nevertheless an appreciable quantity. To give it
primary or unique importance would however seem a sign of
Philistinism: as it would be to deny the elegance of a façade
because a number of windows are boarded up, or to ignore the
sweep of a row of columns because one or two of them are
replaced by iron stanchions.

Let us look first at the verse, since a satisfactory account of
this may, in case of necessity, do duty for an account of much of
the rest; and time is limited. The verse of the play contains no
ganglia of metaphors such as are typical of the later tragedies.
Such of its metaphors as are given any development are allowed,
as it were, ample space and room:

> No, come thou home, Rossilion,
> Whence honour but of danger wins a scar
> As oft it loses all: I will be gone;
> My being here it is that holds thee hence:
> Shall I stay here to do it? No, no, although
> The air of Paradise did fan the house
> And angels officed all. (III. ii.120ff)

Note how the poetic radiation, if the phrase may be allowed, is
from the passage as a whole (and of course, from the longer
passage from which it is taken) rather than from any part of it;
note how, in so far as centres of radiation can be distinguished,
these are widely spaced; note the nature of these centres – the
bare bestowal upon Bertram of his territorial title; the restrained
handling of the war, with the giving and the taking of a single
scar; the verb 'fan', bringing air into the palace of Rossilion
not for an idle purpose but, as [?use] the angels to do an 'office';
note finally the connections of this word with the commonplace,
the humdrum and at the same time indispensable – all combining
with the connotations of the word 'Paradise' to give a picture
of home. And to this home Bertram belongs because, of course,
he is Rossilion. Elsewhere, metaphors are developed along so
narrow a portion of their possible extent that, at first sight, it
may appear no development is intended but only repetition: as
in the third line of the following speech of the King's:

> Let's take the instant by the forward top:
> For we are old, and on our quick'st decrees

> Th'inaudible and noiseless foot of time
> Steels ere we can effect them. (V. iii. 39)

But the line is not redundant, and the King is saying that, if the foot of time is inaudible because we do not hear it, neither could we hear it however much our senses were sharpened, for it makes no noise that might by any agency be heard. As physical beings we are at the mercy of Time: which dominates physical nature without the restraint of physical laws. In other passages there would appear to be no metaphor at all:

> In argument of praise, or to the worth
> Of the great Count himself, she is too mean
> To have her name repeated; all her deserving
> Is a reserved honesty, and that
> I have not heard examined. (III. v. 59ff)

And here a Wordsworthian character is perhaps particularly apparent. But it is also I think to be discerned in other passages not quite so distinguished, but on that account more typical of the play:

> This is not well, rash and unbridled boy,
> To fly the favours of so good a King,
> To pluck his indignation on thy head
> By the misprizing of a maid too virtuous
> For the contempt of empire. (III. ii. 26ff)

Here such metaphors as are introduced remain, so to speak, unripened in single words; while for whatever effect the passage may produce, these words can claim no greater credit than can the adjectives 'good' and 'virtuous'. Worn with frequent handling, such commonplace adjectives are often fatal to poetry; in *All's Well*, however, as in the best of Wordsworth, there shine through them, not the debased notions of goodness and virtue as hurriedly elaborated in haphazard living, but as they once existed and may be restored to existence in an ordered work of art.

But to illuminate this point, which may be important, it will perhaps be better to abandon for the moment the comparison with Wordsworth. Turning to *King Lear*, we shall be working not only with a drama, but with a Shakespearian drama; that is, *in pari materia*. As has often been remarked, on awaking from his madness Lear speaks in a language [different] from that he was earlier wont to employ. It is in fact a language similar to that of which we have found examples in *All's Well*:

King Lear	Be your tears wet? Yes, faith. I pray, weep not.
	If you have poison for me, I will drink it.
	I know you do not love me; for your sisters
	Have as I do remember done me wrong:
	You have some cause, they have not.
Cordelia	No cause, no cause. (*King Lear*, IV. vii. 71)

The rhythm is different, presumably for reasons which may become apparent later, in another connection; the style however is non-figurative, and the vocabulary commonplace and predominantly monosyllabic. Yet the passage is felt to be of a tremendous force, such as the monosyllables in their own right could hardly possess. What merit the latter have of their own would appear to be that of offering no obstacle to a force which the play has generated throughout its length and which is, so to speak, discharged through them instantaneously. Something of this kind, I suggest, happens in the last passage quoted from *All's Well*; it also happens, and to a much more striking extent, in the passage I am about to quote, occurring not at the beginning of Act III but from the end of Act V – at a time, that is, when the play has had opportunity to gather the greater part of its force. Everyone except Diana supposes Helen to be dead, but she has just entered:

King	Is't real that I see?
Helen	No, my good lord;
	'Tis but the shadow of a wife you see,
	The name and not the thing.
Bertram	Both, both. O pardon! (V. iii. 30ff)

Helen is but the shadow of a wife because Bertram has neither acknowledged nor, as he thinks, used her as such. It becomes clear to him (hitherto we have spoken of 'radiation'; now perhaps we should speak of the whole play 'focusing' at this point), that, without being publicly acknowledged, she has submitted to such use. At the sight of such humility where he had least reason to expect it, Bertram is crushed: his pride, his selfishness vanish, he himself is humbled; and like Cordelia, he goes near to losing the power of articulate speech. Yet the broken exclamations of both of them, though commonplace

enough, because of the circumstances in which they are introduced, transmit an agony.[1]

Let us retain the comparison with *King Lear*, for it may
give further help. Both Lear and Bertram attain to humility
and, having attained it, speak a language similar in some
respects. They attain it however by different paths, and while
treading these paths their language is very different. It is
dangerous to throw off summary judgments about Lear but,
for the purposes of this paper, I may perhaps be allowed to call
him, above all, audacious. Publicly he defies the laws of nature,
physical and moral. Publicly he demands from his daughters
protestations of affection which cannot, with any honesty, be
given. Rejected on that account by his honest daughter, he
ranges himself publicly on the side of the dishonest. They too
reject him, whereupon he seeks alliance of the physical elements, of which he demands that they destroy the world, his
daughters and himself. They do nothing of the kind: they
destroy what remains of his audacity, but only at the cost of a
temporary destruction of his sanity. His progress to humility
lies through an increasing darkness: from self-deception such as
cannot flourish except in obscurity, and from an early to an
advanced stage of this, up to a final obscurity which blots all
but the outlines of his former existence, which covers with
oblivion all but his essential self – and this, having shaken off
'sophistication', is of course humble. By humility, it may not be
superfluous to remark, nothing Uriah Heep-ish is meant:
nothing, that is, akin to an affected lowering of oneself below
what one thinks one is; but rather a discovering of what one is,
followed by a lowering of oneself to that.

The last fault of which Bertram can be accused is audacity.
He has not even courage – moral courage, that is; for of physical
courage (and the point is of some importance) he would seem to
have an adequate supply. He flees from moral conflicts as long
as it is possible to do so; except from those immediately
consequent upon his passions, and from these he has not the
courage to flee. '[I'll] write to the King', he says, 'that which
I durst not speak.' (II. iii. 254f). To Helen, rather than repeating the boast he has made to Parolles,

[1] The text of this essay up to this point is taken from a long-hand revision probably
made during the last few weeks of James Smith's life. From here onwards it is
taken from two corrected typescripts composed many years earlier. (E. M. W.)

> Although before the solemn priest I have sworn,
> I will not bed her –   (cf. 265f)

he proffers excuses couched in verse contrasting perceptibly
with the clarity and the freedom usual in the play:

> You must not marvel, Helen, at my course,
> Which holds not colour with the time, nor does
> The ministration and required office
> On my particular. Prepared I was not
> For such a business   (II. v. 58)

and so on; winding up with

> And rather muse than ask why I entreat you,
> For my respects are better than they seem,
> And my appointments have in them a need
> Greater than shows itself at the first view
> To you that know them not.   (*ibid.* 65ff)

A mystery-monger, who speaks with wool in the mouth; or as
Fabian says of Viola, 'a coward, a most devout coward,
religious in it'. In the same spirit or lack of it, when first it
appears that, upon the mere profession of repentance, he is to be
forgiven his dereliction of duty, he is ready with a lie to account
for the dereliction; and later with lie upon lie, when it becomes
clear that forgiveness is to be obtained on no such easy terms.
For the King recognizes Helen's ring and – a more urgent
matter – Diana enters, claiming fulfilment of a promise of
marriage. First he denies he has done anything but 'laugh with'
such a 'fond and desperate creature'; (V. iii. 177f) then, on
being accused of having seduced her while a virgin, thinks it
wise to admit to fornication. Thereby he may elude the graver
charge; and the fornication, committed as he avers with 'a
common gamester of the camp', (*ibid.* 187) may be held to
have been the lapse of a moment,

> Natural rebellion, done i'th'blaze of youth.   (*ibid.* 6)

It is revealed however that, to buy the favours of this common
gamester, he has not refused to part with a 'monumental ring'
(259): how can he explain that? He shifts his ground: 'certain it
is I liked her', he admits,

> And boarded her i'th'wanton way of youth –

his sin, that is, cannot have been impulsive merely, for he

persisted in it over a period. But for the length of that period, he claims, Diana is responsible, not he; since she abused his inexperience with

Her infinite cunning with her modern grace.   (*ibid.* 215)

Parolles now comes on the scene, not without malice but ready to swear that, if inexperience was concerned at all in this unsavoury business, it was so on Diana's side rather than on Bertram's; that any cunning deployed was not hers, but his. To induce her to yield, a promise of marriage did pass. Could Bertram find any answer to this? It would appear difficult: and if the crime with which he has been charged has not been fully proved, its ugliness, or rather Bertram's, has been but the more fully revealed by his attempts to veil it. Had he retreated rapidly and in a single movement, his pursuers might have followed with equal rapidity: as it is they have had opportunity, and have been obliged, to reconnoitre every corner of the sorry landscape he has exposed. But he is spared the embarrassing necessity of looking for a subterfuge, and the more embarrassing knowledge of no subterfuge being available, by Helen's rising, so to speak, from the grave. The sin he has committed in thought; which he himself believes he has committed, not only in thought but in fact; which had he committed in fact, would have brought ruin on others besides himself: this sin he is now revealed as having had no opportunity, other than in thought, of committing, And the opportunity has been closed to him by the devotion of his wife; who in return for contempt has put it in his power to fulfil a duty rather than violate his faith, to confer a benefit rather than inflict an injury. The effect of this discovery on Bertram has already been noted.

Any wrenching of the phrase *felix culpa* from its traditional context is rightly regarded with distrust; perhaps however the traditional should be kept in mind, if the last scene from *All's Well* is to be appreciated – or, by implication, the whole play. For in it Shakespeare would seem to seek, and in no small measure to gain, a close co-operation with the more fundamental of Christian doctrines, the more essential of Christian practices. A verse which seems to prove this will be quoted elsewhere in this paper; for the moment, it is perhaps sufficient to refer to the close similarity between the scheme or course of the last scene, and that of an examination of conscience such as prepares and qualifies for the sacrament of penance. On the one hand, the King embodies the fixed demands of justice; on the other, Diana represents the stirrings of conscience – set into motion, perhaps, by the recognition of Helen's ring. And between them both, Bertram is so pressed and squeezed that, as from Stephen Dedalus in the confessional, 'his sins trickle from his lips one by one, trickle in sinful drops...sluggish, filthy'. At the end of the process they stand revealed, not only to others, but to Bertram himself; stand revealed, not merely in outline but in depth. It is the light shining from Helen, the light of her humility and her charity which has, so to speak, this stereoscopic effect; and which, falling upon Bertram when he has at last been made ready to receive it, causes his heart to crumble and himself to be contrite. So that, if Lear's path to humility lies through increasing darkness, Bertram's would seem to lie through increasing light: first the light of natural reason which establishes beyond cavil what acts he has done, then a supernatural light which discovers to him the moral quality of these acts – the heights humanity in others has attained, the profundities to which in him it has descended.

And here, I think, a number of reasons suggest themselves for a difference between the verse of *All's Well* and that of the earlier part of *Lear*. One may be singled out as immediately relevant. Bertram's path to contrition is the more normal, Lear's is a path reserved for a small number of men. Verse in so close a contact with the commonplace as that of *All's Well* would seem inappropriate to Lear. The latter's movements, it has been emphasized, are public: that is, they are such as to call attention to themselves and are intended to do so. On the part of other agents in the play, whether moral or natural, they are met by movements equally public. Between the two the clash cannot but be spectacular, the result of the clash anything but catastrophic. In consequence, it is necessary that the verse should move rapidly, even violently, and be capable of large sweeps and brusque transitions. Not that it need be any the less precise: but obviously, precision is a quality which manifests itself differently in different subjects – in, say, a heroic fresco and in the painting of an interior. It is perhaps to the latter that *All's Well* is to be compared. For the aspects of Bertram's movements which are of main concern to the play are those which give on his interior – they are not the public but the private aspects. His heart is shattered, not so much by blows which beat upon it from without, as by solvents which work from within. And further his movements are hidden, not only from the public but in some measure from himself; since the majority of them he makes, less from any ripely considered motive, than hurried into them by the circumstances in which he finds himself, by the passions which these circumstances provoke. To convey action at this half-blind or fumbling stage, the verse in *All's Well* would seem, precisely because of its contact with the commonplace, peculiarly appropriate. As its general level is low, attention is immediately called to the slightest change in this level; as its surface is smooth and almost featureless, it permits the briefest ripple to define itself.

If Bertram's actions are fumbling as suggested, that need not of course imply they are incapable of moral qualification. Whether or not, during their performance, he is clearly conscious of where they are leading him, he cannot fail to be so once they are performed; and as he never, until the close, takes the trouble to depart from any new position he has occupied, he must be held responsible for wherever he finds himself. From considerations of this kind, however, it would seem to follow that the moral quality of his acts is dependent on his circumstances, so as to vary with the quality of these; that in other words, the Captain's diagnosis of the human situation as exemplified in Bertram – his speech about the 'web of life', quoted at the beginning of this paper – is to be taken as a fairly exact one. Some of Bertram's actions which prove to be vicious might, in other circumstances, have been the contrary; some of them which in fact cherish, might conceivably have served to whip, his vices. In effect therefore it is his virtues which are whipped: not because they and his vices have roots in common – for in themselves, such roots are good – but because, by their own growth, his virtues have increased the vigour of these roots, only to see it expended to wrongful ends. As the Countess says (and her words also are now revealed as fairly exact), virtues do not only or always operate as virtues: they are traitors too.

Bertram's attempts to free himself from Diana, for example, though not more successful are more persistent than those to

free himself from Helen. In both predicaments his action springs,
as from a root, from his combative instinct, and that in the mean-
time would seem to have been invigorated – perhaps on the
battlefields before Florence, where he has served as commander.
Abstraction made of circumstances, obedience to a natural
instinct, contains in itself the germ of good; and Bertram would
cut a sorrier figure than he does, were he to run away from his
final ordeal. Hitherto he has always run away. Fortunately this
is no longer possible; unfortunately however his circumstances
now are such as to choke any germ of good which his actions
may contain. No honourable man would be found in such circumstances; or if he were as a consequence of exceptional misfortunes to do so, he would put aside all promptings to combat,
and think only of submission. On the battlefield, on the other
hand, the honourable man is at home; the air and the soil
provoke the flowering and the fructifying, the good implied in
all attack however unscrupulous, in any wile that is adopted for
the purposes of defence. And so the twisting and turning such
as, before the Siennese as enemy, covered Bertram with glory,
before the King as judge involve him only in contempt.

Or to take a second example: the words with which Bertram
opens his wooing of Diana are such as to win him the momentary
sympathies of the reader, in spite of the desertion he intends:

> But, fair soul,
> In your fine frame hath love no quality?
> If the quick fire of love light not your mind
> You are no maiden but a monument.
> When you are dead, you should be such a one
> As you are now, for you are cold and stern;
> And now you should be as your mother was
> When your sweet self was got.   (IV. ii. 3)

Sexual passion can carry men out of their normal and often
contemptible selves; and Bertram's obedience to it, precisely
because immediate and unquestioning, blinds him to the
circumstances of his wooing so that his verse acquires a
disinterested, almost a generous quality – he is, for instance,
so far detached from his passion that he can treat of it with
playfulness. With little or no alteration, the speech might have
been addressed to Helen. And as such, it would have been
disinterested in fact, for it would have invited to the pursuit of a

common good. But as addressed to Diana, it proposes not only
that Helen shall be injured, but that Diana shall 'forsake herself'
(*ibid.* 39). She on her part is not slow to urge this on Bertram;
who therefore, as the dialogue proceeds, is compelled to allow a
voice in it, not only to sexual passion but to selfishness. And as
he cannot hope to impress Diana in the way he would with a
naked selfishness, he seeks to blend the latter with his passion;
producing the confused or bleared form of passion which we
know as sentimentality. To a mention of Helen, he replies:

> No more o'that.
> I prithee, do not strive against my vows.
> I was compelled to her, but I love thee
> By love's own sweet constraint, and will for ever
> Do thee all rights of service.   (IV. ii. 13)

When further Diana alleges Bertram's obligations, not only
to Helen but to God, he must blend selfishness with argument
to produce sophistry:

> Be not so holy-cruel, love is holy.   (*ibid.* 32)

From which the descent is easy to a hypocritical representation
of himself as an object worthy of Diana's pity:

> Stand no more off,
> But give thyself unto my sick desires
> Who then recover.   (*ibid.* 34)

Bertram has now abandoned the pretence of integrity, even to
himself; so that, when Diana demands a family heirloom as a
pledge of faith, he can no longer pertinaciously refuse it, nor
yield it up with dignity and with grace. He does so abjectly
and with a grudge:

> Here, take my ring.
> My house, mine honour, yea my life be thine,
> And I'll be bid by thee.   (*ibid.* 51)

Such slight, swift but significant changes in mood and temper
are what the verse in *All's Well* is admirably suited to capture.

It has been suggested that the connection which, in this
dialogue, Bertram endeavours to establish between holiness
and sexual satisfaction is likely to be too indiscriminately
approved by a pious form of pornography; now perhaps it is
opportune to refer to the pornographic form of impiety, likely
to condemn it no less indiscriminately. Such impiety, according

to which holiness is incompatible with the satisfaction of sex, has shown itself a principal obstacle to an understanding of the play. It may therefore be repeated that the attitude illustrated by Bertram towards the instincts in general, and towards the sexual instinct in particular, is by no means peculiar to him among the characters. The Captain implies it in the 'keynote' speech about the genetic relation between virtues and vices, so too does the Countess in hers about the treacherous possibilities in virtue; and the Countess, whose delicacy is usually conceded to be above suspicion, has other words on the topic – words which are less equivocal. She compares sexual desire or fancy (the Elizabethan term is useful, as at once morally neutral and scientifically imprecise) to a thorn, hinting thereby at the harm which it may work; but also, she associates the thorn with the rose, thereby implying that the former as well as the latter is necessary to the perfection of the plant which produces both:

> thorn
> Doth to our rose of youth rightly belong.
> Our blood to us, this to our blood is born.
> It is the show and seal of nature's truth
> When love's strong passion is impressed in youth.
>
> (I. iii. 124)

And Helen has words which are less equivocal still. She adjures the Countess, by the success the latter has made of her life, to help her (Helen) to a like success. And the particular kind of success which she at once admires and envies is one which depends, not on the eradication, but on the proper cultivation of fancy. 'If yourself', she says, (*ibid.* 204)

> Whose aged honour cites a virtuous youth,
> Did ever, in so true a flame of liking,
> Wish chastely and love dearly, that your Dian
> Was both herself and love, O then give pity.[1]

Finally, Helen illustrates this attitude, not only by her words but by her actions. If she does not succumb to temptations similar

---

[1] I. iii. 206ff. The *New Cambridge* editors follow Malone and read 'Love chastely and wish dearly'. 'The transcriber has obviously transposed *wish* and *love*', they say, 'thus making nonsense of the passage.' This is rather strongly put. Take *so* in the second line of the quotation with *that* in the third, and all would seem to be clear. Further, to reduce the identification of Dian and Love to the status of an object of the Countess's wish (she may have wished for something impossible) is, as suggested above, a notable weakening – perhaps indeed, a perversion – of the sense.

to Bertram's, she shows herself by no means insensible to them; and her vacillation in their presence conveys perhaps more convincingly than any words, how closely good and evil are intertwined in the yarn of life; how great the danger, even for the well-balanced and disciplined, of mistaking one for the other.

Helen not only disguises grief at Bertram's departure under tears which, she allows to be supposed, are shed for her father's death; for the sake of Bertram, she becomes oblivious of her father:

> What was he like?
> I have forgot him; my imagination
> Carries no favour in't but Bertram's.   (I. i. 79)

And such a father, the reader reflects, who has just listened to the Countess's eulogy of Gerard de Narbonne. The solid science acquired by the latter, the virtuous dispositions he has been able to bequeath, appear only the more commendable by contrast with the superficial charms which alone Helen is able to plead on Bertram's behalf:

> 'twas pretty, though a plague,
> To see him every hour, to sit and draw
> His arched brows, his hawking eye, his curls
> In our heart's table.   (*ibid.* 90)

It is of course natural for Helen to abandon a father for a lover; and here as elsewhere, *All's Well* shows a peculiar faithfulness in following nature. But nature has her more pathetic manifestations; and if the fancy Helen has taken to Bertram is in itself pathetic, since it persuades her into assuming obligations towards one who, as it seems, will scarcely have the grace to acknowledge them; in so far as it lures her into disavowing obligations which she herself should acknowledge, it threatens to become ridiculous, even repulsive. If not on the verge of losing her balance, Helen is at any rate losing something of her sense of proportion; and it is in this mood that she is approached by Parolles.

With him she engages on the notorious conversation about virginity which, according to Professor Brander Matthews and Miss Bradbrooke, is 'impossible to a modest-minded girl'. One hesitates to assert the contrary, since there are more ways than one of being mealy-mouthed; a great part of the indecency, however, would seem to be injected into the conversation by Parolles, whom Helen has already decided to 'love' for Bertram's sake. This shows the loss of a sense of proportion, already referred to; but not necessarily, one would think, a loss of modesty. Admitting however that the conversation is in a measure indecent: that surely is the point of its introduction, or part of the point. Under the demagoguery of fancy, Helen's little kingdom is suffering an insurrection, or is menaced with an insurrection; as a consequence of which it lies, for the moment, open to marauding attack – to attack from Parolles, or from temptations to rash and possibly vicious action such as Parolles, not unplausibly, commends. Yet for no more than a moment: for long before Parolles has made an end,[1] Helen has ceased to attend. In thought she has followed Bertram to Paris where, in the 'learning-place' of the Court (*ibid.* I. i. 173), she sees him busied about a thousand possible rivals to herself – rivals to please whom it will be necessary for him to master the witty, elegant, if at times foolish, jargon of the country and the period the

> world
> Of pretty fond adoptious christendoms
> That blinking Cupid gossips.   (*ibid.* 169ff)

Brought into contact with such a world and with that of the Court, with its variety, splendour and at any rate outward decency; confronted with the human dignity and the mutual respect among humans which such a decency, however remotely, implies: Bertram himself, Helen's fancy for Bertram, shrink to something like their true proportions. On the chance of immediately gratifying fancy, Helen can no longer contemplate forfeiting the world's good opinion; for which that of Parolles appears – and she has the grace to make the comparison – an

---

[1] I. i. 161ff. Parolles would seem to notice Helen's distraction and to summon her to answer with the phrase: 'Will you anything with it?' She replies irrelevantly and at first sight not very intelligibly:

> Not my virginity yet.
> There shall your master have a thousand loves.

The antecedent to 'There' is the Court of France which, if present to Helen's thoughts, does not appear in the text until l. 173. Therefore the *New Cambridge* editors suspect that the passage has been revised or patched. It may have been. Revision however is not necessarily for the worse; nor would it seem safe to assume that obvious results of whatever revision has taken place were not among those intended by the reviser. What would seem such an obvious result is suggested above: the stressing of a piece of dramatic business important, and perhaps essential, to the understanding of the text.

inadequate substitute. Rather she will engage upon a train of action calculated, in the first place, to win her the favour of the Court and of the world. She will attempt to cure the King; and if, by succeeding in doing so, she also succeeds in winning Bertram, so much the better.

In part, Helen's temptations are now over. Instead of falling a victim to the demagogue fancy, he is to fall a victim to her, at least for a while; and in the first place, his exuberant vigour is to be directed, not to a possibly shameful action of his own choice, but to an action which she herself has chosen and of which neither she nor anyone need be ashamed. And yet, in a conversation with the Countess which immediately follows, she would seem ashamed in some degree. She does not, for example, volunteer a statement about her plans for Paris; nor, when forced to acknowledge that she has a special regard for Bertram, does she paint this as it is, but first as a maternal (I. iii. 182), then as a romantic affection (*ibid.* 190ff): that is, as one which cherishes no hopes of attaining its end. The explanation may be the nature of her plans: which, if they include, after the curing of the King, a forcing of herself upon Bertram whether he will or no, she has every reason to conceal from others – even, so far as she can, from herself. In that case, her proceeding will be of the half-blind or fumbling nature previously attributed to Bertram. But this fact if true, or if not the mere possibility of this fact, suggests a second and perhaps a fuller explanation, neither excluding nor excluded by the first. The reader is in the presence of a further instance of the play's faithfulness in following nature. Human beings do not immediately adapt themselves to the consequences of resolutions taken by the reason, however firmly these are taken; nor are they always aware of these consequences. Additional stimulus may be necessary that the consequences may be discovered and then that they be dealt with. A sharp rebuke from the Countess – who receives the hint of romantic love in a contemptuous silence – provides such a stimulus; after which, a sympathetic attention to Helen's recital of her hopes and fears, brought at last into the open, encourages her in the process of self-knowledge, confirms the re-establishment, within her little kingdom, of the monarchy of the reason. From this moment onwards it is never again seriously threatened. Helen is to show an increasing self-mastery in whatever company she finds herself, whether in that of the Countess or of the King; or, at the other end of the social scale, of the poor Widow of Florence.

Such self-mastery is to stand her in good stead at Court, where the second and more severe part of her temptation awaits her. Or rather, where it would await her, had she not yet become the mistress of herself that she is; for temptation is something relative, which exists only for those more or less likely to succumb to it. Bertram's family, Bertram's overlord encourage her to marry him; Bertram's contemporaries envy him the prospect of such a marriage – and Bertram is foolish in disregarding, in so weighty a matter, the opinions and the wishes of his contemporaries, overlord and family. But if Helen were to marry him with the goodwill only of these and without Bertram's own goodwill she would be more than foolish. First therefore she makes it her business to ascertain whether she has it or not:

> I dare not say I take you, but I give
> Me and my service, ever whilst I live,
> Into your guiding power.   (II. iii. 102)

She does not ask for him, she offers herself, and it is open to him to refuse the offer. He does refuse; whereupon Helen releases the King of his promise:

> That you are well restored, my lord, I'm glad;
> Let the rest go.   (*ibid*. 147)

But the King's honour, which she has unfortunately involved in the matter, cannot let it go, and at least a form of marriage must be celebrated. As penance, it would seem, for the imprudence on her part which has brought this about, Helen accepts the disabilities which marriage imposes while renouncing any of the rights it should confer. Bertram needs but to express a caprice, however cruel, for her to obey. As we have seen, he does so hypocritically, and without the courage of his cruelty; this cannot be hidden from her who is now so sensitive to her surroundings, yet she refrains from reproach. He sends her from the Court, and she goes. When it appears that her residence in his home is exposing him to danger, she abandons it, though it is her home too; and takes on a life of wandering. In future, she is to intervene in Bertram's affairs only when his own good imperatively demands it.

If hitherto Helen has been open to the suspicion of respecting, in the first place, Bertram's rank, henceforward she respects him also as a man. She avoids, not only actions which might diminish his social dignity, but also those which, even in a remote degree, might encroach upon his individual autonomy. If in the early days at Rossilion she considered him as a toy to be seized upon for her own ends; after the visit to Paris she desires him as a companion which whom to pursue ends in common. So much would seem to be apparent, not only from her actions, but from her verse; and we are still, nominally at least, considering the verse of the play. There are for example the lines in which she takes occasion to refute the slanders which, she hears, Parolles is spreading about her. The quiet tone of the passage, the third person in which it is couched, are admirably suited to temper, and so to accredit, both the indignation and the humility with which she speaks: indignation towards Parolles, humility towards Bertram. Humility is the only possible attitude she can assume towards one who rejects her as a lover, and by whom she would not be accepted except for his own free will:

> In argument of praise, or to the worth
> Of the great Count himself, she is too mean
> To have her name repeated. All her deserving
> Is a reserved honesty, and that
> I have not heard examined. (III. v. 59)

The passage has been quoted already; but can bear quotation a second time, both because of its intrinsic excellence and because now perhaps the point is clearer than earlier in the paper, how by means of words commonplace in appearance, something is conveyed, from which the commonplace is far removed. Far removed and yet, of course, near: this is the paradox which, it was suggested, is largely responsible for the general misunderstanding of the play, and which in any case makes it difficult to write about. The paradox is none of Shakespeare's making, but inherent in his theme; his faithfulness to which is nowhere more apparent than in the emergence of the paradox from whatever point of view the play is considered. It is for example tempting to say that, in the above speech, Helen rises to a great humility. Yet obviously, one does not rise to humility; rather it would seem one sinks to it. In truth one does neither: one remains, as Helen does, within oneself and within the com-

monplace by which one is conditioned. And with the co-operation
of grace –
> The greatest grace lending grace –

one transfigures it.

The cause or at least the concomitant of this development in
Helen's feelings would seem to be indicated in another passage
of verse. Looking back to the night which Bertram has spent
with her under the delusion that she is Diana, she exclaims:

> But O strange men,
> That can such sweet use make of what they hate,
> When saucy trusting of the cozened thoughts
> Defiles the pitchy night! so lust doth play
> With what it loathes, for that which is away.　(IV. iv. 21)

Bertram has, in thought, committed a sin so black that it defiles
the pitchy night; in part, he has committed this sin against
Helen so that, it would seem, he has forfeited every title to her
sympathy and respect. Yet she is moved to consider, not only
that he has thought to cozen others, but that in such a thought
he himself was cozened. Her condemnation of him is made
dependent upon, and is qualified by, a larger commiseration: a
commiseration so large that it embraces many besides Bertram.
'O strange men...' Men hate evil, yet they are cozened into the
use of it, as Helen herself stood in danger of being cozened; and
even so, this use is sweet. To receive the force of the passage,
this last word should perhaps be taken, not only in its sense of
'pleasant', but also in that of 'sound, wholesome, free from
taint'. In itself the satisfaction of a natural instinct is good;
good and evil, in the yarn of life, are closely intertwined. It is a
deeper and deeper penetration with this general truth, and with
the particular truth that by grace alone has she been able to
weave the yarn of her fancy into a good web – the evil in it is not
to be disentangled, and remains at least potential in her – which
inclines or if not inclines, accompanies her to humility. And in
its turn, humility inclines her to charity: as she is liable like
other men to the cozenage of evil, she is compelled to believe
that, but for grace, she would have been cozened worse than
they. And so in the last scene there shines from her that light
which, it has been suggested, falls with incomparable benefit
upon Bertram.

Helen recoils from an act of rashness once its nature is made clear to her by the light of reason; Bertram, who would not seem over-endowed with reason, is in need of lengthy persuasion before recoiling. But both recoil, whereas Parolles does not; or at least, not so whole-heartedly. It would seem a serious mistake to dismiss Parolles as an excrescence on the play: rather, he is essential to its pattern, and one of the most tragic, if not the most significant, figure in it.

For he is old in rashness, and in itself this implies grave sin. Experience alone would suffice to make clear to him that nature of his acts, were reason incapable of doing so; whereas, in his case, it would seem quite capable. In the form of mother-wit, he has reason enough; only he uses it, not to restrain his instinct but to provide them with a course as free as possible from restraint. With its aid, he can pass himself off as a traveller, though of travel-talk he has 'vent' (cf. II. iii. 200f) for two ordinaries only; though helpless on the battlefield, in the palace he can pose as master of 'the whole theoric of war...and the practice' (cf. IV. iii. 138). The impulse to play a part in the world, and to be known as the player of such a part, is a natural impulse, and contains therefore the possibilities of good; these however Parolles chooses to neglect, developing only its possibilities for evil. Not pausing to consider what parts it is proper for him to assume, he offers at false parts; in consequence o which his whole life, indeed the whole of existence becomes for him a falsehood. As such, it provides no canon according to which he might choose among its various manifestations, leaving him to his own convenience or to his caprice for a guide; and the former, as often as not, proves another name for his indolence, the latter for his lowest impulses. At Court where, as was to be expected, he seeks to play the part of a courtier, he does not give himself to the imitation, even at a remote distance, of sensible discourses like those of the King, but of the vapid phrases of the King's hangers-on;[1] and these the Clown can

[1] II. iii. 1–49. It hardly seems possible that Parolles's partner in conversation in this part of the scene should be a Lord who elsewhere shows himself so comparatively sensible and accomplished as Lafeu. If not the cream of the Court, neither is Lafeu the dregs; and towards the end of this scene (ll. 187ff) he shows himself, not tolerant, but impatient of Parolles: and cf. l. 48, where Parolles's partner expresses surprise that the King's she-doctor should prove to be Helen; whereas it was Lafeu who introduced her as such to the King. Perhaps the parts of Lafeu and of Parolles's partner were doubled. It is dangerous for a layman to attempt the manipulation of bibliographical evidence; but it would seem at

imitate as well as he – or better, for the Clown does so with an intention of irony. The elegance of courtly clothes impress him more than the elegances of courtly speech; the

world

Of pretty fond adoptious christendoms   (I. i. 169f)

used by courtly lovers arouse in him no enthusiasm and, attaching himself to the seamy side of courtly as of all love-making, he prefers to call his sweetheart a 'kickie-wickie' (II. iii. 276). As the Clown says (and it is a second mistake, it might be noted, to dismiss the Clown as an excrescence; he directs a pointed commentary on Parolles) the 'brains of his Cupid's knocked out' (III. ii. 14ff), and he can love only 'as an old man loves money, with no stomach'. But the fact is that Parolles has 'no stomach' for anything; so steeped is he in falsehood, that he would no longer seem to have the faintest notion of what it might mean to him to be a true lover, a true soldier, a true traveller, a true courtier. So long as the pretence is not discovered, he is content to go through the motions of being the one or the other; though these motions cannot attain the end to which they profess to be directed, and though he is aware that they cannot.

A strange fellow, my lord, that so confidently seems to undertake this business, which he knows is not to be done.   (III. vi. 81ff)

Parolles is in a more parlous state than Bertram; is indeed in so parlous a state that only with the aid of the portrait of himself as of a diagram can it be conceived. The portion of 'sweetness' which his actions contain, and which as human actions they cannot but contain, has been reduced to the smallest possible amount; so that, it would seem, it must long ago have palled. Yet he continues with them. In consequence, if the spectacle of Bertram moves the Captain to pity – 'as we are ourselves, what things

least worth noting that, in the Folio, the speeches of Parolles's partner are headed *Ol. Laf.*, not *Laf.* merely, as are Lafeu's speeches from l. 167 onwards and elsewhere in the play. Perhaps *Ol. Lo.* has been misread as *Ol. La.*, to which, under the influence of the doubling of the parts, an *f* has been added. This of course implies that the stage-direction at l. 167 needs altering. Parolles's partner should be given an exit some lines previously, and Lafeu an entry. The former is quite possible, as the partner has not spoken since l. 102, where his speech is headed *Ol. Lord*. In any case, there is something wrong with this stage-direction; for whoever the characters may be who either enter or "stay behind", they do not do the one or the other for the purpose which the stage-direction prescribes, i.e., a 'commenting of the wedding'.

91

are we!' (IV. iii. 18f) – that of Parolles provokes him to astonishment: 'It is possible he should know what he is, and be that he is?' (IV. i. 44) If the latter exclamation implies contempt, it implies horror also, and a measure of fear. Bertram illustrates the impotence of man, unaided by grace, to initiate a good course of action; Parolles, man's power of persisting in an evil course though it has been recognized for such, and though the hollowness of evil has revealed itself in experience.

There is one hope for the reclamation of Parolles. As he has closed his eyes to reason, first he must be made to open them; and this can only be by punishment. His poltroonery having been exposed to the army it will, he is assured, be published in France. Relieved at having escaped the sentence of death with which he had been threatened, Parolles reflects:

> Yet am I thankful: if my heart were great
> 'Twould burst at this. Captain I'll be no more
> But I will eat and drink and sleep as soft
> As captain shall: simply the thing I am
> Shall make me live. Who knows himself a braggart
> Let him fear this; for it shall come to pass
> That every braggart shall be found an ass.
> Rust, sword! cool, blushes! and, Parolles, live
> Safest in shame! being fooled, by foolery thrive!
> There's place and means for every man alive.   (IV. iv. 319)

Much in this speech would repay a careful analysis. Its most notable characteristic would seem to be its wide range of tone: a beginning not without awe, as at a situation whose gravity is recognized; an ending not without smugness, or satisfaction at a self admitted to go little way towards justifying such a satisfaction; and between the two, a phrase like

> simply the thing I am
> Shall make me live,

which might be either. A conflict has been started in Parolles, and this in itself, however doubtful the issue, would seem an improvement on his former indifference. If, having nothing else left to brag about, he inclines to brag about his folly, this indicates he has taken at least a step in the direction of humility; for folly is more closely akin to 'the thing he is' than were the themes of his former brags. Many steps remain to be taken – how many, may be seen by a glance at the phrase of the professional fool:

honesty...will wear the surplice of humility over the black gown of a big
heart,
(I. iii. 90ff)

a phrase of unhesitating and joyous, rather than reluctant and
defiant acceptance; coloured by self-criticism – 'am I, after all,
any better than the Puritans?' – then by self-satisfaction. But
the Clown, like many of his fellows in Shakespeare, is so to
speak contrite by office; and to compare him in this respect
with Parolles is unfair to the latter. If not yet contrite, Parolles
is at any rate attrite: if his heart has not yet been crushed, it has,
at least, been bruised. And attrition is a title to the remission of
guilt, if not of punishment. Therefore Lafeu, hitherto the most
active in procuring the condemnation of Parolles, ceases to harry
him on observing his at any rate outwardly humble behaviour
on his return to Court. Lafeu will see that he has the opportunity
to work out his punishment: 'though you are a fool and a
knave, you shall eat' (V. ii. 50).

An admirable act of charity on Lafeu's part, which at first
sight may cause surprise. And yet perhaps it should not: the
reader has been prepared for it in a number of ways; among
them, Helen's charity towards Bertram which, if measured by
the same standard as Lafeu's, must appear yet more surprising.
And to apply a different standard is perhaps to mistake the play;
to continue, for example, under the influence of some such
interpretation as the *Arden* editor's of the 'keynote' speech,
according to which men can allow themselves to be consoled for
their vices by the thought of their virtues. If they have no
virtues, or only insignificant ones, they are presumably deprived
of all consolation; and men fall into different classes, of whom it
would be unfair to expect the same mode of behaviour. But, it
has been suggested in this paper, virtues and vices cannot be
balanced one against another in this way; nor are virtues, to
their possessors, so much a matter of consolation as of concern.
Neither the virtuous nor the vicious receive consolation in the
thought of anything but grace, and this is open to all if they co-
operate with it. Now Lafeu, though he does not co-operate to an
extent at all equal to that of Helen, neither does he industriously
postpone co-operation as do Bertram and Parolles. There would
therefore seem to be no reason why his behaviour should not imitate Helen's, even at her noblest; imitate after his manner and so
far as his natural disposition permits, but imitate it nevertheless.

A brief comparison with *Measure for Measure*, with which, of all the plays in the canon, *All's Well* is most easily confused, may help to illustrate this point. In *Measure for Measure* the existence of distinct classes of men, which has just been denied in *All's Well*, would seem to be generally assumed. In the eyes of a fellow-character, for instance, Isabella is 'a thing enskyed'; and in her own eyes she enjoys the privilege of observing laws 'set down in heaven'; laws proper to earth may be recommended to observation by others. The tension which results threatens to disjoint the universe of *Measure for Measure*, so that the direct intervention of Providence is necessary, in the person of the Duke,[1] to restore the appearance of integrity – which perhaps after all, is not much more than an appearance. *Measure for Measure* announces *King Lear* and the tragedies, where salvation must come by extraordinary means, if it is to come at all. But in *All's Well* which never for a moment threatens a universal catastrophe, ordinary means are relied on from beginning to end. Helen is not too self-righteous to avail herself of them; nor is Bertram nor Parolles too persistently self-opinionated. Before the end, both range themselves alongside their fellows; do so, moreover of their own free will and, so to speak, in their right senses. Bertram at least does not need to be beaten out of his senses, as was Lear; nor does Parolles need to be pressed to death, whipped and hanged as is Lucio. Contentment with the ordinary because, if rightly approached, it is seen to imply something beyond itself; confidence in the commonplace, not because it inspires presumption, but because it forbids despair – this would seem to be the peculiar 'note' of *All's Well*.

From the first scenes the sounding of this note is entrusted to the verse. Previously we have ascribed to the verse, and to the use it makes of the commonplace, the function of providing a neutral background against which Bertram's movements – and, of course, Helen's – clearly define themselves. Now we may add that it imparts to these movements an air, not only of plausibility (for a fairy-tale may be plausible in its kind), but of familiarity – and the familiar inspires confidence. Much of course depends on the way the commonplace is handled; for there

---

[1] In 1972 James Smith told me that he no longer looked on the Duke in *Measure for Measure* as a providential figure. (E. M. W.)

would seem to be at least two ways of doing this – either with patience and respect, as Wordsworth does; or with a brusque off-handedness, after the manner of Donne. The former allows the commonplace to assert to the full its quality of familiar; the latter obscures this, as though from the fear that what should inspire confidence may exceed its commission, producing rather complacency. It is Donne who springs to the mind on reading certain passages in *Measure for Measure*, which accordingly tend to jar – not inappropriately, if the play is at all as above sketched:

> liberty plucks justice by the nose,
> The baby beats the nurse, and quite athwart
> Goes all decorum.   (*Measure for Measure* I. iii. 29ff)

The verse in *All's Well* has quite an opposite effect. In the last scene which Helen has alone with the Widow and Diana, the latter, asked whether she is willing to suffer further in the cause of justice, promises martyrdoms. But Helen deprecates heroics, which are discordant with her own temper and with that of the play:

> Yet I pray you:
> But with the word the time will bring on summer
> When briars shall have leaves as well as thorns,
> And be as sweet as sharp. We must away,
> Our waggon is prepared, and time revives us.   (IV. iv. 30)

Diana shall suffer, but suffering is a common lot and therefore not to be romanticized. Within or behind romanticism there lurks an element of fear; whereas common suffering, if approached with a common steadfastness, brings in its train common joys. The moral is ordinary and almost trite; the metaphor is ordinary and on the point of extinction; the rhythm is ordinary and nearly jog-trot. Almost, but not quite. Wherein the difference lies may be left to a close study of this kind of verse and of Wordsworth.

The verse in *All's Well* succeeds to such an extent in its task of inspiring confidence that the reader, at no stage of Helen's progress from moral bewilderment to moral mastery, feels her to be engaged on a sort of Red Queen flight, hurtling from peak to isolated peak. Rather he feels that her feet remain close to the ground; and this at times she is seen, at all other times is assumed, to be measuring with familiar steps. Nor does Helen herself appear a creature such as to require, for her engendering, the impossible congress of two peaks: not a monstrous compound of immodest wench and paragon of wives, fit only for a Jacobean tragi-comedy, but what an attempt has been made to present her as in this paper, what critics from Coleridge onwards have proclaimed her to be, a character in every way worthy of Shakespeare. The verse achieves a yet more notable triumph: for not only Helen's progress but Bertram's also, though more hazardous and more violent – for in a shorter time than she, he covers a longer distance – is followed by the reader with a measure of confidence. The latter's emotions are deeply stirred, without his fearing that they are being stirred wantonly. Some measure of the achievement of the verse in this respect may be obtained by reflecting that an examination of conscience, such as is forced upon Bertram, is not usually undertaken, is indeed usually prohibited in public. The slightest forcing of the pace in the last scene, the least raising of the tone would cause it to be rejected either as unendurable, because too close a copy of such reality as is not proper to be copied; or as preposterous, because too fantastically remote from any reality that can be conceived.

In the pursuit of these effects, however, the verse does not operate alone. Presumably they are beyond the power of any verse. In *All's Well* it has the aid of the construction of the play: a vast topic which we approach too late to do it anything like justice, but which it would be unjust wholly to neglect. Perhaps the most expeditious way of dealing with it is to baptize the society which *All's Well* brings on the stage with the name of the Court: as I think is allowable, for the Court is the dominating member of that society. And having done so, immediately we gain an insight into the complexity of the construction. For the Court, as the Clown expressly informs us and as in any case we should assume, is inhabited by pomp and by pride, who are the devil's nobility; and as we see from the example of Lafeu among others, no more than anything else on earth is the Court free from containing, as a condition of its existence, both 'good and ill' (cf. IV. iii. 68f). Further, it contains this good and ill, not as remotely separated extremes, but 'together'; not only in its web, but in its yarn. At times Lafeu is vulgarly officious, at times indecently facetious; yet from the King downwards, everyone treats him not only with tolerance, but with respect. Before passing comment upon him, the King waits until the stage is empty; and the comment, when it comes, implies approval rather than condemnation:

> Thus he his special nothing ever prologues.   (II. i. 91)

Evidently Lafeu's familiarities are taken as directed, not to the discomfiture, but to the relief or diversion of his sick master; who yet is as sensitive as anyone to vulgarity and indecency. And again, if Lafeu's formulas of courtesy appear at times stilted and mechanical, at others, and especially when addressed to his social equals, they become supple with life, and sparkle with understanding. So exquisite indeed is his courtesy towards the Countess that the *New Cambridge* editors[1] have been led to suspect behind it some private understanding between the two, a whole history of private intrigue. Probably unnecessarily, for there need lie behind it no more than the public history of the Court, which experience has led to elaborate such formulas as conducive to its own interests and to those of its members. They are to be accepted as commonplace at Court, and reassuring as such. Even when not reassuring in themselves (and they often are), they represent a permanent possibility of behaviour which at least is dignified, and may be much more than that. By them, and not by the example of Helen alone, the reader is prepared for Lafeu's magnanimity towards Parolles; by the variety of effects they produce on the lips of Lafeu, the fact is made plausible that a single strand of the web of the Court – say, that of gallantry – can make upon different persons widely differing impressions. Gallantry, or addiction to finery in words and in speech, cannot but be prominent in a courtly web: upon Bertram it would seem to have no good effect; Parolles, by close and continued contact with it, is plunged the deeper into vice; yet the mere thought of it, as we have seen, helps to rescue Helen for virtue.

It is somewhat on these lines that, in the great speech which

---

[1] IV. v. 87–90. See their note *ad loc.* – Though the King has promised to 'stop up the displeasure he hath conceived against' (IV. v. 72) Bertram, nevertheless he may put the latter through an unpleasant quarter of an hour. The Countess asks Lafeu to be present at the interview, to smoothe over whatever difficulties arise. He replies that he had intended to do so, but wondered whether he would be welcome. Thus he puts the Countess in the position, not of receiving, but of conferring a favour; who, not to be outdone, refers him to his 'honourable privilege' – his privilege, that is, as a friend of the family and as a gentleman.

opens the series of scenes at the Court, the King makes an express apology for gallantry. In approaching this speech, we leave the topic of construction to return once more to that of the verse. The play however is so subtly put together that any division of topics, however necessary for the preliminaries of discussion, reveals itself as unsatisfactory once an attempt is made to bring the discussion to a close.

This speech is patient enough in its *tempo*, respectful enough in its tone: Q, for example, remarked upon its note of 'easy-going conversation', its 'large, habitual politeness'. But the speech is not merely easy-going; and its politeness, which is a form of respect shown by the King to his hearers and to the subject they treat in common, is made to appear amply justified by the latter. At once simple, verging on the banal, and yet profound, it both discourages complacency and inspires confidence. Conveying a complicated content while avoiding all superficial complexity, the speech is one of the masterpieces of the canon. The King is holding up the old Count of Rossilion, Bertram's father, as his ideal courtier; and quoting words of the latter, takes occasion to condemn gallantry. Gallantry is proper to the young:

> younger spirits, whose apprehensive senses
> All but new things disdain; whose judgments are
> Mere fathers of their garments: whose constancies
> Expire before their fashions.   (I. ii. 60)

But in doing so, the King makes it clear that he is far from merely echoing the Duke in *Measure for Measure*, who rejects 'witless bravery' without making towards it a single gesture of benevolence; who complains that 'novelty is only in request', without admitting a possible merit in novelty. For the speech of old Rossilion from which the King is quoting is one made, not in condemnation, but in praise of youth; or at least in envy of youth, and envy is a practical form of praise. Further, old Rossilion praises youth for that quality in which gallantry has its proximate source:

> Let me not live, quoth he,
> After my flame lacks oil, to be the snuff
> Of younger spirits, whose apprehensive senses
> All but new things disdain; whose judgments are
> Mere fathers of their garments; whose constancies
> Expire before their fashions.   (*ibid.* 58)

These words uttered 'on the catastrophe and heel of pastime' (*ibid.* 57) – that is, when sport or pastime has resulted in the exhaustion of all who share in it, especially of the old. At such a time the superiority of the young to the old is most painfully apparent. Pursuit of novelty as such may be an evil, but it is at least good that there should be pursuit; and there is the danger that, in ceasing to pursue novelty, age may cease from pursuing anything – not because it does not wish to do so, but because it cannot. The King makes old Rossilion's words his own, in their positive as well as in their negative moment:

> this he wished.
> I after him, do after him wish too
> (Since I nor wax nor honey can bring home)
> I quickly were dissolved from my hive
> To give some labourers room. (*ibid.* 63)

Yet 'I fill a place, I know't', he adds: if age lacks the vigour of youth it also lacks the vagaries, time which has robbed it of vigour having endowed it with wisdom. Age as well as youth fills a place at Court and in society; along with its evil too, good is intertwined.

The speech of the King's is of course far more than an apology for gallantry. Much more adequately, it is to be described as an apology for the whole play: all of whose themes it gathers up, submitting them to a preliminary appreciation. The central position which it thus occupies is bound up with that of the King, who rather than to a keystone, completing and supporting a single arch, is to be compared to the boss of a vault, which supports and completes many. But this will be dealt with more fully in the following paragraph. For the moment let us consider an arch that has already attracted our attention. If Lafeu's conduct towards Parolles has been described as an imitation of Helen's, in a much more literal sense it is to be described as an imitation of old Rossilion's. For in holding up the latter as a model, the King has prescribed a mode of conduct which Lafeu observes. Old Rossilion refused to tolerate the slightest departure from the standards of justice and of good behaviour:

> his honour,
> Clock to itself, knew the true minute when
> Exception bid him speak: and at this time
> His tongue obeyed his hand. (*ibid.* 38ff)

And accordingly once satisfied of the falsity of Parolles, Lafeu is prompt to rebuke him. He does so, it is true, with the contempt and bitterness which old Rossilion avoided except to his equals; but for this apparent discrepancy, a twofold explanation is at hand. First, as has been noted already, in all his actions Lafeu is limited by his own capacities and disposition; and obviously, he lacks the fineness and delicacy of old Rossilion. And secondly, there is the social metaphor in which the speech is cast. The false and the evil are worthy of contemptuous and bitter rebuke only in so far as, by defying the good, they vaunt themselves their equals. Bearing these two facts in mind, Lafeu's reception of Parolles to mercy is seen to be a recognizable, if remote, imitation of the rest of old Rossilion's conduct to his fellows:

> who were below him,
> He used as creatures of another place,
> And bowed his eminent top to their low ranks,
> Making them proud of his humility,
> In their poor praise he humbled. (I. ii. 41)

'Poor praise'; once again, the social metaphor should not mislead. The praise bestowed by old Rossilion is 'poor', not because it is bestowed on poor men; but because it is all the praise which any men, whether rich or poor – for all contain 'good and evil together' – can deserve. Yet as praise, when deserved it must be bestowed ungrudgingly. And so Helen, though rich in virtue, bows her 'eminent top' to the poverty-stricken Bertram.

Like old Rossilion, the King is old. Both have been 'worn out of act' by 'haggish age' (cf. *ibid*. 29f). If, towards the end of the play, stress is laid upon the apparent youth of the King – he is, says Lafeu, 'of as able a body as when he numbered thirty' (IV. v. 77f) – he himself stresses the limited security which this affords. Upon youth as well as age there steals

> Th'inaudible and noiseless foot of time: (V. iii. 41)

both therefore are poor in opportunity, and must exploit to the full whatever opportunities fall to them.

> Let's take the instant by the forward top. (V. iii. 39)

In this way the King, though old, symbolizes youth as well as age; and his symbolic value is increased by the fact that,

if worn by age, he is yet more worn by disease. Even in its
physical form, this can afflict the young as well as the old;
and there are, as we have seen, moral as well as physical
diseases – Bertram complains of his 'sick desires' (IV. ii. 35)
– to which the young are especially prone. The King's disease
is beyond cure:

> our most learned Doctors leave us, and
> The congregated College have concluded
> That labouring art can never ransom nature
> From her inaidible estate.   (II. i. 115)

And so the play opens with the King, a symbol of humanity
whether young or old, whether sick or well, lying under an
apparently unavoidable sentence of physical and moral destruction.

In the course of the play, and by 'the help of heaven' or, in
other words, of grace, the sentence is made void. So too, and by
the same means, the sentence is voided which lies upon Bertram.
But the King's relation to the latter is not only that of a symbol
or type; he is also a necessary agent in Bertram's cure. And he is
so in at least two capacities; for as well as an earthly magistrate,
he is, like many of Shakespeare's Kings and Dukes, the bearer
of a commission from heaven. He is

> One of the greatest names in Christendom,   (IV. iv. 2)

before whom even Helen must kneel. If Bertram is to receive
from him a merciless questioning, calculated, in the name of
earthly justice, to drag his crimes into the open, once Bertram,
not entirely as the result of this questioning, acknowledges his
crimes, he is to receive the benefit of words of an entirely different nature already uttered by the King. They are such as of
themselves to justify, and even to demand, the attempt made in
this paper to treat the last scene as the dramatization of a
sacrament;
> All is whole,
> Not one word more of the consumed time.   (V. iii. 37)

These are words to be spoken, not by a magistrate, but by a
priest.[1] They declare, not that the past is forgotten, but that it

---

[1] V. iii. 37f. If the words are taken as those of a magistrate, then it is necessary to
complain, along with Dr Johnson, that 'Bertram's double crime of cruelty and
disobedience, joined likewise with some hypocrisy, should raise more resentment

is abolished; not that Bertram's breaches of integrity are condoned, but that his integrity is restored. If the King is cured of a physical evil, beyond hope and, it would seem, beyond belief, Bertram's moral evil is cured, not only beyond belief but beyond comprehension. The construction contrives, not only that the lesser cure prepares for the greater, but that the greater should be performed by him in whom the lesser has been performed. If it has recourse to grace, wounded humanity can minister to itself; but those who minister, have no less need of grace than those who receive their ministrations. Good and evil are mingled, even in the most highly privileged, who therefore have no excuse for presumption, or indeed for anything but humility and charity. And that means they have no excuse for despair; for charity, both in those who show it and in those to whom it is shown, is a good far outweighing the evil which, in human beings, seems indispensable to invigorate, if not to provoke it. After a painful journey, all ends well – unbelievably, incomprehensibly well; and the end is not to be attained except by undertaking the prescribed, the ordinary, the commonplace journey.

If, for the sake of rounding off the paper, it is permissible to suggest yet another subtlety in the construction, it must be this. While performing the functions of a delegate of heaven, the King still retains his character as head of an earthly society. By disregarding the warnings which such a society delivers in abundance – inarticulate warnings by way of its habits and institutions, articulate warnings which drop from the lips of its members – Bertram runs into much tribulation. Yet by the agency of its highest officer, who because such an officer is also something higher still, this same society in the end rescues Bertram from tribulation. And so the confidence in the co-operation of grace and nature, with which the Countess opened

... his king should more pertinaciously vindicate his own authority and Helen's merit.' The King does not do so, according to Johnson, because Shakespeare is in a hurry: 'he wanted to conclude his play'. But this explanation will not fit the facts, for the words are spoken, not at the end, but at the beginning of the last scene. This is of some length, the greater part of which must appear otiose to those who do not take it as the dramatization of the struggles of an unwilling and, in the first place, sham penitent. Q, for example, dismisses the intervention of Diana as that of 'a clamant young woman, shouting alternately her wifehood and her maidenhood'. But the writing of the scene is too terse, too obviously purposive for this flippant treatment.

the play, justifies itself in the end: justifies itself not only with respect to Helen, of whom she had never despaired, but also with respect to Bertram, despair of whom – for the Countess too has her admixture of evil – she had not always been able to avoid.

5

'MEASURE FOR MEASURE'
– A FRAGMENT

The outburst of the Duke in Act V, that 'disguised as a looker-on here in Vienna' he has

> seen corruption boil and bubble
> Till it o'er-run the stew; laws for all faults,
> But faults so countenanced that the strong statutes
> Stand like the forfeits in a barber's shop,
> As much in mock, as mark – (V. i. 315)

this outburst is often quoted in studies of *Measure for Measure* but hardly perhaps as often allowed the importance which it would seem to deserve. For though it paints vigorously, it is no mere painting of a background against which the story develops; rather its vigour is due to a sentiment which the background, among other things, provokes, and by which the story is propelled. Here the propulsion is so decisive that, in scarcely more than a moment, catastrophe is at hand. Because of a 'slander to th' state' (*ibid*. 320) which Escalus detects beneath the outburst, he orders the arrest of the speaker; because the speaker resists, Angelo invites Lucio's help; in the course of rendering help Lucio drags off the speaker's hood, thereby revealing the face, not, as he and everyone expected, of some 'bald-pated lying rascal' (*ibid*. 350), but of their earthly lord and master. Their consternation is great.

It is as great as their reverence for their lord, and this in turn can be measured by the speed with which he thinks it advisable to pardon the indignity offered him, though unintentional; and by Isabella's begging for pardon

> That I, your vassal, have employed and pained
> Your unknown sovereignty. (*ibid*. 384)

He is not to be treated as ordinary men, nor required, though he may condescend, to perform their tasks; for he is 'the demi-god Authority' (I. ii. 112), by whom rather than upon whom justice operates, and to whom ordinary men look to guarantee

conditions under which these tasks shall be capable of performance. Even Angelo, though Authority does not permanently
inhere but lodges no more than temporarily within him, is
raised so high above the possibility of ordinary treatment that,
to forestall murmurings which he foresees and fears, the Duke
hastens first to assure Claudio that 'Angelo had never the
purpose to corrupt' Isabella (II. i. 160); and then the Provost
that, if Angelo sternly corrects Claudio for unchastity, he 'doth
with holy abstinence subdue' all unchastity 'in himself'
(IV. ii. 79). But in presuming to offer these assurances, the
Duke offends against truth, and truth avenges itself by pointing
ever more insistently towards Angelo as more in need of correction than any. So that the Duke himself is reduced to murmuring
and worse, and finally to the outburst just quoted. As we have
seen its immediate effect is to secure the return of Authority into
the Duke's hands out of those of Angelo into which, for a while,
it has been alienated. It has been so, in order that the Duke
might have opportunity to learn how, under earthly conditions,
Authority may best assert itself. In this he partially succeeds, so
that there opens before Vienna the prospect of at least a
measure of peace.

Such, in rough outline, is the story of the play as it will
be treated in this paper. Or rather the outline which, if never
possessed by, was originally intended for, a play which, to our
misfortune, has come down in imperfect or mangled form. To
change the metaphor: already in Act III false notes begin to
sound; by Act IV these have, in number if not in resonance,
increased to such an extent as to produce little but a jangle:
and if in Act V harmony is restored, this is poorer, if more
immediately attractive or flattering, than that of Acts I and II.
Some of the bells booming in a tower, it might be said, seem to
have been replaced by bells that tinkle in the hand.

It is not my purpose to inquire how or why these changes
have been effected. The study of history, even the history of
books which is bibliography, appears to me the idlest of occupations. If at times it may render aid, this can be of no more than a
servile nature. Care must be taken lest history be allowed to
rank alongside the study of the meaning of texts which, as it is
the most difficult, is the most serious of occupations that can be
pursued: for it imports the survival of humanity. And if two

studies that differ so widely are accepted, though no more than occasionally, as of equal value: then something like Gresham's Law comes into operation. The serious tends to be neglected in favour of the trivial.

This law may account, at least in part, for the fact that critics, so far from attributing any particular importance to the sentiment which the Duke's outburst expresses, incline to discount that importance whenever the sentiment is expressed. Yet this occurs not infrequently, and as early, for example, as I. iii. Here the Duke, closeted with Friar Thomas, laments

> We have strict statues and most biting laws...
> Which for these fourteen years we have let sleep,
> Even like an o'ergrown lion in a cave
> That goes not out to prey –   (I. iii. 19)

with the result that, as he continues,

> our decrees
> Dead to infliction, to themselves are dead,
> And liberty plucks justice by the nose,
> The baby beats the nurse, and quite athwart
> Goes all decorum   (*ibid.* 27)

But here, it has been suggested, the Duke (or perhaps rather, Shakespeare through the mouth of the Duke) is doing something quite other than impress upon the reader the deplorable results of a slack or ill-informed administration of justice. Rather he is fabricating an excuse for the sudden exaltation of Angelo from obscurity into eminence: an exaltation which would normally be dismissed as improbable, but for which a temporary toleration must be secured, since the reader is to be entertained with its consequences. If obscurity has given Angelo the opportunity to elaborate false theories of human nature, eminence confronts him with the obligation to put these theories into practice. And so he discovers, in the old as well as the new sense of the word, their falsehood to be of such enormity as to threaten with destruction, not only persons with whom eminence has for the first time brought him into contact, but also himself. Though he might be supposed to have had sufficient contact with himself as long ago to have learnt what is best for him, he no less than they needs to be rescued from a capital sentence which his theories demand. And so, according to critics who follow this tendency, the story of *Measure for Measure* deals with a private, not a public misfortune; it starts, in other words, from a regrettable state of affairs not so much in a commonwealth, as in the mind of an individual. And, in spite of the opening verse, one of its purposes is not

> Of government the properties to unfold (I. i. 3)

Or, in so far as it is – since Angelo's theories are not wholly without reference to the government of men – then the play discourages a preoccupation with lawsuits and the whole paraphernalia of justice: the latter, it inculcates, should be not so much administered as superseded by another virtue supposed to be incompatible with justice, and to which these critics give the name of mercy.

If they are right, then it must seem a remarkable coincidence that, at two such critical points of the play as just after the beginning and just before the end, the same sentiment should efface itself as of passing, and no more than passing, importance. And if its importance is in truth of such a kind, then its reappearance at any other point can hardly be regarded as anything but an oversight on the part of the dramatist: since the best that could happen to an excuse proffered for what would otherwise be inexcusable is that, once its purpose has been served, it should be forgotten – just as, when a shoe has been coaxed onto the foot, the shoehorn is immediately withdrawn and not against inserted, lest it interfere with the walking for which the shoe is intended. But, as has been stated, the sentiment reappears at many more points than two: so many indeed, that it might be said to echo down the play, and not only from the lips of the Duke but also of characters who are by no means always in agreement with him. It echoes, for example, from those of Lucio (of all people!) who, when explaining Claudio's plight to Isabella, goes near to repeating the very words and image of the Duke. Angelo, Lucio says,

> to give fear to use and liberty
> Which have, for long, run by the hideous law,
> As mice by lions, hath plucked out an act
> Under whose heavy sense your brother's life
> Falls into forfeit (I. iv. 62)

And if, at the beginning of Act II, Angelo does not repeat the image, what he does is as good or perhaps better: for he provides s second image by which that of the Duke is reinforced.

We must not make a scarecrow of the law,

he protests to Escalus,

> Setting it up to fear the birds of prey,
> And let it keep one shape, till custom make it
> Their perch and not their terror.   (II. i. 1)

In view of Angelo's propensity to 'heading and hanging' (II. i. 204), this may not perhaps appear remarkable; but if so, then it must be recognized as all the more remarkable that, by the end of the Act, Escalus is found speaking in Angelo's support. He is entirely free from the latter's propensity and yet, to an otherwise unknown official who complains that 'Lord Angelo is severe', he returns the answer, 'It is but needful' (*ibid.* 279).

And if he goes on to explain the answer –

> Mercy is not itself that oft looks so;
> Pardon is still the nurse of second woe –

the reason for this is not far to seek. It is not of course to warn critics against too ready a use of the word 'mercy' – though they might benefit by the warning – but to prepare for a similar explanation when advanced by Angelo in his first interview with Isabella, and so to secure its readier acceptance. For by the time of the interview Angelo has come to be eyed with a measure of mistrust, so that anything he advances runs the risk of meeting with a consideration less than its due. The reader has observed Angelo's behaviour towards Pompey, when brought up for judicial examination; he has heard Lucio caricature Angelo as

> a man whose blood
> Is very snow-broth; one who never feels
> The wanton stings and motions of the sense (I. iv. 58);

and from a person far more worthy of credit than Lucio, from the Duke himself, he has caught a hint that Angelo may be no more than a 'seemer' (cf. I. iii. 51). By the workings of envy, if nothing else, the reader may be induced to magnify the importance of this hint, and to diminish that of the same Duke's inclusion of Angelo among 'spirits...finely touched...to fine issues' (I. i. 35); to neglect the testimony that even Lucio finds himself compelled to bear, that Angelo

> doth rebate and blunt his natural edge
> With profits of the mind, study, and fast   (I. iv. 60):

to forget, if he ever remarked, the common sense and everyday wisdom of which Angelo not infrequently gives proof, and of which more than one example is shortly to be quoted.

On the other hand, a natural sympathy may lead to a concentration of the reader's attention upon the youth of Claudio, and upon Lucio's readiness to do him service. In any case, this precious pair are to some extent clarified by their association with Isabella whom, because of her imminent renunciation of the world, one of them calls 'a thing enskied and sainted' (I. iv. 34); so that it is quite possible, if not indeed customary, to overlook the nature of the use to which they propose that Isabella shall be put. This has little, if anything, to do with her saintliness. 'In her youth', says Claudio,

> There is a prone and speechless dialect
> Such as move men (I. ii. 179) –

in other words (taking 'prone' to mean, as I think it must, 'appealing because apparently helpless'), she is a piece of flesh of the sort men find difficult to resist; 'of the sort men ought to resist', corrects the more cynical Lucio – does so, at least, in effect. 'Go to Lord Angelo', run his instructions to Isabella,

> And let him learn to know, when maidens sue
> Men give like gods; but when they weep and kneel
> All their petitions are as freely theirs
> As they themselves would owe them (I. iv. 79).

If however all these considerations are borne in mind and balanced one against the other, and if Escalus's admonition about the nature of mercy is added: then perhaps it becomes impossible to deny that, in at least one passage between Angelo and the supposed saint, it is Angelo who obtains a crushing victory. When he has repeated – yet again! – the substance of the Duke's outburst:

> The law hath not been dead, though it hath slept   (II. ii. 91)

and when Isabella has nevertheless persisted in her plea that he 'show some pity' (*ibid.* 100), then he replies in words that, without apparent effort nevertheless place themselves beyond the reach of contradiction. It is common sense that crushes Isabella:

> I show it most of all when I show justice,
> For then I pity those I do not know.   (*ibid.* 101)

The rest of this speech, it is true, makes a somewhat different impression. 'When I show justice', Angelo in effect continues, 'then I pity those I do not know', but also

> do him right that, answering one foul wrong,
> Lives not to act another. Be satisfied;
> Your brother dies tomorrow, be content

– the ending of which is curt, to say the least, and through it impatience peeps; through the suggestion that, to save a fornicator from backsliding it is praiseworthy to put him to death, an inhumanity worse than impatience not only peeps, but thrusts itself head and shoulders. But my purpose is not of course to maintain that Angelo's temper is throughout perfect, still less that his conduct towards Isabella is at all points blameless, not even that his decisions are always correct. But whatever his shortcomings may be I reserve for later consideration; and meanwhile think it not wholly idle to stress that, at one period of his career, some at any rate of his principles are undoubtedly sound, and some of his utterances marked with what I have already called common sense and everyday wisdom. An Elizabethan audience at any rate could not fail to appreciate the common sense of the verses quoted at the end of the preceding paragraph: by now it is a commonplace that anarchy resulting from a failure to enforce the law was, of all things, what they most feared and despised. And not, of course, the Elizabethans only: memory of the anarchy of Stephen's reign, for example, not only raises the style of the Peterborough chronicler to a high pitch of eloquence, but also sharpens it to a fine point of irony at the expense of those who believe in 'mercy' as a panacea. The chronicler writes: 'When the traitors realized that the king was a mild and gentle and good man, who never inflicted the punishments required by the law, then' – did they follow the king's example, and so procure their own happiness and that of all with whom they had to do? Quite the opposite: 'then they committed every kind of atrocity'.

Private reflection upon a comparably limitless licence would seem, for a moment at least, to plunge the Duke into the deepest pessimism. When Escalus, by way of polite conversation, puts the question: 'What news abroad in the world?' (III. ii. 215), the Duke replies with an earnestness all the more striking

because unexpected and perhaps inopportune: 'None, but that
there is so great a fever on goodness that the dissolution of it
must cure it.' Or in other words (I give a paraphrase because
the sense, obvious as it may seem, has not escaped misrepresentation): goodness is now in so desperate a state of health,
that no cure short of killing can be hoped for. And if the evils
which the Duke goes on to instance speak rather of irresponsibility or hypocrisy than of a physical mischief, that is because the
level of manners has risen since Stephen's day. Not of course the
level of morals, which on the contrary has sunk: for it is not less
but more reprehensible to ruin a man by cunning or by carelessness than to do so by violence. 'Novelty is only in request',
continues the Duke (*ibid.* 217), 'and it is as dangerous to be
aged in any kind of course as it is virtuous to be constant in any
undertaking. There is scarce enough truth alive to make societies
secure, but security enough to make fellowships accursed. Much
upon this riddle runs the wisdom of the world' – of a world,
that is, which has grown so unfamiliar with justice as to be
capable no longer of preserving but only of destroying itself.

But of course, the significance of the Duke's outburst in Act V
is placed in the clearest light, not by the previous sayings of
himself or others, but by this own subsequent actions. The
immediate cause of the outburst is an impunity enjoyed by
evildoers within the city, its immediate effect a return of power
over the city into the Duke's own hands. Whether the outburst
is calculated or involuntary, whether its effect is foreseen or
comes as a surprise: the Duke avails himself of the effect to take
long steps towards a removal of the cause. After the discharge
of a few indispensable formalities, he proceeds to deal with
Angelo, as the principal evildoer at the time before him, and in
the course of his dealing speaks the following words:

> The very mercy [here note the use of the term 'mercy']
>   of the law cries out,
> Most audible, even from his proper tongue,
> An Angelo for Claudio, death for death:
> Haste still pays haste, and leisure answers leisure,
> Like doth quit like, and *Measure* still for *Measure*.   (V. i. 405)

The way in which these words are ordered, as well as their
content, gives them an especial force. The rime by which the last
two verses are bound together is no sign that their tone or

sense may be neglected, as it often is when verses occur towards the end of a scene. In such a position, their sense may be difficult or impossible to establish, either because of an excessive haste in their composition or an excessive condensation in their style; their tone may be offhand or perfunctory. Here on the other hand they are as purposive and as perspicuous as a proverb, and the rime, contrasted with the blank endings of the verses that precede and follow, gives them a proverb's authority. A modicum of authority the verses would in any case possess, since they recall the title of the play; and since the title, in its turn, recalls the Sermon on the Mount.

It would sometimes seem to be assumed that the title, if of any significance at all, is ironically so; since the play, it is suggested, rests upon a Christian foundation, and since the *lex talionis* is incompatible with Christianity. But whatever the truth of the first of these opinions, the second is certainly false. The *lex talionis* is one of the laws, or better, the compendium and archetype of all possible laws, which both by the precept and example of Christ is not to be done away with but rather, down to the last jot and tittle, fulfilled. By misbehaviour, a man arrogates a portion of evil to himself or, in other words, usurps for himself a portion of the miserable patrimony in which alone the devil may take pride. Therefore the devil has a claim to compensation and, since this cannot be satisfied except by a new creation of evil, the man who misbehaves or someone on his behalf must undergo *malum poenae*. This, and the determination to liberate mankind if mankind so wished, was the reason for Christ's undergoing the penalty of the Cross. Since the amount of evil thereby created was infinitely in excess of any to which human misbehaviour could give the devil a claim, Christ might conceivably be charged with an exaggerated respect for the *lex talionis*; but never with having vilified it. Nor does he, in the creation of good for the reward of a man who behaves well; since such a man may be regarded as having, to the profit of others, alienated a portion of good from himself. So that, upon examination, the principle of *measure for measure* reveals itself as a mere re-statement of the traditional definition of justice, *suum cuique reddere*, the restoration to everyman of his own; a definition which has never been repudiated by Christianity but, on the contrary, consistently maintained.

The particular measure due to any particular man may not of course be easy to determine. The difficulty of doing so would indeed appear responsible for the Duke's failure, over a certain period, to enforce at least some of the laws; and for his withdrawal, over a later period, from the enforcement of any laws whatever. But since, as the play progresses, he is able to learn a great deal, by the end he finds himself by no means as helpless as at the beginning. In particular, he has become convinced, for reasons which have been rudely thrust upon him, that the law inflicting death upon a fornicator violates rather than exemplifies the *lex talionis*. It is in consequence an unjust law, such as ought never to have been established, and he disregards it. None of the fornicators coming up for judgment in Act V is menaced with death on that account. How the Duke deals with these and with others of his subjects is most readily understood from his final speech; to which, as it is also the final speech in the play, something like a representative importance presumably attaches.

It begins:

> She, Claudio, whom you wronged, look you restore

(V. i. 521) – 'you, Claudio, have deprived Juliet of public esteem; therefore she is to be compensated out of whatever esteem you yourself enjoy'. A like provision for Kate Keepdown is made at Lucio's expense; and if it appears to the reader that neither she can profit nor he suffer much by the transaction, that is obviously not Lucio's own opinion. For he protests loudly against the enormity of the sacrifice which he is called upon to make. The humiliated Angelo, on the other hand, is unhesitatingly ready to make Mariana all the restitution that lies in his power. After a few more lines, the Duke goes on:

> Thanks, good friend Escalus, for thy much goodness.
> There's more behind that is more gratulate   (*ibid.* 525) –

Escalus's exertions on behalf of the public are, that is, to receive their due acknowledgment. So are those of another servant of the state:

> Thanks, Provost, for thy care and secrecy:
> We shall employ thee in a worthier place.   (*ibid.* 527)

And if the last words spoken to Angelo open before him the

113

propsect of connubial bliss – 'Look that you love your wife',
(*ibid*. 495) the Duke enjoins,

> love her, Angelo,
> I have confessed her, and I know her virtue –   (*ibid*. 523)

this does not occur until it has been made as clear to everyone
as it is to the Duke himself that Angelo is not responsible for
Claudio's death. As long as the contrary could be supposed, the
Duke's sentence ran:

> We do condemn thee to the very block
> Where Claudio stooped to death, and with like haste.
>   (*ibid*. 412)

Short of a Gilbertian ingenuity, it would seem impossible to
adapt measure more accurately to measure. Nor does the Duke
at any time contemplate continuing Angelo in his governorship,
as happened in Whetstone's *Promos and Cassandra* – a touch of
history here, I confess, but it illustrates rather than supplies my
argument. In Shakespeare's eyes Angelo has not deserved well
of the state, and therefore public honours are to be allowed him
no longer.

To some no doubt it will appear that he has deserved ill of the
state, so that a mere cancellation of his honours is too light a
punishment. This objection can be met, if at all, by nothing short
of the whole of my paper, and provisionally I must content
myself with repeating that, for the time at least, some of
Angelo's principles are sound; and that for maintaining such
principles a man merits, not punishment, but reward. And there
are further difficulties connected with act V, the consideration of
which I should be glad to postpone: the Duke's pardoning of
Barnardin, his leniency to the crime of '*lèse majesté*' committed
by Lucio, above all, his failure to deal out any justice to Pompey
and Mrs Overdone. They do not of course come before him to be
dealt with: but it is precisely their failure to do so which seems
to me one of the more disturbing, as it is one of the most
disappointing, features of Act V as we have it. I pass to a
problem which, whether or not it appears more urgent, is
certainly more important than any of these: the problem, namely,
of how Angelo, if as I have suggested endowed with common
sense, everyday wisdom and at least some principles that are
sound, nevertheless behaves in such a manner that, by Act V, he

ranks foremost amongst evildoers. The answer immediately
suggesting itself is of course that of passion: but such an answer
is rarely complete, nor in this case would it seem to be the most
important part of an answer. For already before he yields to
passion, perhaps even before he is attacked by it, Angelo has
associated himself with evil. In an endeavour to make this clear,
I propose to return to the interview between Angelo and Isabella
which, so far, has been no more than touched upon. Only this
time, in order to avoid repetition as far as possible, I shall
begin by stressing rather the weakness of Isabella's arguments
than the strength of Angelo's.

She herself is of course completely unaware of the role for
which she has been cast by her brother and Lucio; that of the
cheese in the mousetrap of illegality into which Angelo is to be
tempted. Nevertheless her opening arguments, though in one
way infinitely more creditable, in another are hardly so. For
the reasons she advances why Angelo should act as she wishes
bear so little relevance to what he deems permissible and therefore possible as to be either no arguments or worse than none.
'I have a brother is condemned to die', she begins (II. ii. 34),

> I do beseech you, let it be his fault
> And not my brother –

thereby confusing the office of moralist with that of administra-
tor. In pointing out the difference, and the impossibility of his
resting content with the discharge of the one when that of the
other is required, Angelo gives proof of patience, perhaps also
of kindness. There follows a short skirmish, the purpose of which
appears to be to induce him both to distinguish between and to
confuse his official and private capacities, so that what is impossible to the one, improper to the other, may come to seem proper
and possible to a capacity which is at once neither and both. In
breaking off the skirmish without comment on its underlying
morality, or lack of it, Angelo once again is at least not unkind.
So Isabella falls back on commonplaces familiar from Seneca:

> No ceremony that to great ones 'longs,
> Not the king's crown, nor the deputed sword,
> The marshal's truncheon, nor the judge's robe
> Become them with one half so good a grace
> As mercy does –

and if Angelo turns a deaf ear to these, it is difficult to see why

115

he should not. Presumably no prudent person has ever taken to commonplaces seriously, Seneca least of all; and if some of the humanists have appeared to do so, that only shows how little prudent they were – how little versed in the ways of men: deserving not so much the name with which they have been dignified as that of cadaverists. Even Portia, it may be suggested, employs the same commonplaces not in the hope of persuading – for she is a cunning lady – but rather of bemusing both Shylock and the rest of her audience, so that the one shall be the more painfully, the others more agreeably surprised when her trap is sprung. And to that end, she has recourse to a battery of rhetorical devices. But Isabella is either ignorant of these or as yet incapable of handling them; with the consequence that her verses resemble nothing so much as a list of the contents of some dusty wardrobe. These she mechanically exhibits, one after the other, without in any way trimming them: unless indeed the adjective 'deputed' is intended to trim the sword for Angelo's use. But if so, why is it not prominent either at the beginning or the end of the list rather than, as at present, buried in the middle?

Dragged hastily from her convent, which limited and clearly defined duties flooded with light, Isabella encounters difficulty in adjusting herself to the penumbra of worldly affairs. As yet she has not succeeded in bringing into focus the obscured and complicated contours of the objects by which, for the first time, finds herself surrounded. Naturally she fumbles, speaking from a prompting that it is necessary for her to do so, rather than from any conviction either of the truth or of the appositeness of whatever, in her bewilderment, it may occur to her to speak. No verses could be more perfunctory than those with which she opens. And of this Lucio, if not the critics, is uneasily aware; for more than once he urges greater warmth upon her.

> If you should need a pin,

he says,

> You could not with more tame a tongue desire it.   (*ibid*. 45)

But, it will be maintained – at least, it has been maintained – this coldness and mechanism of utterance yields to the fullest life when Isabella, abandoning the words of Seneca, pleads the example of Christ:

116

> Why, all the souls that were, were forfeit once,
> And he, that might the vantage best have took,
> Found out the remedy. How would you be
> If he, which is the top of judgment, should
> But judge you as you are? O think on that,
> And mercy then will breathe between your lips
> Like man new made.   (*ibid.* 73)

With respect to these verses however a difficulty arises which Dr Johnson noted as affecting all verses that treat of a religious theme. In itself, he said, the theme is such as to monopolize attention, leaving little or none available for the elaboration of the verse – or, we may add, for its estimation. Critics who highly praise these verses of Isabella may, very possibly, be attending to the theme alone. But obviously, as literary critics, they should not; or if in practice, and above all in this particular case, the implied distinction is too subtle to be insisted on, let me say that as dramatic critics they are forbidden to attend exclusively to the theme. For the dramatic importance of the latter depends, not on itself alone, but also on the context, so that attention needs to be divided between the two. And once this division is effected, then I think the theme is seen to be irrelevant: so irrelevant indeed that its introduction into the context amounts to an irreverence on Isabella's part. I make no doubt that this is involuntary, since it proceeds from what I have called her bewilderment; once she is engaged on it, however, it cannot remain wholly hidden from her. And this perhaps explains her use of the curiously infelicitous verb 'found out', not so much because of its cacophony, as because of its utter failure to suggest the swiftness and the sureness with which Christ moved to the redemptive act, or the love and wisdom on which alone it may with any propriety be represented as depending. If Angelo should stumble on a means of sparing Claudio, or if he should discover a means by dint of such 'pains' as are recommended to Escalus in V. i. 245, then he might with some exactness be said to 'find it out'; what however he found out by such devious methods could not, without an equal or yet greater degree of inexactness be described as a 'remedy'. It would in fact be the opposite. The debt incurred by Claudio would not have been paid, nor the injury he had inflicted on the devil have been cured, but rather left to fester. And with regard to the *lex talionis* Angelo would have implied that it needs not so much a fulfilling as a forgetting. As we have seen, the implication of Christ's words and deeds is of a different tendency.

Isabella, in other words, after using Senecan claptrap goes very near to making a claptrap use of Christianity. If her subsequent lines are no longer quite so dead as those with which she opened, such life as they possess is capable of producing only a false, and not a true order; to which, considered in itself and not in so far as it might promise better things, the original confusion is to be preferred. To Christ, she applies a verb applicable rather to Angelo; and to the action for which she pleads to Angelo, she applies a noun applicable rather to the action of Christ. This violent juxtaposition of the two agencies does nothing but force into an absurd relief the difference between them; so that once again Angelo can be understood as moved by kindness – at least he moves to her relief – when he repeats that his personal agency does not come into question:

> It is the law, not I, condemn your brother.   (II. ii. 80)

Whatever Christ's example may require of a man, of the law – and with regard to Claudio's fate Angelo speaks as the law – it requires no more and no less than that it should continue its strictest self.

If I examine the text of this interview with a degree of closeness, it is partly because, by common consent, it is of the greatest importance for the play; but also because, in spite of that consent, it would not always seem to be sufficiently closely examined. So often is it represented as a dialogue from a mediaeval morality: in which Isabella speaks like a figure called Mercy, while Angelo replies like a figure called Justice or Authority. Or like a figure called False Authority: this has been suggested perhaps as an acknowledgment of the fact that a morality written by Shakespeare should after all be somewhat more subtle than one written in mediaeval times. But in *Measure for measure* this particular subtlety is obviously out of place, since Angelo's authority, received directly from the Duke, could require no fuller legitimation. Of itself, in any case, the subtlety is far from adequate for the sort of interpretation which the interview demands. Neither partner to it is completely black or white: each is of a peculiar shade resulting from a blend of blacks and whites of differing intensity and differing extent. Isabella for example speaks not only out of mercy, whatever that may mean, but in part out of sisterly affection; in part, out of inexperience of the world, natural in one confined to the cloister; in part, out of spiritual experience, leading to humility, such as the cloister as naturally provides. Humility together with in-experience of the world make her doubtful whether or not she is right in yielding to sisterly affection so far as to plead for Claudio; make it indeed possible for her to plead, only because she is in doubt:

> There is a vice that most I do abhor,
> And most desire should meet the blow of justice:
> For which I would not plead but that I must,
> For which I must not plead, but that I am
> At war 'twixt will and will not. (*ibid.* 29)

So that, when Angelo assures her that pleading will in any case be vain, she immediately acquiesces:

> O just but severe law!
> I had a brother then: heaven keep your Honour. (*ibid.* 41)

Fortunately she has worldly experience at her side in the person of Lucio, who effectively if inelegantly brings her to realize that, in the world if not in the cloister, the decisions of authority are not always beyond question and therefore irreformable. Lucio's presence is on the other hand unfortunate to an equal if not a greater degree, since his experience is not sufficiently complete or sufficiently digested to indicate how authority may be appropriately questioned, but only how importuned. Such a task is quite incompatible with humility: and this is another reason for what I called Isabella's speaking for the sake of speaking, her speaking without conviction. In part too it explains the immediately succeeding confusion of her speech, since she becomes aware of the inadequacy of Lucio's tuition before ceasing to feel the need of it. All these movements within her seem to be essential parts of a complex movement taking place within the scene as a whole, the other parts of which they help to define. Only perhaps in contrast to the emptiness or confusion of Isabella's verses do those of Angelo fully reveal their substantiality and their orderliness:

> Be you content, fair maid:
> It is the law, not I, condemn your brother.
> Were he my kinsman, brother, or my son,
> It should be thus with him. He must die tomorrow.
>
> (II. ii. 79)

Their surface is smooth, like a healthy skin; and like such a skin, it bounds and controls a unity which, though of opposites, is easy because natural. One and the same set of verses suffices to convey Angelo's courtesy and his firmness, a consideration for his petitioner and a respect for himself. As yet he enjoys a calm composure, based on the unshaken belief that not only are his general principles sound but his particular decisions also, and such that both himself and all others of goodwill must find them easy, even pleasant to obey. When a person of apparent goodwill such as Isabella persists in a reluctance to do so, then indeed he begins to show impatience, and upon this more than a hint of inhumanity immediately follows. The substance of his verses shrinks, their surface cracks:

> Be satisfied:
> Your brother dies tomorrow. Be content. (*ibid.* 105)

The greatest contrast provided by the scene however is that between, not Angelo's earlier verses and his later, nor between any verses of his and those of Isabella, but rather between those which she begins and those which she ends by speaking. After the failure of her misjudged attempts either to secure Angelo's complicity in defrauding the law, or to defraud both him and the law together, she would seem to pause in order to take stock of the situation as it now presents itself:

> So you must be the first that gives this sentence,
> And he, that suffers. (*ibid.* 107)

Then something happens. As a consequence, her eloquence opens, and verse pours from her as precipitous as previously it had been sluggish, and because of its precipitation as varied in its forms, lights and colours as it was previously dull:

> O it is excellent
> To have a giant's strength, but it is tyrannous
> To use it like a giant... (*ibid.* 108)

> Could great men thunder
> As Jove himself does, Jove would ne'er be quiet,
> For every pelting, petty officer

Would use his heaven for thunder,
Nothing but thunder   (*ibid.* 111)

and so on.

In large measure, credit would seem to be due to the passage
of time. Gradually Isabella's eyes have grown accustomed to the
penumbras in which henceforth she moves, so that she no longer
depends upon Lucio or anyone for seeing; and with the power of
the spiritually trained, she sees further, deeper than most. But
partly perhaps also, she is helped by the change in Angelo which
has just been noticed: the cracking of his composure makes it
easier to see what is necessary to be seen, if her situation is not
to continue intolerable. For that is how it has come to appear.
In his fidelity to the law, Angelo is formally right; and yet, if
Claudio is to escape death as sisterly affection demands – and
worldly authority, upon close acquaintance, no longer awes such
affection into silence – Angelo must also be wrong, at least
materially. While on the other hand, if Claudio succeeds in
escaping death, then though she has been formally wrong –
indeed, gravely so – in seeking to tamper with Angelo's fidelity,
from the beginning she must also have been materially right.
This is a riddle to which a solution must be found. As her
insight becomes more and more accustomed to a worldly atmosphere, and therefore less and less hampered in its operation, it
does not in the end prove unequal to the task. At the very heart
of Angelo it discerns something by which the riddle is explained.

Like many others of her gifts and training, however, Isabella
does not find herself immediately capable of expounding what
she discerns. She can point to it, compare it to other things, give
it therefore a name and indeed a number of names, but analysis,
definition, understanding – these are only slowly achieved, and
in a haphazard rather than a systematic fashion. Even so, she is
not always careful to make clear the stages of her achievement.
That after all is neither her purpose nor her office: her one goal
is, not to instruct anyone, but to wring from Angelo a single
boon. That she now recognizes as an act, not of favour for Claudio,
nor of mercy falsely conceived, but of justice. Towards that end,
once she has glimpsed it, and regardless of all other things, she
drives headlong.

When she compares Angelo to a giant, it is the giant of
classical mythology she has in mind: who uproots forests,

oversets mountains, chokes the rivers and the seas, all for a selfish lust – say, that of vainglory. As yet unaware of any other lust at work in Angelo, she immediately proceeds to compare him to the tyrant which a classical giant would become, should he succeed in displacing Jove. A yet more startling example of a tyrant would however be provided by one who, displacing Jove, contrasted with him not only as the giant does, in lacking wisdom, but also in lacking power. Hence the reference, in a verse which shortly follows, to a 'pelting, petty officer'. And with this reference, Isabella takes perhaps her first step towards understanding. As pelting and petty, the officer resembles the soft myrtle, for he is easy to destroy: therefore in directing his 'sharp and sulphurous bolts' against the myrtle rather than the 'unwedge-able and gnarled oak' (*ibid*. 117), he sets a precedent for his own destruction. Likewise the 'angry ape' (*ibid*. 121), towards whom for a moment Isabella turns her glance: an additional comparison serving, if not to advance her thought, at least to fix it at the point to which an advance has already been made. By the 'fantastic tricks' with which the ape hopes to win the admiration of beholders, he succeeds only in moving their compassion or contempt: for the beholders are aware, as he is not, that the essence of which he feels 'most assured' is but 'glassy' – but the image of an essence, that is, such as a glass may form (cf. II. iv. 125; *Hamlet* IV. vii. 166). And as the glass distorts, so his assurance is but an ignorance under disguise. Therefore he is predestined to humiliation, in addition to the destruction which the glass, by its fragility, entails.

For the time being, nevertheless, both ape and pelting, petty officer maintain themselves in existence. The only possible explanation is that of a special status which they usurp, an exceptional treatment to which they lay claim. They themselves are exempted from the blows, whether physical blows or blows of ridicule, which they deal out to others. Something like a solution of the riddle has now been approached, something (at any rate) like the definition of a tyrant. But Isabella, moving swiftly so that the reader swallows her breathless, indicates this only by a regretful negative:

We cannot weigh our brother with ourself. (*ibid*. 127)

If we are to escape the imputation of tyranny, we should

accord to our brother the same treatment as, were we in his
position, we should deserve. The difficulties in the way of doing
so are however enormous – and especially for great men, who
have more than anyone else to accord. It is impossible they should
enter into the position of one who is accused of a crime

> Because authority, though it err like others,
> Hath yet a kind of medicine in itself
> That skins the vice o'th'top.   (*ibid.* 135)

Whatever the nature of this medicine – the immunity of the
great from punishment, their provision with blinkers against
criticism, their continual, indeed inevitable, exposure to
flattery – it is powerful, so that a correspondingly powerful
effort is necessary for its neutralization. Leaping over all
intermediate stages, Isabella summons the great men before
her to an effort of this magnitude:

> Go to your bosom,
> Knock there, and ask your heart what it doth know
> That's like my brother's fault. If it confess
> A natural guiltiness, such as is his,
> Let it not sound a thought upon your tongue
> Against my brother's life.   (*ibid.* 137)

One of the intermediate stages is of course a proof of tyranny
in Angelo. But, from the terms of the summons, it can readily
be supplied. He is a tyrant because the law is such to which, in
his fidelity, he clings. In demanding the death of any and every
fornicator, the law not only permits but demands of all by whom
it is administered that they employ a double set of measures:
one for the prisoners before them, another for themselves.
Humanity's proneness to sin, and the persistence and pervasive-
ness of temptation to carnality is such that, were only a single
set of [?measures] available, administrators would be cleared
from the earth as soon as prisoners – or sooner, since they are
fewer to begin with. Their mere survival, like that of the pelting,
petty officer and the ape, is sufficient proof of their tyranny.

Since the law is tyrannical, it is not, in any proper sense, a
law; and so, already at the beginning of Act II, Isabella has
reached a conclusion towards which the Duke does not advance –
or which, at any rate, he does not proclaim – until Act V. But
it is not only the rapidity of her performance which indicates her

superiority of insight over one who has known the training, not of the cloister, but of the world only; the play provides another indication, and of a somewhat more lugubrious kind. Before coming to his conclusion, the Duke has need of evidence not only considerable in extent, but distressing in quality: the spectacle of brothels in Vienna, their exploitation by Pompeys and Mrs Overdones, their patronage by Lucios and Froths: and yet further, an attempted seduction on Angelo's part, a bribe offered in order to accomplish the seduction, a murder planned in order to cloak the bribe. When launching her charge of tyranny Isabella is possibly – indeed, very probably – unaware of the first of these two groups of horrors; of the second she can have no inkling, since Angelo has not as yet so much as hinted at a desire to seduce her – nor, for anything that the text contains, has such a desire crossed his mind. She accuses him of tyranny therefore not as he is himself, still less as he is to show himself to be, but as she might accuse anyone else who, standing in his place, attempted the task which he attempts. Not that 'natural guiltiness' – original as distinct from personal sin – of itself suffices to justify the accusation: but the vice of which Isabella caught a glimpse, and which led her to compare Angelo to a giant – the vice for which I suggested the name 'vainglory': the vice at any rate which, blinding a man to what in him is 'natural', lures to a hoisting of himself above his natural state.

To a novice fresh from the cloister, such a vice can be no less abhorrent than any other. That, once it is diagnosed in a human being, he should not recoil from it, is impossible for her to conceive. So that, at the opening of the second interview between the two, and when, for the first time since her denunciation of tyranny, Angelo announces his intention of maintaining the death sentence upon Claudio, her immediate reaction is to cut the interview short (cf. IV. iv. 34).[1] No human means, it appears to her, can prevail against such obstinate, such wilful blindness. Fortunately for Claudio and for herself, fortunately too for the play.

[1] *Note.* In the original typescript the words 'That, once it is diagnosed...cut the interview short' are lightly cancelled in pencil. I have let them stand as J. S. did not live to replace them. (E. M. W.)

6

THE WINTER'S TALE

We can perhaps consider *The Winter's Tale* as a sort of comple-
ment to *King Lear*. The two plays, I would suggest, deal with
the same topic, but under different aspects. The topic is
imbecillitas humana: the folly or weakness because of which,
unless men are prudent (and so few of them are), they begin to
play fantastic tricks as soon as they have any authority to play
with. In so far as they do so before high heaven they are unworthy of their theatre, and the likely result is tragedy. In so
far as they are men, the tricks are inadequate to the ends they
hope to gain: and so furnish promising material for comedy. If
you object that *The Winter's Tale*, along with a measure of
comedy, contains an abundance of something else: that, I think,
might form part of my argument. Owing to human imbecility,
it is necessary to distinguish between aspects of the theme
which imbecility itself provides. But to distinguish need not
mean to separate, and two aspects of the same thing remain in
communication through the thing to which they belong. Hence
a play based upon one of them smacks of the other: tragedy of
comedy, and *vice versa*. It is now some years since Professor
Wilson Knight, I think with justice, drew attention to what he
called a comedy of the grotesque in *King Lear*. It would not seem
difficult to discern, in *The Winter's Tale*, a tragedy of the grotesque; or at least, a grotesque element that borders upon tragedy
very closely.

All this is highly general, and whether you consider it
important must depend on the help it brings to a study of
details. Let us take two of these, such as are not usually
considered grateful to study: on the one hand, Gloster's
supposed precipitation of himself from Dover cliff, and on the
other, Hermione's apparent return from the dead.

Gloster, finding himself sound in wind and limb after, as he
thinks, a fall of some hundreds of feet, allows himself to be
persuaded that there has been a special intervention of Providence
on his behalf:

Think that the clearest gods, who make them honours
Of men's impossibilities, have preserved thee

(IV. vi. 73f)

Consequently, he begins to believe in Providence or, if he believed before, revives and invigorates his belief; and abandoning the Stoic pride which he has recently affected – and which I would call *fustian*, if only because it is so patently false: 'I shake patiently my great affliction off', he said, when he was the reverse of patient – abandoning this Stoic pride, he replaces it with a humility as near as makes no difference to the Christian: it teaches him to be honest with himself, and yields a degree of patience as its fruit. 'I'll bear affliction', Gloster resolves,

till it do cry out itself
Enough, enough, and die (*ibid*. 75f)

Gloster's having a right conclusion foisted upon him, by a deduction he is encouraged to make from premises that are manifestly, pitifully and absurdly wrong – this humiliates him more, I think, than if he himself were infected by the wrongness. In that case, he would be being deceived, as by an equal; in fact, he is being humoured, as a mother might her child. It is being assumed that, of his own efforts, he is incapable of reaching a conclusion of which he stands in need. It would perhaps be difficult to illustrate imbecility in a manner more apt.

So apt indeed that, for the moment, the spectator may feel inclined to laugh, or even to turn disgustedly aside, as from something that outrages the dignity of a fellow human. In doing so, I do not think he would be wholly unjustified: scarcely however would he be paying due regard to the gravity of what lies at stake. And as though to keep the spectator in mind of this gravity, Lear immediately enters. The effect is at least twofold. First, Gloster is brought to realize yet more clearly the fustian quality of his Stoicism. Under its influence, he had prided himself on bearing as much affliction as could be expected of a man: now he is confronted with a greater affliction, which nevertheless a man is bearing. And secondly, I would say, the spectator begins to suspect, and from this point onwards suspects with increasing certainty, that Gloster's absurd adventure has been put before him for more than its own sake. It adumbrates an adventure of Lear's which, as it takes place not in the physical but in the moral world, cannot be presented to the eye. A physical analogue is at least useful to direct attention towards this adventure; to ensure a real as distinct from a merely notional apprehension of it, a physical analogue is perhaps indispensable.

Like Gloster, Lear believes that he has fallen from a height. And in a sense, of course, this is true: once a king, the fount of honour and the source of justice, now he is an outcast – an object of contumely to whom nothing seems more fitting than that justice should claim him as a victim;

> If you have poison for me, I will drink it. (IV. vii. 72)

At first stunned, then dazed, gradually he recovers the use of his faculties. And when he has done so, he finds that they are what they were. He is still the Lear he was, he has survived his fall. What then, we ask, does he conclude? It is here, perhaps, that Gloster's adventure is of particular value as a pointer. In his own case, Lear would seem to reach the same conclusion as, under the compulsion of ocular evidence, the spectator reached in the case of Gloster. Neither in the one case nor the other was there, in any real sense, a fall. While yet king, and in his own eyes deserving of envy and admiration, in fact and in the eye of Heaven Lear was already an object of contumely; in reality he was already, though he imagined himself the creditor, no more than the debtor of justice. Therefore he embraces a humility equal to Gloster's, and embraces it more closely, both because his is the more thorough spirit, and because he has been more thoroughly chastened. Not only has he been treated as a child, it is impossible he should be unaware of the way in which he has been treated. Of himself he has learnt not only what Gloster learnt – namely, that a Providence exists powerful, among other things, to nullify the effects of a fall; but also what blindness prevented Gloster from learning – that never, except in his own conceit, had he attained a height from which a fall was possible.

The spectator, it was suggested, might be tempted to laugh at Gloster. The first person tempted to laugh at Lear must be Lear himself: not necessarily, of course, with laughter of the same sort. The spectator's sprang from a sense of superiority to a man, the momentary absurdity of whose situation excluded him from sympathy. Though there is a sense in which Lear might be said to feel superior to himself – superior at least as he now is to the Lear he used to be – any failure to sympathize with the one-time Lear would imply a division within him, manifesting itself either as self-pity or as self-contempt. Of neither does he show the slightest trace.

Take for example a scene towards the end of the play in which Lear does laugh: the scene after the British defeat which must, it seems to me, be accepted as the culmination of the tragedy. It will be remembered that news of this defeat caused Gloster to threaten a relapse into pride. To Edgar's urging that he should put himself in a place of safety he replies:

> No further, Sir. A man may rot even here. (V. ii. 8)

– a reply which earns the rebuke 'What, in ill thoughts again?' (*ibid*. 9). Upon Lear the effect is as different as it well might be. He shows no stubbornness or will to resist, he is all acceptance. In prison, he says to Cordelia,

> We'll live,
> And pray, and sing, and tell old tales, and laugh
> At gilded butterflies (V. iii. 11ff)

– laugh, that is, not out of superiority as an adult might, but as children whom considerations of superiority and its opposite have not yet darkened. If the spectator wished to turn aside from Gloster, if in this scene he has no wish to turn aside from Lear – and it seems scarcely possible that he should – he must be prepared to revise his opinion of the Gloster who was subjected to mothering. The spectator must admit what Lear has already admitted: that to be childlike is not necessarily to impair humanity. In prison, Lear and Cordelia will beguile the time with what they regard as toys; they will play at children's games –

> [We'll] take upon's the mystery of things
> As if we were God's spies. (*ibid*. 16ff)

The charm of such games, as for instance that of soldiers, is that the children know they are not soldiers at all, of whose function therefore they enjoy the excitement and the splendours, while remaining secure against its danger and responsibilities. In the same way Lear and Cordelia know – or at least Lear knows, for Cordelia (perhaps significantly) keeps silent – that they are not God's spies, not at all in God's confidence: rather they are removed as far as possible from being so, since they are amongst the paltriest of God's creatures. Souls so completely purged of pride are, in Lear's words, fit not to offer but to receive incense: fit, that is, to enter heaven – but hardly, alas! the fitter to hold their place in the world. Immured in his cell, however, Lear belongs to the world no longer, and that he should be removed from it by death is a matter of no concern to the play. What follows upon his exit to prison is irrelevant, and might with advantage be omitted.

'But what follows is so heart-rending!' Exactly: unless Aristotle and all reputable theorists of tragedy are at fault, words which merely rend the heart are not suitable for utterance on the public stage. Questions such as

> Why should a dog, a horse, a rat, have life
> And thou no breath at all? (*ibid*. 306f)

– questions irrepressible and unanswerable as an agony: these are to be canvassed, if canvassed at all, only in the secret of the confessional or the closer secret of the heart. On pain of ceasing to discharge the function of alterative that, at its best tragedy has always discharged, it needs to acknowledge a limit to its licence to perturb; just as its partner, comedy, has never in effect put forward more than a limited pretension to soothe. Emerging by favour of fortune from a series of trials, comic characters imply they are to live happily ever after – that, in the words of one of the gentlemen in *The Winter's Tale*, henceforward they are to light 'nothing but bonfires'. But the audience knows, and the author knows, that the implication is false; or rather, that it would be false if the characters were not what they are, but real men and women. As long as life endures, these are to light bonfires perhaps, but along with them fires of a destructive intent. To this fact comedy, because of what it is, is compelled to close its eyes. Not only are tragedy and comedy not the same as life but, no more than any other form of art, are they capable of digesting everything that insistently, persistently thrusts itself upon the living.

Of all its congeners, *The Winter's Tale* perhaps endeavours to keep its eyes open as long, and as widely, as possible. Its central character is Leontes who, having caused much suffering at the beginning of the play, himself continues to suffer to within a few verses of the end. He is stricken with remorse for the deaths of his wife and son, both of which he believes, and in one case rightly, he has brought about; and for plotting a death, that of Polixenes, which he proved unable to compass. Learning of these facts, both the real and the supposed, Paulina impulsively condemns him to 'nothing but despair' (III. ii. 210); alarmed by signs that show him close upon despair, as impulsively she changes her tune: 'What's gone and what's past help', she coaxes, 'should be past grief. Do not receive affliction...take your patience to you' (*ibid.* 222ff). As yet it is too early for Leontes to respond to cajolery of this kind. Nor sixteen years later, is it early enough for him to yield to the sober reprimand of Cleomenes:

> Sir, you have done enough, and have perform'd
> A saint-like sorrow...
> Do as the heavens have done, forget your evil;
> With them, forgive yourself. (V. 1. 1ff)

– a reprimand that rises to the reasonable when Cleomenes, citing the dangers of a doubtful succession, exhorts Leontes to marry a second time. Against any such project, it is true, Paulina stoutly protests, and so appears to sing yet another tune. By now however she is laying a plot of her own, for a purpose to be revealed at the close of Act V.

Until the revelation, Leontes finds himself in a very human perplexity – no doubt an exaggerated version of this perplexity: but the intention of Shakespeare the exaggerator is that humanity shall more readily recognize itself. The perplexity is consequent on man's dual nature, denizen at once of a physical and of a moral world. As the former, it is eminently desirable that Leontes should not, in the words of Time the Chorus, 'shut up himself' (IV. i. 19) – should not, that is, withdraw himself from State affairs and the affairs of his fellow-men. To do so might be accounted a form of pride, since he would be over-rating the physical consequences of acts performed by an individual – even by a king – in a world which, as the well-nigh perfectly prudent Camillo puts it, is a world of 'infinite doings' (I. iii. 253). On the other hand, to follow the advice of Cleomenes would be to engage on an immeasurably more dangerous form of pride, that of under-rating an individual's moral liabilities. The forgetting of one's sinfulness is not an earthly but a heavenly privilege: a privilege Leontes has clearly no intention of usurping. He has learnt the lesson of penitence. He must now learn that of practical wisdom, and combine the two. Or rather, the word 'combine' is misleading, since it suggests that the two lessons, lying side by side, may be studied separately. In truth, they interfuse to constitute a single lesson, as the single human being is constituted by the interfusion of what is physical and what is moral about him. Leontes must habituate himself to a kind of practice that, without sacrifice of efficacy, shall at the same time be a penitence; to a kind of penitence that shall permeate practice, furthering rather than hindering it thereby. The lesson is of a subtlety far exceeding that learnt by Lear; and rather than to be mastered within a man, it would be truer to say that a man must be mastered by the lesson – the whole man, that is, down to his very centre where, presumably, the physical and the moral lie as yet undifferentiated. As such a centre remains inaccessible both to the intellect and to the imagination, it would seem doubtful whether the mastering could be played out on the stage of the moralities; on the Shakespearian, it would seem impossible. Yet Shakespeare has his own way of doing things.

At first sight, it might seem that in *The Winter's Tale* he intends employing very much the same device as in *King Lear*: by denying the reality of an external happening, that is, to body forth a happening internal to one of the characters. In *The Winter's Tale* however the happening to be denied belongs, not to the present, but to the past: whence there rise a number of difficulties. A character such as Gloster, for example, turns out to be of no further use: for however easy to deceive a blind man about what is going on around him, about what went on years ago, or at any time before his blinding, he is as likely to possess sound ideas as anybody. Nor could the unsuspected survival of a well-informed witness to the past prove of much help in the theatre; for any long recital on his past, troublesome enough at the opening of *The Tempest*, would prove insufferable towards the close of *The Winter's Tale*, as of any other play. Partial and broken recitals, for example, are sufficient to stir impatience during the last Act of *Cymbeline*. And it is easy or – once again with *Cymbeline* in mind – at least it is pleasant, to assume that, by the time he wrote *The Winter's Tale*, Shakespeare had determined upon the renunciation of ghosts, gods and the like who might be credited with a capacity to draw the past from behind its veil. Willy-nilly therefore it would seem that he is forced upon an inversion of his device in *King Lear*: a happening internal to a character is to be presented in a sufficiently plausible and probable light as to deprive a sudden unveiling of the past of any tendency to offend or shock it might possess – to cause it on the contrary to be welcomed, either rapturously or as a matter of course. Willy-nilly, I said a moment ago: on the other hand, Shakespeare may have addressed himself with eagerness to a task permitting or inciting him to a study to which he seems to have felt inclined: a study, that is, of the fascinating if vexatory relation between physical and moral worlds. In either case, the task cannot have been other than one of extreme delicacy. Let us see how Shakespeare sets about it.

First, he does all that he can to remove any doubt that might hang about the death of Hermione. It is impossible to agree with Coleridge that mere oversight is responsible for the Oracle's failure to foretell reunion for the spouses. Towards the close of the very scene in which the Oracle is made public, Leontes asks to be brought

> To the dead bodies of my queen and son;   (III. ii. 235)

in the last speech of the play he affirms that he was so brought: 'I saw her', he says, 'as I thought, dead.' Then there is the vision with which Antigonus is visited upon the Bohemian coast: a vision which he interprets, and according to all normal canons interprets rightly, as importing the death of Hermione. Finally Paulina, in pursuance of the plan she is secretly elaborating, is as ruthless in her characterization of what Leontes supposes his misdeed as Edgar was hair-raising in his account of what Gloster supposed his fall. 'She you kill'd', says Paulina of Hermione. 'Kill'd?' asks Leontes, 'She I kill'd?' and answers, 'I did so' (V. i. 15ff). Until very nearly the end of the play, that is, Leontes and everyone except Paulina – and this 'everyone' includes the spectator, who is not yet in Paulina's confidence – continues in the conviction that he is a wife-murderer.

As for the easily deceived Gloster, Shakespeare replaces him, I think it must be said, by the multitude of courtiers. There is safety in numbers, but safety can hardly be – obviously is not – Shakespeare's sole reason for adopting this policy. For he shows the courtiers as, unlike Gloster, not so much deceived as deceivable; and he permits of a doubt whether they are not deceivers also. Gloster's example might perhaps be pleaded as evidence of an advantage, possibly of a virtue, to be found in deceivability; whether the example of Edgar as deceiver might be pleaded to a similar effect is more than doubtful. Discussion of the question would lead into a maze of casuistry from which there would be no chance of my emerging. I content myself therefore with a general, and I hope generally accepted, observation. For its maintenance, society requires a deliberate exploitation of make-believe; a willing submission to what is to be distinguished from deceit – if it is to be distinguished at all – only on the closest inspection and by the sharpest wit.

It must, for example, be feared that society as we know it, or any form of society we should find tolerable, could not survive the increase, cannot perhaps survive the continuance, of what at times is praised as the 'frankness' of recent novels. Certain things, it has hitherto been assumed, are as little to be talked of as if they did not exist; and are to be acknowledged as existing only under conditions of absolute necessity or guarded secrecy, such as the bedchamber, the brothel, the latrine or the professional consulting room provides. Nor on topics very different from those reserved for privileged places – topics of an importance varying from the paramount to the minimal – not even upon these is it commendable to blurt out the truth: if only to avoid a ruffling of the composure, a diminution of the geniality, which are – or used to be – demanded by good breeding. And as it is about private joys and sorrows, whether one's own or those of other people, that umbrage is most easily given and most readily taken: for this and for another reason to be considered shortly, an individual's affairs are either not to be handled in conversation, or to be handled only in the most gingerly fashion. Yet conversation cannot be allowed to languish: society would disintegrate if everyone were to follow what seems to have been the example of Leontes for sixteen years: to commune, that is, with himself alone.

With the courtiers about, society is threatened by no such danger, for they manage to keep up a conversation as continuous as it is lively. They are enabled to do so by an exaggeratedly artificial language with which Shakespeare rigs them out – I had almost said, availing myself of what I take to be a coinage of Laforgue's, *les enchasuble*: because of which he has been accused of pandering to a taste for the burlesque. Once again, however, Shakespeare's exaggeration must be allowed not to lack a purpose; and the purpose, once again, is to focus attention on what, though familiar, is as familiarly ignored. Whether out of imbecility or its opposite – out of the pained consciousness, that is, of a dearth of topics threatened by considerations such as were listed in the last paragraph – we spend a great deal of our time chattering about things of little significance to our interlocutors or to ourselves; we proffer statements not intended to be taken at their face value, nor are they in fact so taken. Nevertheless, we should resent no value being attached to them at all; and should feel ourselves fools if our chatter were dismissed as wholly meaningless. The question rises – it has been posed already by the accusation that the courtiers are burlesqued – whether they are not running, whether they have not already run, upon a fate of this kind.

For who, without previous knowledge of the play, could feel confident that reunion between Perdita and Leontes had actually taken place, depending as he must on what he overhears of the courtiers' effusions? Their minds seem to accommodate objects as many and as various as a curiosity shop, a selection from which – bonfires, ballads, fish-hooks, weather-beaten conduits, the colourings of marble – they parade with such industry as to obscure their professed theme; they employ hyperboles so preposterous as to cast doubt on what otherwise might be accepted as the plainest statements. 'The king and Camillo', according to one of them, '...looked as though they had heard of a world ransomed, or a world destroyed' (V. ii. 10, 14f). 'One of the prettiest touches', interjects another, was 'how attentiveness' to Leontes' relation of the death of Hermione 'wounded his daughter; till, from one sigh of dolour to another, she did, with an "Alas!" I would I fain say, bleed tears...if all the world could have seen't, the woe had been universal' (*ibid*. 80, 85ff). But it is a third who, while exemplifying, also epitomizes this quality of the courtiers' speech. 'Such a deal of wonder is broken out in this hour', he exclaims, 'that ballad-makers cannot be able to express it' (*ibid.* 23ff). 'Cannot be able' and not merely 'cannot': not only is a fact denied but, it would seem, even the possibility of conceiving the fact. Yet if Autolycus's summary of his wares has enabled the spectator to conceive anything, it is that nothing to be found this – or any – side of reality baffles the ballad-makers' facundity.

Shakespeare's intention however can hardly be to mislead his audience. Rather I think it is to bewilder or at least bemuse, for the sound and – for the purposes of his play – imperative reason that men reflectively given are continually, all others at least occasionally, bemused at 'the strangely equivocal nature of the universe' in which they find themselves. The equivocality rests on the interfusion of the physical and the moral worlds already referred to: an interfusion which, though incomprehensible, is everywhere and at all times conspicuous. It allows, or provokes, a lump of clay to stand up and call itself a man; to engage upon actions for which it claims or must accept responsibility; and by these actions to effect not only physical but moral changes as well: an agent's intention is able to metamorphose apparent cruelty into kindness, apparent (because material) falsehood into veracity. Intentions are, however, evident to the Deity alone, mankind having to content itself with what knowledge can be inferred – often hazardously inferred – from overt acts. Here equivocality would seem to raise itself to a second power or (perhaps rather) to turn round upon itself, like a kitten upon its tail; since in disproof of appearance it finds nothing to offer save appearance alone. Here too there presents itself an immensely more powerful reason than any previously put forward for avoiding, as far as possible, discussion of an individual's affairs. Here, above all, there appears a dividing line between tragedy and comedy: or rather, as no such line can be hard and fast, there opens between the two a stretch of no man's land, belonging as yet to neither, but over which the one or the other eventually asserts control. For intention transforms, not only apparently evil acts into good, but *vice-versa*: if Paulina helps towards the salvation of Leontes by concealing the survival of Hermione, by disclosing the 'country disposition' of Venetian ladies (*Othello* III. iii. 205), Iago propels Othello downwards towards destruction. From some such point as this onwards, the dramatic territory to be traversed grows ever murkier: though, as no human act was ever performed except in expectation of a good of some kind, light continues to shine, fitfully and dimly perhaps, yet sufficiently to play a multiformity of tricks. If Cordelia's harshness towards her father – a harshness in which, towards her sisters, she persists to close on the very end of her life (*King Lear* V. iii. 7) – if this can unmask itself as the tenderest of charities, why not that of Goneril, or that of Regan? The question must be left for decision to powers higher than human, who have so disposed of the facts. Even after Lady Macbeth's devotion of body and soul to the most diabolic of superhuman powers, her yearning for what is sweet in goodness endures in such strength that, overhearing her last words, a doctor of physic – in spite of the 'general scandal' attaching to his profession – is moved to utter a prayer on his own behalf as well as hers: 'God, God forgive us all!' (*Macbeth* V. i. 727). And indeed, on the very extremity of the moral landscape on which Lady Macbeth has come to poise, no help is to be looked for except from the Highest Power of all.

Fortunately – or so at least we flatter ourselves – Lady Macbeth is an exception. The greater part of mankind, it seems to us, pass the greater part of their time in a twilit region, perhaps even in the better illuminated part of that region where, if already possible, it is hardly as yet likely that 'fair is foul, and foul is fair'. Even so, they sense a fog, however tenuous, that envelops them and that, for its defeat, calls for some kind of strategy. If fate has been unkind enough to hoist them on to the judge's bench or to dice them into a jury box, their only strategy can be to take upon themselves the superhuman power to distinguish between potential Cordelias and Regans: not for nothing did King James I and his like relish repetition of the Old Testament verse (Ps. 82: 6) in which no less a personage than the Deity addresses magistrates as gods. And even those lucky enough to avoid involvement with the law courts may, by a sudden or exceptional crisis, find themselves placed in the dilemma of either, at enormous risk, assuming authority as of the gods, or ashamedly confessing ineptitude. But for the more fortunate many, a strategy similar to that adopted by the courtiers would seem very suitable. It may be divided into two stages. First, the courtiers choose a language sensational enough to fill them with the necessary courage, which may be great, to spite the fog by keeping their noses in the air; too sensational however to inspire others with confidence, while insufficiently so to compel mistrust. In this way the courtiers secure the widest scope for such manoeuvring between scepticism and credulity as future circumstances may require. And secondly, of course, they must develop a weather eye for observing and a memory for recording these circumstances: ransacking the physical world, it might be said, so as to leave little or nothing in it that, either in itself or in any moral relationship, might spring a surprise. If the bizarre lingo cultivated by the courtiers does indeed work in this sort of manner, then might it not serve as a faithful exponent of the parlous condition of Leontes, if only he would expound it? or of the parlous condition of mankind, in so far as Leontes is a representative figure? In any case, it is partly, if not greatly, to the prevalence of this lingo that Leontes is to owe his ultimate salvation.

But this is to anticipate. So far, we have taken a glance at no more than the hyperboles which the courtiers employ; it is high time therefore to make some measure of acquaintance with the curious and intimate concern they manifest for the physical world. A piquant example is provided by the speech already quoted, in which an episode of the reunion with Perdita is singled out as 'the prettiest touch'. This touch, a courtier goes on to say (in words that have not been quoted as yet) 'angled for mine eyes (caught the water though not the fish)' (V. ii. 82ff). The well-bred joke is to be noted: well-bred because it aims at geniality, relieving without discrediting seriousness. But far more clamorous for notice is the commonplace and callous image under which the courtier chooses to represent one of the tenderest and most recondite of all phenomena: Perdita's inner wounding and the sympathy it provokes. If it existed by itself, the image could only be condemned as barbarously, even brutishly inappropriate: it exists however in a context crowded with images of a similar kind. The context even includes a statement that, at moments of deep and violent disturbance, not only human feelings but human beings are to be recognized only by their physical accompaniments: 'There was casting up of eyes, holding up of hands, with countenance of such distraction, that they were to be known by garment, not by favour' (*ibid.* 47ff). Here the spectator – or listener, as it seems more proper to call him, since we are dealing with a scene, the appeal of which is not to the eye, but to the ear alone – here the listener naturally, I think, turns his thoughts to the arts for which physical accompaniments are of prime importance, to the plastic arts, that is; and especially perhaps to sculpture as practised in the sixteenth, seventeenth and (in Germany) the eighteenth centuries. By their beckonings across and athwart, groups of figures produced at that time confuse the beholder, unless he takes up a carefully calculated point of view; and if incautious enough to examine the figures separately, he is as likely to be filled with disgust as with delight – so violent are the contortions of both feature and limb.

According to the courtiers, this second misfortune certainly overtakes those principally concerned in the reunion with Perdita. Paulina, for example, they describe as having ' one eye declined for the loss of her husband, another elevated that the oracle was fulfilled' (*ibid.* 74ff) – a description often likened to that given by Claudius of himself, when marrying Gertrude

With an auspicious and a dropping eye. (*Hamlet* I. ii. 11)

But it is difference rather than likeness that strikes the awakened ear. Only one of the adjectives employed by Claudius has a physical reference and that, because of the inevitable association 'dropping' with 'drooping', no more doubtful. Whereas both the adjectives used of Paulina's eyes belong uncompromisingly to the drawing board, so that the poor lady appears to undergo a punishment like that of the rack, or of a rending asunder by horses. Nor do the King and Camillo present an attractive spectacle when seeming 'almost, with staring at one another, to tear out the cases of their eyes' (V. ii. 11ff). And when a courtier reports of Leontes (*ibid.* 54) that he 'worries' his daughter as a dog might worry a bone, the listener, I think, involuntarily shudders and compresses his eyelids. Fortunately for him – and for Leontes also, as it turns out – the latter recedes so far into the throng of courtiers as to be lost in it. 'Thither', says a member of the throng, pointing to Paulina's sculpture gallery, 'thither (with all greediness of affection) are they gone' (*ibid.* 101ff) – they, not he, not even he as one of them, but only they. And they are gone 'with all greediness of affection' – with all 'eagerness of natural love', translates the recent Arden edition but, it is to be feared, much in the manner that Bottom was translated. For a word such as 'greediness', specifying a physical appetite, is precisely what the rest of the scene insists upon, and what is at last consistent with the conclusion of the courtier's speech: 'Thither (with all greediness of affection) are they gone, and there they are to sup.'

There follows an interlude between Autolycus and the Shepherds, which may be compared to a glass of water taken after one tipple of strong wine to clear the palate for the next. This next proves unexpectedly strong: for with few and short exceptions, dialogue is confined to Paulina and Leontes, and Leontes has undergone an astounding transformation, not only from the silent solitary of some sixteen years back, not only from the 'gross and foolish sire' (III. ii. 197) of yet earlier times, but also from the melancholy if communicative invalid of the opening scene of Act V. Towards the end of that scene, it is true, the meeting with Perdita stirred him to an activity that the observant jealousy of Paulina found alarming (V. i. 223ff); and whatever else the courtiers' galimatias in scene ii may conceal, at least it makes clear that recognition of Perdita as his daughter raised Leontes' activity to a point of frenzy. Yet it would seem that immersion amongst the courtiers influenced him most, for he issues from it as from a legendary bath – not of course rejuvenated, but primed with all the courtiers' alertness to the physical world, and wariness of the marvels which, in conjugation with the moral, it may engender. When led before the statue of Hermione, for example, does or does he not believe it to be no other than it appears? He calls it a 'royal piece' (V. iii. 38) – in the sense of 'masterpiece', according to the Arden editor, and this is quite possible. But it is also possible for the spectator to recall that, in an earlier scene, Perdita was called 'a piece of beauty' by Florizel (IV. iv. 32), and by Polixenes a 'piece of excellent witchcraft' (*ibid*. 423ff). And though both Leontes and Paulina refer to the statue as a 'stone' (V. iii. 37, 58, 99), a stone which, though 'dear' (*ibid*. 24) is also 'cold' (*ibid*. 36), this idea of coldness is roused in Leontes by what he remembers of the warmth of Hermione: may therefore – it would seem a fair presumption – be no more than what he thinks proper to impute to a stone, so long and in so far as he considers it as such; no more, for example, than that possessed by the stone to which he compares Perdita, benumbed at the first sight of her mother;

or by that to which he reproachfully compares himself, for not reacting to the sight as impassionately as he would wish, or thinks he ought (*ibid.* 36ff). Yet he reacts, it would seem, impassionately enough: as Perdita needs to be restrained from kissing the hands of the statue, so he from kissing the lips (*ibid.* 46, 80). And though held motionless and at a distance by fear of marring what he covets and adores, his senses continue to work, and to work feverishly: scrutinizing so closely the statue's every detail, down to the veins and the wrinkles, that he might be said to devour it. He himself employs the figure of ingestion: the 'affliction' prepared for him by Paulina he compares to a 'cordial comfort' (*ibid.* 77), the 'taste' of which is so 'sweet' that he would not cease from sipping it 'these twenty years' (*ibid.* 84). Thus there is justified the word 'greediness', proleptically employed by the courtier; who proves mistaken, not in the fact, but only in the timing of a banquet. This does not follow, but is contemporaneous, indeed identical with a viewing of the sculpture. Leontes enjoys his banquet now. Nor is the banquet as yet at its height: upon a course to dazzle the eye there follows a second to quicken the ear – music sounds (*ibid.* 98); finally there is served a course of magic which, though 'lawful as eating' (*ibid.* 111), cannot have been devised for the sole satisfaction of the tongue. It is of course a cozenage of Paulina's, the consummation in fact of the plot she has for so long nursed in secret. Its success however rises far above anything to which she herself might have aspired: for, without the co-operation unconsciously lent by the courtiers, how could a self-convicted wife-murderer have failed to retreat before the descent of that wife from her pedestal – repeating the acknowledgment of himself as 'offender', wrung from him by the merely imaginary, not the real, presence of his wife (V. i. 59), fearing that though he had refrained from a second marriage, she must, if not 'shriek' (*ibid.* 65), at least murmur reproaches in his ear? But Leontes' submission to – or, to establish a parallel, however remote, between him and Lear, I think we may now say his humbling himself before – the courtiers' acceptance of a universal perplexity has allowed any and every perplexity of his own to be subsumed and so vanish within it. He has been moved down to the very centre; his whole being has been changed, so that the physical and the moral now move in harmony within him.

Therefore he welcomes the descent, and does so not only with rapture but – what Paulina must consider the greatest of her triumphs – as a matter of course.

Relieved for the first time of the burdens of the world by imprisonment, Lear laughs; habilitated for the first time for those of king, husband and father, though Leontes does not laugh, he overflows like Lear with joy; and as Lear sought to associate Cordelia with his laughing, so Leontes would have his joy freshen those about him. He commands the marriage of Camillo and Paulina. This, I suppose, might be taken as a mere application of the lesson he has learnt, that nothing, neither mistaken pride nor impossible loyalties, can be of so indubitable a nature as to excuse anyone from taking part in the 'infinite doings' of the world. The heart however goes out to Paulina who, while lamenting a 'mate (that's never to be found again)' (V. iii. 34), suffers another mate to be forced upon her; and the mind boggles at the prudent Camillo assenting, without more ado, to an offhand flouting of ceremony. Yet does he assent, and does she suffer? The play contains no word of either's attitude to the marriage. Save as a mere name, or *flatus vocis*, the marriage lies outside the play, so that speculation about it is not so much superfluous as unwarranted. The inclusion of the name I look upon as a concession to the convention of a happy ending; as part of the price – by no means a large one – which *The Winter's Tale* must pay for classing itself as a comedy.

The price is not large when contrasted with the wealth that is hoarded by *The Winter's Tale* as a whole. So far it has been comsidered no more than in part; and I am uneasily conscious that this part, treated as it has been – strung along the sole and slender thread of the courtiers' conversation – may appear somewhat spidery. I would therefore recall a remark made a while ago, about groups of sculpture produced in the baroque period. Considered separately, I said, figures in such a group might repel, and as a whole the group must confuse, unless viewed from a carefully calculated point. *The Winter's Tale* has suffered in both these ways: for lack of a proper point of view it has been accused, not only of burlesquing the courtiers, but of jumbling the affairs of Sicily with those of Bohemia, the fortunes of Leontes with those of Florizel; of presenting Leontes' jealousy of Hermione in an incredible, his reconciliation with her in a fantastic, light; and, in spite of all that prudence over whispered, or common experience loudly trumpeted, of hailing the passion of Florizel for Perdita as of salvific potency for everybody. None of these features should however be considered by itself: all must be viewed together, as can be possible only from a point that lies beyond, or rather above them all – the point which is provided by human imbecility. Then it will be seen how the features work upon and modify one another, each requiring the rest to be taken into account if it is to be understood as Shakespeare intended, and as it really is. I know of no play which is richer in content that *The Winter's Tale*, and at the same time more skilfully and scrupulously organized – not only every Act and every scene, but every speech within a scene playing a due and necessary part. Within the limits of a single paper I cannot do more than indicate this closeness of texture, if indeed I can do as much. But let me endeavour to do what I can.

First, I would point out that Act I opens with a conversation between courtiers cut to exactly the same pattern as that of the courtiers in Act V. Curious comparisons are sought for: the Bohemians, for example, trust to 'sleepy drinks' (I. i. 13) to match in the Sicilians the stupefaction which Sicilian generosity has induced in themselves. Outrageous over-statements are flung out: Leontes and Polixenes are said 'to have seemed to be together, though absent; shook hands as over a vast, and embraced, as it were, from the ends of opposite winds' (*ibid.* 29ff). Nor, lest the pattern, though in small, be incomplete, is the well-bred joke neglected. Camillo, having allowed a more than usually glaring absurdity to escape him, is challenged by Archidamus. 'They that went on crutches before [Mamillius] was born', Camillo brags, 'desire yet their life to see him a man.' 'Would they else be content to die?' asks the sly Archidamus. Gracefully and good-humouredly, Camillo confesses that he has received a body-blow: they would be so content, he answers, 'if there were no other excuse why they should desire to live' – and, of course, there always is.

In Act V, the continuous and careful practice of this form of conversation is shown as leading, with Fortune's aid, to the happiest of results; in Act I neglect of it precipitates, without any aid from elsewhere, results which could not be more horrific.

Prevented by business or, as he may think, dispensed by rank from practising conversation as he ought – and a third and less creditable reason, to be mentioned later, may perhaps come into play – Polixenes makes but a poor fist of disguising in a polite form his longing to be loose from Sicily. By his second speech (I. i. 10ff) he has succeeded, if in anything, only in disguising the disguise he has chosen: a fear, namely, both of outstaying his welcome and of untoward happenings in Bohemia. Yet it is Leontes who, of the two Kings, behaved by far the more culpably: for he does not so much betray a neglect as flaunt a scorn of conversational decencies. To Polixenes' series of fumblings he returns what are, in effect, curt refusals to take them into due account. Exasperated by what can only be called a display of ill-breeding, Polixenes summons whatever powers of plain speaking he possesses; and if, in the light of later information, his plain speaking does not appear wholly honest, we should bear in mind what has previously been said of the precarious nature of all judgments passed upon human motives. ' My affairs ', insists Polixenes,

> Do even drag me homewards; which to hinder
> Were (in your love) a whip to me; my stay
> To you a charge and trouble: to save both,
> Farewell, my brother.   (*ibid*. 23ff)

Such a resolute and coherent declaration no longer admits of being brushed aside and so Leontes, apparently incapable of anything different, is fain to turn for help to Hermione. Thereby he sets that unfortunate lady's steps in what is to prove her Way of the Cross.

For she is a simple creature: of a simplicity that would be fitting and admirable in the seclusion of a prison cell like Lear's, or in a lower order of society preserved from dissension by the example – or the main force – of an order which is higher. But in such a higher order, simplicity blinds Hermione to the complexity and latency of motives. There looms before her nothing but the duty of satisfying, as best she may, the wishes of her husband who is also a master. Inevitably if innocently, she overtrumps him in ill-breeding; since she does not so much disregard one of the polite pretexts of Polixenes, as give it the lie. Only yesterday, she blabs, news arrived that all goes well in Bohemia (*ibid*. 30f). Then, sensing that an impropriety has been committed (as simplicity, like an animal, may sense, without conceiving why) she endeavours to divert attention by a sort of gambolling around Polixenes:

> Verily!
> You put me off with limber vows; but I,
> Though you would seek t'unsphere the stars with oaths,
> Should yet say 'Sir, no going.' Verily,
> You shall not go: a lady's Verily's
> As potent as a lord's. Will you go yet?
> Force me to keep you as a prisoner.
> Not like a guest: so you shall pay your fees
> When you depart, and save your thanks

and so on. Such gambols are ungainly in the human adult. Indeed, when Hermione imagines her husband's ends have been attained and with mock eagerness begs to be crammed with praises like a goose (*ibid.* 91f), when she crows like an infant over a feigned discovery that she 'has spoke to th' purpose twice' (*ibid.* 106) – then she calls down upon herself one of the most disagreeable of all adjectives that can be applied to an adult: she is *arch*.

Not that her native simplicity does not at times break through. When she prompts both Leontes and Polixenes with words such as the following:

> To tell, he longs to see his son, were strong;
> But let him say so then, and let him go;
> But let him swear so, and he shall not stay,
> We'll thwack him hence with distaffs –   (*ibid.* 54ff)

then the homely noun and verb in the last line, and the picture they evoke of a righteous, not monstrous regiment of women: these refresh like contact with a healthy peasantry. The refreshment however quickly passes, because of a puzzle which the verses pose. From the opening of the play Polixenes has been searching for an excuse to depart without offence to his hosts; such an excuse is here presented to him by one of the hosts themselves, and yet he ignores it. Why?

An answer is perhaps suggested somewhat later when the two kings, the difference between them outwardly composed yet both of them inwardly seething, the one with frustration, the other with an emotion yet to mention, fall back on the topic on which, according to Jane Austen, ladies in embarrassing situations have the custom of falling back: the topic of their children. On behalf of his little son, Polixenes puts forward the breath-taking claim:

> He's all my exercise, my mirth, my matter – (*ibid.* 186)

breath-taking because no adult in his senses can or should find 'all his matter' in a child. Is it however possible to bestow the honourable title of 'adult' on Polixenes? Serious doubts are raised by his attempts at self-justification: for these read more than somewhat like an impeachment. His son, says Polixenes, 'makes a July's day short as December' (*ibid.* 169): now, no mature person, conscious and proud of his opportunities, ever found time to hang upon his hands – rather than of a lack of affairs with which to fill up time, his continual complaint is of a lack of time with which to deal with affairs that, either as delights or duties, press upon him. The 'varying childness' of his son, Polixenes goes on, 'cures in me Thoughts that would thick my blood' (*ibid.* 170f): but what – our ruminations up to this point provoke us to ask – what is the quality of this cure? For there is a thinness of blood that threatens as many dangers of at least a similar magnitude, if of an opposite kind, as any thickness. And the imminence of such dangers is at least suggested by the contrast Polixenes draws between July and December: for though this is restricted by his words to length of daylight, it seems impossible that the restriction should not be set aside by his thoughts, as it certainly is by those of the spectator. July the month of luxuriance and satiety, December of nudity and famine: if the latter is in truth the object of Polixenes' preference, then we light perhaps at last upon the third reason which, it was suggested above, might account for his social inadequacy – not merely a lack of practice in conversing, but a more deep-seated and general inadequacy which, however much he practised, must for ever keep him from conversing as he should. The burdens of adult life he finds too heavy to bear: no more imbecile than Leontes, as compared with Leontes he suffers the disadvantage of an awareness of imbecility. Enviously therefore and in thought he turns towards his little son, of whom nothing but imbecility can as yet be expected: while fearfully and in fact he keeps his son at a distance, lest the difference between their ages and consequent obligations should leap into a prominence impossible even for himself to ignore.

Weighty backing is I think given to these deductions by the more than Arcadian, by the paradisal memories which Polixenes entertains of his own and Leontes' boyhood. He tells Hermione

> We were as twinn'd lambs that did frisk i'th'sun
> And bleat the one at th'other –   (*ibid*. 67f)

creatures, that is, incapable of rising into the rank of sinners; but also (though he does not use the words, the context amply justifies their being supplied) creatures incapable of descending to that rank, since they hymned and fluttered like cherubs. Unfortunately, Hermione's simplicity defeats Polixenes of whatever end he may have hoped to attain by this *fantasia*: incapable of recognizing in what he says anything but a violation of common sense, archness prompts her to make fun of it. Such evident preoccupation with sin, she teases, suggests an uneasy conscience. It is dangerous to come between a luckless man and the dream from which he derives consolation. 'O my most sacred lady', begins Polixenes, with a heavy irony,

> O my most sacred lady,
> Temptations have since then been born to's; for
> In those unfledg'd days was my wife a girl,
> Your precious self had not then cross'd the eyes
> Of my young playfellow.   (*ibid*. 76ff)

'Grace to boot!' protests the alarmed Hermione,

> Of this make no conclusion, lest you say
> Your queen and I are devils.   (*ibid*. 80f)

But whether Polixenes considers them devils or not she is never to learn, fortunately perhaps for the secrets of the bedchamber; for Leontes interrupts the dialogue.

While Polixenes and Hermione torment or puzzle each other, Leontes has been the reverse of unobservant: he has noticed the two 'making practis'd smiles As in a looking-glass' (*ibid*. 116) and – if the conclusions we have so far drawn are at all correct – has been right in his noticing. Hermione arch, Polixenes hiding a plurality of vexations: neither is behaving in a natural but in an affected manner. Add the inferiority Leontes cannot but be conscious of to both, since he felt the necessity of appealing to the one for help against the other; add the boorishness he has evidenced from the moment of his entry upon that stage: and little if anything further is needed to generate jealousy – a few customary gestures perhaps that Leontes, being so inclined, may interpret as 'paddling palms and pinching fingers' (*ibid.* 115). But it is Mamillius who, as a sort of catalyst, brings jealousy to the point of explosion. In spite of the agreement expressed in lines 71ff – an obvious excuse for getting rid of a presence by now obnoxious – Leontes' attitude to his son 'divides more wider than the sky and earth' from that of Polixenes. Admiring Mamillius both for physical qualities – he has a 'welkin eye' (*ibid.* 136) – and for those of spirit – he'll not 'take eggs for money' (*ibid.* 136) – Leontes is vividly aware, not of any difference between himself and his son, but of a likeness amounting very nearly to an identity: 'Twenty-three years' back, he reflects, 'How like...I then was to this kernel, This squash, this gentleman' (*ibid.* 155, 159ff) – a series of appellatives of which the last is no more than partially dictated by condescension or mockery; twenty-three years later the two are universally pronounced 'Almost as like as eggs' (*ibid.* 130). Indignation, resentment that such a magnificent creature as Mamillius reflects should be made a fool of before his own eyes – this lets loose the tirade containing the line:

> Affection! thy intention stabs the centre.   (*ibid.* 138)

Though the tirade suffers under the reputation of obscurity, at least as much sense can be made of it as is to be expected from a man who is out of his senses. Whether the word 'centre' is here used to mean the centre of the universe, as elsewhere in the play (II. i. 102), or as elsewhere in this paper the centre of a man's being; whether the apostrophized affection is jealousy or lust, whether in consequence Leontes comminates objects of his enmity or commiserates himself, as an object deserving pity: of all these cases, the upshot is the same. The foundation of things, or of Leontes' conception of things has been removed; all laws of likelihood have been abrogated so that, as it is put in *Macbeth*, 'nothing is but what is not'. Leontes may give rein first to his unsavoury, then to his savage, imaginings. These rise, or descend, to the poisoning of Polixenes, and to the burning of Hermione alive.

The jealousy swells very quickly, but no more quickly than it collapses when Mamillius dies (III. ii. 145) – another proof of the importance this young man possesses for his father. Shakespeare has a large stretch of ground to cover, and the speed at which he does so is, I think, less deserving of remark than the perfect balance he manages to maintain. Of the comic element in *King Lear*, Professor Wilson Knight observed that it was treated with a sureness of touch sufficient to retain it, without toppling over, on the border between comedy and tragedy. The same is to be said of *The Winter's Tale* where the toppling, if it happened, would of course take the opposite direction. Two outbursts on the subject of lust may, if laid side by side, illustrate both the likeness and the difference between the plays. 'Let copulation thrive', Lear blusters (IV. vi. 117); 'no barricado for a belly', laments Leontes (I. ii. 204). Considered by themselves, both might seem utterances from the same mouth; taken in their contexts, they diverge widely. Before the mind of Lear, all creatures without exception and therefore himself (IV. vi. 118f, cf. III. iv. 76f) indulge in lustful orgies: for which reason his hand, no less than anyone else's, smells of mortality (IV. vi. 133). Leontes is embarrassed by no such smell, for unlike Lear's 'simpering dame', his Sir Smile represents, not the whole of humanity, but humanity with a single exception: Leontes himself. In consequence, Sir Smile personifies, not offences committed against the Deity, but only the offences – or the offence – of which Leontes imagines he has to complain. Such self-righteousness I would call grotesque and big with tragedy. Another incident, at least equally grotesque, occurs when Leontes, with real or feigned reluctance, yields to the courtiers' plea that the sentence of instant combustion, passed on Perdita, shall be commuted. 'I am a feather for each wind that blows', wails Leontes (II. iii. 153); though as the courtiers know only too well, and as he himself can hardly help knowing, he is of no weight to float, but to crush anyone on whom he chooses or happens to fall. Had he shown any tendency to joke, or the slightest taste for play-acting, at this moment he might be reluctantly admired as a resuscitated Richard III: his self-righteousness however forbids anything of the kind. His wail must therefore be taken seriously: implying, in addition to self-righteousness, a self-deception that hints at a tragedy yet more cruel than Richard ever suffered or perpetrated.

Hermione at least entertains no doubt of Leontes' self-

righteousness: though he fails to understand her, she understands him. However little simplicity may see, what it does see
it sees clearly; the vision of boorishness is invariably blurred.
As therefore she unhesitatingly obeyed his command to retain
Polixenes, she resolutely refrains from defending herself. 'It
shall not boot me', she explains at her trial,

> To say, not guilty. Mine integrity
> Being counted falsehood, shall, as I express it,
> Be so receiv'd. (III. ii. 25ff)

Like Cardinal Newman – another simple soul, as inept in the
management of his life as skilful in that of his pen (contrast
Cardinal Manning!) – like Cardinal Newman when under attack
from Kingsley, Hermione complains that the wells have been
poisoned. Nor would an *Apologia* be of use to her, even if she
had time to develop it; for Leontes has made sure that her
audience shall consist of Kingsleys alone. By insistence on his
absolute authority, he muzzles all such protests as the courtiers
began by raising on Hermione's behalf. 'What need we
Commune with you of this?' he asks. '[We] rather follow Our
forceful instigation. Our prerogative Calls not your counsels...
We need no more of your advice' (II. i. 161ff). And so all stand
by, with tacit if not vocal approval, while (could anything be
more tragically grotesque?) he plumes himself in his 'natural
goodness' (*ibid.* 164), on his scrupulous avoidance of 'wildness'
in 'an act of [such] importance' (*ibid.* 181) as the arraignment
of Hermione.

All, it may be objected, except Camillo, Paulina and Antigonus.
By the time of the trial however Camillo is no longer to be
found in Sicily; nor has Paulina as yet established herself as a
figure of anything like commanding importance. Her attempt to
discharge the role of champion of chastity and protector of
innocence earns nothing but such titles as 'mankind witch...
most intelligencing bawd' (II. iii. 67f); for inability or unwillingness to control her, Antigonus is berated as 'lozel' (*ibid.* 101),
as 'dotard...woman-tir'd, unroosted By [his] dame Partlet'
(*ibid.* 74f). None the less – and before any command is laid upon
him, to be discharged on pain of his own life and Paulina's – he
declares a readiness to 'pawn the little blood' left in him to save
Perdita (*ibid.* 165f). Returning to the terminology employed in a

previous paragraph he might be said to raise himself thereby to a superhuman level: to a level, at any rate, far higher than that of the rest of the courtiers who, confronted by the rage and folly of Leontes, find their customary strategy of no avail. Accordingly they degrade themselves to what Paulina scorns as obsequious shadows of Leontes (*ibid.* 34f). And yet – such are the enigmas with which life confounds us – it may be they who, with their habit of hovering between scepticism and credulity, preserve in the secrecy of their minds (where, of course, it is of no immediate use) a greater independence and therefore soundness of judgment: a vision would perhaps have convinced them somewhat less easily than it convinced Antigonus, not only that Hermione is dead but that she died an adultress.

Camillo has fled because warned by his prudence that Leontes' jealousy, like a July sun, is soon to shine too hot for life beneath it to be tolerable. Not that the same prudence allows him to except in Bohemia a December such as Polixenes dreamt of: for Decembers of that sort are not to be found in any calendar. As the sun of one passion declines, that of another arises, and in due time Bohemia is to be threatened with a conflagration by Florizel. No greater misconception of the architecture of the play could be implied than by a contrast between Bohemia as a reserve of pastoral innocence and Sicily as a den of courtly vice. If not a geographical, the two countries preserve a moral and emotional continuity. The first Bohemian to set eyes on Perdita shares the conviction of the last Sicilian to leave her: 'Sure some scape', reflects the Shepherd, 'though I am not bookish, yet I can read waiting-gentlewoman in this scape: there has been some stair-work, some trunk-work, some behind-door work' (III. iii. 71ff). And so far from cherishing illusions about males at Florizel's stage of development, the Shepherd would, if he could, suppress them entirely: 'I would there were no age between ten and three-and-twenty... for there is nothing in the between but getting wenches with child, wronging the ancientry, stealing, fighting' (*ibid.* 59ff). Similar notes are sounded by Autolycus, by the Clown – who, it is interesting and important to note, insists (IV. iv. 244) that, in their public conversation, his social equals observe artifice and deceit corresponding to those of the courtiers – and, most impressively of all, by Florizel.

But, setting him apart for the moment, let us note how other characters already known to us comport themselves in Bohemia. Camillo whom, Leontes protested, 'I have trusted

> With all the nearest things to my heart, as well
> My chamber-counsels, wherein, priest-like, thou
> Hast cleans'd my bosom: I from thee departed
> Thy penitent reform'd –   (I. ii. 235ff)

this same Camillo earns no less enthusiastic praises from Polixenes. 'The need I have of thee', declares this latter, 'thine own goodness hath made...[Thou hast] made me businesses, which none without thee can sufficiently manage...the very service thou hast done...if I have not enough considered (as too much I cannot) to be more thankful to thee shall be my study' (IV. ii. 11ff), and so on. And, jumping a little ahead, as Camillo may be said to have betrayed Leontes for the best of reasons, so in time, and for reasons that are not quite so good, he is to betray Polixenes. Yet these reasons are by no means wholly reprehensible: for when touched as he imagines in his honour, Polixenes reveals himself the equal of Leontes in savagery: the old Shepherd he regrets 'that by hanging...I can but shorten thy life one week' (IV. iv. 422f), Perdita's beauty he threatens to have 'scratch'd with briars' (*ibid.* 426), and herself, should she continue to receive Florizel, with 'a death as cruel for thee As thou art tender to it' (*ibid.* 441). Under these menaces, Perdita carries herself with the somewhat stolid, because unimaginative, steadfastness of her mother:

> I was not much afeard; for once or twice
> I was about to speak, and tell him plainly
> The selfsame sun that shines upon his court
> Hides not his visage from our cottage,   (*ibid.* 443ff)

while her response to Polixenes' plea on behalf of gillyvors borders on the contemptuous: 'I'll not put The dible in the earth to set one slip of them.' Fortunately, along with the steadfastness, she inherits none of the archness of her mother: Camillo's sole attempt at gallantry –

> I would leave grazing, were I of your flock,
> And only live by gazing –   (*ibid.* 109f)

meets with the response dictated by common sense:

151

Out, alas!
You'd be so lean that blasts of January
Would blow you through and through.   (*ibid.* 110f)

But what of the above mentioned plea on behalf of gillyvors?
Might it not appear that, in Bohemia, Polixenes has acquired a
command over language which in Sicily we felt proper to deny
him? Two facts are to be borne in mind: first that, as he has no
reason to doubt of the inferiority of Perdita's birth, not the
remotest fear of inadequacy can arise to unnerve him when, with
her, he deigns to bandy words; and secondly, that his words are
no more than bandied, for they are entirely forgotten when the
supposedly unnatural procreation of gillyvors as theme gives
place to the possible procreation of children by Perdita and
Florizel, which for him would be unnatural beyond all doubt.
And so we return to Florizel.

Most of the exchanges between him and Perdita are 'so
lovely fair and [smell] so sweet' as to cause the senses to ache.
They have been sufficiently, if no more than rightly praised;
planted therefore so deep in every reader's memory that, without any fear of their erasure and consequent distortion of the
balance of the play, we can pass them by. And time is growing
short, though there is great need of it for the due consideration
which a speech of Florizel's, however celebrated, would seem
so far to have escaped.

The speech is that with which he endeavours to reassure
Perdita when, in spite of her customary staidness (staidness is
the ally of steadfastness of a worthy kind) she has allowed the
wish to pass her lips of holding Florizel 'quick, and in [her]
arms' (*ibid.* 132). Half playfully, she excuses herself: 'sure this
robe of mine Does change my disposition' (*ibid.* 134). 'What
you do', Florizel comforts her.

Still betters what is done. When you speak, sweet,
I'd have you do it ever; when you sing,
I'd have you buy and sell so, so give alms,
Pray so and, for the ord'ring your affairs,
To sing them too: when you do dance, I wish you
A wave o'th'sea, that you might ever do
Nothing but that, move still, still so,
And own no other function. Each your doing
So singular in each particular,
Crowns what you are doing, in the present deeds,
That all your acts are queens.   (*ibid.* 135ff)

The speech is one of Shakespeare's prosodic masterpieces, rising to a climax in the treatment of the wave: a creature whose essence is motion (if ever there was one), but which the poetry, while preserving the essence, nevertheless immobilizes. A more truly metaphysical sequence of verses could not well be imagined: it recalls the Thomistic definition, according to which motion, while both actual and potential, is yet neither. Such a seeming self-contradiction supplies substance to almost all – to all, that is, except the first and the last few lines – of the speech: for Florizel's exhortation, 'when you sing, I'd have you buy and sell so' bears a very different meaning – I hope the remark, as over-officious, will not offend – from the Clown's to Autolycus, that he 'approach singing' (*ibid.* 214). The Clown requires no more than that Autolycus shall sing while he approaches; but Florizel, that Perdita's buying and selling shall not accompany but, while remaining what they are, themselves be a singing. And so of her speaking, almsgiving, praying and the rest. All these are to be blended – or, much better, summed up – into and by a single act, which alone, and never any other, she shall perform. Thereby it is rightfully to acquire the title of queen, and ostentatiously discharge a royal function: throning in solitary state and (as they say of the Popes) gloriously reigning.

All of which implies that, in enjoying Perdita, Florizel aspires to enjoy the whole of life perfectly and at once – or in other words, to enjoy what Boethius defined as eternity. Boethius, it is true, prefixed the adjective 'endless' to the noun 'life': but that need not concern us, since it could not concern Florizel – for what young man, or at any rate, what young man in love, ever troubled himself with the problem whether life is doomed to an end or not?

Yet however much in love, not even Florizel can remain blind to the fact – for it is clear as noonday – that in this world nothing is to be enjoyed 'save under the condition of time': neither simultaneously, that is, nor as a whole, but only in such portions as are doled out by successive moments. At first, he seeks to evade the fact by contrasting the past with the present: in the past Perdita may have engaged on a plurality of doings, but this plurality, as belonging to the past, can in no way impugn the unity, the uniqueness of what she is doing now. Then there follows the memorable justification of this unity and uniqueness: the justification itself however implies the existence of a need for it – at least of an appearance of plurality, which it is necessary to argue away. Unfortunately, things that are merely argued away have the habit of fixing themselves all the more firmly in the mind: whence perhaps the somewhat peculiar lines

> Each your doing
> So singular in each particular

Does not the adjective 'each' imply more doings than one? But is not this implication denied by the adjective 'singular' following so closely upon it? And in its turn, this 'singular', is it not denied by a repetition of 'each'? At this point however Florizel might attempt a *distinguo*: on its second occurrence, he might claim, 'each' applies not to a doing itself, but to its 'particulars' – by which, I suppose, he means its properties or qualities. Thereby he sacrifices the unity of a doing – it is no longer one, but a bundle of things – in the hope of preserving its uniqueness. No stratagem could be more futile: no Fifth Columnist works with swifter efficiency than plurality, once admitted into a stronghold. As soon as properties or qualities are allowed a separate existence, they demand that this existence shall be independent also. And so, at the end of his penultimate line, Florizel allows the plural 'present deeds' to escape him – the deed now being done is no longer even unique, for as well as predecessors it has contemporaries. And if, in the line with which he concludes, Florizel persists in talking of queenliness, he has to distribute it among rivals, thus abating the dignity of the title, and casting doubt on its legitimacy.

These nervous, almost spasmodic movements of Florizel's thoughts bestow a pathetic, or rather a dramatic quality on the speech; and because of the nature of the foreshadowed drama, danger too is foreshadowed.

Florizel labours beneath a violent tension between his inescapable subjection to time, his intense longing for what is to be had only in eternity. The intensity of the longing causes the succession of moments to appear unendurably slow, the portions which they dole out exasperatingly small. In spite of the smallness, the exasperation provokes the temptation to seize upon one of the portions – and probably the least commendable, since its immediate appeal is the strongest – in order to use or abuse it as though it were the whole. Thereby – at least for the time being – all claim is forfeited to the enjoyment of what is truly eternal.

With the sharp-sightedness inherited from her mother, Perdita senses the danger. Rather than reassured, she is alarmed by Florizel's eloquence. 'With wisdom I might fear, my Doricles', she murmurs, 'You woo'd me the false way.' To his credit, Florizel also senses the danger, but maleness commands that, instead of alarm, he display pride. As he boasts to the disguised Polixenes,

> had [I] force and knowledge
> More than was ever man's, I would not prize them
> Without her love; for her, employ them all,
> Commend them and condemn them to her service,
> Or to their own perdition.   (IV. iv. 375ff)

Here the word 'perdition' acknowledges an extremity of danger; the word 'condemn' – by its similarity with 'commend' forcing its way in, it might seem, in Florizel's despite – admits the wrongheadedness with which danger is defied. And wrongheadedness itself comes to be boasted of when, Polixenes having thrown off his disguise, danger has become obvious to all. By contrast with the mildness of Camillo's warning 'Be advis'd', Florizel's reply might be said to rise to a scream: 'I am [advised]', he brangles,

> and by my fancy. If my reason
> Will thereto be obedient, I have reason;
> If not, my senses, better pleas'd with madness,
> Do bid it welcome.   (*ibid.* 484ff)

As this outburst of Florizel's is often, perhaps usually, assimilated to another of Leontes', and as the assimilation threatens with collapse the cunningly contrived architecture of the play, it deserves – at the cost of a digression – at least a moment's notice. Leontes' outburst comes when Paulina proposes to curtain off the statue of Hermione, fearing – or simulating a fear – he may be 'so far transported that He'll think anon it lives'. 'O sweet Paulina', implores Leontes,

> Make me to think so twenty years together!
> No settled senses of the world can match
> The pleasure of that madness.   (*ibid.* 70ff)

The speeches of Leontes and Florizel certainly possess in common the words 'senses' and 'madness'. But the most cursory inspection suffices to discern that, in intention, they are diametrically opposed. Florizel refuses to abandon something he already possesses, *although* it be a madness (which it is); Leontes yearns for something he does not as yet possess, even *if* it prove a madness (which it does not).

In the economy of the play, Florizel acts neither as a replica of Leontes, nor as his antithesis. The part assigned to him is at once more supple and more subtle: much as Act IV provides a practicable bridge between Acts I–III and Act V, so Florizel interprets – I can think of no better word – between Leontes at the two ends of the play. Florizel's ardour – the persistent and defiant passion he suffers for Perdita – suggests an explanation at once of the violence of Leontes' jealousy, and of the tenacity with which the courtiers and Paulina, though unknowingly to each other, labour not only to annul but to reverse the effects of that violence. To this reversal Camillo contributes, good fortune contributes, and also Florizel contributes, though to a small degree – no doubt, lest young humanity should be misrepresented.

Little confidence is to be placed in Perdita's assurance of Florizel's uprightness – 'your youth', she tells him,

> And the true blood which peepeth fairly through't
> Do plainly give you out an unstain'd shepherd –   (*ibid*. 147ff)

for assurances of that sort are common form with spellbound young women; still less confidence is commanded by the assurance proclaimed by Florizel himself – 'my desires', he asserts,

> Run not before my honour, nor my lusts
> Burn hotter than my faith (*ibid*. 33f)

– for that too is common form, and a form too commonly violated. By his actions nevertheless Florizel furnishes proof that he is upright in some measure: and chiefly by his consenting – once his screaming fit has subsided – to pay attention to Camillo. Camillo imposes by his age, by the reputation he has long borne of wise and faithful counsellor – 'it is my father's music', Florizel acknowledges, 'to speak your deeds' (*ibid*. 519) – but most of all by his diplomacy – or, recalling an apparently unkind word used when we first dealt with the courtiers – shall we say his deceitfulness? At any rate, he flatters Florizel to the top of his bent: crediting him with a 'ponderous and settled project' (*ibid.* 525) only a few lines after Florizel's admission that he envisages no more than a 'tug' with fortune (*ibid.* 498), only a few lines before he confesses that himself and Perdita are but 'the slaves of chance, and flies Of every wind that blows' (*ibid.* 541). There follows the conclusive argument: though successive moments supply no more than portions of love-enjoyment, portions of other substances are also supplied – and without such portions nothing, not even love-enjoyment, can persist.

> Prosperity's the very bond of love,
> Whose fresh complexion and whose heart together
> Affliction alters.   (*ibid.* 574)

Though Perdita demurs in favour of the constancy of the heart, and though she is often praised for this demurrer, I look upon it as another inheritance from her mother, and this time an unfortunate one: of her mother's short-, rather than clear-sightedness. And in Camillo's approval of her I can see nothing but irony, nor anything but diplomacy in the laudations of her which he prolongs. At any rate they serve their purpose: so that at last Camillo succeeds in shipping Florizel and Perdita off to Sicily, resolving at the same time that he and Polixenes shall follow as soon as possible. And once arrived in Sicily all four, and all characters left behind when they sought refuge in Bohemia – all these are, according to the convention of comedy, to live happily ever after.

Not however without the aid of fortune. As was mentioned only a moment ago, as was hinted when comedy first came up for discussion, without favour from fortune the convention remains inapplicable. In a play which borrows as much as does *The Winter's Tale* from the tradition of Greek romance, it might seem superfluous to stress the fact, or impossible to separate instances of good fortune due to this tradition from those which the comedy as comedy demands. Yet a rough and perhaps serviceable distinction can be attempted. On the one side are to be found the Oracle (the importance of which to the play appears to me heavily over-stressed), the discovery of an abandoned infant in a desolate spot, and the preservation of garments, jewels and the like by means of which the infant's identity is at length established. Opposed to these are Paulina's timely discovery (of which no account is given) that Hermione's death-swoon is no more than a swoon, the unconcerted co-operation she receives from the courtiers, and the dependence of Camillo (of all people!) upon (of all people!) Autolycus for clearance from the charge which, in the final Act, Florizel is only too ready to bring against him:

> Camillo has betray'd me;
> Whose honour and whose honesty till now
> Endur'd all weathers.   (V. i. 192ff)

For in his longing for 'the sight again of dear Sicilia, And that unhappy king my master' (IV. iv. 512f), the prudent Camillo had overlooked the improbability or rather the impossibility that a mere crossing of the ocean should eradicate Polixenes' prejudice against what he supposed the family connections of Perdita. Yet without its eradication, Camillo would not have been able to fulfil his undertaking that, in Sicily, Florizel should 'enjoy [his] mistress' (*ibid.* 529). He can do so only because Perdita's true origins are discovered; and that in turn is possible only because Autolycus, of his own accord, shanghaied the Shepherd and the Clown on to the ship bearing the lovers (*ibid.* 837).

When first mentioned in this paper, Camillo was described, not as 'perfectly prudent', but as 'well-nigh perfectly' so. Hence his part subjection to imbecility; hence the need of good fortune which is his no less than that of other men. How great must be our own need, who not only cannot benefit by the convention of comedy, but live in an age when imbecility of hitherto unknown proportions reigns over areas of an extent hitherto unknown. Watching by a civilization sicker even than Lady Macbeth, we can only repeat with her physician: God, God forgive us all!

7

THE TEMPEST

To judge from the pleasure it has given in wide circles, and the respect it has enjoyed in exalted ones – circles as wide and as exalted as can be – Prospero's speech about the 'cloud-capp'd towers, the gorgeous palaces' is as important and integral to *The Tempest* as the soliloquy 'To be or not to be' to *Hamlet*. Yet in the eyes of the New Cambridge editors, the speech is no more than an 'irrelevant philosophical rhapsody'; other critics, both before their day and since, have dismissed it as a patch – a patch remarkable perhaps for its texture, but in its function, which is that of hiding a hole, no more than a patch.

The presumption is that such critics are mistaken. And even a superficial examination would seem sufficient to make the presumption stronger. Very obviously, for example, in at least one important respect the speech is not discontinuous from the context, but of a piece with it. It is, or at least begins as, consolatory in intent:

> You do look, my son, on a mov'd sort,
> As if you were dismayed: be cheerful, sir. (IV. i. 146)

And consolation is what Ferdinand, to whom it is addressed, stands most in need of.

Until a moment ago, his eyes were filled with a 'most majestic' masque, and his ears were 'charmed' with its harmony. From his father-in-law, to whom he turned for enlightenment, he learned that, though but a 'present fancy', the masque is enacted by spirits summoned from their confines for no other purpose but that. 'Let me live here for ever', Ferdinand exclaims in consequence:

> So rare a wonder'd father and a wise
> Makes this place Paradise. (IV. i. 123)

He is speaking with emotion, yet at the same time with precision. Prospero is a wondered father, in the sense of having wonders at his call; if nevertheless he shows himself to be wise, as wonder-workers rarely are, he continues uninterruptedly content. For no desire that he may have will be unworthy of satisfaction; and if incapable of it, he will choose for enactment such fancies as soothe, rather than those which exasperate, desire. In a strict sense of the word, that is, Prospero leads an existence comparable to the paradisal, and in it those in whom he takes a benevolent interest may hope to share. Filled with a joyful anticipation of this kind, Ferdinand restores his attention to the masque.

Suddenly it is shattered. Of itself, that would be sufficient to cause him dismay; but on turning again to his father-in-law, Ferdinand's dismay is many times multiplied. For not only has all trace of wisdom vanished from Prospero's countenance, it has been replaced by anger. And if wisdom supported by magic power promises a blissful future, at the mercy of an angry man this power threatens the reverse of bliss.

Dismay indeed hangs everywhere like a cloud, and it seems a singular perversity to suppose that, because one of the persons present is affected by it, none of the others need or can be. Not even the spirits who perform the masque escape the feeling. They do not, as the verb might suggest, 'vanish' instantaneously and impassively but, as the stage-direction prescribes, 'heavily', in sorrow that is and with reluctance; nor do they vanish silently but with a groan or, to quote the stage-direction again, with 'a strange hollow and confused noise' (IV. i. 138).

Out of this cloud it is Prospero who first emerges; or rather, who makes the first effort to emerge. As still the wiser or, at any rate, the elder of the two, he provides Ferdinand with an enlightenment somewhat different from what he looked for. Prospero utters the famous speech, expounding the opinion to be held of the masque and how, in consequence, Ferdinand should behave. As for himself, Prospero admits that, for the moment, 'infirmity' prevents him from behaving as would be proper; in order to clear his old brain, and re-establish mastery over its 'beating', he must first take a turn or two. Whether Ferdinand on his side is able to profit by the speech we do not know, for Prospero dismisses him. As a courteous young man he accepts the dismissal without question and without delay.

Yet apart from blindness or obstinacy of his own, there would seem no reason why he should not profit. By the common consent of readers, the speech is worthy of Shakespeare at his best. Its words have established their capacity at once to enlighten, to captivate, to control. In a matter ultimately one of taste, it is no doubt tasteless to deny Aldis Wright's assertion that the line

> You do look, my son, in a mov'd sort

'can scarcely have come from Shakespeare's pen'. However, it is perhaps allowable to protest against the line's condemnation as 'halting prosodically'. The prosody in question was unknown in England until imported by the humanists (cadaverists rather) of the sixteenth century, and when at his best, no succeeding poet has allowed himself to be hampered or even guided by it – least of all, Shakespeare in *The Tempest*. If the line is complained of as short, so are others in the play; the word 'mov'd' however is such as of itself to be capable of expanding the line to any desiderated length. If it is the lack of iambic movement which causes complaint, it may be asked where in the play is the iambic movement observed – except in passages of lowered tension, where the sing-song of comparatively listless speech has occasion to assert itself. But

> In the dark backward and abysm of time   (I. ii. 50)

or

> This music crept by me upon the waters[1]   (I. ii. 395)

these are not iambic, and any attempt to conceive them as such is to misconceive them entirely.

The particular movement possessed by

> You do look, my son, in a mov'd sort

would seem suitable both to the meaning of the line itself, and to the part which it plays in the context. The sharp interruption after 'look' is as it were contradicted by a compassionate lingering over 'mov'd', which yet echoes 'look' so that sharpness and compassion are reconciled: while both together prepare for the invigorating, or at any rate comforting roll – 'be cheerful, sir' – with which, after yet another pause, the following line

---

[1] J. S. misquoted this line in his typescript: 'This music crept by me on the waters.' I do not think that that fact affects his judgment on the non-iambic nature of the line. (E. M. W.)

ends. A similar effect is obtained later in the speech, where the coalescence of the 'l's in 'little life' increases, by the delay which it imposes, the comfort of the roll 'Is rounded with a sleep' – though rather than invigorating, the comfort here is a cradling one. Not that, here or anywhere, sound or movement have a value apart from meaning, or meaning apart from these, or indeed that any one of the three can be apprehended apart from the rest. Perhaps however one of them may be abstracted, to serve as guide to the value which all possess together.

But meaning having once been mentioned, it may be objected that, whether abstraction or not, it provides the chief obstacle to recognizing the speech as anything other than a patch. Granted that Ferdinand stands in need of consolation, granted too that what he needs consoling for is the shattering of a belief that spirits, as they are submitted to Prospero's wise control, guarantee his happiness at the moment and for ever: to attribute the shattering, not to a failure of Prospero's wisdom which might be accidental, but to what in the spirits cannot change, namely, to their nature – this is not to lighten but to aggravate grief, not to soften but to harden it into permanence. And to proceed, as Prospero immediately does, to an insinuation that not only are the spirits 'baseless' and 'insubstantial' but also

> The cloud-capp'd towers, the gorgeous palaces,
> The solemn temples, the great globe

and even Ferdinand himself, so that he and they like the spirits will melt 'into thin air' – all this too closely recalls the *infinita vanità del tutto* of the nineteenth-century poet for it to be a source of consolation, or of anything short of black despair.

Shakespeare however did not write in the nineteenth century; and had he done so, he might, like the poet referred to, have considered consolation and despair to be by no means incompatible. Here rises the problem of the relating the speech to the context for and in which it was written. By 'context' I am not of course so ambitious as to mean the seventeenth century as a whole: but however narrowly the term is interpreted, the problem remains of a magnitude that allows no hope of an immediate solution. At the outset of an essay, it must therefore be sufficient to point out that the relations between the speech and the rest of *The Tempest* – even the immediately obvious relations, such as strike the cursory eye – are in fact numerous, and of such a kind as, in all probability, to be important.

Time and time again in the play experience – in the sense of what is seen or heard or felt and, as such, is suffered or rejoiced in – time and time again this is compared to a dream; a number of times too it is implied, once at least it is stated, that experience is not on that account to be shunned, but the more readily encountered. For as dream-like it is the more easily forgotten, while as experience it might be dangerous to remember.

The boatswain and the master, for example, are separated 'as in a dream' from their companions at the ship. Since they had supposed these companions to be drowned, the separation causes them to 'mope': whatever that may mean, either 'amazement' according to the stage-direction, or 'sorrow' according to commoner usage. The question is not of much importance, since both are forms of distress and neither lasts long: master and boatswain need but to cast eyes on their 'king and company' for them to be restored to the gaiety with which one of them, at the sight of the ship, had 'capered'. Then again, Ferdinand says that, as a consequence of the spells either of Prospero's magic or of Miranda's beauty or (more probably) of both, his spirits 'as in a dream, are all bound up' (I.ii. 491). Within that dream, his experiences are to prove by no means pleasant: for they include monstrous accusations which he is not permitted to refute, outrageous insults which he is compelled to swallow, and heavy labour which he is obliged to perform. Yet by the beginning of Act IV he seems to have entirely forgotten all unpleasantness of the kind: so that it is perhaps allowable to wonder why commentators, who would not seem to have noticed the stress laid upon forgetting, have not, among the various scenes which they postulate as once forming part of the play, included one in which Ferdinand should complain, however courteously, of his treatment, and Prospero, however inadequately, should excuse it. Yet again, Prospero himself compares the liberation of his victims from their spells to a process of awakening: 'My charms I'll break', he says,

> their senses I'll restore,
> And they shall be themselves,   (V. i. 31)

or more explicitly,

> The charm dissolves apace;
> And as the morning steals upon the night,
> Melting the darkness, so their rising senses
> Begin to chase the ignorant fumes that mantle
> Their clearer reason. (V. i. 64)

And once they are awakened – this is the statement referred to – he warns against a pondering upon what, under the influence of the spells, they may have seen and heard. 'Sir, my liege', he says to Alonso,

> Do not infest your mind with beating on
> The strangeness of this business...
> ...be cheerful,
> And think of each thing well. (V. i. 246)

The adjuration is virtually identical with that closing the speech following the masque.

In the lines which I have omitted, Prospero does it is true undertake to 'resolve' any doubts which Alonso may harbour over 'these happen'd accidents'. But obviously, he considers this no pressing matter, for he is to discharge the undertaking only 'at picked leisure;' obviously too, the matter is not without peril in his eyes, for it is against an 'infesting' of the mind that he warns. To infest is to poison in peculiarly effective because peculiarly loathsome manner. Gonzalo's mind would quite conceivably be infested should he 'beat on' the 'torments, troubles, wonder and amazement' which led him to long for a 'heavenly power' to guide him from the island. Ferdinand's mind would without doubt be infested should he renew his thoughts and feelings when

> With hair up-staring – then like reeds, not hair – (I. ii. 213)

he was the first to leap from the ship. For at that moment, as is shown by his cry of 'Hell is empty, and all the devils are here', (I. ii. 214) his mind was in truth infested, since he was mad.

But, it may be answered, all these experiences are the experiences of spell-bound men and as such, in some sense or other, 'unreal'. Therefore they have no title to lodgment in the memory, from which it is quite proper to expel them. Rather I think the conclusion should be that they stand in no need of expulsion; I have however no intention of embogging myself in psychological or epistemological argument. It is sufficient for

my purpose to point to Alonso who, long before coming within
the range of Prospero's spells, committed acts the recollection of
which has already caused him torment and which, as he fears,
will continue to do so for ever. They are brought vividly before
his mind when Miranda is presented. 'O how oddly it will
sound', he laments, 'that I must ask my child forgiveness.'
'There, sir, stop!' breaks in Prospero,

> Let us not burthen our remembrance with
> A heaviness that's gone.   (V. i. 198)

'Be cheerful, sir' – once again Prospero's recommendation to
Ferdinand is recalled, and not merely I think by the metre.

Yet another example remains to be quoted, which is perhaps
the more instructive in that, while pointing to the same
conclusion, it sets out so to speak from an opposite quarter. It is
an example of men, not waking with difficulty out of a dream,
but more or less complacently falling into one. These men are
Antonio and Sebastian. Around them Alonso and his courtiers
lie asleep, and are so, as Macbeth would say, 'in double trust':
for not only has Sebastian invited them to sleep, not only has
Antonio promised them protection meanwhile, but also,
Alonso is Sebastian's brother. Yet Antonio proposes that
Alonso's throat shall be cut, in order that Sebastian may wear
his crown. At first, the latter dismisses the proposal as he ought
and, since he ascribes to it a dream-like quality, can do so with a
degree of cheerfulness. 'Do you not hear me speak?' asks
Antonio impatiently. 'I do', comes the mocking reply,

> and surely
> It is a sleepy language, and thou speak'st
> Out of thy sleep. What is it thou didst say?
>   (II. i. 207)

Sebastian however pauses to consider the problem which any
dream presents:

> This is a strange repose, to be asleep
> With eyes wide open; standing, speaking, moving,
> And yet so fast asleep.   (*ibid.* 210)

The pause is fatal to him: not having been instantly dismissed,
the dream has opportunity to sink into his mind and there take
possession. All trace of a waking cheerfulness has disappeared

from his next utterance, which has already put on something of a dream's uneasiness. 'Thou dost snore distinctly', he says to Sebastian, inviting him to elaborate the proposal, 'there's meaning in thy snores'. From that moment onwards, a dream wraps the two more closely round, until in the end they imagine that they alone, of all with whom they have to deal, are awake. Then they are infested with that peculiar form of madness which believes itself the only sanity.

Enough perhaps has been said to render it at least probable that, if meaning alone is sufficient for the rejection of Prospero's speech, then many other passages in the play should be rejected likewise; so many indeed that little of the play can remain but tatters. It is the main purpose of this essay to suggest that *The Tempest* is no such tattered thing. Of itself, the purpose seems to me worth pursuing; but I confess that I have in part been led to do so by the opportunity it seemed to offer of vindicating the play as an entertainment. As such it was composed, as all plays are or ought to be; but the evident fact seems to have been forgotten of recent years. I do not of course wish to deny seriousness to the play, nor indeed seriousness of the highest kind; but a kind of seriousness I do – that which, however appropriate to a tractate or a homily, when hung upon a play gives it a pathetic or a silly appearance, as would an ill-fitting garment. I think *The Tempest* presents such an appearance when interpreted in the way that, if not begun, was much encouraged by Mr Colin Still; who called it – as far as I remember, these are his very words – 'Shakespeare's essay in comparative religion'. I think too that the appearance results from Professor Curry's interpretation according to occultist principles; or at least, from the elaborations and deductions therefrom which have been made by his disciples. For having completed his interpretation, Professor Curry took the precaution of shutting *The Tempest* up in the refrigerator provided by Croce for all works of art. There it froze into an impregnable or rather ineffable solidity: for no adjectives can enter the refrigerator or, if they do, they also become works of art and, like the notes from Munchausen's bugle, freeze in the air without attaching themselves either to one another or to anything. But for some time now I believe the doors of the refrigerator have stood open, with the result that Professor Curry's *The Tempest* has begun to melt and, to certain eyes at any rate, to reveal its occultist framework. As was inevitable, it has been assimilated with works to which such a framework is proper; and Shakespeare takes his place among the forerunners of, *proh pudor*! Madame Blavatsky. It would seem desirable above all things to remove him thence: for – to return to the reflection with which this section began – Shakespeare's reputation, wide as the world and as exalted as learning, this might possibly be compatible with his being not so great as dramatist as has been thought, perhaps even with his being not so great a poet – but it is not conceivably compatible with his lacking plain sense.

II. ANTONIO DE ESLAVA

To justify itself, a new essay upon a Shakespearian play needs to discover in it new qualities, or to present qualities already discovered with a freshness or a newness upon them. To that end it is desirable for the essayist to see the play in a new light. But it is also desirable, if not necessary, that the light should not be an artificial one, or of his own devising. For if it is, the tricks which come within his scope surpass those of a photographer.

Light independent of the essayist falls upon a play, as upon any work of art, from its congeners. If however these belong to a remote country or time, the essayist may, and perhaps rightly, be accused of dragging the play he is studying into a light for which it was never intended. Therefore he will be better advised to set it alongside only such congeners as are its neighbours and contemporaries. Best of all will be to restrict himself, if he finds it possible, to the light shed by contemporary congeners which philological research suggests that the playwright may have used as sources. For in that case, though the efficacy of the essayist's proceedings remains in question, it will hardly be possible to doubt their honesty.

Of course, not all sources are congeners, while some are congeners in a much slighter degree than they are sources. From these facts arises the danger with which, as is often stressed, philological research may threaten literary criticism. The stress is justified; perhaps however the danger may be averted, if only the concepts of source and congener are kept distinct. In the case of encyclopaedic works, for example, from which the playwright can have taken only a scrap of information, or maybe a whole heap of such scraps, it is impossible for the danger to arise: no one can suppose Muenster's *Cosmography*, or Gessner's *Book of Fishes*, to have influenced significantly, if at all, the form of *The Tempest*, or the end which Shakespeare proposed to himself in writing it. If on the other hand doubts arise whether an influence of that kind was exerted by Jakob Ayrer's *Die Schoene Sidea*, or by certain scenari of the *commedia dell'arte*, they can for all practical purposes be set at rest – and criticism is a practical affair – by considering the form and the end of these compositions. Is it such that they and *The Tempest* can be accepted as, however remotely, aesthetically akin? If not, then Shakespeare can have taken from them no more than scraps of information, or what corresponds to such: stage themes or devices which, in their complete lack of form or adaptation to an end – and in their lack of the uniqueness which is characteristic of historical scraps – he might just as well have found elsewhere, or even in his own head. That I would say is true of *Die Schoene Sidea*, which bears as much resemblance to *The Tempest* as crude carpentry does to a live dog. It can shed as little light on an aesthetic object as on a biological; except of course that through the darkness which it sheds, the object's own light shines yet more brightly, thereby establishing itself as aesthetic. I come to somewhat a similar conclusion about the scenari of the *commedia dell'arte*, though for a different reason. For they themselves are different from *Die Schoene Sidea*: as sophisticated as that is crude, and further, at first sight they appear to have many more things in common with *The Tempest* – not only a couple of warring parents reconciled by the marriage of their children, an exiled princess and her father, a prince who carries logs, which are all that *Die Schoene Sidea* possesses: but a whole list of devices or themes – a lovelorn swain, an amiable maiden, a group of shipwrecked masters, a corresponding group of drunken servants, a wild man from the woods and a magician who, starting out as the lord of an island, ends by abandoning both his lordship and his art together. Yet when pared of any vestige of adaptation to an end, not only the lovelorn swain and the amiable maiden among these but all the rest I think appear such as might either have been encountered anywhere or, in case of not being encountered, might have been invented. It is the fact that all occur together in the scenari which suggests the latter as important for a criticism of *The Tempest*: it is however precisely this fact which the critic must refuse to consider. For the way in which they are together, the pattern which they form, is generically distinct from the pattern which *The Tempest* presents. The latter can be as little illustrated by the scenari, as a Titian by a kaleidoscope.

Thus I emphatically, but not I hope unscrupulously, repel the danger which, by my mention of the word 'sources', I may appear to have invited, of projecting on to *The Tempest* anything of the crudity or woodenness of *Die Schoene Sidea*, anything of the instability or tenuity of the *commedia dell'arte*. I might also appear to have excluded the hope with which I started of obtaining light from the sources of *The Tempest*. For I have exhausted the list – at least the list of sources for the play as a whole – which English editions usually recite. There remains however a possible source which, though these editions mention it either not at all or only disparagingly, has after consideration forced itself upon me as congeneric. This is the fourth *novela* of Antonio de Eslava's *Noches de Invierno*, first printed at Pamplona in 1609. I do not of course wish to suggest that, as an aesthetic triumph, this *novela* is remotely comparable with *The Tempest*: nevertheless it can and ought I think to be considered as a member of the same family – if only as the bilberry-bush is akin to the oak. It possesses a sophistication of which Ayrer had no inkling, it aspires at least towards a stability of which the *commedia dell'arte* had no care. At any rate, I have found it to shed what seems to me revealing light upon *The Tempest*. Therefore I propose to refer to it not infrequently; that I may do so with profit, I must beg for patience until it is summarized. So far as I know, it is not accessible in English; nor indeed in the original, which has not been reprinted in modern times, is it accessible with ease.[1]

The novela runs as follows, Nicephorus, Emperor of Greece, summons Dardanus, King of Bulgaria, to renounce his throne in favour of one of Nicephorus's sons. Dardanus very naturally refuses, but offers to marry Seraphina, his only daughter and heiress, to the elder of these sons, named Valentinian. The proud and arrogant Nicephorus declines to hear of any such

---

[1] A modern edition *is* available: edited by Luis Mª Gonzál Palencia (Madrid, Editorial Saeta, 1942). (E. M. W.)

compromise and waging ruthless war upon Bulgaria, drives Dardanus and Seraphina into exile.

Taking temporary refuge within a thick wood, Dardanus reflects aloud and at length on the vanity of the things of this world. All creatures, from the elements upwards, are he says engaged upon mutual strife, so that rest and quietness are to be looked for nowhere. Least of all are they to be looked for among men, whose company therefore he renounces. And taking eternal Chaos as his witness, he vows that nevermore will he inhabit the fertile earth.

By his magic, he informs Seraphina, he is able to erect on the bottom of the sea a palace where he claims it will be possible for them to live, not only in greater quiet but in greater comfort than before. The young and beautiful Seraphina is inclined to demur, and Dardanus himself laments she should be cut off from the many knights and princes who hitherto have paid her court. But his oath forbids him abandoning his resolution, nor does Seraphina venture to suggest that he should do so. None of this would have happened, Eslava explains, if Dardanus had made use of his magic powers. For he is the greatest magician of his age. He has however bound himself by an oath never to have recourse to magic when in defiance of the law of God, or to the prejudice of his neighbour.

For the first two years she is conscious of no reason for regret. The palace on the sea-floor proves to be not only comfortable but magnificently built. Round its courts run Corinthian columns, down its corridors finely carved vases. One of the walls is adorned with a frieze of the Pharsalian wars, one of the ceilings with a representation of the heavenly bodies. The doors are encrusted with jewels, the walls with silver, and the ceilings with gold, ivory and mother-of-pearl. For twelve miles in all directions there stretch gardens beautified with every variety of plant; springs bubble, brooks flow, collecting here and there into pools filled with every variety of fish. Over all there arches a vault which has the appearance of a huge diamond, for it is formed by the waters of the sea.

Seraphina is entertained, not only by these wonders, but by the melodies of nymphs, so soft and so sweet as to enrapture all who hear them. Growing weary nevertheless, at the end of two years she summons up courage to make the following representation to her father. 'All things, dear father', she says, 'are in the course of nature moved to love: it is therefore neither new, nor in any degree to be wondered at, that your lonely daughter should find herself moved in the same manner. Please do not think me immodest because I speak thus openly; since I am forced to do so by the impossibility even of hoping to see another of my kind, so long as I continue imprisoned, as I am now, in the depths of the sea. Therefore I earnestly beg of you that, as you are the cause of my girlhood's fading away in this your magic palace – I beg of you to provide me with a husband suitable to my age and rank.' Though, or perhaps because, Dardanus has expressed a belief in universal strife rather than in universal love, he finds himself compelled to admit the reasonableness of this complaint. He promises that his daughter's request shall be granted.

Meanwhile Nicephorus has died, and bequeathed his dominions – both Greece which he has inherited, and Bulgaria which he has conquered – to Julian his second son. This Julian possesses an unscrupulous temper similar to his father's, such as presages an equally successful reign. Valentinian the elder son, on the contrary, is mild and courteous. Reluctant nevertheless to give up his rights, he determines to seek an ally in the Emperor of Constantinople.

For that purpose it is necessary to cross the Adriatic. He can find no other vessel than a small boat, and no other rower but a grave old man. And when they have completed half their journey, he is alarmed to see the old man, who is Dardanus in disguise, abandon his oars for a wand. With this he strikes the waters, which, thereupon, form themselves into a wall on either side, flanking a path down which the boat glides down to the magic palace, at the sight of which Valentinian's alarm changes to delight; when he meets Seraphina, delight changes to ecstasy. Immediately he petitions for her hand, and Dardanus makes no difficulty about granting it. He resolves to celebrate the wedding with splendid festivities, for by his art he is able to gather together the kings and princes who, along with their beautiful consorts, dwell in the ocean isles.

These festivities are interrupted by a storm. A furious northeast wind lashes the waters into a frenzy; in a moment the blackest and thickest of clouds veil the sky; one wind contends with another so as to snap the stoutest of masts or to wrench it from its holding; pulleys groan and cables whistle, tillers are lost. The prows of ships are lifted up to the heavens, their poops sink down to the centre of the earth. Their rigging is rent, and the clouds shower stones, fire and lightning down upon them. Most are swallowed up by the hungry waves; of the rest, a great number are set on fire by the infinity of thunderbolts – to four only do the heavens show mercy, and these bear the Emperor Julian, his newly wedded wife and his courtiers, who are making their first journey to the capital of Greece. The burnt and the broken ships crash down to the sea-floor, rousing the indignation of Neptune. He threatens to sink those still afloat, but Dardanus persuades him that to do so would be beneath the dignity of a god. Instead, Dardanus shows himself above the waters, astonishing and abashing Julian with his white hair, long beard and fiery eyes, and with the reproaches which he hurls against the insatiable ambition of Nicephorus and of Nicephorus's successor. Not content with devastating the earth, says Dardanus, Julian is seeking to bring confusion into the bosom of the sea. But his tyrannic and usurped power will not be left to him for long: and with that prophecy, Dardanus plunges back again beneath the waters. The imperial company continue staring over the ship's side as though they themselves were turned to wood.

Dardanus's prophecy is rapidly fulfilled, for upon arriving at his capital Julian succumbs to an illness. This untimely death is interpreted by the inhabitants as a mark of divine displeasure at the policies of Nicephorus, especially the conquest of Bulgaria and the exclusion of Valentinian from the succession. So they send messengers to look for the latter in all quarters of the earth. But the messengers are unnecessary, for by his art Dardanus has been kept aware of the course of events. He has caused his magic palace to vanish as quickly as it rose, and embarked himself, his daughter and his son-in-law for the capital. Immediately upon their arrival, not only Valentinian but Seraphina is hailed as a sovereign, for Dardanus regards himself as bound by his oath to keep aloof from human society. Wishing nevertheless to remain as close as possible to his children he has a wooden palace built, which he floats on five ships and anchors in the port of the capital. There he lives out the rest of his days.

III. THE VIRGINIA NARRATIVES

The similarities between Eslava's story and that of *The Tempest* are obvious. Those who require it will find an exhaustive list of them in Menéndez y Pelayo's *Orígenes de la Novela*. On the points of difference however Menéndez y Pelayo is hardly so satisfactory: for he contents himself with attributing to Shakespeare and denying to Eslava 'all that is profound and symbolical, anything that is musical and etherial', together with a power of 'plunging the reader into an ecstasy which it is impossible to describe'. This last phrase comes close to repudiation of criticism, the main business of which it is to describe, so that judgments of value, otherwise exclamatory, may acquire articulacy to a certain degree. The task, a difficult one, may however be lightened by, among other things, diligence and care in the use of congeners. When these have ceased to shed light by their similarities, then by their differences they begin to do so. Against a background of similarities, these differences stand out clearly, serving to call attention to the quality, the group of qualities, the purpose and the nature peculiar to the congener to which they belong.

An early and obvious difference between Shakespeare and Eslava is the lodging each assigns to his magician: the one a submarine palace, the other an ocean island. A moment's consideration suffices, I think, to show the reason for Shakespeare's preference. If by comparison with figures of the *commedia dell'arte* those of Eslava appear not filaments but surfaces, not transitory but permanent: on comparison with those of *The Tempest*, these surfaces reveal themselves as accompanied by little or no depth, their permanence to be the result, not so much of resistance to opposing forces, as of a complete absence of these. Down on the sea-floor, Dardanus and Seraphina are deprived, as Seraphina complains, of such opportunity of exercising their mental and moral powers as would be provided by contact with their kind; nor do they enter into contact with the physical objects by which the remaining powers of a human being are normally exercised – even the waters are separated from them by a distance of twelve miles. Yet it is by such exercise that, in art as in life, a human being shows his possession of solidity. In *The Tempest* as elsewhere,

Shakespeare intends his characters to be solid. By entering into their company his readers are to exercise as many as possible of their powers and so be profitably entertained. Eslava on the other hand seems satisfied to exercise no more than his readers' sense of sight. In the company of Dardanus and Seraphina it is necessary to use the eye but hardly any other organ. In *The Tempest*, moreover, Shakespeare pursues an end which is peculiar to the play. It is that at which the opening section hinted, of examining the dream-like quality of experience. Therefore it is necessary for him to stress the reality in which experience is grounded; since if that grounding were not clear, by frequent association with a dream, experience might appear to dissolve in it. If that happened, a comparison between the two would become meaningless, or rather impossible, for it would have collapsed into an equation.

Information about some of the forms of moral and physical resistance required on an ocean island Shakespeare found in the so-called Virginia narratives, which are in part accounts of the wreck of the ship the *Sea Adventure* in the year 1609. In large measure they are sources merely, and as such would not call for notice. But some of them are congeners in some respects, and one in a respect which seems highly important. It would therefore be imprudent not to notice them with some care.

The wreck of the *Sea Adventure* had two strong claims upon the attention of contemporaries. In the first place, it happened in the Bermudas, hitherto supposed to be habitable, not by men, but only by fairies and devils. The intricate reefs by which the islands are surrounded seemed to make it impossible 'to bring in a bable boat, so much as of ten ton, without apparent ruin'; the 'hellish sea, for thunder, lightning and storms' which was believed to prevail in the neighbourhood prevented mariners from attempting to do so. Yet when the company of the *Sea Adventure* was washed up there, they discovered 'many fair harbours for the greatest English ship, yea the argosies of Venice'. They were welcomed by a 'rich, sweet and healthful climate', and regaled by an abundance of delicious food – fruit, fish and flesh. As for the supposed supernatural inhabitants, 'all the fairies of the rocks were but flocks of birds, and all the devils that haunted the woods were but herds of swine'.

Then again, not only did the *Sea Adventure* carry the Admiral of a fleet of nine, but also the Governor, Lieutenant-Governor and the principal commissaries – all the officers, in short, to whom the task of the fleet had been entrusted. And this task was an invigoration of the colony of Virginia, which men of the most diverse callings, in Church, State, City and at the Court, had for the moment agreed to regard as of major importance. 'Virginia was a thing so full of expectance not above three years since', wrote William Strachey in 1612, 'as not a pilgrimage to a Roman Year of Jubilee could have been followed with more heat or zeal.' 'As to the voyage' of 1609, asked the author of the *True Declaration*, 'what swarms of people desired to be transported? what alacrity and cheerfulness in the adventurers by free-will offerings' to contribute, if not to the manpower, to the finances of the fleet! So loud was the roar of enthusiasm, as temporarily to drown the voices of those inclined by temperament to carp at enterprise in general, or obliged by conscience to criticize colonial enterprise in particular.

In the shocked silence following the news that the *Sea Adventure* had been lost, these voices had opportunity to re-assert themselves. Providence, they claimed, had condemned the enterprise by a sentence as clear as its execution was rapid, for the fleet had been decapitated at a single blow. Nor did these voices subside upon its being learned that, though the Admiral's ship was lost, his company was saved. For the means of their safety – not only a wreck, but a wreck upon the 'hideous and hated Bermudas' – was so incredible as to raise the cry of a miracle; and a miracle can be interpreted as a sign of divine wrath as well as of divine favour. At any rate, carpers and critics could point out, if Governor, Lieutenant-Governor and the rest had at last been able to reach their destination: they had done so only to discover that the task entrusted to them was no longer capable of accomplishment. Owing to the months during which they had been deprived of authoritative supervision, not only the stores but the colonists shipped from England had scattered, melted and rotted away.

Here was ample matter for a dispute, and the dispute provided opportunity for pamphlets designed to profit by the public interest, and faced those anxious to guide that interest with a necessity for pamphlets. An example of the first is Silvester Jourdan's *Discovery of the Bermudas*, the dedication of which is dated 13 October 1610. Neither in quantity nor in quality is it much more than a broad-sheet, but it has a corresponding liveliness and is, moreover, authentic – Jourdan having been a passenger on the *Sea Adventure*. It is possible that Shakespeare took from him a number of details. Most of these however are included in *A True Declaration of the Estate of the Colony in Virginia*, entered at Stationers' Hall on 8 November 1610, and this is usually considered Shakespeare's more likely source. In scale, manner and purpose it is widely different from the *Discovery*. For it is an official publication, intended to put carpers and critics to silence. The author is fitted for his task by, among other things, a sharp wit, skill in the use of figures such as antithesis and paranomasia, and command of a wide range of tones, from the expository to the hortative. Few more competent pieces of propaganda can have been issued. I dwell on it at no greater length, because it will return for consideration later.

Meanwhile, it may be noted that the *True Declaration* drew, not only upon the *Discovery*, but also, and very much more largely, upon a letter finished about the middle of 1610, and addressed by William Strachey, Secretary to the Council in Virginia, to a 'noble lady' in England. Because of its frank account of the vices and the follies of the colonists, this was withheld from publication until 1625. In that year Purchas, having baptized it *A True Reportory of the Wreck and Redemption of Sir Thomas Gates*,[1] included it in his *Pilgrims*. But from the first it circulated among those interested in Virginia, among whom Shakespeare is known to have had friends. In any case, it seems certain that a manuscript copy came into his hands, for the *True Reportory* possesses in common with *The Tempest* a number of details absent from both the *Discovery* and the *True Declaration*. Referring to the editions of the play for a full list of these, I quote a single detail only; and do so, not so much for its value as evidence, as for a purpose which will, I hope, become apparent shortly. In reporting to Prospero his performance in the storm Ariel describes how he played the part of a corposant or St Elmo's fire. 'I boarded the king's ship', he says,

> now on the beak,
> Now in the waist, the deck, in every cabin,

[1] *Hakluytus Posthumous or Purchase His Pilgrims* (Glasgow, 1906), vol. 19, p. 5 *et seq.* (E. M. W.)

I flam'd amazement; sometime I'd divide,
And burn in many places: on the topmast,
The yards and boresprit, would I flame distinctly,
Then meet and join.   (I. ii. 195)

'Upon the Thursday night', Strachey had reported, 'Sir George Summers being upon the watch, had an apparation of a little round light, like a faint star, trembling and streaming along with a sparkling blaze, half the height upon the main-mast, and shooting sometimes from shroud to shroud, tempting to settle as it were upon the four shrouds: and for three or four hours together, or rather more, half the night it kept with us; running sometimes along the main-yard to the very end, and then returning.' Of themselves, these words suggest the mysterious mobility with which Shakespeare endows Ariel; and if they make mention of no more than a single flame, that occurs a few lines later, where the corposant is given its classical name of Castor and Pollux. But, adds Strachey, it is only when one of the twins appears without the other that the sailors look upon him as of evil omen. Shakespeare makes use of the corposant as such an omen, attributing to it at the same time not so much a double as a multiple flame. Thereby he flouts both nautical tradition and nautical experience; but also, I imagine, he deepens the mystery surrounding Ariel.

It must of course be admitted both that the corposant is in itself mysterious, and that other voyagers besides Strachey are by no means sparing in their accounts of it. But as I said, I have quoted only one piece of the evidence connecting *The Tempest* with the *True Reportory*. In any case, it is not as a source that I am interested in the latter, but as a congener. Whatever may be true of it as source, as congener its importance would appear to be great. For like *The Tempest* and none the less efficiently because implicitly, the *True Reportory* would seem to exploit the comparison of experience to a dream.

Perhaps I had better repeat my disavowal of any intention to suggest that Shakespeare found the comparison in Strachey. That would be to confuse the two notices of source and of congener which, as I have urged, should be kept distinct. And in its naked form at any rate, the comparison lay in many places to Shakespeare's hand; nor in such a form was he entirely incapable of drawing it for himself. It is the use to which he and Strachey put the comparison which is of interest to criticism. Up to a point this use is the same, and the two compositions show, up to the same point, a similarity. Once that point is passed, they diverge and, since Shakespeare is in question, they do so widely and with speed. That as completed wholes they differ is of course apparent from any point of view: but only perhaps as seen against the similarity upon which it follows and out of which it grows does the difference define itself. As thus defined, it continues the flow of light started by the preceding similarity; perhaps even the flow is increased. But whether it does so or not, is a matter for our later concern. First, the similarity which needs to be established and put to such exploratory use as proves possible.

The *True Reportory* is at once a narrative and an admonition. In both capacities it is quite admirably served by Strachey's turbulent prose. But as an immediate clarity is hardly to be numbered among the virtues of the latter, I shall allow myself a certain liberty in the order in which I present quotations. The liberty will not I hope be abusive.

I begin with Strachey's recital of the reasons why, from the beginning of the storm, the men on board the *Sea Adventure* found their senses 'troubled and overmastered'. The first was the fear of death. 'For surely, noble Lady', he says, 'as death comes not so sudden and so apparent, so he comes not so elvish and painful (to men especially even then in health and perfect habitudes of body) as at sea; who comes at no time so welcome but our frailty (so weak is the hold of hope in the miserable demonstrations of danger) it makes guilty of many contrary changes and conflicts.' The second reason was more commonplace, but possibly more immediate in its workings. 'No such unmerciful tempest' as that overtaking the *Sea Adventure*, laments Strachey, but 'is compound of so many contrary and diverse motions . . . that it worketh upon the whole frame of the body, and most loathsomely affecteth all the powers thereof; and the manner of the sickness it lays upon the body, being so unsufferable, gives not the mind any free and quiet time to use her judgment and empire.'

Yet the circumstances of the men were however such as to call loudly and continually for judgment to be used. Not only the mental world in which they moved, but the physical also seemed troubled and overmastered. The elements, departing

178

from their accustomed seats, no longer presented their accustomed faces. 'Heaven...like a hell of darkness turned black upon us', reports Strachey, '...the sea swelled above the clouds, the waters like whole rivers did flood the air.' The question rose: to what extent were such-like phenomena really occurring? to what extent were they the fantasies of nauseated and terrified voyagers? the latter found it a matter of increasing difficulty to reply. 'For four and twenty hours the storm in a restless tumult had blown so excedingly, as we could not apprehend in our imaginations any possibility of greater violence, yet did we still find it not only more terrible but more constant, fury added to fury, and one storm urging a second more outrageous than the former; whether it so wrought upon our fears, or indeed met with new forces.' But the most convincing if only because the most startling proof of their debility was borne in upon them when a huge wave 'broke upon the poop and quarter'. Covering the whole ship 'from stern to stem like a garment or vast cloud', it not only 'rushed and carried the helm-man from the helm...our Governor from the place where he sat, and grovelled him and all us about him on our faces, beating together with our breaths all thoughts from our bosoms else, than that we were now sinking – for my part', interjects Strachey, 'I thought her already in the bottom of the sea–' not only did the huge wave do this, but also, 'it so stunned the ship in her full pace, that she stirred no more than if she had been caught in a net, or than as if the fabulous remora had stuck to her forecastle. Yet without bearing an inch of sail, even then she was making her way nine or ten leagues in a watch.'

Confronted as it seemed with a ship that, though halted, continued to advance; with a wave that sank the ship to the bottom while keeping her afloat; with a wind that could not conceivably increase in violence and yet persistently did increase: the men on board the *Sea Adventure* were baffled. Thwarted in their expectation of what, according to previous experience, should follow upon the experience of the moment, their doubts whether the latter could be determined seemed confirmed. In *The Tempest*, Shakespeare shows his characters as baffled in a similar way. What these appear to learn from one sense is contradicted by what another sense tells them; at the same time, the same sense may tell contradictory things to different people;

nay, the same sense may refute what, a short while ago, the same person appeared to learn from it. And so at times he may appear unable to learn anything at all. Strachey's purpose in thus plunging his people into the perplexities of a dream is obvious: it is to allow, or perhaps rather to compel, his reader to share in a particular experience, one quality of which was to perplex. His example entitles us, perhaps, to assume that Shakespeare's purpose was of a similar kind. In *The Tempest* he is not, as some have thought, quaintly defying experience or, as some have feared, wearily neglecting it; he neither intends to produce a fairy-story nor is he content with a piece of dotage; still less is he constructing an allegory having reference to experience, if at all, through the teachings of comparative religion or of occultism: rather his purpose is to introduce the reader to an experience of a particular kind, and then to force him through it.

The latter will be possible only in so far as the former has been achieved. The task of criticism is to ensure that it shall be more readily, more widely so. The necessity of such a task illustrates its difficulty. But having been helped so far on our way by a comparison between the *True Reportory* and *The Tempest*, a contrast between the two may help us further. For it is from this point onwards that the two compositions cease to be similar. If each adopts the same device for introducing a particular experience to the reader, the experience which each introduces is different. And we may perhaps begin to gain a notion of the difference by considering yet another instance of bafflement, as known on board the *Sea Adventure*.

'In the beginning of the storm', says Strachey, 'we had a mighty leak... the ship in every joint almost having spued out her oakum.' Yet so occupied were they in observing other things, or so incapable were they already grown of profitable observation, that for a long time it escaped their notice. So that, when at last it was forced upon them, it seemed to make the ship 'five foot suddenly deep with water above her ballast'. Once again their expectations were thwarted. 'We almost drowned within', groans Strachey, 'whilst we sat looking to perish from above.' The immediate consequence was that the confusion, already in possession of their mental and physical worlds, seemed to seize upon their moral world also. 'There might be seen master, master's mate, boatswain, quartermaster,

coopers, carpenters and who not, with candles in their hands,
creeping along the ribs and viewing the sides, searching every
corner and listening in every place if they could hear the water run.'

What Strachey is here describing is not merely an abandonment of their proper tasks by members of the ship's hierarchy,
such as happens on a number of occasions during the voyage.
Strachey highly approves of it when voluntary and deliberate, as
it may be either for the performing of an urgent task, or for
setting an example in the performance of tasks which are least
congenial. By contrast, what follows upon the leak is involuntary
because unthinking; it is the concentration of all upon a single
task; it is an abandonment of the notion of hierarchy or, as has
been suggested, a confusion.

When Ariel plays the corposant, confusion of a kind seizes
upon the companions of Alonso. But the kind is at once more
disturbed and more disturbing, for no one concentrates upon
anything. 'Not a soul', says Ariel,

> But felt a fever of the mad, and played
> Some tricks of desperation. (I. ii. 208)

While on the other hand, no such tricks are played on board
the *Sea Adventure*. The difference between the behaviour of the
two companies may perhaps be compared to that between a
dream and a nightmare. A dream baffles by a continual changing in the presentations it brings before the mind. The latter
has no sooner convinced itself of the necessity of attending to
one of these, than it is confronted by another, possibly widely
different. Yet a dream can do no more than baffle, because its
presentations can do no more than change. Those of a nightmare,
on the other hand, not only change but, in spite of an apparent
impossibility, they also persist. The mind is required to attend
to two, three, any number of incompatible presentations at the
same time. It finds itself dragged in contrary directions, the
consequent threat to its integrity filling it not so much with
bafflement as with alarm; when the threat seems no longer
resistible, it now yields to *Angst*, madness or, to use Ariel's
exactly chosen word, desperation. From just after the beginning
until close on the end *The Tempest* is haunted by madness or
nightmare; from Ferdinand's cry of 'Hell is empty!' (*ibid.* 214)
to Alonso's Lear-like apology,

> Th'affliction of my mind amends, with which,
> I fear, a madness held me.   (V. i. 116)

But it does not enter the *True Reportory*.

And yet, so extreme is the distraction of the men on board the *Sea Adventure* that it might appear likely to enter; or even bound to do so, in so far as the men were not sunk beneath their distraction into a bestial apathy or soared above it by a saintly disregard of their worldly fate. Strachey does not portray the men as either saints or beasts; he might therefore appear to be under the suspicion of falsifying a record of the voyage. A number of reasons can be imagined why he allowed himself to falsify, chief among them perhaps vanity, a jealousy for his own and for his companions' reputation.[1] I do not know whether a passage such as the following might not, at a first reading, appear to strengthen the suspicion. 'I am not able to give your Ladyship every man's thought', he writes, '...but to me, this leakage appeared a wound given to men that were before dead. The Lord knoweth, I had as little hope as desire of life in the storm, and in this it went beyond my will, because beyond my reason, why we should labour to preserve life; yet we did.' So far, the passage might be taken as preparatory of a nightmare: with its talk of men who, though dead, are yet capable of a wound, and who, though dead and wounded both, are yet obstinate in their efforts to live. But all expectations of the kind are immediately and, as it might seem, deliberately destroyed: for Strachey proceeds to advance reasons for conduct which, at the time when it happened, he has just admitted was unreasonable. 'Yet we did labour to preserve our lives', he continues, 'either because so dear are a few lingering hours of life to all mankind, or because our Christian knowledges taught us...not...to neglect the means of our preservation; the most despairful things being matters of no wonder nor moment to Him, who is the rich fountain and admirable essence of all mercy.'

No unfavourable account of the passage can however survive

---

[1] I have tried here to follow two long-hand slips of paper inserted into one of the carbon copies. I cannot guarantee the correctness of every word because of the difficulty of James Smith's handwriting. The first begins: 'It finds itself...' and continues as far as '...*Angst*'; the second begins: 'And yet...' and continues to '...his companions' reputation'. (E. M. W.)

a second reading, certainly not a second reading in the origina context. Of this context I am afraid my quotations have given an inadequate idea. They have been few and short, since my theme is not the *True Reportory*; as I have warning, I have at times rearranged them; often, as I have endeavoured to make clear by suspension points, I have omitted phrases, even lengthy clauses, from their centre. My excuse has been what I called the turbulence of Strachey's style. But this turbulence, if it prevents the ready comprehension desirable in a critical essay, may assure an original composition of something which is of greater value. And in Strachey's case I think it does. It binds the *True Reportory* together, from the first word to the last; clause thrusting into clause weaves a single structure which, to be appreciated, needs to be known as such. None of the fragments into which, with difficulty, it may be broken down can give the remotest notion of it. I can therefore only express the conviction that the *True Reportory* possesses a unity, such as to forbid any hypothesis of its being falsified as a record might be. For then it would contain a heterogeneous part or parts, and these would stand out as such. No part does in fact do so: in spite or because of its inner turbulence, the *True Reportory* presents a uniform surface, and it is quite remarkably homogeneous throughout.

If that is the case, and if Strachey, as he confesses, weaves into it reasons of which he did not become aware until after the events which they explain, the date of these events cannot be that of the experience which the *True Reportory* conveys. Nor do I think it is. What Strachey enables or compels the reader to share is the complex of his thoughts and feelings, not as he lived through the storm, but as, having survived it, he reviewed it in his memory. His attitude and intent are not those of a recorder but rather of an interpreter: of one who has before him, not a continuing, but a concluded series of events; who therefore knows or thinks he knows the relations of any of them to the rest and in consequence the meaning of them all. In so far as an interpretation of this kind necessarily involves falsification, then Strachey must be adjudged guilty of it; of any cruder sort he may be acquitted.

That he contemplates the series of events from a position outside and not within it is I think particularly obvious from a number of things; among them, the second reason he advances for the obstinacy of the dead men.[1] These he not only describes as taught the sinfulness of suicide; he goes on to suggest, and to suggest as strongly as may be while avoiding the explicit statement, that they were taught to expect a miracle. And this they could not be, at least by 'Christian knowledge'; since according to Christianity, miracles are the least covenanted of mercies. But to the Strachey who saw the storm in retrospect, it seemed that a miracle had in fact saved the company on board the *Sea Adventure*. They must therefore have been worthy of it, as they would not have been had they yielded to madness or desperation. For that would have implied either that they mistrusted God, or that they had forgotten Him. Yet the only ground for believing that they had been miraculously helped was that they were completely incapable of helping themselves: desolate that is to the point at which desperation seizes upon most men. The only solution to the problem thus posed was that, on board the *Sea Adventure*, the company was endowed with a composure already in itself miraculous: they knew, although they had not been taught, that they might count on a

[1] (Again there are two slips of paper inserted in carbon copy with a draft of the rest of this paragraph. I do not know whether they represent an earlier or a later version of it:)

'. . .the dead men. These he describes as taught not only, or not so much, the sinfulness of suicide as its folly – its folly, that is, from a worldly point of view. For 'the most despairful things. . . being matters of no wonder nor moment' to a merciful God, his very despairfulness, he implies, brings a guarantee that may well be miraculously [metamorphosed] into things of hope. Such a guarantee, however, is what no beings of any kind can bring; since once to their knowledge, miracles are the least covenanted of all mercies. Their full occurrence can under no circumstances be present, only their post-occurrences under particular circumstances can be confirmed. It was only in retrospect that Strachey could argue the certainty of having been saved by a miracle. From this certainty to the further certainty that, from the outset of and throughout the storm he and his companions were destined to a miraculous rescue was a practicable step. But in projecting these certainties back into his narrative of the storm, when they would not as yet have been acquired, Strachey abandoned all claim to be a [?witness]. Inevitably he represented himself and his companions as possessed of a composure which, as it was neither saintly nor bestial, was only the more inhuman, since it is not human to remain composed when destruction appears inevitable. But Strachey's narrative was all the more homogeneous; and at the same time it provided shipping reading-matter written for the 'noble lady' and her friends in London. The British interest, it appeared, or at any rate the British interest bound for Virginia benefited by a peculiar privilege. The future of Virginia was therefore a matter of certainty; and the *Sea Adventure* would secure its two-fold end, that of an admonition as well as that of a narrative, while retaining an unbroken unity.' (E. M. W.)

salvific miracle. As thus interpreted, the history of the wreck provided edifying reading matter for the adventurers in London. It seemed that colonists need never fear and need fear nothing, so long at any rate as they were making for Virginia. And so Strachey's *True Reportory* could serve the two purposes already referred to, that of a narrative and that of an admonition, while attaining an unbroken unity.

The particular experience communicated by the *True Reportory*, I conclude, is secondary, in the sense that it is the recollection and the accompanying experience of a primary experience. *The Tempest* on the other hand communicates an experience which is primary, and this is the main difference between the two. If the statement appears too abstract to be of interest, one or two concrete conclusions can I think be drawn from it and immediately verified. The first is that, in spite of the turbulence of its style, the *True Reportory* is more perspicuous than *The Tempest*; and also that, in spite of its supposedly classical structure, *The Tempest* is less shapely. Or rather, it has no shape at all. I do not imagine that any reader of *The Tempest*, during the time of his reading, is impressed by or even aware of the fact that it observes the three unities; nor would he ever be, were it not for the remarks of classically minded critics. But in mentioning the unities in connection with *The Tempest*, these critics show as little concern for the characteristic merits of the latter, as does the housewife for those of a portrait, when she commends its harmonizing with the wall-paper. A remark much more relevant is that made by Mr Morton Luce: 'Few if any of Shakespeare's plays have so little dramatic action', he says, 'the plot, if there is one, is obvious – the story dies in the telling; progressive movement, incident, suspense are almost entirely wanting.' The story, in other words, has no shape, since there is hardly any story: and what *The Tempest* impresses upon the mind is not so much a visual image, such as might have a shape, but an image at once more penetrating and less graspable. What this image might be is a matter for future investigation; it may however be suggested as having more relation to the auricular sense, than to that of sight. As such it is not grasped by the mind, in the sense of being understood; is *The Tempest*, in consequence, perspicuous?...

The lack of perspicuity has been not so much overlooked as

deplored, and it is I imagine one of the reasons why attempts have been made to erect – so to speak – within *The Tempest* scaffoldings such as those which comparative religion and occultism can provide. In that way the drama appears to become an object suitable for grasping. But what is a matter of fact is that the drama ceases to be what Shakespeare made it. In particular, it is deprived of that quality for which Shakespeare did not hesitate to sacrifice shape and perspicuity: the quality namely of reality, which is also the quality of truth. For, we must now admit, all interpretation such as Strachey indulged in does falsify, since it sets out from a supposition which itself is false. The experiencing subject cannot cut himself off from his experience and view it from a distance, as if it were separated from himself as an object appears separated from its surroundings. All experience maintains a continuous connection with the subject as long as the latter exists. He cannot view it, or become aware of any shape that it possesses until he dies. Then and then alone does it acquire a shape: as it does so suddenly, the shape is, disagreeably or otherwise, a surprising one.

The reality or the truth of *The Tempest* is shown by a vividness rising to the point of pain – as, for example, in the madness or the nightmare which it contains. Not that these in themselves are valuable. But they may be of value compared with a composure resting upon the expectation of a miracle. As the latter is unjustified and unjustifiable, not only may it be shattered in a moment and the composure along with it; but also, while it endures, it attracts unjustifiable companions to itself. Of these, the first and most obvious is spiritual pride. A hint of this, and perhaps more than a hint, is by no means absent from the *True Reportory*; as we shall see, by the time of a later work of Strachey's, it had grown to a disconcerting extent. *The Tempest* discourages any such a growth, while relying at least as firmly on the doctrine of Providence. It does so however for an opposite purpose; not in order to foretell the future confidently, but rather to forget the past – not to discount miracles, but to write off evil.

Once more I find myself making abstract statements; and of course, on such topics as the general qualities of *The Tempest* I must do so, since *The Tempest* has not yet been studied in detail. Let us then return to the topic to which we have devoted as much time as we can afford, and close this section with something as concrete as possible: a further illustration of the difference between the *True Reportory* and *The Tempest*. This will be the more instructive, the more closely it shows the difference to be connected with a preceding similarity – to grow from it, as has been suggested. Therefore I take the passage in which each composition makes mention of the corposant. It has already been shown that these passages coincide closely in their sense; now I think it will be possible to show how, in their function, they widely diverge.

In *The Tempest*[1] the function of the corposant is as evident as its activity is brief: it precipitates a panic. It is not however *The Tempest* but the *True Reportory* which gives expression to one of the most powerful reasons why it should do so. This is its fleeting resemblance to other luminaries, the regular rise and fall of which provide the most soothing of all sights at sea; since they assure mariners of an ability to return whence they came.

The relevant paragraph in the *True Reportory* begins with a regret that these luminaries were not visible from the deck of the *Sea Adventure*. 'During all this time', says Strachey, 'the heavens looked so black upon us that it was not possible for the elevation of the Pole to be observed; not a star by night, not sunbeam by day was to be seen.' What was to be seen instead was the corposant, of which there follows the description already quoted. After discussing the superstition according to which, with a double flame, the corposant augurs fair success to a voyage and, with a single flame, a success which shall be foul, Strachey continues: 'Be it what it will, we laid other foundations of safety or ruin' – not however than the flame's singleness or doubleness, but – 'than. . .the rising or the fall of it.' This is perhaps the most striking of the many striking phrases to be found in the *True Reportory*. By an attempted assimilation of the corposant to the heavenly bodies Strachey illustrates the impossibility of such an assimilation. But at the same time he illustrates the desperate position of the man on board the *Sea Adventure*: to whom it could, even for a moment, occur to look to the corposant for that guidance which only the heavenly bodies can provide. Strachey shows the corposant as mocking

---

[1] From here to the end of this section of the essay I have used what seems to be a revised version of the text I am following. (E. M. W.)

the men with an illusion of that they most needed. Such mockery is, of all things, most calculated to destroy composure.

But in the *True Reportory* composure is not destroyed; and because it is not destroyed when everything indicated that it would be, it appears increased. Rather than allowing themselves to be mocked by the corposant, the men on board the *Sea Adventure* make a mock of it. 'Could it have served us to take a height by', continues Strachey, 'it might have struck amazement or reverence in our devotions, according to the due of a miracle. But it did not light us any whit the more on our known way'; and therefore, after their mock, the men dismissed it from their minds. Strachey too dismisses it from the pages of *True Reportory*: where it has served not, as in *The Tempest*, to mark the outbreak of a panic; but rather that miraculous composure of the man – a composure which, as has been said, is neither bestial nor saintly nor human, and which renders them immune from outbreaks of any kind.

'We run now as do hoodwinked men, at all adventures', Strachey concludes. In so far as both are baffled, the phrase might describe the men in *The Tempest*, as well as those in the *True Reportory*. But it is a phrase that no one in *The Tempest* could have used either of himself or of his fellows. For if hoodwinked, they are unaware of the fact. They cannot therefore, like the men in the *True Reportory*, wait with as much patience as they can muster for the hood to be lifted from their eyes. Rather, for ought they know, their blindness is a seeing and they must endeavour to make use of it as such. In other words, theirs is the torment of men in a nightmare, to whom it never once occurs that they are not awake. Since their nightmare is the nightmare of life, the torment must continue for ever; or until they learn the proper use to which to put the doctrine of Providence.

IV. CALIBAN

According to the last section, characters in *The Tempest* are subject to perplexities. Certainly commentators on *The Tempest* have shown themselves to be so: among them Mr Morton Luce, although he takes high rank precisely because he pays the perplexities a proper attention. But as a result of his doing so he does not so much offer an explanation of the play as confess

that it is inexplicable: *The Tempest*, he concludes, is 'ideal' –
itself a perplexing adjective. By it Mr Luce would seem to
mean a number of things, between all of which it is not necessary
for the moment to distinguish: but two things at least which he
does mean are 'praiseworthy' and 'vague'. It is difficult to
conceive of a play being both together, or at least to conceive of
its being the one because of the other. But in any case, it has
already been suggested in this essay that *The Tempest* is not ideal
but real; and now I proceed to the suggestion that, whatever
else it may be, it is the opposite of vague. Such perplexities as it
produces have their origin rather in an abundance than a
paucity of details. Whereas a single account of an object or
event might have sufficed, two are given. These accounts are
contradictory, and so the object appears now to exist, now not to
exist: in other words, it is dream-like. Or a single account may
be so full of details that these sway hither and thither like a
swarm: the mind has difficulty in deciding whether it is faced
by one thing or by many, and if by one thing then what is its
head, tail or centre. Now the mind is attracted by what seems
to be one of these parts, now by another; or what seems to be
the same part now attracts and now repels the mind. The object
in short appears to exist and not to exist at the same time; it
provokes reactions so complex and so incompatible as to put on
the appearance of a nightmare.

The first of these cases is that of Alonso's ship. Mr Luce
finds a difficulty in some witnesses describing it as split, others
as foundered. A landsman sees no objection to its being both:
it may, for example, split against a perpendicular rock, and the
resulting fragments be immediately swallowed up. What moves
even a landsman to objection, is the ship's splitting or founder-
ing and at the same time remaining intact and afloat. Yet that is
what is reported. According to the cries of those who are on
board, both passengers and crew, the ship is about to split;
according to Miranda who is on shore, but near enough to hear
the cries, it does split; according to Ariel, who also is near
because he is everywhere, it arrives safely in harbour. And later,
the same crew who 'gave it out as split' are compelled to agree
with Ariel, for the ship is exhibited to them as

> tight and yare and bravely rigged as when
> We first put out to sea.   (V. i. 226)

Presumably the passengers agree also, for they find the ship 'tight and yare' enough to embark on it for Naples. Here are flat contradictions between what is seen by the same people at different times, and by different people at the same time.

Nor are such contradictions in any way concealed from the reader. Rather they are paraded before him. For example, they furnish the main matter and, as it would seem, the main motive for some hundred lines of dialogue at the beginning of Act II. When Gonzalo and Adrian maintain that the island provides 'everything advantageous to life', that the grass is lush and lusty and green, and that the air breathes sweetly upon them, Antonio and Sebastian immediately deny all these statements. According to the latter speakers, means of living on the island are 'none or little', the grass is neither lush nor lusty because there is only 'an eye of green in't', the ground is tawny, and the air stinks like that from a fen. This dispute Mr Luce seeks to dismiss as a quibble; but of all possible ways of dealing with it this would seem the least admissible. For it is of the essence of a quibble that, of the two parties to it (if there are no more than two) one at least should be recognized as in the right; while if each of the parties can be recognized as having right on his side, in however different a sense or way, then so much better the quibble. But as between Gonzalo's party and Antonio's, the reader is possessed of no means whatever of deciding, for he knows nothing of the subject of the dispute except what these parties tell him. And if he would seem to know something of the appearance of the company's garments – since in the preceding scene he has heard Ariel assure Prospero that, in spite of their immersion in sea-water, these garments are 'fresher than before' – nevertheless the reader hesitates to come to a decision when this in turn becomes a subject of dispute. For, amongst other things, he notices an uncertainty in Gonzalo, who from a boast that his doublet is 'rather new-dyed than stained', descends to an admission that it is fresher only 'in a sort'. It seems all the more remarkable that he should insist on any sort of freshness. If so weak a disputant is pertinacious in disputing, the reader concludes that dispute between the characters is inevitable.

In any case, the reader is soon, and often, forced into a dispute with himself. After the opening storm he gathers, I think, the impression that the weather on the island is set fair. Yet at the beginning of the second scene of Act II he is startled with the sound of thunder; during the course of the scene, he is informed by Trinculo, the sky is covered by clouds as black as bombards and as ready to shed their liquor. Immediately the scene is over fair weather sets in again: although no interval of time divides it from its neighbours – rather it would seem to be contemporaneous with at least part of them.

Caliban the reader hears complaining of being confined to a 'hard rock', and Prospero he hears confirming this complaint; yet Caliban also boasts of having access to 'every fertile inch' of the island, and Ariel mocks him for forcing access to inches fertile enough at least to bear

> Tooth'd briars, sharp furzes, pricking goss and thorns
>
> (IV. i. 180)

Then there is the contradiction between Miranda's remembering 'rather like a dream' that once she had four or five women to attend upon her, and her denial that she remembers any woman's face but her own. She is similarly inconsistent about her acquaintance with the other sex: until Ferdinand's arrival, she says on one occasion, she has seen no man but her father; on another she admits having seen two men, her father, namely, and Caliban.

This last inconsistency may however depend upon another which, according to Mr Luce, is the most striking in the play. 'If all the suggestions as to Caliban's form and features and endowments...are collected', he says, 'it will be found that one half render the other half impossible.' If that were true, then Caliban would be, in Mr Luce's terms, a 'vague' or an 'ideal' figure; in language which we have striven to make more exact, he would be dream-like. But as a matter of fact he is not: rather he is one of the most obviously nightmarish figures in the play.

The point is important, not only because of the prominence of the part played by Caliban, but also because it is a part with nothing corresponding to it in the play's congeners – not, at least, in the two we have so far considered. To us therefore it constitutes a characterizing difference of *The Tempest*, and we may hope to gain some light from it. It is necessary for us to study Caliban carefully.

Having addressed ourselves to the task, we find ourselves I

think obliged to regret that, in his anxiety to establish a vagueness or ideality, Mr Luce should have overstated, if not mis-stated, the evidence before him. At least he has overstated such of it as concerns Caliban's 'form and features'. For as a matter of fact, very few suggestions about these are thrown out. Stephano it is true addresses Caliban as a cat, and Prospero as a tortoise, while Trinculo upbraids him as 'puppy-headed'. Very possibly however none of these is more than a figurative term. In spite of Caliban's long nails, Stephano may mean no more than that, once wine is poured down his throat, he will begin to 'speak after the wisest'; Prospero probably means no more than that Caliban is lazy, Trinculo than that he is foolish.

Leaving aside all descriptions either obviously or possibly figurative, we are left with two only: Caliban has the form of a fish, say Antonio and Trinculo; many other characters imply, though they may not say – yet some of them do say – that he has the form of a man. And of these two descriptions one, I think, upon examination very soon ceases to appear as such.

'A plain fish and no doubt marketable' (V. i. 268), is Antonio's exclamation when he first sets eyes on Caliban. It might seem easy enough to interpret; Antonio however is speaking not so much to inform as to distract himself and others. Those whom he is addressing have no need of information, for Caliban is before them. And whatever kind of fish the latter may be, he is certainly not a plain one; nor is he any more plainly a fish than he is anything – otherwise it could not have entered even Mr Luce's head to call him 'ideal'. Perhaps therefore it is safer to take the term 'fish', on Antonio's lips at any rate, as another rhetorical figure. As such it is not infrequent in common speech, in which something may be called a 'fish', not because it has gills, but because it is strange.

Therefore Trinculo would seem to be a more useful witness. As he is alone at his first encounter with Caliban, he speaks to distract no one, unless possibly the audience. 'What have we here?' he ruminates, 'a man or a fish?' (II. ii. 25) and following his nose, he decides for the second. 'An ancient and fish-like smell' is however no impossible mark of a human being; as Trinculo himself discovers when at last he ventures to peep beneath Caliban's gaberdine. For then he becomes aware of legs like those of a man, and of fins which are not fins but arms. He needs do no more than touch the body – 'warm, o' my troth' – for him to abandon the notion of its fish-like nature. Nor does he ever return to it. If he seems to do so when he calls Caliban 'thou debosh'd fish', (III. ii. 26) it should be remembered that with this phrase he is seeking to requite what he considers to be abuse. Either the adjective or the noun must be figurative and, in view of the fact that the three companions have long been drinking, the odds are heavily in favour of the noun.[1]

With the same phrase, Trinculo seeks to assert superiority by the exercise of his wit. In so far as Caliban is partly a fish he is not wholly a monster, to that extent therefore disqualified for the publishing of lies so monstrous as that Trinculo is 'not valiant'.

But in so far as Caliban is only partly yet not wholly a fish, he is not the less but the more monstrous; and Trinculo is allowing his wit to run away with him. The very insecurity of the joke however serves to make clear the fact that, by the time of its making, the term 'monster' has established itself as a proper appellation for Caliban. As a matter of fact, his most constant companions, who are this same Stephano and Trinculo, only exceptionally call him anything else.

The term can be applied to any kind of creature, whether legged, winged, finned or merely rooted, so long as this creature is not so much unfamiliar as unexpected or improbable in appearance. Men with heads beneath their shoulders, fishes with eyes in their tails, mandrakes bearing rose-blossoms are all in the same sense monsters. This wide variety does not however imply any vagueness in the name which they bear in common, but rather the opposite: since only a precise meaning could first gather and then keep them together. A monster is one of nature's failures or mistakes. It is a creature which, in consequence of some mistake, has failed to reach one of the perfections intended by nature for her creatures. Either the material submitted to her for elaboration was insufficiently responsive, or she herself was insufficiently inattentive during the process of elaboration, or the time for that process was cut short. Or, more briefly, a monster is an abortion, something which should not have been born either as or when it was. This

---

[1] From here onwards I have followed a single unemended and almost uncorrected typescript. (E. M. W.)

sense may not be so readily accessible to a modern reader as to an Elizabethan; that Elizabethans so unlearned as Trinculo and Stephano were perfectly familiar with it is shown by their occasionally varying their name for Caliban from 'monster' to 'moon-calf'. A moon-calf is a calf, or any kind of offspring, that was born before sufficiently ripe. The weakling moon seems therefore to have operated on it and not, as should have been the case, the potent sun: *Homo hominem generat et sol*.

Since we have dismissed the supposed fishiness of Caliban, and since the only alternative description proposed for him was that of a man, we may I think without more ado assume that he is a human monster. In other words, the perfection for which he was intended and of which he fails is that of humanity. And this is where his nightmarishness enters. To a degree all monsters are suitable for figuring in a nightmare, since at the same time they rouse an expectation and they baulk it. But the contradictory feelings roused by a human monster are exceptionally strong and exceptionally complex. Since the expectation which he baulks is of a perfection similar to our own, at best he seems to mock us; at worst, he may direct a reproach against us, or even an accusation. For no man is absolutely perfect; nor is the division between perfection and imperfection marked by a line, but rather by an area of indeterminate extent, at any end and at every point in which perfection and imperfection blend imperceptibly the one into the other. Or if they are divided by a line, then this is no more stable than the crest of a wave or the boundary of a colour on the pigeon's neck. On this line in one of its positions each of us has his place: but Caliban has his place on the line also, and therefore we are akin to him not only by his humanity but by his monstrosity. No wonder he alarms, as would the most nightmarish figure. Or if we make a laudable attempt to repress this alarm, in the end we succeed in nothing but in replacing it with bafflement. The more details we note about Caliban that make for his monstrosity, the more we find that call to be noted as making for the opposite. We begin to doubt whether we have one thing or many before us, whether we have anything at all. We find ourselves in short in the position of the men on board the *Sea Adventure*, when their mind had lost its judgment and empire.

Let us nevertheless preserve that empire as long as we can,

meanwhile noting as many details as possible about Caliban. The first among these would seem to be his physical ugliness, since that is the first to be impressed upon the reader. And the impression is intended to be deep, for Ariel is dressed as a water-nymph and called back upon the stage for no other purpose than, by the contrast he offers to Caliban, to make it so. Yet the ugliness would seem to be of a softer kind, rather ludicrous than horrific: of all the other characters only Miranda and Prospero hinting anything to the contrary, either by action or by word. And of these, Miranda has a special reason for so doing, since in her memory the appearance of Caliban is associated with an attempted rape. As for Prospero, he would not seem to make any clear distinction between disgust at the physical and the moral Caliban. In any case, his solitary reaction cannot be considered to have a significance equal to that of so many others who, rather than turning their eyes away, allow them to dwell on Caliban: either to their scornful or to their tolerant amusement.

A ludicrous ugliness is a heavy cross for a man to bear; not however large enough, if he is a man, to hide the fact. Accordingly, we find the fact recognized not only in the conduct but in the words of the other characters. It must however be admitted that they show no great eagerness to do so: their attitude, rather than one of a decided acceptance or a decided repudiation of Caliban's human appearance resembling that of the reader's hitherto – that is to say, it is an attitude of bafflement. Thus only once does Stephano, the most kindly disposed of all towards Caliban, gratify the latter with the name of 'man-monster'; only once does he go ever so far as to call him 'Monsieur Monster'; for the most part of the time he is content with the name 'servant monster', the anthropomorphic suggestions of which are no more than slight, if indeed they exist. And if Prospero on one occasion allows himself to group Caliban along with Stephano and Trinculo as 'men', and again, a few lines later, as 'fellows', he would seem on that occasion to be attending chiefly to other thoughts; normally at any rate his language is of quite a different kind. On the other hand, Miranda allows herself to compare Caliban with Ferdinand, the paragon of men, and to do so with respect to physical form. And yet, as we have seen, she is also capable of omitting Caliban from the list of men.

Perhaps I had better warn against any attempt to solve the problem of Caliban by putting him down as an ape. However easy, in these days of evolutionism, the solution may appear, it is forbidden not only by chronology but also, I believe, by evolutionary orthodoxy. Of evolution the Elizabethans suspected nothing; in any case it does not proceed, if it does proceed, by way of abortions. Further, there are no creatures of whose difference from himself Caliban is more convinced than he is of that of apes. These he not only fears because they are employed to torment him, he also despises them for the way they 'mow and chatter' (II. ii. 10); 'thou jesting monkey' (III. ii. 45) is the most satisfying insult he can find when Trinculo has given him the lie on the matter nearest his heart; the punishment he most dreads, along with that of being immobilized into a barnacle, is that of degradation into an ape 'with forehead villainous low' (IV. i. 249). Caliban's forehead, it may be presumed, was a perceptibly high one.

A reminder of the fact is not inappropriate as preparation for a study of what Mr Luce calls Caliban's endowments. For of course it is only mental and moral endowments which are in question. Of the physical, Caliban quite obviously possesses at least his proper share. He can eat – he makes his first entrance eating; he can sleep – Prospero reproaches him with sleeping too much; he can move himself and other things – this capacity for locomotion is exploited to the full by Prospero; he is philoprogenitive – according to Prospero, excessively, even unscrupulously so.

Among mental endowments, he possesses to a notable degree that of cunning. Given an end, he is never at a loss to devise the means for obtaining it. The end which he takes as given, and architectonic to all others, is that of vengeance upon Prospero. Accordingly he notes the time at which access to Prospero is least dangerous, and how to circumvent such danger as remains. First Prospero must be deprived of the books which are his weapons of defence; then, and then only, are offensive weapons to be used – a log, a stake or a knife. These Caliban knows himself too cowardly to wield: he is too cowardly to attack even Trinculo, until someone else's blows have lamed the latter. But Stephano, Caliban thinks, is brave; and not altogether foolishly, since the valour of a man when drunk is not necessarily a drunkard's valour. And so Caliban proceeds, by bribery, to devise yet another means to his revenge. Stephano shall have Caliban as a servant, Miranda as a consort, and the island as a kingdom, only if he will consent to act as executioner. He does consent, only, as the reader knows, to fail in the office.

The manner of his failing is such as, by contrast, to suggest that Caliban is endowed not only with cunning but with prudence, and indeed with quite a high measure of it. For having devised means to an end, he remains constantly aware of the temporal priority of the former, and exercises self-control in refraining from any attempt upon the latter until the means have been secured. Stephano on the other hand would seize upon the ends without delay. No sooner has he heard Ariel's music than he is off in pursuit.

> This will prove a brave kingdom to me,

he says,

> Where I shall have my music for nothing. (III. ii. 142)

'When Prospero's destroyed', rings Caliban's warning cry; but Stephano will have none of it, preferring to heed Trinculo's 'Let's follow' the music, 'and after do our work.' He commands Caliban to lead the pursuit but Caliban refuses, lagging disconsolately behind. Such at least is a possible interpretation of the speech-headings and, it seems to me, the most plausible one.

Nevertheless he does not abandon Stephano, on whom all his hopes are fixed; he knows of course of no one else upon the island on whom he might fix them. When we next see him, he is exercising a self-control that is nothing less than extra-ordinary: for he is patient under reproaches that he has done nothing to deserve. It is he, say both Stephano and Trinculo, who is cause of their shins having been pricked with thorns and their noses having been offended with a filthy pool. And yet, as we have seen, Caliban did not lead the chase which brought them to these misfortunes; nor did he tell them that Ariel's music was harmless to follow, only that it was harmless to listen to. The immediately subsequent behaviour of his companions calls for, and meets with, a self-control which is even greater. For they rush upon the glittering garments which Prospero has hung out 'for stale'. Caliban gives expression to anger no more violent than is necessary to restrain them, were they capable of restraint. The garments he condemns as 'trash' or 'luggage';

Trinculo he calls a fool for laying a hand upon them; he himself will have 'none on't'. And he proclaims the punishments to which they are exposing themselves. All is useless, and Caliban must face the punishments along with the other two. He does so in a silence which, like all negatives, can bear no weight of interpretation; it cannot however be interpreted as undignified.

Caliban's self-control and prudence should be borne in mind when his moral endowments come up for consideration. Meanwhile, it may be noted that they are in no way incompatible with ignorance of astronomy. Trinculo may affect to think so; but then Trinculo is a parasite upon learning as upon many other things, and in order to increase his own importance is led to overprize it. Caliban may very well believe both that there is a man in the moon and that Stephano is such a man, without ceasing to be as cunning and as prudent as a number of men, indeed leaders of men, known to history. On the other hand, what might seem repugnant to his possession of any mental or moral qualities whatever is the aphasia with which, according to Prospero (or Miranda), he was once afflicted.

> I pitied thee,
> Took pains to make thee speak, taught thee each hour
> One thing or other: when thou didst not, savage,
> Know thine own meaning, but wouldst gabble like
> A thing most brutish, I endow'd thy purposes
> With words to make them known.[1]   (I. ii. 354)

In interpreting this passage however the philological uncharitableness should be borne in mind which, though at times ascribed as a monopoly to the Greeks, has manifested itself in most places and continues to do so down to modern times. Any unfamiliar speech is readily dismissed as a 'gabble'; so that Prospero's evidence need not be taken to imply that Caliban was ever speechless. In any case, by the time the play opens he has long ceased to be so; and in recognizing that, with a new form of speech, new powers have been conferred upon him he would seem to give invincible proof of the possession of an intellectual nature. In recognizing that he has abused these powers he would seem to prove that he possesses a moral nature also:

> You taught me language, and my profit on't
> Is, I know how to curse.   (*ibid.* 364)

[1] This speech is attributed to Miranda in the Folio and in *N.C.S.* (E. M. W.)

Like Prospero's speech with which this essay began, this utterance of Caliban's has echoed throughout the world; it can hardly have come from a brute.

Yet a brute is what, according to Prospero, Caliban undoubtedly is; or if not a brute then he is a devil, which is something worse. Either that is he is beneath morality, as incapable of it; or he is averse from it, as incurably malicious. It is scarcely necessary to quote Prospero's fulminations to this effect. 'Abhorred slave', he says,

> Which any print of goodness will not take,
> Being capable of all ill! (*ibid.* 353)

or again,

> A devil, a born devil, on whose nature
> Nurture will never stick; on whom my pains,
> Humanly taken, all, all lost, quite lost!
>
> (IV. i. 188)

It is however rarely possible to accept fulminations at their face value; and of itself, the wording of Prospero's makes it clear that they cannot. If Caliban is a 'born devil', then he is no devil except figuratively, for devils are not born. And once attention is fixed upon this figure of Prospero's, he reveals himself I think as failing to justify it. For the charges which he alleges in its support are two: of lust, and of ingratitude.

> I have us'd thee
> . . . with human care, and lodg'd thee
> In mine own cell, till thou didst seek to violate
> The honour of my child. (I. ii. 346)

If both charges are grave, neither lies beyond the reach of merely human wickedness. And of this truth no one, it would seem, is more aware than Prospero himself. For, to take the less serious charge, he does not think it superfluous to warn Ferdinand against the sin of lust: Ferdinand, whom no one has suspected of falling outside humanity, who on the contrary has enjoyed the highest rank within it, who has received the most careful moral training that men can devise, whom Prospero himself has submitted to a moral probation and whom, in consequence, he has thought worthy of his daughter's hand. Yet even so, he delivers the warning not only once but twice, and then weaves a third repetition of it into a masque provided for Ferdinand's entertainment. Admittedly, the gulf between liability to lust and lustful sin is such as, in the eyes of justice, it cannot be bridged: those under the liability may however bridge it in a single moment, and with a single act. Recognition of them as such would therefore seem to entitle them to charity, at least in speech; however firmly Prospero may be convinced that, with respect to Caliban, he functions as an officer of justice. But it is precisely in speech that Prospero is most notably lacking in charity. As for the second and more serious charge of ingratitude, a similar comment on it is provided by one of the phrases contained in Prospero's warning to Ferdinand. 'The strongest oaths', he admonishes the latter, 'are straws to th'fire i'th' blood' (IV. i. 52). If the strongest oaths, then the closest obligations also; and other passions besides lust may cause these obligations to burn away like straw. If all are to be considered as brutes or as devils who, under the persuasion of passion, have shown themselves ungrateful, then a great part of what is usually considered human history should be called by another name. Indeed, Prospero's vehemence towards Caliban shows itself upon scrutiny as so far beyond justification as to raise the doubt whether the passion which Caliban does entertain towards him, the passion of hate, is not all too easily explicable.

Explicable and no more, for justified it cannot be. It is a completely ruthless hate. The lines in which he not only issues but savours his instructions for the murder of Prospero are by far the most brutal in the play:

> there may'st thou brain him,
> Having first seized his books; or with a log
> Batter his skull, or paunch him with a stake,
> Or cut his wezand with a knife.   (III. ii. 87)

However, they are not the most diabolic lines; the credit or the shame for uttering which must be allowed to a gentleman of Ferdinand's rank and training: the usurping Duke of Milan who, when reminded that, as a human being, he is supposed to have a conscience, replies:

> I feel not
> This deity in my bosom. Twenty consciences,
> That stand 'twixt me and Milan, candied be they
> And melt ere they molest.   (II. i. 274)

The treachery involved in his plot to murder Alonso has already, in the opening section, been the subject of remark. Therefore perhaps it is sufficient here to add that this treachery is beyond all possibility of explanation. Neither Alonso nor Sebastian has suffered any uncharitableness at Prospero's hands, nor claims to have done so. The sole motive to their crime is, they confess, ambition.

Caliban is then less diabolic than either Antonio or Sebastian. As no one doubts that these are men, it follows that Caliban is not a devil at all. Prospero's alternative suggestion remains to be considered, that he is a brute. And about this the first remark to be made would seem to be that no one brings evidence in its favour, save Prospero himself. Nor would that evidence, from the language in which it is couched, seem to be above suspicion. On the contrary, the whole of Prospero's demeanour towards Caliban rouses suspicion of the strongest kind. If he really believed Caliban to be a brute, for example, he would not rail at him as he does: for it is not intelligent to rail at a brute for the evil he may do, any more than it is to rail at a river for the way in which it flows. If the flow displeases, dykes and dams are constructed to control it. Similarly a brute, if he displeases, is confined and beaten, without apologies to him, to oneself or to anybody. And much of Prospero's railing has the air of being an apology addressed to the universe. These, it may be objected, are merely negative considerations. Positive ones in the same sense are however not lacking. Caliban, we have seen, possesses the power of intelligent choice, which brutes do not: and when this choice is between means and ends, he is capable of standing by a choice of the means, however strongly the ends may attract him. His chief end, the murder of Prospero, must be admitted to be evil. If however he has not, like Antonio and Sebastian, stifled his conscience in order to be free to pursue it, that need not imply he is brutish because of an absence of conscience. He may very well have a conscience and this, as often happens in men, be blinded or blunted by passion to the evil on which he is engaged. Further, there would seem to be occasions when he is not so blinded or blunted. As has been noted, he regrets his cursing: which if he does not clearly repent of, at least he recognizes that repentance would be proper. And if, from the play's opening, he shows himself as, in his conduct towards Prospero, entirely governed by hate, there was a time, he claims, when this was not so: a time when Prospero invited love and gratitude –

> and then I lov'd thee,
> And show'd thee all the qualities o'th'isle,
> The fresh springs, brine-pits, barren place and fertile.   (I. ii. 337)

Prospero does not venture to deny the claim. And that the fount of love and gratitude, though no longer flowing in Prospero's direction, is by no means dry in Caliban's heart is shown by his conduct towards Stephano. The latter hardly needs do more than make a few amiable gestures, utter a few not obviously harsh words to Caliban, for the latter to embarrass him with professions of love:

> I'll show thee every fertile inch o'th'island...
> I'll show thee the best springs; I'll pluck thee berries,
> I'll fish for thee, I'll get thee wood enough...
> I prithee, let me bring thee where crabs grow;
> And I with my long nails will dig thee pig-nuts;
> Show thee a jay's nest, and instruct thee how
> To snare the nimble marmoset; I'll bring thee
> To clustering filberts, and sometimes I'll get thee
> Young scamels from the rock. Wilt thou go with me?
>
> (II. ii. 153 ff.)

The litany is pathetic, both in its own eloquence and in the indifference of him before whom it is poured out.

Caliban is pathetic too in his offer to worship Stephano, for which he has often been condemned. Yet the offer does not hold for long: Caliban is intelligent enough to learn from experience, and when he has done so rapidly degrades Stephano from god to king or lord. Nor while it lasts would the offer seem to be to Caliban's discredit, but rather the opposite. A god is the strongest possible source of authority, and a recognition of authority, together with a willingness to submit to it, is a necessary preliminary to the moral life. For conscience is nothing if not authoritative. Even the mild authority of Alonso is unbearable to Antonio and Sebastian, who stifle conscience.

The moral life is a conflict. Accordingly, those who engage upon it are in need of encouragement, and this they find in the prospect of a time when the causes of conflict shall have been removed. Caliban too enjoys such a prospect. The music of Ariel not only gratifies his senses, it conjures up a vision of paradise:

> Sometimes a thousand twangling instruments
> Will hum about mine ears; and sometimes voices,

> . . .and then, in dreaming,
> The clouds me thought would open, and show riches
> Ready to drop upon me.   (III. ii. 135)

Nevertheless he does not follow the music, for he knows that, in this world, paradise is to be enjoyed in prospect only. Thereby as we have seen he shows himself superior in prudence to Stephano and Trinculo. Now I think we may add he shows himself superior to Ferdinand also: at least at the moment when Ferdinand, not content with a passing snatch of the spirits' music, would have them gratify all of his senses for ever. For that is to demand a paradise on earth.

But it is time to halt in our investigation. Having started from a consideration of Caliban's monstrosity, we seem to be on the verge of concluding that no other character in the play is human in a like degree. If so far we have avoided bafflement, it may be we have done so only at the cost of taking a corposant for a planet. Shakespeare is proving his power over us; it was not however part of his intention that his readers should fall victims to a nightmare. And that they should not do so, he provided objects other than Caliban for them to consider. It will therefore be wise for us to change the object before us.

V. THE SPIRITS

In spite of the recommendation with which the last section closed, I find it necessary to return to Caliban. But only for a moment, since my sole object is to get rid of the notion that he is a supernatural being. Mr Luce put it about that he was, or at least one aspect of him: but then Mr Luce held that Caliban was vague, and we have seen that he is rather the opposite; Mr Luce also assumed that the word 'vague' has as synonym, not only the word 'ideal', but the word 'supernatural'. And few would agree with him in this.

Supernatural beings are, not ideal, but at least as real as any other; nor are they vaguely, but at least as precisely known. They can be so, because in no part and in no respect are they compounded of matter. Hence they may be called spiritual substances but, in order to distinguish them as clearly as possible from the spirits which play a prominent part in *The Tempest*, it is perhaps desirable for us to call them 'intellectual substances'. As such, they can exercise control over the world and its inhabitants, in so far as these are not intellectual but material. The purely intellectual substances include God, the good and the evil angels, and the devil as the chief of the latter.

Prospero calls Caliban 'a devil, a born devil' but, as was pointed out in the last section, this cannot be more than a figure of speech. Nor may his description of Caliban as a 'demi-devil', a 'bastard devil' or 'got by the devil himself' by any more than such. Caliban's mother, we are told, was a witch; and witches, we know, were in the habit of accepting devils as their lovers. But it was not inevitable that they should do so, and Sycorax may have been more fastidious or more recalcitrant than the majority of her kind. If indeed Sycorax was a witch – a question which may occupy us later. But whatever answer we may be compelled to return to it makes no difference to the answer required of us now. For the offspring of a union so unnatural as that between a devil and a witch is nothing above nature, but something within nature if not in accordance with it, something preternatural to use the technical term or, to fall back on the term with which we are already familiar, a monster. The characters in the play are fully aware of the important difference between monsters on the one hand, and devils on the other. Stephano, for example, is quite happy to divert himself at the expense of a creature with four legs and two voices so long as, however abnormally shaped, it appears to him normally animate. When however one of the voices addresses him by name, he recoils in fear. For, as he is ignorant that any of his fellows has been washed up on the island, it seems to him that knowledge of his name can have been acquired only by an intelligence surpassing the natural. 'Mercy, mercy', he therefore cries, 'this is a devil and no monster. I will leave him, I have no long spoon' (II. ii. 100).

Stephano's reaction is to be noted, for it is the reaction of all and any characters in the play when they find themselves or believe that they find themselves in the presence of the supernatural. They acknowledge its powers: inclining themselves in reverence and humility if these appear powers for good, recoiling in fear and horror if they appear powers for evil. In the latter case the evil characters, who have set themselves up as rivals to the devil, do not recoil as far as they should; still, they do not deny the existence of the intellectual substance whom they rival. Antonio and Sebastian, when they hear a recital of the crimes they committed long ago and far away from the island, like Stephano conclude that the devil is at work. Unlike Stephano, they do not withdraw but express a wish to fight the devil. Such a wish is absurd, and the condition they seek to impose, that the fight shall be a fair one, only makes the absurdity clearer. As Gonzalo notes, Antonio and Sebastian are 'desperate' – mad, that is, with the same sort if not the same degree of madness as was Ferdinand, when he threw himself out of the ship. He was led to do so by the sight of disturbances in physical nature which seemed to him beyond the power of anything natural to produce. So too the proximate causes of madness is the appearance of Ariel as a harpy and of the 'strange shapes' which, having brought in a table with 'gentle actions and salutations', remove it 'with mocks and mows'. Like the disturbances of the storm, these shapes vanish, and the madness with them. Yet the belief remains, in virtue of which they were able to cause it. When Prospero, somewhat later in the play, hints that, if he wished, he might recite crimes not yet committed but only plotted by Antonio and Sebastian, the latter whispers to the former: 'The devil speaks in him' (V. i. 129). Thereby Prospero is for the moment disconcerted for, as we shall see later, nothing is further from his intentions than to appear as an agent of the devil.

It is as condensations of a firmly held belief in the supernatural that figures of speech such as Prospero's 'born devil', 'bastard devil' are to be explained. No notion can be admitted of explaining the belief itself as a construction upon the figures; for that would be to explain it away, and in consequence the figures would lose much, if not indeed the whole of their force. If Prospero did not believe in the devil's existence, a form of words such as 'born devil', which would then be an empty form, would provide no relief for feelings as vehement as those which he nourishes towards Caliban. Even trivial expressions such as Trinculo's 'The devil take your finger', or Stephano's 'Where the devil should he learn our language?' (II. ii. 68) should not be assumed to coincide with apparently similar expressions on the lips of an unbeliever. For they are different in form, if not in the words out of which they are put together: they are animated by a belief, however sluggishly, at the moment, such a belief may be functioning.

That there can be such moments is proof, paradoxical perhaps but palmary, that the belief is capable of functioning with force. Those who are aware of the supernatural as existing about them everywhere and at all times are under what seems to them the necessity of referring frequently to it. Should time or energy be lacking to do so with a proper formality, they make the reference in a summary way. In consequence they may appear to others, or even to themselves, to treat the supernatural with an undue familiarity: in their eyes, familiarity is not such an offence as neglect would be. For neglect may lead to a weakening of belief, and perhaps to its disappearance. The principle does not need to be argued, perhaps indeed it hardly needs to be stated: for its workings are observable in everyday life. From the conversation of those whose belief in God and the devil is but faint, these names are banished as indecencies; in the conversation of those with a lively faith, on the other hand, God and the whole heavenly hierarchy are liable to be invoked on what might seem indecent occasions.

The principle should be borne in mind when considering the meaning to be attached to such exclamations as Miranda's 'O heavens!' or 'Heaven thank you for it!' It may seem of little importance that these should be dismissed as tricks of speech or empty verbal forms: the critic who allows himself to do so may however find himself similarly dismissing Gonzalo's 'Good angels preserve the king!' (II. i. 304) or the king's own 'Give us kind keepers, Heavens!' – and that is not quite so obviously of little importance. On the other hand, the importance would seem quite sufficiently obvious of allowing a measure of force to Prospero's asseverations that he and Miranda were guided to the island 'by Providence divine', or that, during the voyage thither, she was

> Infused with a fortitude from Heaven,   (I. ii. 153)

the sight of which roused in him

> An undergoing stomach, to bear up
> Against what should ensue.

Most obviously, it would seem most important of all to acknowledge that when Prospero, observing the promise of marriage passed between Ferdinand and Miranda but himself unobserved, uses the words:

> Heavens rain grace
> On that which breeds between them! (III. i. 75)

– that then he is uttering, not a mere wish or a hope, but a prayer; that when, bestowing Miranda upon Ferdinand, he calls out

> afore Heaven
> I ratify this rich gift! (IV. i. 7)

he is not merely protesting the sincerity of his intentions, but taking an oath to that effect; and that when he insists Ferdinand shall not untie Miranda's virgin-knot before

> All sanctimonious ceremonies may
> With full and holy rite be ministered,

he is moved by an anxiety, not merely that human convention shall not be slighted, but that supernatural ordinance shall be obeyed. For if it is not obeyed, supernatural sanction will follow. As Prospero himself says: should Ferdinand defy the warning which is being delivered to him, then

> No sweet aspersion shall the Heavens let fall
> To make this contract grow.

I imagine that no critics would dismiss the appeal to Heaven in this last line as a form of words which is wholly empty; but no critic, I also imagine, can appreciate the force which fills it unless he allows that all the lines quoted in this paragraph are equally full. Yet if he does not, neither does he appreciate the play, one of the central themes of which is Prospero's manner of securing his daughter's happiness. Since that happiness is earthly, it can never be rendered absolutely secure; Prospero however must be understood as rendering it as secure as he thinks he can. According to his ideas, things earthly are secure when set in the supernatural which, in so far as they are good, will protect them; in so far as they are evil will, by its sanctions, procure either their correction or their destruction.

And once it is recognized that the characters in the play conceive of themselves as surrounded at all times and in all places by a supernatural which they must either gratefully respect or desperately fear: then and then only, it seems to me,

does another important truth about the play become apparent.
This is the truth that Prospero's spirits have nothing to do with
the supernatural at all. They are no more supernatural than is
Caliban: or rather, they are less so. For if and in so far as he is a
human creature, he can enter into relations with the supernatural;
whereas the spirits cannot even do that. The proof is that no
one in the play regards the spirits as in themselves objects of
either respect or fear. At least, no one does so in so far as he
does not mistake the spirits for angels or devils, for the supernatural or intellectual substances, that is, which they are not.
The newcomers to the island are of course particularly liable to
such a mistake, and as we shall see, Prospero encourages them
in the making of it; the old established residents of the island
on the other hand hardly allow themselves to be aware of the
spirits. For these are too insignificant to be worth notice.
Caliban for example treats them with the indifference, if also
with the tolerance, with which he would treat a band of his own
brothers. Of themselves, he says,

> they'll nor pinch,
> Fright me with urchin-shows, pitch me i'th'mire,
> Nor lead me, like a firebrand, in the dark
> Out of my way. (II. ii. 4)

Unfortunately, Prospero employs the spirits as his tormentors,
and so by association they become objects of fear to Caliban.
That is the reason why, having mistaken Trinculo for a spirit,
he throws himself flat upon the ground, and before being
touched, perhaps even before being observed, he moans out:
'Do not torment me, O!' His fear is abject, like that of a nervous
patient at the dentist's. But it is a fear that the spirits inspire
only accidentally and not by their nature; so that, however
abject, it can occasionally be laid by. To music that the spirits
play, Caliban can listen more than contentedly. When towards
the end of *The Tempest* he has his first sight of the courtiers of
Naples and Milan, he mistakes them, as he did Trinculo, for
spirits: nevertheless, he can spare a moment for their fine clothes.
'O Setebos, these be brave spirits indeed' (V. i. 262), he exclaims.
But fine clothes do not soothe him as music can, and so the fear
of punishment returns.

The only reference to spirits made by a second old-established
resident, Miranda, would seem indifferent to the point of

contempt. When Ferdinand is for the first time exhibited before her, 'Believe me, sir', she acknowledges to her father, 'it carries a brave form. But 'tis a spirit', she adds, with the implication that it can be of no possible concern. (I. ii. 415).

Of all the islanders, it is of course Prospero who has most dealings with the spirits. And certainly, he is not to be described as indifferent to them. His dealings are however not only so numerous but so varied that they must be left for a later discussion. At the moment, we may content ourselves with noting that he exploits the airy quickness of Ariel with as little compunction as he does the earthy slowness of Caliban; and that if from time to time he allows himself to express satisfaction with Ariel's services, or amusement at his tricks – 'that's my dainty Ariel!' – nevertheless he does not hesitate, when occasion seems to him to call for it, to abuse Ariel as 'malignant'.

Two speeches of length, and of an importance equal to their length, are I am aware often quoted as proving either that the spirits are supernatural, or that in some way or other they are related to the latter. These are the speech of denunciation delivered by Ariel as a harpy, and that of farewell addressed by Prospero to the elves. Neither however is easy to interpret, nor are we as yet fully prepared to do so. Therefore I must pass them by, confining my attention to whatever other evidence seems to point to the same conclusion. It is neither plentiful nor impressive.

First perhaps should be taken Caliban's claim that his master's art is of such power.

> It would control my dam's god Setebos.   (I. ii. 374)

As this art finds its chief or perhaps sole ministers in the spirits, here it might be thought we have an instance of the spirits entering not only into relations but into relations of superiority with the supernatural. The divine status of Setebos is however by no means clear. It may be worth noticing that, according to Pigafetta (from whom, through Eden's translation, Shakespeare took the name) he is provided with two horns to his head, hair down to his feet, and the power to cast out fire both before and behind. It is moreover his habit to shake until they burst the bodies of those who make the sign of the cross in his presence. Shakespeare gives no hint that, though encountered in Patagonia, he is possessed of such familiar attributes. It may therefore be Shakespeare's intention that, unlike other pagan gods, Setebos should not be considered as entering into the Christian pandemonium. Perhaps rather he is the sort of god which Caliban, for a passing moment, offers to make of Stephano: a living god, a human idol. In that case, any power which the spirits might exercise over him presents a problem no different from that presented by the power which they actually exercise over Stephano. Or again, Setebos may be of the same nature as the spirits themselves. In any case, he is too obscure to shed light on that nature, or on anything.

Further pieces of evidence might seem to be supplied by Ferdinand. After listening to Ariel's first ditty, he concludes:

> This is no mortal business, nor no sound
> That the earth owes. (I. ii. 411)

And if earth does not own it then, it would appear, either Heaven or Hell must do so. Ferdinand however is repeating the mistake which we have already observed Trinculo to make on one occasion, and on another Antonio and Sebastian. 'The ditty does remember my drown'd father': unaware of the presence on the island of anyone with a perfectly natural knowledge of that father, Ferdinand falsely attributes a supernatural intelligence to the singer.

Of the salutation with which he greets Miranda:

> Most sure,
> The goddess on whom these airs attend – (*ibid.* 427)

it is I fear at last possible, and perhaps it is necessary to complain of as a trick of speech, and an empty verbal form. Among the other advantages of his rank, Ferdinand has enjoyed a classical education, and this encourages the habit, as it confers the power, of elaborately saying little or nothing. *O dea certe* the address of Aeneas to Venus was the more irresponsibly copied, as no responsibility was felt towards the godhead of Venus. Nor does Alonso feel any such responsibility when, as in courtesy bound, he repeats his son's salutation towards the end of the play. Ferdinand has no need to assure him that Miranda is mortal; nor would it occur to Ferdinand to do so, were it not for the antithesis with 'immortal' which he intends in the following line.

The last scraps of possible evidence which occur to me are one or two utterances of Miranda's. But almost before examination they reveal themselves as no evidence at all. When for example she says of Ferdinand:

> There's nothing ill can dwell in such a temple.
> If the ill spirits have so fair a house
> Good things will strive to dwell in it,   (I. ii. 462)

she is using the term spirit, not in what might be called the technical sense peculiar to this play, but in a sense more widely familiar. Christian teaching is in her mind and in particular, I imagine, the parable of the room swept and garnished. Nor when she calls Ferdinand 'a thing divine' is she contrasting him with spirits such as Prospero's, for not even the relation of contrast is possible between these and divinity. As has been pointed out, if Ferdinand were a spirit, he could not be a subject for her concern. He has become very much a subject of that kind; and therefore she contrasts him – her own words make it clear – with all other natural things that are known to her.

Provisionally then I conclude that the spirits have nothing to do with the supernatural. The question rises, with what have they to do? and what are they?

It is a question of extreme difficulty. Usually two answers seem open to the critic, when called upon to specify the dwelling-place or exercising-ground of beings who appear properly to belong neither to earth, Heaven or Hell. He can lodge them in, so to speak, the interstices of the earth; the gaps which, however narrowly, none the less effectively separate one natural kind from another. There Caliban dwells, in so far as he is a monster and not human; there too I suppose dwell the witches of *Macbeth*, in so far as not merely human instruments of the devil. But however important the part assigned to the witches, it is a strictly limited one: confined to the emission of alluring if alarming howls, and to an emission so occasional that no one is much troubled to know exactly whence it proceeds. As for Caliban, he is sufficiently inert to be content with an interstice. But it is impossible for the spirits to be so: they themselves, and not merely their voices, rise and shoot through earth, air and sea, and they do so at all times.

Perhaps then it is necessary for a new earth, air and sea to be created, which shall be a habitation as proper to them as it is to Prospero, Miranda and the rest of the characters. An answer of this kind inherits from a critical tradition at least as old as the eighteenth century. It would seem none the more satisfactory. To a dispassionate examination, the so-called creative powers of the artist reveal themselves such as to be mocked by the name. For they are no other than powers, not of making what is new, but of selecting and combining what is old. And if exercised in such a manner as temporarily to hide this their dependence on the old, what they produce may certainly appear new, but as certainly it appears insignificant. An extreme but all the more instructive proof of this is supplied by Eslava who, it will be remembered, permits his Dardanus to exercise magic nowhere but on the bottom of the sea. Thereby he avoids all but the remotest suggestion of a conflict between natural powers and those of magic; but also, as has been pointed out, nature is all but abolished by him. And now it may be added that magic too is all but abolished: the submarine palace is called into existence and later caused to vanish, Dardanus, Seraphina and Valentinian have their entrance to and their exit from the palace, but while in it, they witness even fewer magical happenings than they do natural. The water-nymphs attendant upon Seraphina let nothing be known of themselves but their voices; nor do these voices lure Seraphina to action nor alarm her for having acted – they merely lull her to peace. In *The Tempest* on the other hand the spirits not only lull but enliven, when indeed they do not torment; they not only sing but do things, and some of the things they do are of a stupendous violence. Yet all have their place, or seem to have it, neither beneath the sea nor in any newly created world, but in a world which is old and familiar because, in the strictest sense of the word, it was created once and for all.

The problem of the spirits becomes all the more difficult of solution. Examination has indeed scarcely begun before it appears impossible. For turning to Prospero who, as master of the spirits, may be expected to have the fullest and most reliable information about them, we overhear him remark of Ariel that he is 'but air'. And by 'air' Prospero means 'nothing'; at least he does so in so far as, in non-philosophical conversation, the two terms are distinct. After listening to Prospero's consolatory speech to Ferdinand, as we did in the opening section of this essay, the remark should not of course surprise us: for already on that occasion we learnt that, as the spirits are 'baseless' and 'insubstantial', they and anything (such as a masque) for which they are responsible must be expected at any moment to melt into thin air. Yet by this reminiscence our difficulty is only increased: on the one hand, nothing can come of nothing; on the other, from Prospero's spirits there comes, or there seems to come, a very great deal. And after all, even a masque is something.

But Prospero's spirits can do much more than represent a masque. They cannot only cause to appear things which are not – Iris, Ceres, Juno, nymphs, reapers, strange shapes that 'mock and mow' – they can also cause things that are to change their appearance, and even at times to disappear. Before the astonished eyes of Alonso and his courtiers on land, they can bring in a table and remove it; before the affrighted eyes of the same Alonso and his courtiers at sea, they can raise the waves 'to the welkin's cheek', and can cause the welkin to pour down 'stinking pitch' in return. They can cause the lightning to flash, the thunder to roll and the winds to roar. And they can either cause Alonso's ship to appear to split and founder, or having caused it to do so in fact, they can raise and reintegrate it again. And also they can utter sounds which allay both the fury of waters and the sorrow of men. They can speak words by which men are stung either to humble remorse or to defiant rage. Nay, they can affect not only men's sight and hearing but also the most stolid and apparently most reliable of their senses, that of touch. Caliban complains that the spirits pinch him, or prick him as though they were hedgehogs, or wound him as adders might. In the form of dogs, they are set to hunt Caliban, Stephano and Trinculo; and in respect of these three, goblins receive a charge to

> grind their joints
> With dry convulsions, shorten up their sinews
> With aged cramps, and more pinch-spotted make them
> Than pard or cat o'mountain. (IV. i. 259)

Apparently the goblins are equal to the charge, for at his next entrance Stephano complains of being so sore that he is no longer Stephano 'but a cramp'.

These facts are puzzling, yet other facts, still more puzzling remain. The spirits, though nothing, cannot only affect things which are something; these things which are something can affect the nothing of the spirits. Ariel's being but air presented no obstacle to his being imprisoned for twelve years in a cloven pine nor to his suffering, over these twelve years, 'a torment' fit 'to lay upon the damn'd' (I. ii. 289). And the torment is at least likely to have been a physical one, for under the stress of it he uttered groans so physcial that they

> Did make wolves howl, and penetrate the breasts
> Of ever-angry bears.

Nor in the presence of the spectators does he show himself wholly exempt from the sort of accidents to which only physical or partly physical natures are usually held to be liable. At the sight of the distractions of Alonso, Sebastian and Antonio he feels such a 'tenderness' that Prospero, who is normally tender to nobody but Miranda, considers himself thereby rebuked. More frequently, Ariel shows himself as moved to hilarity: his delight in 'playing the Jack' is indeed so great that he ventures to do so with the most unlikely persons, and on the most unpromising occasions. He challenges, however gently, the portentous solemnity of Prospero – 'Do you love me, master? no?' – in his first ditty he mocks, however gently, the grief of Ferdinand. But then, the whole company of spirits performing the masque could not, we remember, pretend an impassivity when the masque was destroyed: they vanished 'heavily, to a strange, hollow and confused noise'. Remembering these spirits, yet another difficulty comes to our mind. We have now learnt that they are nothing: how then is it possible that, as Prospero informed Ferdinand, they should inhabit 'confines'? However spacious these may be – the whole expanse say of an element – it would seem as impossible for nothing to be placed there as Ariel in his pine. But Ariel too performed a part in the masque: therefore he too has his 'confine' – and as a consequence, not of violence, but of his nature! Yet there is nothing he longs for more constantly than to be free; and he is promised by Prospero that, as a reward for diligent service, he shall be 'free as the mountain air'.

A recital of these difficulties prompts perhaps the reflection that, if the critic himself is not mad, then some person or persons in the play must be so. I know not what stout authority might be pleaded in support of a suggestion that, say, Stephano, Trinculo and Caliban labour under no more than a strong persuasion of being hunted by dogs. If the persuasion is strong enough they may feel, and not merely imagine that they feel, the dogs' teeth piercing skin and flesh; if in its turn the feeling is strong enough, it may produce discontinuities in skin and flesh that are deep and wide enough to remain open for many a painful day. Although in the opening section I declared that epistemological and psychological discussion was to be excluded from this essay, I should perhaps devote a moment's consideration to a theory of this kind. For hallucinations on the part of some or other of the characters in *The Tempest* may appear so plausible that, if I neglect them, I may seem to do so not so much out of scorn as out of fear.

A hallucination that serves as the spring of either the whole or the major part of a dramatic action must either be confined to a single character or, if a number share in it, then all must share in it to the same degree. In other words, the hallucination must be either private or collective. For a stage upon which a number of characters were acting each in accordance with a hallucination either wholly or partly his own would hardly provide an entertainment in the modern sense of the word; rather it would afford a disedifying glimpse into Bedlam. In spite of its date, *The Tempest* has I think given satisfactory proof of being the former.

Of these two possibilities, that of a collective hallucination would at first sight appear the more useful to us. For not only one but all the characters in *The Tempest* are to some extent affected by the spiriting of Ariel and his colleagues: even Miranda, in so far as she is a spectator of the storm and of the masque. But Shakespeare would seem to have taken a step which puts any such possibility out of the question. For at the beginning of Act II he shows various characters unable to agree on what is before their eyes. Whatever else may have happened to them, therefore, they have not been collectively hallucinated. If all are so, then each lies under a different hallucination, and at once the dispute between them becomes disedifying. And this Mr Luce seems to have felt when he – ill-advisedly, as has been shown – sought to be rid of the dispute as a quibble. If on the other hand, only one party is hallucinated, it does not really matter which: for in both cases the result is the same. Both parties are where they are, and able to engage on the dispute, merely as a consequence of the wreck. But this wreck is the work of Ariel or, in other words, hallucinatory. The party who is free from hallucination should not therefore have been affected by it; he should not find himself where he is; he should not be disputing at all. Or should we say that, while immune from some of the delusions spread by Ariel, he is susceptible to the rest? If so, to which is he susceptible, and to which not? But it is useless to continue with this series of questions, which might be prolonged indefinitely. Obviously, we are circling the edge, not so much of a dramatic Bedlam, as of a dramatic Chaos.

Any theory that the hallucinations of a single person are responsible for the action in *The Tempest* implies Prospero to be that person. For he alone is sufficiently constantly in contact with the other characters for his mental state to have significance for them all. Though the theory may seem preposterous, in that it reverses the parts of hallucinated victim and hallucinating victimizer, it is as a matter of fact the least difficult to defend of all that are based on psychopathology.

For Prospero is a magician, and one of the ways of explaining a magician's feats was to say that he forced his hallucinations upon the world. The ideas and images before his mind were thought to have such power that, when projected out of the mind – as they might be by words which the magician had the skill to discover – they could alter other things into their own likeness. Now there would seem to be one or two indications in *The Tempest* that Prospero shares in a notion of this kind.

I pass over the suggestion of the New Cambridge editors that the line

> Come with a thought; I thank thee, Ariel: come   (IV. i. 164)

should be amended to read

> Come with a thought; I think thee, Ariel: come.

I pass it over, although it seems to me highly plausible. But it suits my present purpose so aptly that, were I to make use of it, even I should cease to trust myself. And also I pass over Prospero's injunction to Ariel:

> Be subject
> To no sight but thine, and mine: invisible
> To every eye-ball else.   (I. ii. 301)

This has appeared an absurdity to editors from Johnson downwards. If however Ariel is a projection of Prospero's, the
injunction acquires a clear sense, if a strange one: for at his
whim, the latter may or may not make Ariel visible to himself.
But the text would seem to be uncertain, and in any case the
injunction is of minor importance. On the other hand, the
undoubtedly important speech in which Prospero bids farewell
to the elves would seem relevant to our present point. Consideration of this was previously postponed on the ground of its
difficulty; but now our section is drawing to a close, and the
difficulty cannot be put off for ever.

The most striking thing about the speech is the wide range of
tones through which it runs, and the direction of its running. If
its first evocation is of the calm attendant upon 'hills, brooks,
standing lakes and groves', and its second of the sparkle with
which a playful Neptune ebbs and flows, these are rapidly
succeeded by the dimness of a maleficent moonshine, and a
blackness through which the curfew tolls and in which midnight
mushrooms are fostered. And when, from a description of the
dwellings and offices of the elves, the speech passes to a list of
Prospero's own achievements, these are such as to startle from
the first; they end by revolting the reader. 'I have bedimm'd',
says Prospero,

> The noontide sun, call'd forth the mutinous winds,
> And 'twixt the green sea and the azur'd vault
> Set roaring war.   (V. i. 41)

This perhaps the reader is willing to accept as an account, if a
somewhat highly pitched one, of the opening storm. But when
pitch is yet further raised, and Prospero boasts

> To the dread rattling thunder
> Have I given fire, and drifted Jove's stout oak
> With his own bolt. The strong-bas'd promontory
> Have I make shake and by the spurs pluck'd up
> The pine and cedar –

at this point the reader finds himself protesting that he had no
idea of the storm being so wantonly destructive, or indeed
destructive at all. It is true that the only assurance he has

217

received to the contrary is a limited one; he had however assumed that, if Prospero gave no other comfort to Miranda than that of perdition not having

> Betid to any creature in the vessel,

it was because Miranda had expressed no other concern. And surely she would have done, had she seen pines and cedars hurtling through the air. In any case, Prospero has posed as universally benevolent – benevolent even to Caliban, if Caliban would let him. And not even Prospero could complain of pines and cedars as opposing obstacles to the exercise of virtue. The reader begins I think to suspect it may be necessary to revise the opinion which hitherto he has held of Prospero. On arriving at the latter's final boast, however, he doubts, if he does not despair, of the possibility of any revision which might be of use. For, the list of achievements conclude,

> graves, at my command,
> Have wak'd their sleepers, oped and let 'em forth
> By my so potent art.

The man who complacently recounts so unsavoury, not to say unholy, exploits would seem to be irreconcilable with the one who valued 'sanctimonious ceremonies...with full and holy rite'. Uneasily going back over the whole speech, the reader notices yet other things about it which are, to say the least, surprising. As a leave-taking it should, according to all normal notions, be such as to gratify rather than offend those to whom it is addressed. Yet Prospero thinks it opportune to observe that, though the elves to whom he has been obliged for assistance may be 'masters', none of them is more than a 'weak' master. And not content with describing as 'puppets' those who

> By moonshine do the green-sour ringlets make

he reduces them to the stature of 'demi-puppets'. However appropriate the name may be to elves in so far as they are known to English folk-lore, it would hardly seem to be so in so far as they are possessed of powers to which Prospero has found it necessary to have recourse. The old man recalls a megalomaniac who, on an occasion calling for a graceful acknowledgment of dependence, finds himself incapable of anything but a graceless vaunting of self-sufficiency.

Having arrived so far in his reflections, the reader remembers almost with relief that self-sufficient is what hitherto he has always supposed Prospero to be. As will be mentioned later, the latter is helpless without book, wand and robe: once however such equipment is at his disposal, he never hints the slightest doubt of his ability to perform whatever he has undertaken to perform. He has no need of elves nor of any other beings as allies; for Ariel and the spirits are not allies, but mere instruments. They do no more than Prospero tells them, and they do it all. And if Ariel wields an authority over the lesser spirits, he does so by grant from Prospero: they are the 'rabble', over whom Prospero has given him power.

Must then the reader assume that, when delivering the farewell speech, or at any rate the first part of it, the old man suffers from an hallucination? and that he is seeking to project this hallucination, not so much on the present, but rather on the past? The conclusion seems fantastic; but then, all other possible conclusions seem equally so. These are two: either the speech must be accepted at its face-value, or it must be dismissed as a verbal [trick?], an empty form. As has been seen, the first of these threatens not so much to transform as to destroy all the notions the reader has so far been able to build up for himself about the play. To the second, objections are so obvious that perhaps it is not wholly a waste of words to point out what might be said in its favour. Like Ferdinand, Prospero would seem to have received a classical education. His address to the elves is as closely modelled on Medea's tirade when about to 'renew old Aeson', as Ferdinand's salutation to Miranda is modelled upon that of Aeneas to Venus. As the young men of the time, because Venus was no more than a name, felt themselves free to find a goddess in any young woman they met, and the more fleshly the better: so perhaps the old men, precisely because they were innocent of any intention or hope of perpetrating Medean horrors, may have considered it permissible to mouth out Medea's words.

Of course, the explanation is fantastic. But, I repeat, so are the other two: and for the moment I do not venture upon any decision between them. Our discussion has not however been wholly useless; for now I think we are able to confirm what from the beginning of it we suspected was the truth – that like epistemology and psychology, psycho-pathology also must be excluded from a critical essay on *The Tempest*.

As has been pointed out, if any character is hallucinated, this must be Prospero. Assuming that, as a magician, he is successful in projecting his hallucinations on the world, we are left with the problem why he should permit, or perhaps prefer, that world to contain a creature as repugnant to himself as Caliban, an action so generally repugnant as the plot of Antonio and Sebastian against Alonso. The only way to solve a problem of that kind would be to unveil, or rather to invent, the conflicts raging in Prospero's 'unconscious'. And however proper to a scientific tractate, that would be disedifying in a critical work. If on the other hand Prospero fails as a magician, the failure is skilfully hidden both from himself and from the audience: a number of the characters must therefore have banded themselves together to that end. But that is beyond all conceivable absurdity; and for the moment there is nothing left for us to do but to treat the activities of Ariel and of his fellow spirits with exactly the same seriousness, the same respect, as we do those of any other character. That is, we must assume that the spirits produce something, although we now know that they themselves are nothing. And with that not very satisfactory conclusion our discussion must I am afraid be broken off.

VI. FERDINAND AND MIRANDA

If our survey of the spirits has had a somewhat dizzying effect – 'Prithee do not turn me about', begs Stephano of Trinculo, 'my stomach is not constant' (II. ii. 118) – let us steady ourselves by attending for a while to characters who, beyond any possibility of doubt, are something, and that something flesh and blood. I mean Ferdinand and Miranda.

There is an obvious and possibly illuminating contrast between each of them and the corresponding character in Eslava's *novela*. Whereas Ferdinand is not approved of as a husband until he has successfully undergone a test, Valentinian's worthiness is assumed from the first. Whereas Miranda is surprised at the appearance before her of a young man suitable as her husband, Seraphina asks that one should be brought.

The test undergone by Ferdinand is a carrying of logs, taken over, it is often supposed, from *Die Schoene Sidea*. At the risk of digressing (but here almost certainly we have an instance of

Ayrer's darkness allowing the light of Shakespeare to shine more clearly) I think it perhaps not uninteresting to remark that *Die Schoene Sidea* contains no test of any kind. In that play, log-carrying is imposed on a captive prince merely as a vindictive, or at any rate as a retributive punishment. His father has made successful war on the father of the princess, driving the two latter into exile: therefore when the prince is captured he is condemned to hard and humiliating labour, and the princess awarded the satisfaction of acting as his taskmistress. Only as she is doing so, does the thought of a marriage occur to her or to anyone: as daughter of an exiled king, she reflects, her future is hardly likely to be as pleasant as that of a wife, whose princely husband is safely established in his court. So she proposes a bargain: she will free the prince from his task, if he on his side will take her home and marry her. Without difficulty he agrees; just as, having reached home without the princess, he has no difficulty in forgetting the bargain. But she succeeds in tracking him down just in time to prevent him from marrying another woman. He is full of apologies, and puts the position of wife once more at the princess's disposal.

In Ayrer, it will be seen, the log-carrying of the prince and his marriage to the princess are connected by a chain of accidents which might be broken anywhere, and which towards the end comes near to being so. There is no necessity that such a marriage should have been preceded by a log-carrying, nor even any probability that it was; conversely, the log-carrying is such that neither necessarily nor probably does it precede a marriage. In Shakespeare, on the other hand, the two are so intimately bound together that, it is hardly too much to say, the one becomes an aspect of the other, or functions as a symbol of it.

As has been pointed out in the previous section, Ferdinand's wooing begins with a courtly compliment: 'Most sure, the goddess...' (I. ii. 426). The next step is the offer, on conditions, of courtly splendours:

> O, if a virgin
> And your affection not gone forth, I'll make you
> The queen of Naples. (*ibid.* 452)

It ends with Miranda unconditionally assuming, not the privileges of sovereignty, but the duties of servitude:

> I am your wife, if you will marry me;
> If not, I'll die your maid. To be your fellow
> You may deny me, but I'll be your servant
> Whether you will or no –   (III. i. 83)

while on his side, Ferdinand claims the servitude for himself:

> My mistress, dearest,
> And I thus humble ever.

The change has come about through the log-carrying, which Miranda has witnessed, not in an official capacity, but stealthily. Authority does not command her to do so, charity constrains her. And charity works so strongly in her that, at the spectacle of Ferdinand's labours, she not only

> weeps...and says, such baseness
> Had never like executor,   (III. i. 12)

but offers to execute it herself. It would, she affirms, cost her less suffering than it does to Ferdinand:

> I should do it
> With much more ease, for my good will is to it,
> And yours it is against.   (*ibid.* 29)

But, replies Ferdinand, it causes him no suffering, or at any rate no balance of suffering: as imposed by her father, and as performed in her presence, it is a source rather of delight:

> The very instant that I saw you, did
> My heart fly to your service, there resides
> To make me slave to it, and for your sake
> Am I this patient log-man.   (*ibid.* 64)

And thus the idea is built up of a marriage which, in spite or rather because of the suffering it may occasion, shall be delightful. The idea is summed up in the final words of the wooing, when Ferdinand offers his hand

> with a heart as willing
> As bondage e'er of freedom.   (*ibid.* 88)

'Although I am entering on a bondage', is a primary implication; almost immediately overwhelmed however by an implication secondary in time but not in importance. The bondage in question is of itself such that no freedom, even as freedom, could be equally satisfying. Before the log-carrying begins, Ferdinand and Miranda have only changed eyes; when it is

over they have changed – that is, they have interchanged – their
selves. And they have done so the more readily because it has
been made clear to them that such an interchange, like all
sacrifice of the self, requires effort, implies pain.

The Virginia narratives, commentators on *The Tempest* have
pointed out, unanimously attribute the failure of the colony to
an unwillingness on the part of the colonists to accept the effort
and the pain implied even by partial self-sacrifice. Not so much
their idleness is to be condemned, according to the author of the
True Declaration, although this idleness, allowing every man to
'shark for his present booty', rendered him 'altogether careless
of succeeding penury'; not only the treasons as a consequence of
which 'unhallowed monsters...forsook the colony and exposed
their desolate brethren to extreme miseries': but rather the
temper which made idleness appear praiseworthy and treasons
permissible – 'every man overvaluing his own worth would be
a commander; every man underprizing another's value, scorned
to be commanded'. In the *True Reportory* William Strachey, who
also has idleness and treasons to lament, finds the same temper
to be responsible. 'The major part of the common sort' of
those wrecked upon the Bermudas, 'and perhaps some of the
better sort' too, conceived he says that design of 'ever inhabiting
there', and of violating in consequence their obligations to the
fleet already arrived in Virginia, to the London adventurers who
had fitted out the fleet, and to the King who had armed the fleet
with his authority. It was the prospect of freeing themselves
from the latter by which they were most strongly tempted, for
they imagined that, on the Bermudas, it would prove possible,
without 'wanting...or watching...or any threatening and use
of authority', to enjoy 'at ease and pleasure...a plenty of
victuals'.

For a particular illustration of this temper and its opposite,
Strachey has recourse to a task which involved the carrying of
logs. In order to escape from the Bermudas, it was necessary to
build vessels which should replace the *Sea Adventure*. But 'an
ill qualified parcel of people...were hardly drawn to it, as the
tortoise to the enchantment, as the proverb is'. Whereupon the
Governor, not content with issuing invitations and commands,
himself set the example of 'felling, carrying and sawing cedar,
fit for the carpenters' purpose'. By doing so he proved himself,

in Strachey's eyes, worthy of the office with which he had been entrusted: 'Sure it was happy for us, who had now...fallen, into the bottom of this misery, for we both had our Governor with us, and one solicitous and careful'.

Thus it would appear at least likely that Shakespeare found the log-carrying in Strachey, without consulting *Die Schoene Sidea*. In the latter it functions, as has been said, as a punishment only; in the former it is already a test and a proof of social fitness. And the likelihood is the greater, because the marriage of Ferdinand to Miranda, of which he proves himself worthy by a carrying of logs, functions not only as a marriage but as a symbol of all social institutions and of society itself. *The Tempest* has an abundance of characters – Ariel, Caliban, Stephano, Antonio and Sebastian – who are either reluctant to offer service or who refuse it. They do so of course with greater or with less excuse: *The Tempest* does not fail to emphasize the duties of governors towards the governed. But its doing so is only another reason for emphasizing the duty of the governed as such. That it does both is another instance of what, in the opening section of this essay, was called its realism: it is filled with the strains and stresses of everyday life, without which social institutions would be inconceivable. Society as such demands service and sacrifice.

Once more Eslava shows himself to be comparatively empty of such stresses. So far from functioning as a symbol of anything, the marriage of Seraphina and Valentinian hardly functions as itself: for the *novela* tells us as little of it as would an *avis de faire part*, received from total strangers.

But it is perhaps in Shakespeare's and Eslava's dealings with the princess in each of their stories that this difference comes out most clearly. There would seem to be little danger that Seraphina's request for a husband should appear immodest, as she thinks fit to regret: rather it is the sort of request which calls neither for the epithet 'immodest' nor for that of 'modest', but merely for the epithet 'proper'. It is proper as a proposition in Euclid is so. And as the latter owes its enunciation to the exigencies of points that have no length, lines that have no breadth, surfaces that have no body: so Seraphina's request is due to nubility – the idea of nubility, that is, bare of any of the concomitants with which alone it can emerge into reality.

Eslava does indeed inform the reader that, before her banishment from the upper world, Seraphina was surrounded by suitors. But he does no more than inform, and informs of no more: the reader is required to imagine for himself the feelings which these suitors may have aroused within her. But the reader hesitates to do so, for the idea of nubility, any more than a point, a line or a surface, is not capable of feeling.

In so far as Miranda can be associated with the idea, that is because Shakespeare shows the process of its entering her mind, and there providing itself with concomitants of such number and variety as itself to become real, and to render the mind yet more so. For such an undertaking, Shakespeare might seem to be placed at a disadvantage by the isolation of Miranda who, until Ferdinand, has met no one who might stir up thoughts of marriage; nor does she, until the marriage is concluded, meet anyone who might act as Ferdinand's rival. As usual, Shakespeare converts an absence of opportunities into a freedom from distractions. He concentrates his whole attention on the process and, dealing justly with each of its stages and aspects, deals only the more justly with the whole which they prepare or constitute.

The first impulse to the process is desire. This Shakespeare catches in its nascent state, when as yet neither selfish nor unselfish. 'Lord, how it looks about!' (I. ii. 415) cries Miranda on her first sight of Ferdinand, eagerly identifying the life which is within him with her own. But that the two are separate and distinct is indicated by Ferdinand's form, towards which in consequence she might be expected to conceive a degree of resentment. As yet however she lies under the notion of his being a spirit and so, ungrudgingly if resignedly, she can allow that the form is 'brave'. When Prospero proceeds to undeceive her, there is nothing for her left to do but to recognize the form as divine: as having authority over her, that is, for an authority that we accept is in some way identified with us, however great the distance to which at the same time it may be removed. At this moment, Ferdinand catches sight of her. In him desire has long since passed out of its nascent state, and therefore he begins with a compliment. Unaware of the possible worthlessness of compliments, Miranda is abashed; and modesty, if it demands that she should acknowledge herself a maid, also forbids that she should accept the appellation of 'wonder'. But soon her self-confidence is in a measure restored, for it becomes apparent that, however divine, the being to whom she has conceded authority suffers from misfortune. As he thinks, he has lost his father. 'Alack, for mercy!' (*ibid.* 441) Miranda exclaims. A few minutes more, and further misfortune seems to threaten Ferdinand, this time at the hands of her own father. She develops cóurage for his defence:

> There's nothing ill can dwell in such a house. (*ibid.* 463)

From this point onwards, she remains torn between two affections, both strong within her: on the one hand she would comfort Ferdinand, on the other placate her father. In the latter hope, at any rate, she is unsuccessful and Prospero – it springs from something curiously insensitive or curiously incomprehensible within him, which we shall need to notice later – permits himself to punish her presumption with a taunt:

> Thou think'st there is no more such shapes as he,
> Having seen but him and Caliban! foolish wench!
> To th'most of men this is a Caliban,
> And they to him are angels. (*ibid.* 483)

Hitherto she has been meekly dependent, now she is stung to a defiance of him. And the irony into which good manners bid her compress the defiance only makes it the sharper:

> My affections
> Are then most humble; I have no ambition
> To see a goodlier man. (*ibid.* 487)

Since experience has taught her nothing of the goodliness possible to men, she reveals herself as stung to rashness as well. But the test which Prospero imposes on Ferdinand gives her time to inquire of herself, not only whether she wishes to be a wife – that aspect of the dialogue has been dealt with already – but whether it is in truth Ferdinand whose wife she wishes to be. The answer being positive, rashness becomes fortitude; and fortitude, rather than putting modesty to flight as an enemy, bids it, as an ally, to stay. And so swearing by her modesty, Miranda can make the frank declaration to Ferdinand:

> I would not wish
> Any companion in the world but you,

> Nor can imagination form a shape
> Besides yourself, to like of. (III. i. 54)

He replies with words of a similar intent, and Miranda weeps; condemning herself while she does, for her heart is glad. And yet of course she is right to weep, since the source of her gladness is at the same time the source of her tears. I weep, she says,

> At mine unworthiness, that dare not offer
> What I desire to give; and much less take
> What I shall die to want. (III. i. 77)

By the interchange of selves, which has now been accomplished, what normally appear the most incompatible things have become reconciled: not only gladness and tears, but modesty and pride, gratitude and generosity, servitude and sovereignty, protectiveness and worship. But the most remarkable reconciliation of all is that between the full development of desire, which demanding an interchange of selves presupposes a distinction between them, with its own nascent vigour, for which no such distinction can exist. That this vigour survives is shown, simply yet effectively, by Miranda's choice of the word 'die'.

It is useless to spend more words on this passage; my fear is that I have spent – and wasted – far too many. I have risked the reproach of doing so in the hope of suggesting, however faintly, that the passage is indebted for its beauty to the elements of nature or reality which it contains – elements the presence of which in Shakespeare is glaringly illuminated by their absence from Eslava.

I return for a moment to the part played by Prospero in shielding Miranda from the harm which, as a consequence of her own rashness, she might inflict upon herself. In the case of a young woman growing up under normal conditions, this part would in large measure be played by society: by its religious and civil institutions, and by its conventions. By precept and example, such a young woman would be taught that the indications of desire are neither immediately nor inevitably to be trusted. But Miranda has grown up in solitude, and therefore Prospero must function, not only as father but also as society on her behalf.

And he does so too in shielding her from the harm which, because of the same rashness, she might suffer at the hands of others. As has been remarked, it is impossible that, in her inexperience, she should realize how little the compliments of others need have the significance of her own; how deeply a young man, when he acclaims her as perfect and peerless, may be deceiving her – and even himself. For desire can blind to honesty as to any other virtue. And therefore Prospero, in imposing the test, is acting not only on Miranda's behalf, but also on Ferdinand's own. Not only is the latter required to prove his sincerity; he is given the opportunity to inquire into it.

For of course his sincerity can never be proved with certainty; not at any rate – as Solon said of happiness – [?until] he is dead. As desire may blind to the virtues, so it may dull to physical pain. It is conceivable that, once relieved of the weight of his logs, Ferdinand should rush all the more impetuously into a lustful orgy. This Prospero fully understands, and hence his thrice repeated warning against lust; a warning which, as has been noted already, he does not consider superfluous although Ferdinand has satisfactorily performed the test.

As regards his children, in sum, Prospero shows possession of both an extraordinary breadth and an extraordinary closeness of understanding; his attempt to safeguard their future is wise and scrupulous to an equally extraordinary degree. It is the more surprising that, as regards Caliban, he should show an understanding apparently so deficient. That Caliban and Ferdinand are associated in his mind, and not only by contrast, is revealed by his taunt to Miranda; in the spectator's mind they are associated in that, but also in other ways. For both serve Prospero as slaves and, at Prospero's bidding, each in turn enters upon an empty stage bearing a log. Whatever excuse it is either necessary or possible to provide for Caliban's yielding to desire, Ferdinand would seem to provide. And perhaps even Miranda; she and Caliban have the vigour of desire in common, and the charm of her 'I shall die to want' is heard, however faintly, through Caliban's triumphant guffaw at the thought of his peopling the isle (I. ii. 351). Can it be that Prospero, functioning partly as society towards Ferdinand and Miranda, towards Caliban functions wholly as such? For society neither has nor can have mercy on those who ignore the rules by which it subsists. It may however be doubted whether Caliban has in fact done anything of the kind: Prospero's undertaking towards him, at any rate, would seem to have been that of educating him, not within, but for society. But about Prospero there are a number of things which as yet we do not understand. It will be as well to submit him to the sort of examination to which we have submitted others.

VII. PROSPERO

Applying a method which has I hope shown itself not wholly useless, I compare Prospero to Dardanus and note, first of all, a difference between the powers assigned to each. Those of Dardanus appear without limit, Prospero's by contrast severely limited.

The former are at any rate sufficiently nearly limitless for Dardanus to be a source of embarrassment to Eslava. Not only has a hero who can do everything nothing further to do, since he has done it already: he communicates a similar torpor to all who come into contact with him. If they are his friends, he has already gratified their desires; if his enemies, their desires have been thwarted without their being able to stir a limb. And so, in order to allow of someone doing something in his *novela*, Eslava must either isolate Dardanus, or deprive him, if only temporarily, of his powers.

Out of abundant caution, he does both. Dardanus is bound by an oath never to employ his magic either in defiance of the law of God, or to the prejudice of his neighbour. And that, says Eslava, is the reason why he failed to rout Nicephorus, although it would have been very easy for him to do so. But as the divine law is not defied by self-defence, nor a neighbour prejudiced when restrained from crime, the logic is not pellucid. It is, I am afraid, typical of Eslava.

Exiled from Bulgaria by Nicephorus, by a second oath Dardanus exiles himself from the earth. As in doing so he rids himself of all possible neighbours, the exercise of his powers may be restored to him. The first and almost the only use to which he puts them sufficiently illustrates their extent, for it is nothing less than the creation of an earthly paradise. In spite of Renaissance furnishings such as carved vases, Corinthian capitals, Pharsalian friezes and the like, the submarine palace which Dardanus evokes is but a late example of the earthly paradises imagined by mediaeval writers. These blended pagan fantasies with the visions of St John: similarly, the trees adorning the gardens where Dardanus, if he wished, might enjoy a pagan recreation are offshoots from the Tree of Life, the brooks by which the gardens are watered flow from the Fountain of Life, the jewels studding its doors and roofs – the pearls, the emeralds, the jacinths, the agates and the sapphires – are those which sparkle in the Apocalypse. Moreover, Dardanus is the typical guardian of a paradise, above all by his inactivity. Having at a single stroke put himself into possession of all things desirable, he cannot be moved to take a second. Not, at least, by anything within himself. If he sets out to seek Valentinian, it must be at Seraphina's request; if he rises to rebuke Julian, it is to oblige Neptune. Nor, though Julian is his enemy, does he either launch him on the sea or overwhelm him with a storm; if he foretells the death of Julian, he neither raises a wand nor utters a syllable to hasten that death. And his children succeed Julian on the throne without his exerting himself more than to procure them a comfortable journey home. If paternal affection somewhat inconsistently rouses him to share the journey, he quietens it while still at a safe distance from the shore; at a distance, that is, where the paradise may continue to cling around him.

By contrast with Dardanus who, because he can do everything, needs do nothing, Prospero is obliged to plan and to labour if he would do anything; nor is it inevitable even then that he should succeed. As Caliban knows, he is 'but a sot' without his book – perhaps also, we should add, without his robe and his wand. Presumably because these did not lie within his reach, he had no hope of resisting the Neopolitan occupation of Milan. Nor, though they were slipped into his boat, did he show himself capable of either setting or keeping a course. The 'rotten carcass of a butt' (I. ii. 146), it would seem provided neither the room nor the stability essential for conjuring. That became possible only after 'Providence divine' had landed him on the island. Even so, the spells he was able to work were of no more than a restricted potency: if he has no difficulty in mastering the island and its inhabitants, with regard to other regions and those who move there he remains as powerless as before. He cannot, for example, set out like Dardanus and seek a son-in-law; rather he must wait until 'bountiful Fortune' blows or washes one into his neighbourhood. In the same vessel, she brings the enemies who expelled Prospero from Milan. That he successfully exploits the opportunity thus provided, every reader knows.

But, I repeat, it was not inevitable that he should do so. Continually throughout the play he utters exclamations of delight: 'All goes on...as my soul prompts it', 'my charms crack not' – and this it would not be reasonable for him to do, were the delight not accompanied and at least in part occasioned by surprise. Continually he thanks the spirits for 'doing well' or 'bravely performing' the tasks which he has appointed: all of which implies that their doing so is not a matter of course. Once indeed their readiness and efficiency in service so violently surprises Prospero that he further shortens the already shortened period during which Ariel is bound to obey him; and this, although a few minutes earlier he has considered Ariel to deserve a chiding.

As a magician then he is weaker than Dardanus; but also – and here I come to a second difference between the two – he is more ambitious. His ambition is such that it leads him to attempt a task for which not even the powers of Dardanus would have been sufficient, nor indeed any, short of those of God Himself. For the task is the ordering of consciences other than Prospero's own. Not content with a public and external condemnation such as compels Alonso and Antonio to restore his dukedom, he endeavours that each of these shall, in his own interior, condemn himself. Only 'heart's sorrow' upon their part will, he insists, earn his forgiveness. And at times he talks as if the imparting of this forgiveness were of more importance to him than his return to Milan.

By some I know it is maintained that Prospero himself is divine or quasi-divine. Like other dukes or political heads in Shakespeare, it is said, he is invested not only with civil but with religious authority; and his charge is to procure not only the temporal but the eternal welfare of his fellows. What may be the case of other dukes I do not know: as far as Prospero is concerned, it seems to me that the mass, if not indeed the whole of the evidence weighs against this opinion.

Passages in its support are quoted from the speech in the course of which Ariel describes himself as a 'minister of fate'

(III. iii. 60). If this speech can be taken at its face value, it must of course be admitted to provide solid, if not indestructible, support. For into the astonished ears of Alonso, Antonio and Sebastian, Ariel expounds the workings of destiny; to which if they do not submit they will, he foretells, be subjected to a merciless persecution from 'the powers'. These are the powers that govern the earth, the air and the sea. If Ariel, who is Prospero's minister, is in truth their minister also, then it would seem that Prospero is to be ranged no lower than they; very possibly, he is to be ranged above them.

However, the speech is Ariel's in delivery only. From the first word to the last it is prompted by Prospero, who stands over Ariel during the delivery and, at the end, congratulates him on having 'bated' nothing of what he was instructed to say. Though it need not follow that the speech is false, parts of it would seem to fall in fact not very far short of falsehood. 'Destiny', says Ariel, hath caused 'the never-surfeited sea... to belch up you'; 'the powers', he continues, have

> Incens'd the seas and shores, yea, all the creatures
> Against your peace.   (*ibid.* 74)

If Prospero is to be numbered among the powers or identified with destiny, this is strictly true; yet even so, there would seem to be a certain disingenuousness in not mentioning him by name, since he is to draw profit from the belching and the incensing. This I think is the root of the dissatisfaction which the speech arouses or should arouse; while offering itself as independent testimony to Prospero's deserts, it is something quite different. It is no more than Prospero's testimony on his own behalf. As such, it needs to be carefully examined before it can be admitted.

The briefest examination serves I think to render its admissibility more than doubtful. For it does not stand alone, so much as point the moral of a spectacle or interlude to which Prospero himself refers in terms hardly of respect but rather of irony, if not indeed of contempt. During the interlude the appetites of Alonso, Antonio and Sebastian are whetted by the sight of a banquet; then these appetites are rebuked by the banquet's being snatched away. When all is over, Prospero congratulates Ariel, not only on the delivery of a speech, but on the performance of a part.

> Bravely the figure of this harpy hast thou
> Perform'd, my Ariel: a grace it had, devouring.
>
> (*ibid.* 83)

'You looked as if you were about to gobble the banquet up: you, who of all creatures are the least capable of doing so', would seem to be the implication. Ariel's fellow-spirits also are congratulated on the 'good life and observation strange' – on the verisimilitude and scrupulous care, that is – of their performance. Apparently these surpassed expectation, were they in truth ministers of fate, as Ariel's speech asserts them to be. Nor would it be necessary for them to take any care in the performance of a part which was native to them. Strictly speaking of course it could not be called a part, nor could they be said to perform it. If these considerations seem fairly conclusive, another yet more so is brought by the next scene in which Prospero, grouping the interlude along with the masque of Ceres, describes the latter as a 'vanity' and both of them as 'tricks'. Tricks in the language of Jacobean times need not be trivial, as in that of today: at all periods of the language however it is invariably something, the essence of which is to deceive. As Ferdinand finds to his dismay, the masque deceives for no other purpose than to amuse. The purpose of the interlude may be weightier, but not necessarily, on that account, more praiseworthy. Nor would it seem to be so: for the interlude is intended to encourage Alonso, Antonio and Sebastian in the misapprehension to which, as newcomers to the island, they are liable – the misapprehension, namely, that the spirits are supernatural and their doings, in consequence, of supernatural authority.

Other arguments for the exaltation of Prospero are sought in his relations with Sycorax. It is assumed that, because these two are opposed on certain matters – as, for example, the question of the sovereignty of the island – they are opposed on all. And therefore, because Sycorax, as described by Prospero, was 'a foul witch', 'a damn'd witch', a witch condemned

> For mischiefs manifold, and sorceries terrible
> To enter human hearing, (I. ii. 264)

Prospero himself must be noble, blessed, the author of benefits too miraculous to issue from a human brain. Here the mistake of admitting Prospero's evidence on his own dehalf is not only repeated, but aggravated by neglect of his own admission that, on one occasion at least, Sycorax 'did' something such as to render her execution unthinkable. But any possible weakness in the premisses shrinks into insignificance beside the faultiness of the logic of this argument. Other possibilities exist than that Prospero and Sycorax are wholly dissimilar or wholly alike. The latter they cannot be, if only because Prospero is a Christian, while Sycorax believed in Setebos. But while dissimilar in some respects, they may be alike in others. A rapid scrutiny reveals I think both that they are, and that the respects are numerous in which they are alike.

If, in his first greeting to Prospero and Miranda, Caliban appears undutifully to admit that his mother was wicked –

> As wicked dew as e'er my mother brush'd
> With raven's feather from unwholesome fen
> Drop on you both – (I. ii. 322)

it should be noticed that he takes over this adjective from the summons which Prospero has just addressed to himself:

> Thou poisonous slave, got by the devil himself
> Upon thy wicked dam, come forth.

And from Ariel we know that, no less than Sycorax, Prospero makes use of dew. Whether wicked in itself or not, this dew is gathered at midnight, which is a wicked time, and fetched from the 'still-vex'd Bermoothes', reprobated in nautical tradition as a wicked place. The adjective 'still-vex'd', which might be compared with Sir Walter Raleigh's 'hellish', shows Shakespeare as, in this passage at least, adhering to the tradition. Then as we have seen, Prospero displays no reluctance, but rather an eagerness that is none too easily explicable, in assuming the role of Medea, ancestress of all the Sycoraxes known to literature. Nor does he, in the short moment during which he indulges in playing the role, appear concerned to mitigate its horrors. Or perhaps rather: if at first he makes an attempt at mitigation, his rapid failure to do so throws the horrors into greater prominence. From elves who sport in the daylight, he allows his attention to be drawn by those who, under the dim moon, sour the grass, or who, at black midnight, tend the mushrooms; a third kind of elves he describes as 'rejoicing' in the curfew – in the sound, that is, that lets loose not good but evil spirits upon

the earth. The destructive and unsavoury character of such feats
of his own as Prospero chooses to recite has already been dealt
with.

As Sycorax needed the help of 'more potent ministers' in
order to imprison Ariel, while Prospero unaided can set Ariel
free, it would seem that he is her superior in power. He cannot
however be very greatly her superior, for if he can raise a storm,
she
> could control the moon, make ebbs and flows,
> And deal in her command without her power.

And this same episode of Ariel's imprisonment shows Prospero
as, at least on one occasion, the inferior of Sycorax in temper. A
refusal of obedience she punished with the torture of a cloven
pine; for a mere murmur of discontent, he threatens the torture
of a riven oak. Presumably the latter is the more severe; yet it
is inflicted for the slighter offence.

Of course, if the commands of Sycorax were in themselves
wicked – 'earthy and abhorr'd', as Prospero claims – then the
slightest punishment for resistance to them was unjust. And
if on the other hand Prospero is divine to any degree, then the
slightest resistance to any such commands as he may issue is
deserving of the severest punishment that can be imagined. For
reasons which I hope will appear justified, towards the end of
this essay if not before, I am not concerned to argue against the
former hypothesis. The second I am in process of arguing
against. Perhaps I have already made it seem unlikely; two
further pieces of evidence remain which should, I think, render
it impossible.

The first is, not so much the fact that Prospero abjures his
magic, as the way in which he thinks fit to do so. Immediately
after recital of the destructive and unsavoury feats of which it
has made him capable, he deplores it, not inappropriately it
would seem, as 'rough'; and then he says,

> I'll break my staff,
> Bury it certain fathoms in the earth,
> And deeper than did ever plummet sound
> I'll drown my book. (V. i. 54)

Not only, that is, will he nevermore make use of them himself;
he will take such measures as effectively prevent any use of them
by anybody.

A number of commentators, it is true, expound this abjuration in quite a different way. They appeal to the principles of the occultist philosophy, according to which, it appears, a white or blameless magic moulds the soul of its practitioner into a 'rough' likeness of the Divinity. But if, they go on to explain, the practitioner desires the likeness to be perfect, he must abandon magic entirely; the final stage towards deiformity being traversable with the aid of prayer alone. And obviously, to their eyes, Prospero is making preparations to devote himself to a life of prayer.

I find it difficult to believe that this is obvious to the normal reader of *The Tempest*. The highly metaphorical sense which these commentators give to the adjective 'rough' seems somewhat wilful, when the context so loudly calls for the meaning more nearly literal. Then again, though intending to praise Prospero, they place his burying of the staff and his drowning of the book in an invidious light. If at the stage of perfection which he has reached these instruments can be of no further use to him, they might be valuable to others, in raising them to that stage. Nor would the play seem to contain any clear evidence that Prospero envisages prayer as his sole or even his main occupation in the future. He does indeed announce that, after retirement to Milan,

> Every third thought shall be my grave. (V. i. 313)

But as long ago as the opening dialogue with Miranda he made evident his regret at the inefficiency of which, in the discharge of his duties as prince, he had been guilty; the readiness with which, in the last scene, he not only dons ducal attire but holds something like a ducal levee strongly suggests a determination that the guilt shall not be prolonged.

Accordingly, it is not so much to anything in the play proper to which these commentators appeal, as to the Epilogue. The Folio directs that this shall be 'spoken by Prospero', and it contains the lines:

> Now I want
> Spirits to enforce, art to enchant,
> And my ending is despair
> Unless I be reliev'd by prayer.

This resort to the Epilogue would seem to be a desperate measure, likely not so much to strengthen as to expose the weakness of the opinion in support of which it is made. For the Epilogue is not part of *The Tempest*, as it never is of any Shakespearean play: except perhaps *Henry V*, where the epilogue is not properly speaking such, but rather a final chorus. Nor does the direction in the Folio imply more than that the Epilogue to *The Tempest* is spoken by the actor who takes the part of Prospero. All other actors have left the stage; the play is now over; and he remains behind, speaking henceforward not in Prospero's person but his own. The prayer on which he relies for relief is addressed, not to the Deity, but to the audience; the despair which he describes himself as fearing may be damnation, but only a theatrical one; and the relief for which he hopes is nothing future and spiritual, but the immediate and material benefit of applause. As has been the custom of actors since the earliest days of their profession, he is begging that he and his fellows shall be clapped. Lest the request should weary by its jejuneness, he freshens it by using Prospero's situation as a metaphor of his own. This however he finds impossible without misrepresenting the former, slightly but nevertheless significantly; and of itself, this misrepresentation should I think forbid any quoting of the Epilogue as evidence of what happens within the play. Before granting Ariel his freedom, Prospero took the precaution of requiring 'auspicious gales' for the ship bound back for Naples. But the Epilogue shows him as anxiously uncertain whether or not a gale will be provided. And of course it must do so. An actor supplicating the audience for the breath of its favour cannot at the same time betray a confidence that the favour either has been or will be granted.

I come then to the last piece of evidence that Prospero, though engaging on a task peculiarly divine, has nothing of the divine about him. The evidence, which seems to me irrefutable, is that he fails in the task, as what is divine can never do. Or to put the matter more precisely: though a man may refuse to repent, God, who has the power of reading consciences, is aware of this refusal, which thereby enters into His ordering; Prospero on the other hand misreads three out of the four consciences with which he presumes to meddle. What he imagines to be his ordering of them is in consequence a mere mockery of the reality. As for the fourth conscience, which he reads aright, very possibly its state would have been what it is even if he had not meddled; so that neither in this case is the ordering his own.

The fourth conscience belongs to Alonso, one of whose speeches has already been referred to as 'somewhat Lear-like'. It is that with which, on being restored to his senses, he greets Prospero:

> Whether thou be'st he or no,
> Or some enchanted trifle to abuse me,
> As late I have been, I not know, thy pulse
> Beats, as of flesh and blood; and, since I saw thee,
> Th'affliction of my mind amends, with which,
> I fear, a madness held me. (V. i. 111)

The speech of Lear's which it recalls is of course that in which he too regains mastery of himself:

> Pray do not mock me:
> I am a very foolish fond old man,
> Fourscore and upward, not an hour more, nor less;
> And to deal plainly,
> I fear I am not in my perfect mind.
> Methinks I should know you. (*King Lear*, IV. vii. 59f)

In so far as there is any resemblance between the speeches, between the persons who utter them and between the situations in which these persons find themselves, then Prospero may have a claim to be considered God-like. For the resipiscence of Lear is due to no human agency. The comparison has however only to be stated for Alonso and Prospero to reveal for how little they are able to sustain it. The former has none of the fantastic confidence, the ruthless egoism of Lear. In consequence, if he is made to suffer a storm and, as he thinks, the loss of a son, he is spared any ingratitude on the son's part; instead of the chatter of the Fool and Edgar, he is required to put up with that of Gonzalo; instead of Gloster's 'bleeding rings', he is confronted with harpies and 'strange shapes'. Yet not even these are necessary for his conscience to be troubled. He gives unmistakable signs for its being so from his first entrance upon the stage. For the augmenting of the trouble up to the point at which, finding it unbearable, Alonso resolves to repent and so be rid of it, Prospero's gimcrackery may perhaps deserve a portion of credit; hardly more, however, than the fly deserves for the dust raised by a wheel. At least it would seem so when the incapacity is taken into account, which Prospero manifests in his dealing with other consciences.

Of this, Caliban provides the most obvious instance. From the beginning to the ending of the play Prospero condemns Caliban as beyond hope of redemption:

> Abhorred slave,
> Which any print of goodness will not take,
> Being capable of all ill – [1]   (I. ii. 352)

This is one of Prospero's first accounts of him;

> A devil, a born devil, on whose nature
> Nurture can never stick; on whom my pains,
> Humanly taken, all, all lost, quite lost –   (IV. i. 188)

this is one of the last. At the close of the play, Caliban himself gives all of them the lie. For he expresses, soberly but none the less convincingly, a determination to 'be wise hereafter, And seek for grace'. Prospero's two other failures are Antonio and Sebastian, whom for a long time he has classed along with Caliban as 'devils'. At a point within the last scene, and for no apparent reason whatever, he begins to class them with those who are capable of repentance and who have repented. Unlike Caliban, they have manifested no intention of amending their lives; rather the sole use they have made of their restored senses has been, irrelevantly to their situation as might men in a dream, to make fun of Caliban and the clowns. Prospero nevertheless has no hesitation in including them along with Alonso in the absolution which, as he imagines, he is imparting on the ground of a change of heart alone:

> they being penitent
> The sole drift of my purpose doth extend
> Not a frown further.   (V. i. 28)

His failure with Antonio and Sebastian is indeed remarkable, not so much for being what it is, as for what seems his obvious determination, not only in default but in spite of the evidence, to consider it as a success. This determination is already manifest before Sebastian or Antonio or any of the courtiers has recovered the power of speech. For Prospero, reproving the crime of his own and Miranda's expulsion from Milan, claims

> Thou art pinch'd for't now, Sebastian.   (V. i. 75)

---

[1] As noted earlier, this speech is attributed to Miranda in the Folio and in the New Cambridge Shakespeare. (E. M. W.)

As these pinches are not of the kind inflicted by the dogs on Stephano and Trinculo, but such as only a man's own thoughts can inflict – and a few lines later, Prospero himself describes them as 'inward' – he can as yet have no warrant for this claim. Or if, from the movements of Sebastian's body, it is apparent that he is being inwardly pinched in some way, only the movements of Sebastian's tongue, such as have not yet been possible, could inform whether these are pinches of remorse, inspired by the wickedness of an act, or pinches of regret, inspired by the failure of that act to secure the benefits which were hoped from it. And when Sebastian does at last move his tongue, it is to regret and not remorse, and to the rage consequent upon regret, that he gives utterance. He shows that, as far as it is possible for a human being to judge, his spiritual state continues the same as it was after the show of harpies: which he mistook as a display not (as Alonso did) of the good supernatural powers, and as such intended for his salvation, but of the supernatural which works for evil, and therefore intended solely to thwart him. Similarly, when Prospero hints that accusations additional to those of the harpy might be published against him, his first and his only thought is for the devil. 'The devil speaks in him!' (*ibid.* 129) he whispers to Antonio. The suggestion is so inappropriate to, or rather incompatible with, the state of grace which Prospero flatters himself he is restoring that for a moment even he is disconcerted. But only for a moment: having uttered a 'No!', but finding it impossible because unpleasant to advance down the path into which it leads, he returns – 'gaily' it might almost be said; certainly glibly – to the path which from the first he was bent upon pursuing. He repeats the grant of absolution for the 'rankest faults' of Antonio and, by implication, of the man who whispered to him.

This is an almost, if not quite, pathetic exhibition of gullibility such as is difficult to explain. The only explanation which suggests itself is perhaps that of its resting upon an equally pathetic vanity: experience shall not separate Prospero from the satisfaction he has promised himself in the performance of a divine role. In its turn, such a vanity must rest upon a grossness, a lack of fineness in the perception of what is due from himself, both to the Divine and to others. Prospero forgets, if he ever was aware, that if it is a divine privilege to forgive upon repentance, the human being is bound by the duty of forgiving unconditionally.

Lack of fineness is however what Prospero with frequency betrays. Take for example his dealings with Gonzalo: an amiable creature, of course, but one whose amiability, since it entails an attempt to be all things at all times to all men, is to say the least exaggerated. It is not only on the island that he would plant a commonwealth, providing all the advantages of government with none of the unpleasantness of governing or being governed: he seeks [one] already planted, and everywhere. When therefore he has accepted from Antonio mastership of the design for setting Prospero and Miranda adrift, he slips into the boat

Rich garments, linens, stuffs and necessaries – (I. ii. 164)

but nevertheless he returns to Antonio's service. The latter allows, because unaware of, this manifestation of a loyalty so curiously comprehensive as to embrace its opposite: of the loyalty itself however he is aware, and so he knows that, if Alonso is successfully got rid of, then Gonzalo must be got rid of too. For deprived of any other means of serving Alonso, Gonzalo will seize upon words for the purpose: he will 'upbraid our course' – how he will upbraid! cramming words into the ears, against all stomach of the sense. In time he might be persuaded to cease, if only Antonio disposed of the time (as he would not) and of the energy for persuading. Gonzalo could be led from persistent reproach to persistent praising as easily as Antonio leads from belief in a humming (the humming of Ariel) to belief in a noise similar to that made by 'bulls, or rather lions', and finally to a belief into the existence of the beasts themselves. In the same way, when Sebastian has compared the 'strange shapes' bringing in the banquet to the phoenix and the unicorn, and when Antonio has outbid Sebastian by comparing them to whatever is told by travellers and wants credit, Gonzalo finds himself drawn to outbid them both. Though Antonio's vagueness somewhat cruelly foils him, he does what he can with talk of 'mountaineers Dewlapp'd like bulls' and 'men Whose heads stand in their breasts'. In his own eyes at any rate he is a success; and the resultant exhilaration leads him to join the hitherto reluctant Alonso to taste the banquet. In quite the same way, it might be suggested, Polonius is led from seeing a cloud to seeing a camel, from a camel to a weasel and from weasel to a whale: Polonius of whom Hamlet's description, 'Thou wretched, rash, intruding fool' undoubtedly is harsh, but to whom the Queen's description 'good old man' does quite adequate justice, if not more than justice. As for Prospero's descriptions of Gonzalo, 'a loyal sir To him thou follow'st', an aged man 'whose honour cannot be measured or confined', above all 'Holy Gonzalo, honourable man': these are possible only to one whose perception, either temporarily or permanently, is blunted. In so far as Gonzalo seeks to do good to everybody, his doing good to somebody is inevitable; in so far as he lacks all conception of an opposition between goods, he will not 'take suggestion as a cat laps milk' in order to secure a particular good of his own: but all this is mere amiability, facilitated by fatuity – it is hardly honour, it is certainly not holiness, because it is contrary to plain sense.

With Ferdinand also Prospero's dealings are, in some respects, very far from fine. 'In some respects': the phrase is a reminder how, in this play as in all of Shakespeare's, the complexity and the subtlety of the text forbids almost any qualification of it which, however just, is not at the same time a denial of justice. However, the wisdom and charity with and for which Prospero imposes the test on Ferdinand has already been treated of: the opportunity, indeed the necessity is all the greater for treating of a lack of charity by which that imposition is accompanied. Not only does Prospero assert what he knows to be falsehoods about Ferdinand's overt acts:

> Thou dost here usurp
> The name thou ow'st not, and hast put thyself
> Upon this island as a spy, to win it
> From me, the lord on't –   (I. ii. 457)

he goes on to make equally unscrupulous assertions about Ferdinand's interior. Having reduced him to immobility by means of spells, he both attributes the immobility to an uneasy conscience and seizes upon that conscience as matter for a taunt:

> Put thy sword up, traitor,
> Who mak'st a show but dar'st not strike: thy conscience
> Is so possess'd with guilt.   (*ibid.* 474)

It is possible, though hardly likely, that the falsehoods are necessary for the development of the action; for the taunt any similar excuse would seem to be out of the question. If Prospero's vanity is responsible, then it is indeed great: for it blinds him, not only to the actions of others, not only to his own motives, but to a deliberate action of his own, performed but a moment ago. In any case, he has offered one of those outrageous and superfluous insults which incline to the belief that, even before hearing the consolatory speech which follows on the masque, Ferdinand has already learnt something of the expediency of forgetting.

Towards Miranda, it will be remembered, Prospero indulged himself in a similarly unjustifiable taunt. It is however in his dealing with Caliban that his lack of fineness comes into greatest prominence. Once again therefore I propose that we turn our attention to the latter. In doing so we shall, I hope, cover the last lap of our somewhat protracted journey through and about *The Tempest*.

VIII. PROSPERO AND CALIBAN

Unlike Ferdinand, Caliban has no need to complain of Prospero's behaviour as 'crabb'd and...compos'd of harshness'. The reader observes the fact for himself. No other character but Prospero thinks fit to heap upon Caliban, however villainous or ludicrous in appearance, the burthen of a diabolical ancestry. Even the brutish Stephano occasionally lets fall words of kindness; not so Prospero – or not, at any rate, until the very last scene. And even then, the kindness seems grudgingly measured. To would-be traitors and parricides Prospero grants an immediate remission of guilt; the would-be murderer Caliban must be content, not only with a remission of punishment, but with such a remission in prospect.

Yet by contrast with previous severity, the slightest act of mercy on Prospero's part is such as to startle. Reasons are felt to be required for it; and it is perhaps hardly cynical to suggest that one lies closely to hand. This is the vanishing of an object of dispute between Prospero and Caliban. A few minutes before the latter's entry upon the stage, Prospero has been restored to the sovereignty of Milan. Henceforward the sovereignty of the island is of no interest to him.

In one of his first utterances, Caliban claims that sovereignty for himself, and accuses Prospero of usurpation:

> This island's mine, by Sycorax my mother,
> Which thou tak'st from me. (I. ii. 332)

More than once he repeats the claim and the accusation to Stephano:

> As I told thee before I am subject to a tyrant,
> A sorcerer, that by his cunning hath
> Cheated me of the island (III. ii. 42)

and again,

> I say by sorcery he got this isle,
> From me he got it. (*ibid.* 52)

So strongly convinced is Caliban of the justice of his claim, so deeply wounded therefore at its being ignored, that he develops a litigious fever or madness: in order that the claim may be vindicated, he is willing to forgo all advantages that might result from it. He will make the island over to Stephano, constituting him lord by cession, if only Stephano will undertake that Prospero, who detains the lordship by force, shall be duly punished.

On his side, Prospero gives no sign – at any rate, no immediately legible sign – of being conscious that he deserves punishment. To Ferdinand he presents himself as, without qualification, the lord of the island; to Alonso, he asserts that he was landed there to be the lord – and he regards the landing, it should be remembered, as a directly providential act.

In the pamphlets about Virginia, to which reference has already been made, the sovereignty of newly discovered lands was a topic frequently and laboriously treated of. The critics of colonial enterprise suggested that the English were acting unjustly in intruding themselves into Virginia: for the title to the country, they held, vested not in the English but in the Spaniards; or if not in the Spaniards, then in the native inhabitants.

In so far as the Spanish title reposed, not upon effective settlement, but upon the Bull of 1493, the apologists for the enterprise made, or thought they made, short work of it. Christ's kingdom is not of this world, and therefore the Vicar of Christ – supposing for the moment the Pope to be such – has no authority to give this world's kingdoms away. Nor is the Pope, on the ground that the native inhabitants are idolaters, able to dispossess them in favour of the Spaniards or of anybody. For in the Old Testament we do not see Israel or Judah attacking neighbouring tribes merely on such a ground; nor do Israelitish or Jewish kings, when they themselves fall into idolatry, thereby forfeit their dominion. Gleefully the English Protestants quoted Catholic theologians, such as Vitoria and Cajetan, who had advanced similar views.

However, the main purpose of these Protestants was to justify, not so much the expulsion of the Spanish from the Indies, as the entrance thither of the English. And the more energetically they proclaimed native rights as demanding the former, the more peremptorily did these same rights forbid the latter. In the face of this unsurmountable obstacle, different controversialists adopted different tactics.

William Strachey, for example – of whose *True Reportory* we have already made extensive use – seems to have cultivated a religious rapture such as might, in his own eyes at any rate, raise him above the obstacle and float him over it. In the *History of Travel into Virginia*, which he began about 1612 – and which cannot therefore have had any influence on *The Tempest*; but which I quote as an illustration, and possibly an unusually clear illustration, of a temper of the times – he proclaims as 'the...only end intended by His Majesty, by the honourable Council for the business, by the Lord General, Lieutenant General, Marshal, and such-like eminent officers...together with the general adventurers', not 'common trade and the hope of profit', but 'with all carefulness principally to endeavour the conversion of the natives to the knowledge and worship of the true God and world's Redeemer Christ Jesus'. And if, alongside this 'only end', common trade and the hope of profit happen to be pursued, that he explains is but a consequence of the adventurers' philanthropy. For trade into all parts of the world is the natural right of man, so that, by seeking to prevent it, the natives reveal their ignorance of the 'graces...and particularities of humanity'. Their need of enlightenment on political and social matters is, in short, as great as their need of religious enlightenment. The adventurers regard it as their inescapable duty to confer both: 'to exalt privation', says Strachey, adopting a metaphor from alchemy, 'to the highest point of perfection', to transform the crude earth of the natives into the purest gold. And therefore the cause of the Virginia expedition is not only a 'holy cause', but one of 'the most sacred' to which a man can put his hands. Nor has any man done so, except moved by 'pity and religious compassion'; 'our charity suffereth' for the natives, says Strachey, 'until we have derived unto them the true knowledge indeed'. And on this topic he rises to a pitch of eloquence so high as to halt the reader, who is at a loss to know whether to admire his skill, to pity his folly or to reprobate his blasphemy. Our enterprise in Virginia, Strachey claims, is 'the raising and building up of a Sanctum Sanctorum, a holy house and a sanctuary to His Blessed Name amongst infidels; placing them therein on whom it hath now pleased Him both to be sufficiently revenged for their forefathers' ingratitude and treasons, and to descend in mercy to lighten them that sit in darkness, and to direct their feet in the way of peace'.

The author of the *True Declaration*, as the official apologist of the Virginia Council, addresses himself to a wider and a partly sceptical audience. On that account he thinks it prudent to strike a quieter note. The preaching of the Gospel, he explains, might be accomplished in any one of three ways. But of these, the apostolical is no longer to be thought of, since with the ceasing of the gift of tongues and of that of miracles, the divine commission of the apostles has been withdrawn. The second way is imperial, as 'when a prince conquers bodies, that the preachers may feed their souls'. According to the author, this 'may be a matter sacred in the preachers, but I know not how justifiable in the rulers, who for their more ambition do set upon it the gloss of religion. Let the divines of Salamanca discuss the question', he concludes, levelling a usual English reproach against the Spaniards, but doing so with rather more than the usual skill. There remains the third way of 'merchandizing and trade', whereby the natives are brought into a 'daily conversation' with Christians. This is the way reserved for the English. Trade in general is lawful – how otherwise should it have been permitted to Solomon? – English trade to Virginia particularly so, and for a number of reasons. Chief amongst these is the fact that one of the Virginian kings 'sold unto us for copper, land to inherit and inhabit'. By argumentation of this kind, the author of the *True Declaration* seeks to convince the cooler-headed amongst his readers. The warmer-hearted he condescends to rouse by stressing the miraculous rescue of the company on board the *Sea Adventure*. As 'God commanded Elias to flee to the brook Cedron, and there fed him by ravens: so God provided for our disconsolate people on the island in the midst of the sea by fowls – but with an admirable difference. Unto Elias the ravens brought meat, unto our men the fowls brought themselves for meat: for when they whistled...the fowls would come and sit on their shoulders, they would suffer themselves to be taken and weighed by our men, who would make choice of the fattest and fairest.' After so affecting a mark of divine favour, who can doubt of the future of Virginia? The *True Declaration* ends with an eloquence drawing its warmth from the same source as Strachey's, but which the author, in view of the diversity of his audience, sees fit to temper with a classic frigidity. Thus he achieves a language at once enthusiastic and decent: 'O all ye worthies, follow the ever-sounding trumpet of a blessed honour – let religion be the first aim of your hopes, *et caetera adjicientur.* ...The same God that hath joined three kingdoms under one Caesar, will not be wanting to add a fourth...Doubt yet not but that God hath determined and demonstrated (by the wondrous preservation of those principal persons which fell upon the Bermudas) that he will raise our state, and build his church in that excellent climate, if the action be seconded with resolution and religion. *Nil desperandum Christo Duce et auspice Christo.*'

All this rhetoric is very fine, and that of the *True Declaration* at least very clever: its main purpose however is but to hide the fact that, at the end, the English find themselves in a similar position to those Spaniards from whom, at the beginning, it was their boasted intention to differ. Like the Spaniards, they allow native rights to be overwhelmed by supposedly conflicting rights of the Gospel. If indeed the Spaniards do so: for in one respect these have an advantage over the English. They are commissioned by two masters or, in so far as they are traders, by three: as preachers by the Pope, as conquerors by the King, and each of them as a trader by his private interest. Any conflict between their preaching, conquering and trading may be referred to an easily conceivable conflict between these authorities, existing independently of themselves. But the Englishman claims to be commissioned by his conscience, and so faces the difficult if not repulsive task of identifying his preaching with his trade. And if conquering prove unavoidable, what then? As Strachey foresees that it might, for he considers the possibility of the Virginian natives failing to appreciate the 'graces...and particularities of humanity' which he says trade implies; as the author of the *True Declaration* foresees that it will, for he has no hope of the land bought 'for copper' sufficing for the needs of the colonists. Thereby he abandons the one controversial advantage possibly possessed by the English, and these, he allows, must set about that 'conquering of bodies' which he defied the divines of Salamanca to justify. True, he says that the Virginians will have been the first to engage upon hostilities. But the Spaniards said that also; and when touching upon this topic, the *True Declaration* sounds such a note as might have been sounded by the Spanish conqueror at his reputed worst. The natives, he says, are 'human beasts', in whose fidelity there can be no trust 'except a man will make a league with lions, bears and crocodiles'. The same note had already been sounded by Strachey in the *True Reportory*, towards the end of which he found himself compelled to regret that 'fair and noble intreaty' proved of no beneficial effect upon the Virginians. Rather, it encouraged them in 'the practices of villainy', and so had to be replaced by a 'violent proceeding'. To the stay-at-home Purchas it appeared that this violent proceeding should have been taken from the first; for in printing the *True Reportory* in 1625, he added to the phrase 'fair and noble intreaty' a marginal observation. '*Ad Graecas Calendas*!' he exclaimed, 'can a leopard change his spots?' And so native rights become so entirely overwhelmed as to be forgotten; from the rank of men the natives sank down to that of beasts, incapable of any rights whatever.

It is I think impossible to read the pieces in this debate without being reminded of the phrase which we found in the *True Reportory* on our first dealings with it: 'hoodwinked men'. Only, the participants in the debate are hoodwinked, not as Strachey described the company on board the *Sea Adventure*, but as I suggested the characters in *The Tempest* would prove to be. They are hoodwinked without knowing it, so that it is impossible they should have patience under the disability. Rather than

waiting until they shall see, they must immediately make use of
their blindness as a seeing. The use they make of it is of an
appropriately fantastic kind. Ignorant of their own motives, they
miscall both these motives, the actions which result therefrom,
and the objects upon which the motives are directed. They
reprove the conduct of the Spaniards in the Indies, and at the
same time imitate that conduct. Filled with a Christian charity
towards the natives, at a slight provocation they overflow with a
diabolic hate. Aspiring to exalt the crude earth of the natives to
the purest gold, they are ready to stamp it beneath their feet and
to scatter it to the winds. Like hoodwinked men they keep on
no steady course, but lurch from one side to the other of the
path in which it never occurs to them to halt, because they have
no notion of being unable to walk down it.

In his dealings with Caliban, at any rate, Prospero appears
as a hoodwinked man of this kind. To his making there has gone
a part, indeed I think quite a considerable part, both of the
Virginia controversialists and of the adventurers into Virginia:
some of the former Shakespeare read, with some of the latter
he conversed, for they were his friends.

Prospero is fully convinced of his charity towards Caliban.
He has 'humanly taken' pains on Caliban's behalf:

> I have us'd thee
> ...with human care, and lodg'd thee
> In mine own cell. (I. ii. 346)

Or again:

> I pitied thee,
> Took pains to make thee speak, taught thee each hour
> One thing or other.[1] (*ibid.* 354)

If this charity has not produced the effect which, according to
supernatural authority, it cannot fail to produce, the fault is not
Prospero's, but Caliban's entirely. For neither of them is life
made the sweeter because, says Prospero, Caliban's 'vile
race...had that in't which good natures could not abide to be
with'. That a liability to lust cannot be considered so intolerable
a companion has already been suggested, on the ground that
Prospero shows himself tolerant of the same liability in Ferdinand. But now perhaps it is apparent that the suggestion is more

---

[1] This is taken from the speech attributed to Miranda in the Folio and in the New
Cambridge Shakespeare, see pp. 198 and 239. (E. M. W.)

deeply and widely based: neither Caliban's nature nor anyone's can contain anything capable of giving supernatural authority the lie. What Caliban's nature does contain is something capable of hiding Prospero's own nature from himself. He believes his charity to be perfect, when in fact it is otherwise. This something is, in all likelihood, a title to sovereignty. In its turn, Prospero's imperfect charity blinds him to the existence of the title: for it allows him to describe Caliban as not a man but a beast, or if not a beast, then something worse, 'a devil, a born devil' – something at any rate in which no title can vest. And so Prospero makes a lurch to the opposite side of the path which he is treading: for as a devil or a beast, Caliban is no more a fitting object of charity than he is a fitting sovereign, nor would Prospero ever dream of lodging him in the same cell with Miranda. The hoodwinking continues yet a stage further, as Prospero convinces himself that he is not only charitable but just. Caliban, he maintains, is 'deservedly' confined to the rock and kept from the rest of the island, although if a devil or a beast, it is impossible for him to have deserts. Since human justice recognizes no rights in such beings, neither does it subject them to penalties: and Prospero has once more lurched across his own path.

Whether or not the inconsistencies of his conduct are to be explained only by a hoodwinking of this kind, they are in fact explicable if it has taken or is taking place. And perhaps in one passage of the play we can see it doing so. The complexity of the passage caused the New Cambridge editors to suspect it of being 'patchwork'; rather perhaps that very quality goes to prove its integrity. The passage occurs in the first dialogue between Prospero and Ariel, and runs as follows:

> *Prospero.* ...then was this island –
> Save for the son that she did litter here,
> A freckled whelp hag-born – not honour'd with
> A human shape.
> *Ariel.* Yes Caliban her son.
> *Prospero.* Dull thing, I say so. (I. ii. 281)

'Ariel', say the editors, 'who cleaves to Prospero's very thoughts (IV i 165) is extraordinarily obtuse here.' Or he may, I would suggest, be cleaving more closely to these thoughts than Prospero finds comfortable. Scrupulous to do nothing less,

if nothing more than justice, Prospero has constructed such a
sentence that, if its parts are taken in the proper order, it
concedes humanity to Caliban. 'Then there were no humans
save Caliban on the island.' But Prospero has filled the sentence
with words suggesting that, if a man, Caliban is at the same time
a beast. He is not only a son, but a whelp; if he was born, he was
hag-born; in any case, he was not only born, but littered. Nor
is it easy to grasp the proper order of the parts. A long parenthesis separates subject from verb and, dwarfing the former,
seems to cry for independent consideration. In that case it
implies: 'Nothing that I say can of course have reference to
Caliban.' Or if independent consideration is refused, the first
word of the parenthesis can only with difficulty be made to
depend, as it should, on the last word of the succeeding phrase
('no human shape save Caliban's'), the first word of the phrase
temptingly offers itself as dependent on the last of the parenthesis
('hag-born, not honoured with human shape'). And so suggestion pours in from many points upon the reader – from yet more,
perhaps, upon the hearer – that Caliban is not a man at all; that
those very qualities about him which might make him seem so,
emphasize only the more heavily the fact that he is not; that is,
with one part of his mind, Prospero is anxious to preserve an
appearance of justice, with a larger and a stronger part he is
convinced that the appearance is contradictory of the substance.
And so he comes near to refusing justice openly. Seeing his
master on the verge of an indiscretion, Ariel ventures to correct
him. Nothing is more irritating than that thoughts we have been
at pains to hide should be exposed, not so much to the sight of
others, as to our own. Prospero relieves the irritation with the
adjective 'dull': in itself, as the New Cambridge editors are
right in noting, a surprising adjective to be applied to Ariel;
in the context however perhaps not so surprising, and in any
case hardly more so than the adjective 'malignant', which
Prospero has similarly applied a few lines earlier.

The reader may have noticed, and if so he will have been
amused – indeed, he may have amused himself in this way a
number of times before – that, while berating Prospero for
presuming to spy into the conscience of other people, I do not
appear to have the slightest hesitation in spying into his own.
In so far as this difficulty is raised by the whole of my essay, it

will be proper to consider it when that whole comes up for review, that is, in the concluding section. With regard to the particular instance of the difficulty now before us, I would plead that I have been arguing from a premiss adopted by the Virginia pamphleteers against the Spaniards and, in so far as Prospero has elements in common with the pamphleteers, shared in by himself. The premiss is that the natives have rights. If the pamphleteers and Prospero, setting out from a premiss of this kind, succeed in persuading themselves of an opposite conclusion – if the end of their reflection, like Gonzalo's commonwealth, forgets its beginning – then they invite speculation about their interior. Indeed they demand it, if they are to continue being treated as rational beings and not mere gabblers of the kind to which Prospero, in one of his outbursts against Caliban, would assign the latter. If on the other hand, the premiss may be denied, not shamefacedly and perhaps unconsciously at the end of an argument, but deliberately and boldly at its beginning, speculation such as I have indulged in would be superfluous and therefore impertinent. The consequences of such a denial are both alarming and far-reaching; nevertheless the pamphleteers did not always refrain from it, nor are signs lacking that Shakespeare intended Prospero to be understood as not doing so.

My quotation from Purchas, a few paragraphs ago, was incomplete. In full, the marginal observation which he attached to *True Reportory* runs as follows: '*Ad Calendas Graecas!*' he cries, 'Can a leopard change his spots? Can a savage remaining a savage be civil? Were we not ourselves made and not born civil in our progenitors' days? and were not Caesar's Britons as brutish as the Virginians? The Roman swords were the best teachers of civility to this and other countries near us.' A similar historical reminiscence is made by Strachey himself in his *History of Travel*, when concerned to deny that such violence towards the Virginians as colonization may involve is properly to be considered as an injury to them. 'Had not this violence and this injury been offered unto us by the Romans', he writes, '. . . we might yet have lived overgrown satyrs, rude and untutored, wandering in the woods, dwelling in caves, and hunting for our dinners as the wild beasts in the forests for their prey, prostituting our daughters to strangers, sacrificing our

children to idols.' The far-reaching consequences of the denial
are perhaps apparent: not only the human individual, but whole
groups of humans, such as tribes and nations, are it would seem
to be considered as passing through a period of nonage. And
during that period they are, like the minor under Roman law,
to be exposed to whatever suffering an adult, or at any rate an
authorized adult, thinks fit, for their own good or upon any
other pretext, to inflict upon them. That the consequences are
alarming is equally clear. The human individual defines himself,
but who is to define a tribe or a nation? and until that is done,
how is its nonage to be limited? To Purchas it might seem
obvious that, compared with the Virginians, the English were
adult; to a Spaniard, comparing the spacious decency of the
Escorial with the crowded squalor of Whitehall, the massive
unity of Salamancan theology with the fractious fragments
produced at Oxford and Cambridge, the English might seem no
less obviously minors. And had the Spaniards succeeded in
obtaining a hold on England, they would have lost no time in
exposing Oxford and Cambridge theologians to such sufferings
as the Inquisition thought they not so much deserved as needed.
Yet again, the readiness of the Spaniards to have recourse to an
Inquisition might cause them to appear in other nations' eyes
less adult than they seemed in their own. By the initial denial of
native rights, in short, the chances of a man's being hoodwinked
are very greatly increased, increased perhaps even to infinity:
for the sole cause of hoodwinking is no longer a blurring of
man's sight, on particular occasions or when face to face with a
particular object or group of objects; it is also the blurring of
what on all occasions is the principal object of his sight,
humanity itself. At any time and place, humanity may not as yet
have attained to the perfection of existence, may still remain
involved in the imperfection of becoming. And though this
imperfection may be a falling short of, rather than a deviation
from, the proper end of humanity, as imperfect that latter
resembles Caliban. It both is and is not, it drags him who
observes it in two different directions, it puts on, like Caliban,
nightmarish qualities.

And yet, as I said, there are indications that Shakespeare
intended Prospero to be understood as making the denial.
For not only does the portrait he draws of Caliban closely

resemble Strachey's nightmare portrait of our British ancestors – if allowed no daughters to prostitute, no children to sacrifice, Caliban is very much an 'overgrown satyr'; he seeks his dinner in the woods, at least in so far as it consists of pig-nuts, filberts and 'scamels'; he is endowed with a full measure of crocodile cunning and bear-like savagery – not only does Shakespeare draw this portrait, he allows short shrift to those who assert the impossibility of denying rights to any tribe or nation. Or rather, he allows them no shrift at all, but goes out of his way to consign them mercilessly to the hell which gapes for fools.

In Shakespeare's day, the most notorious example of such an assertion was to be found in Montaigne's essay *On the Cannibals*. The mere title of this essay guarantees its relevance to *The Tempest*, since 'cannibal' and 'Caliban' are in all probability phonetic variants of the same name. Another such variant is 'Caribal' or 'Carib', under which form the name has been assigned by history to that American tribe or nation which offered most effective resistance to European colonizers. Other tribes might flee before the Spaniards or, if they resisted, might be defeated after a struggle lasting days, weeks, months or possibly years; but defeated they would be, and henceforward serve the conquerors. Not so the Caribs, who preferred death to defeat; and who, should they be captured alive, employed every device of savagery and cunning either to make their escape or to render their service valueless. They refused to be Europeanized, and so came to symbolize the colonizing problem, in so far at least as this problem depended, not on geographical but on human factors. But, according to Montaigne's essay, no such problem existed. If the Caribs or cannibals ate human flesh, he maintained, they ate only a very little of it; nor did they so much eat it themselves, as send round the choicer morsels as presents among their friends. And if they executed with a fearsome cruelty their captive enemies, this was no more than they themselves were willing to undergo, should they have the misfortune to be captured. While waiting for the torment, they uplifted both themselves and all who were near them by the songs which they sang. Such songs could not fail of an uplifting effect, since the Carib language employs grammatical terminations similar to those of the Greek. No wife among the Caribs is jealous, no war-lord is ambitious, no member of the nation indeed, of whatever quality, is avid of anything but honour. Yet not even honour leads to strife: 'the very words that import lying, falsehood, treason, dissimulations, covetousness, envy, detraction and pardon, were never heard of amongst them'. In view of all these excellencies, the trouble which the Spaniards were giving themselves to civilize the Caribs could proceed only from a singularly narrow notion of civilization. Undoubtedly, the Spaniards allowed themselves to be unduly impressed by the fact that the Caribs wore no breeches.

Of this rhapsody, Shakespeare shows his opinion by copying out its essential part with hardly more alterations than are required by the metre. Then, not content with entrusting its defence to the fatuous Gonzalo, he permits the worthless Antonio and Sebastian to refute it. That their worthlessness cannot infect and so discredit their refutation, but must rather throw its soundness into relief, is proved by its destiny in the minds and on the lips of generations of Shakespeare readers. They have made it as universally current as is the speech of Prospero's with a consideration of which the present essay began. 'The latter end of his commonwealth forgets the beginning', says Antonio of Gonzalo: and so it must, since the Caribs as Montaigne imagines them dwell in an earthly paradise, and earth in its present state is what paradise has rejected. On such an earth, men's only way of fitting themselves for paradise is to work; which if they neglect, then as Antonio once more observes, they are 'whores and knaves'. Of the soundness of this second part – or corollary – of his refutation, Montaigne's essays themselves would seem to supply a sufficient proof. For written in a library that their [? author] had sought to make as much of an earthly paradise as possible, in large part they record the whoring and the knavery of a mind. But there is no need to go outside *The Tempest* itself for proof. Stephano and Trinculo go whoring after Ariel's music and come to grief. Ferdinand allows his fancy to go whoring after an endless succession of masques to entertain him, and has his entertainment immediately cut short.

Perhaps then Prospero may not be hoodwinked about Caliban, the inconsistencies of his conduct towards whom may be evidence rather of an open-eyedness.

IX. BE CHEERFUL, SIR!

At the end of the last section, we found ourselves faced by an alternative. Either Prospero is hoodwinked with respect to Caliban, or he escapes that fate only by falling into what at first sight seems a worse. He is liable to hoodwinking with respect not only to Caliban, but to himself, to anyone or anything. Let us begin our attempt at a conclusion by enumerating, so far as we can, the respects in which in the course of this essay he has shown himself as certainly hoodwinked, or in all probability so.

First we can make the hypothetic statement that, if the spirits are nothing – and it is Prospero himself who tells us that they are – then he is hoodwinked when he treats them as something. We may go on to the categorical statement that quite certainly he is hoodwinked with respect to the supposed repentance of Antonio and Sebastian. Indeed, this particular instance is so certain that he might almost be accused of carrying out the hoodwinking himself. Then too he is almost if not quite hoodwinked with respect to Gonzalo: an estimable creature, as we have said, but one of whom an estimate such as Prospero's is quite impossible to anyone with open eyes. He pays no excessive attention to Stephano or Trinculo but, in so far he does, few or none will be inclined to challenge the rightness of his dealings. Certainly, Stephano and Trinculo deserve punishment for having allowed themselves to become involved in a project of murder; almost certainly, as king of the island, Stephano would have been a comic failure, Trinculo as viceroy would have been a lamentable one. Towards Ferdinand, Prospero indulges in a superfluous harshness for which it seems hoodwinking of some kind must be responsible; towards Miranda even he lets fly an unnecessary taunt. But of the suitability of Ferdinand and Miranda as man and wife, and of their future happiness together, if he can be no more certain than any other man, he has done as much as man can do to secure a near certainty. That his eyes are open to Alonso there would seem to be not the slightest doubt: he thinks that Alonso has repented, and in fact he has done so.

Alonso would seem to require distinction of a similar kind when we pass from Prospero to consider in what ways and to what extent the other characters in the play are hoodwinked. For they are human beings like Prospero, so that his situation must be theirs. Of all the other characters, only Alonso seems fully aware, or at any rate always conscious, of uncertainty about Caliban. The latter has been a long time before Alonso's eyes without his making any remark; when at last he does so, the remark is a confession of uncertainty:

> This is as strange a thing as e'er I looked upon. (V. i. 291)

The other characters may, as we have seen, either hesitate over the name they give to Caliban or be inconsistent in their use of names; nevertheless, in their actions they do not hesitate. Miranda turns her back on him with decision; Antonio and Sebastian no sooner set eyes on him than they use him as a laughing-stock; Stephano and Trinculo are milder, for they laugh with as well as at him – yet they too allow themselves to be abused. They take seriously the schemes which Caliban propounds for the elimination of Prospero and the substitution of themselves in the government of the island. They would have made a fine job of it, and rapidly become a source of misery to themselves and to one another. But neither would Antonio and Sebastian have been any more successful in their schemes for the elimination of Alonso. They would but have secured their own unhappiness, if not in this world then in the next. Once in the past Alonso allowed himself to be hoodwinked along with this same pair: misery has not only fallen upon him in consequence, but he has recognized it as such. Therefore he has repented, and his eyes are now open.

In view of this series of exceptions we are obliged to make on Alonso's behalf, are we to consider him as the character in the play with whom above all others the reader is called upon to sympathize, the character against whom as a standard all the rest are to be measured? That can hardly be the case, because Alonso is the most passive of the characters. He does [not] so much act, as allow himself to be acted upon. One important act he certainly does perform, his repentance: that however is an interior act, and in drama as in life, characters are expected to engage upon external activity. Because of the marriage which they resolve upon, which is an external act, Ferdinand and Miranda make a far stronger call for sympathy than does Alonso:

257

although, and in spite of Prospero's precautions, they run a risk, if no more than a minimum risk, of being deceived. If no such risk threatens Alonso, it is only because he does nothing.

Often in the course of this essay we have had occasion to remark upon the folly, and even upon the wickedness, of fantasies of an earthly paradise. It is a human duty, as it is the one hope of human happiness, to do things. In so far as he refrains from doing, Alonso is entertaining such a fantasy; for he is implying either that others will do things for him, or that he does not need things done. On the other hand, we have the positive examples of Ferdinand and Miranda, who undertake a marriage; and we have that action of Prospero, undertaken to promote that marriage and to ensure as far as possible that it shall be a success. The question before us is, why did this action seem to us so emphatically worthy of approval? Why in contrast did we hesitate to approve Prospero's actions towards Caliban?

In so far as a man is hoodwinked, what he sees can afford him no safe ground for action. For either he sees nothing, or nothing but images: images that is of nothing, which have as little substance and as little consistency in or among themselves as have those of a dream. On many, if not most occasions, Prospero would seem to be hoodwinked: the actions at those times he engages upon are mistaken. Yet he is not always mistaken in his actions. How do we distinguish between the two? How should he himself have distinguished between the occasions, and so have avoided his mistakes?

As well as the natural, the supernatural affords grounds for action. If nature forces men to act, the supernatural orders that their acts shall be virtuous; if they are otherwise, then it orders them to be repented of. In the light of supernatural commands, natural experience is to be interpreted. Certain elements in the dream of experience are attracted to the supernatural, and so form solid ground on which to take a stand for the purposes of action.

Often interpretation is not easy; at times not even possible, at least to the degree for which men long. That degree is attainable only after death. Until [then] a man must do what he can, and be content with that. As for example Prospero with his measures to ensure his children's happiness.[1]

---

[1] In the typescript at this point James Smith pencilled in (in capitals) the word 'FORGETTING'. (E. M. W.)

It would be an offence against both nature and supernature to allow himself to become desperate because ignorant of the future of the marriage. Desperation forbids action – if it inspires a valour to act, it is only that wherewith 'men hang and drown their proper selves'; on the other hand, even desperation, perhaps [is] preferable to complacency, the complacency with which men flatter themselves they foresee the future: when they have tracked down the intentions of Providence on their own behalf. The complacency of the men on board the *Sea Adventure*. The complacency of Strachey in the *History of Travel*. He is a John the Baptist, announcing the Messiah of Colonialism.

Not that colonialism is wholly or necessarily an evil. What to do with the Calibans? Having pointed out that this is a question, and that the way to deal with them lies neither through desperation nor complacency, an essayist on *The Tempest* may hold himself absolved from going further. That Prospero commits grave errors towards Caliban would seem certain: for whatever may be the truth about Caliban's nature, the supernatural commands charity towards him, which Prospero signally fails to observe. But then Prospero signally fails in his duties on many occasions. He has his complacencies. He was landed by Providence on the island. Providence no doubt is sending him back to Milan. But will he or Milan be happier on that account? He would be a bold or rather a rash critic who would answer with an unqualified affirmative.

Yet it is Prospero who rebukes Ferdinand by reminding him that life is a dream. It is Prospero who consoles Alonso with the same reminder. A man who knows the truth, but who is humanly imperfect in the interpretations he produces in the light of it: not a sensitive nature. He is too humanly capable of being blinded by his passions: his vanity, his ambition makes him forget the truth.

Yet on occasion he can announce it. The great speech – the last lesson to his prospective son-in-law; and the necessity of such a lesson made all the clearer by the approach of conspirators. Ferdinand must be lessoned to take such things with a due mixture of seriousness and lightness. Seriousness perhaps predominates in the aside following upon Miranda's outburst of 'O brave new world!' (V. i. 184) – 'Tis new to thee', remarks Prospero. The due mixture perhaps achieved in his comment upon the wooing: I cannot be as happy as they, but it would be impossible for me to be happier. Not to over-value experience – how foolish to do so, since it is but a dream. But neither to undervalue it: for its very dreaminess may be part of the dream, and may therefore be as little trusted.

The theme of the unsubstantiality of this world, or our experience in it and, in so far as we belong to it, of ourselves, this is not pessimistic, since it is not anti-Christian. A theme rather of the Prophets and of the Psalms and of the Fathers and of the homilists. Familiar outside Christianity also, especially in the East. Through the tale of Barlaam and Josaphat Eastern elements combined intimately with the Christian. And so provided subject-matter (arguments) for a number of mediaeval and Renaissance compositions. With one of these, Shakespeare shows his acquaintance in *The Taming of a Shrew* – the man who dreams he is a prince. That enters into *The Tempest* also: Prospero, whether or not the true Duke of Milan, is only a doubtfully legitimate lord of the island. Caliban dreams he is lord and, at his instigation, so does Stephano. Another argument: the brute a man makes of himself if he goes a-whoring after his dreams, without first allowing them so to speak to precipitate upon the supernatural whatever solid they may hold in solution. Caliban [is] such a brute. So is Segismundo in Calderón's *La vida es sueño*: where also Segismundo is – or for a period thinks he is – the prince in a dream. The part coincides with *The Tempest* at a number of points.

But on one point *The Tempest* is different. And though it is foolish to discuss which of two such eminent masterpieces is the superior, yet in virtue of that point *The Tempest* can, I think, be awarded superiority as a variation upon the argument that life is a dream. For whereas in Calderón's play one character only is shown as dreaming, while the rest are wide awake and so have the opportunity of learning their lesson from him; in *The Tempest* all the characters are involved in the dream contemporaneously. All then must learn their lesson at their own expense; and even Prospero must relearn it, since he forgets it. Hence the realism of the play. It has no more and no less than the dreaminess of life. Hence reading it, the reader too must learn at his own expense. For he is no better off than the characters – and why should he be? Like them he is puzzled to know the qualities of the island; like them he will never be quite certain what behaviour to adopt towards Caliban. If he thinks it worth while to do so, he may ask himself a million times whether or not the spirits are real, whether Prospero really achieves anything with his conjuring. But his enjoyment of the play should thereby be not the less but the greater. He should enjoy it as he enjoys life, of which it is not a representation seen from a distance and therefore falsified, but the rarer perfume when life, because of its dreaminess, is seen to depend completely upon the supernatural. No desperation, no complacency; be cheerful! Tragicomedia?[1]

---

[1] On the back of the penultimate page of the typescript are the following jottings in James Smith's hand:

'Are we right about Gonzalo? Who can choose between Gonzalo and Antonio?'

'Our own enquiry into consciences.'

'Was Sycorax a witch or not?'

'The experience through which the reader is *forced*.'

'DIVERSION'

(E. M. W.)

8

ON METAPHYSICAL POETRY

In literary criticism the adjective 'metaphysical', like the noun 'metaphysics' in philosophy, has had a busy life. It has assumed new meanings before casting off the old, and the separation of old from new is not at all easy. I believe that such a separation is nevertheless desirable: for, though we may not be saying much when we say that a poem is metaphysical, it is as well to know exactly (if we can) what the little is we are saying.

Hobbes in philosophy dismissed new meanings as merely nonsense: 'the term signifieth as much as the books written, or placed after, Aristotle's *Physics*'. Such a proceeding, however tempting, is no longer possible; not, at any rate, in criticism. For nowadays, I think, there is felt to be about the adjective 'metaphysical' a peculiar fitness for the description of a certain kind of poetry, of which the norm is Donne's; and, whatever this fitness may be, it is not to be discovered by an investigation of origins. It was perceived neither by Johnson when he popularized the adjective as a critical term, nor by Dryden when he suggested it.

Johnson had little metaphysics, and much of what he called metaphysical poetry we should now immediately dispose of under other names. We shall glance at it later; here it need not delay us. Dryden, on the other hand, was more cultured, and noticed that in Donne metaphysical propositions are to be found. In this he saw rather a reason for chiding, than for praise: Donne, he says, 'perplexes the mind of the fair sex with nice speculations of philosophy, when he should engage their hearts, and entertain them with the softnesses of love'. It would be strange if a term were felt peculiarly apt for the description of a major poet, when it described, not a source of his strength, but his weakness. Not all, however, would agree with Dryden that there is a weakness here; and a simpler reflection will suffice. It is that metaphysical propositions occur, not only in the poetry of Donne, but in that of (say) Parmenides and Lucretius among the ancients; in Guinizelli, Dante and Petrarch among the mediaevals; in Elizabethans like Sir John Davies and Chapman; even in

Romantics like Shelley and Wordsworth. Some critics have used the term 'metaphysical' with as wide a reference as this; some, I believe, have said that all great poetry is metaphysical. But that is the abuse of a term. To say that Donne is metaphysical is not to say that he is great. It is an endeavour to distinguish the way in which he is great, if he is so, from other forms of greatness. It is, however, an unsuccessful endeavour if it is the same as saying that in his work metaphysical propositions are to be found. For it is not thereby he is distinguished from poets like Parmenides, Petrarch and Shelley.

The phrase, 'metaphysical proposition', is a wide one: to some people it may suggest the ejaculation of a theosophist, to others an axiom from *Principia Mathematica*. If it is made more definite, may it not provide us with the means of distinction we require? Dante and Lucretius, for example, are poets in whom metaphysical propositions abound, and they have frequently been held to be very like Donne – to be, in fact, metaphysical poets *par excellence*. May not they, and Donne, use a particular type of metaphysical proposition, which distinguishes them from Parmenides and Shelley? This, I believe, is an opinion which has frequently been held; but I know of no one who has succeeded in the isolation which it demands of a type of metaphysical proposition. Such a task is one upon which any man may well be reluctant to engage. And I doubt whether it would even be profitable to do so. For to me Dante and Lucretius, together with the lesser lights of the *dolce stil nuovo*, together even with Chapman, seem not very like, but very different from, Donne. Later I will endeavour to make clear what seems to me the nature of this difference; here, as we are discussing metaphysical propositions in poetry, I will only refer to an observation, which I think is just, already made by Professor Praz. It is, that if metaphysical propositions occur in Lucretius, in Dante and in Donne, they occur in Donne in a peculiar way. Whereas Dante and Lucretius take seriously the propositions they quote, Donne does not do so: he quotes them, not as themselves true, but as possibly useful for inducing a belief in something else, which he believes is true. His concern is not with the incorruptibility of pure substances, but with the union of his soul with his mistress's: it is of this that he is convinced, and of this alone does he wish to convince his reader. Professor Praz states his distinction in terms that seem to me not wholly fortunate – they suggest a frivolous attitude to important matters, which I do not find in Donne – nevertheless, I heartily approve of the distinction being made. Dante and Lucretius, it is true, devote themselves to the exposition of a metaphysical system, or of parts of it; and Donne does not. That being so, it becomes at least an open question whether a search for a type or types of proposition common to them all can be of any value, even if it is successful. The use to which they are to put this type or types, when found, would seem to demand at least a prior study.

Even that, however, I do not propose to make. For one thing – and this is a confession which, out of deference to what I think is a widely-held superstition, I have postponed as long as I may – it seems to me that the number of quotations Donne makes from the metaphysicians has been exaggerated. Further – this is a more important, though more contentious, point – there has also been exaggeration of the significance of such quotations as he does make for the poems in which they occur. I cannot hope to prove this now; to do so must be the task of what remains of my paper. My third point, however, should be immediately clear: it is, that if the use made by Donne of such propositions as he does quote at all resembles that which Professor Praz says it is, it cannot be of importance to our present investigation. This starts from the assumption that Donne is felt to be very aptly called metaphysical. A man who pulls down houses, as such, is not felt to be aptly called an architect. If Donne merely plays ducks and drakes with metaphysics, we may as well abandon our investigation; we shall find a perfectly satisfactory account of him in Johnson.

I am therefore forced upon my own resources. This is unfortunate, for the country I have to cross is very extensive, and it is already marked with a multitude of tracks made for any purpose but my own. I will do what I can to follow one track but, if I make unnecessary detours, I must beg my reader's indulgence. My problem at the moment is to know which track to choose to set out on. Perhaps the safest is an opening of that discussion I have already proposed, of the differences between Dante and Lucretius on the one hand, and Donne on the other.

Mr Herbert Read, in a paper on the nature of metaphysical poetry – in which, I must admit, he supported a thesis contradictory of my own – said of Dante: 'the world was not a problem to him'. Nor was the world a problem to Lucretius. To Donne, the world is full of problems. And this remains true, though the world with which Donne is concerned is that of flesh and blood; while Lucretius is familiar with atoms, with the vacuum, with gods, and Dante with Heaven and Hell. To Donne the most important things that exist are himself and his mistress, the most important relation between them the everyday one of love. Lucretius's atoms fall through space, swerve, combine fortuitously to a universe, mind appears and disappears again; Dante finds excellence in Hell, cruelty is exerted by the supreme love, Heaven is extended and has no extent. Yet it is Donne's verse that is disturbed, and his lines that are the battleground between the difficulty of belief and the reluctance to doubt. Lucretius is bellicose, Dante submissive; but both have an assured peace. This is a gross contrast between the poets; but, for the moment, I leave it as such. It provides me with the starting-point I was seeking.

For I think it can be said, of both Dante and Lucretius, that they were not so much themselves metaphysicians, as the disciples of metaphysicians; and disciples have a way of being more certain than their masters. There is, for example, an obvious contrast between Thomism as one meets it in Dante, and as one finds it in Thomas himself. To the lips of those who know Thomas only through Dante, or through compendiums devised for the study of the *Commedia*, there rises inevitably one adjective for the description of his work: the adjective 'neat'. There is, of course, a neatness about Thomas: one of language, which has scarcely, if ever, been rivalled. But his thought, or any fragment of that thought, is rich, suggestive and haunting. It has a thousand ramifications, of all of which the mind is to some degree aware, few of which it can clearly grasp and follow, and these perhaps not to their very end; further, they are fine and interpenetrating, so that they seem to be alive. When en-countered for the tenth or perhaps the twentieth time, they do not impair the unity of Thomas's work: but that unity is still rather felt, than displayed before one, and seen. It is the unity of a vast and not simultaneously demonstrable whole; persuasive in its way, but demanding almost any other adjective for its description, than neat. To say this is not, I think, to say any-thing to Thomas's discredit. For, if it is discredit, then he shares it with all great metaphysicians. In their work, there is the pursuit rather than the attainment of truth; and such value as their work possesses seems to depend wholly on the pursuit. Or, to vary the metaphor (since pursuit without at least the hope of attainment does not seem very intelligible), the value depends on what is held in suspension in their thought, rather than on what is precipitated. Once precipitation takes place, it loses in value; nor has the precipitate a value which makes up for the loss. Yet it is this precipitate that the disciples collect, and of it they make their 'neat' display.

I am aware that at first sight there does not seem to be a great resemblance between Donne's turbulence, springing from his being full of problems, and what we may call Thomas's subtlety or elusiveness. Later I shall suggest that both spring from the same cause; and that the difference between the two, great as it is, is no greater than one would expect, given the very different aims that Donne and Thomas pursue. Here, leaving aside for the moment profounder speculation, I wish to establish one point merely: that turbulence in Donne, elusiveness in Thomas – both are signs of something very different from the certainty to be found in Dante and Lucretius. Lacking such a certainty, Donne resembles Dante's master much more than does Dante himself; in one respect at least, therefore, he is, more properly than Dante, called 'metaphysical'. The question rises, whether this respect is important enough to merit consideration. And I think it is. For I am not suggesting a resemblance between Donne and Thomas in the possession of a negative quality merely. I do not believe that anyone who lacks certainty, who is puzzled and therefore in his account of his studies puzzling – for instance, the cross-word fanatic or the half-wit – is for that reason to be called metaphysical. Metaphysics is 'puzzling', if I may retain the homely word, in a peculiar way. It is not that, to the matters it studies, there is an abundance of clues, so that the mind is lost among them; or that there is a shortage of clues, so that the mind is left hesitant; but rather, that such clues as there are, while equally trustworthy, are contradictory. And again, I do not mean that they are contradictory as are, say, pleas in a law-court. A judge is puzzled if he has before him two chains of evidence, one tending to prove that a certain person was in a certain spot at a certain time, the other that he was not. In cases like this, the contradiction rests upon accidents merely: it is compatible with the nature of the person whose movements are being considered, either that he was, or that he was not, at the given spot. The contradictions in metaphysics, on the other hand, spring from essence. The very nature of things brings them forth. It seems impossible that the nature of things should possess either the one or the other of a pair of qualities; it seems impossible that it should possess both together: it seems impossible that it should not possess both. Concern with problems of this kind gives a quite peculiar air of being puzzled; it is only in possession of this air, and not of any other, that I wish to say Donne and Thomas resemble each other.

I should like to give this air a name – say, the 'metaphysical note'; describe it generally, as that it is a note of tension, or strain; and merely affirm that it is to be found in Donne. The note is so distinctive that, once it is perceived, it is impossible not to recognize it again; and I am willing to trust my own judgment in the matter. But others would not; and fortunately there is, I think, other and more obviously firmer ground on which I can rest my case. This is an enumeration of the subjects of Donne's greater poems. For problems of the kind mentioned in the last paragraph are not infinite in number or variety. It has been held, indeed, that there is only one of them: the problem of the Many and the One, as old as Plato, but still, the argument goes, the concern of metaphysics. This is probably true; but whether true or not does not much affect my case. For, whether the problems discussed by metaphysics in its long history are or are not derived from that of the Many and the One, they resemble it in the nature of their difficulty, and they are restricted in number. At times the individual has fought against, and depended upon, its fellow individual, much as multiplicity unity; or the individual has fought against the universal; or against the universe, or against God. Or the here–now has risen up against its natural ally the then–there, and both have risen up against eternity. Or the spirit, partaking of the universal, has had nothing to do with the flesh; and the flesh, primed with the certainty of the here–now, has dismissed the spirit as a fable. And so on. I do not wish to give, nor indeed am I capable of giving, a complete list. The existence of problems of this kind is well known, their general nature, I hope, clear. Should anyone however make such a list, I am sure that in it would be found every one of the subjects of Donne's greater poems. Donne does not write about many things: he is content with the identity of lovers as lovers, and their diversity as the human beings in which love manifests itself; the stability and self-sufficiency of love, contrasted with the mutability and dependence of human beings; with the presence of lovers to each other, their physical unity, though they are separated by travel, and by death; the spirit demanding the succour of the flesh, the flesh hampering the spirit; the shortcomings of this life, summarized by decay and death, contrasted with the divine to which it aspires.

Donne's choice of subjects may of course have been dictated by chance, and a quality they have in common may be no sign of a quality common to his poetry. But I prefer to ignore this possibility; and taking my courage in my hands, to venture upon my own definition of metaphysical verse. It is, that verse properly called metaphysical is that to which the impulse is given by an overwhelming concern with metaphysical problems; with problems either deriving from, or closely resembling in the nature of their difficulty, the problem of the Many and the One. The definition sounds spare, but that I do not look upon as a defect. It is at any rate fairly clear. I would point out that it is by no means improbable, but rather the reverse, that poetry of the kind postulated by the definition should exist. For metaphysics, while highly abstract, is by the very reason of its high degree of abstraction intimately concerned with the concrete. It concerns everything, because it studies reality, not in this or that thing, but in everything or, as the phrase goes, 'in itself'. It is impossible to take a single step in any direction, without brushing against metaphysics. Now reality is a word of great emotional significance. Before a thing can completely command a man's attention, he must be assured at least of this about it, that it is real. To most people, of course, this assurance is not difficult to obtain; others, aware of a difficulty, do not find their daily life disturbed thereby. They are the metaphysicians, who like any other scientist, distinguish clearly the problem to which they devote their professional hours from the immediate problems of living. It is conceivable, however, that there should be a few who, aware of the difficulty of metaphysical problems, see them lurking behind any action, however trivial, they propose. Such people will be in a state of great disturbance or at least excitement. Such excitement may well be an impulse to poetry, and the poetry it generates be metaphysical. Such a course of events, I repeat, is at least possible. From the example of Donne I am convinced not only that it is possible, but that it has occurred.

A definition, if a sound one, enables the student to give more satisfactory accounts of the things it purports to define. It has been led up to by the study of such things; but, once arrived at, leads back to them and illuminates them. The definition I have proposed does this I think with the poems of Donne. Take for example *The Good Morrow*, which now usually stands at the head of the *Songs and Sonnets*. I am relieved, in the accounts I give of it to myself, to feel myself no longer obliged to attach prime importance to the last three lines, where the mention of a metaphysical doctrine – the incorruptibility of pure substances – occurs. The doctrine seems to me more or less extraneous to the poem, hanging on to it as a grace, perhaps not in the best fashion; and it is brought in so late – the poem, in my opinion, being for most purposes over before the last three lines are reached. What stands in the foreground of my attention are the two hemispheres in the lovers' eyes, dependent on each other, and together making up a world; the conceit of the little room, which is 'an everywhere'; or that dim time of forebeing, which is nevertheless so real that in it the lovers snorted in their den. And behind all these I see most clearly the metaphysical problem of the lovers who are two, and yet one; who are mortals, and yet have no fear; who are circumscribed beings, and yet a universe. This problem dictates the very plan of a poem. In the first stanza the past is considered, the time before that of Donne's love: it comes up for consideration because that love, to all appearances an earthly phenomenon, must have antecedents. Confronted with the present, however, the past cannot claim an equal reality: it must sink to the level of a fancy or a dream, that is, to a level consistent with its deriving such reality as it possesses wholly from the present. Note, however, that at the same time it is an infancy, with its gross pleasures, and an adult sleep, with its grosser manifestations. When we come later to study the conceit, we shall see that it is an essential property of Donne and his like to maintain as even as possible the balance between two rival claimants to reality. In the second stanza there is a shift from time to space: the present itself is considered, and in the present, while there is no question of a before, there is one of an elsewhere. Donne and his lover are themselves the world; but also they are in 'one little room', and outside that room there is a vigorously active world – one that, as a result of voyages of discovery, is even expanding. Yet it too, like the past into the present, is absorbed into the little room, which becomes an everywhere. In the last stanza the future is glanced at, but no more than glanced at. For those who have the convictions of the first two stanzas the future can hold no terrors. It is in connection with the future that metaphysical dogma is brought in, but brought in, now I think obviously, not to establish a conclusion, but to lend what support it can to a conclusion that is already established. Or take *A Valediction, forbidding Mourning*. That the oddity of the image of the compasses has nothing to do with the poem's being metaphysical, it is perhaps not necessary to insist; that, however, it is very important to the poem still seems to be widely believed. Comparisons between Donne and Browning, on the ground that both use images that are unusual or at first sight unpoetical, are still common – Professor Praz, for instance, makes them. Why Browning drags the everyday and the familiar into his poetry is not always easy to see: I suspect it is the debauchee's device, of gaining interest for the habitual by giving it a new setting. In Donne the reason is always clear. The subject of this poem, for example, is again a metaphysical problem: that of the union of the lovers even when they are separated. The union is not such as would have satisfied a Romantic, in thought merely or imagination: Donne, as Courthope says, 'works by abstraction', and is not interested in a solution of his problem resting on the fallacy of the accident. It is in the very respect in which they are separated, that he wishes to show his lovers are united. Their souls are one substance, which has the invisibility of air, but also the obvious unity of a lump of gold. It is to stress this last point that the compasses are brought in. For gold, though originally solid enough, falls under suspicion of being likely to vanish away, once it has been compared to air. Compasses do not vanish: they have not the remotest connection either with physical or metaphysical subtlety. Hence, once the needful subtlety has been expounded, they close the poem and symbolize it – not, however, by their oddity. Or take, finally, the two *Anniversaries*. Of these Professor Praz made a confessedly unfavourable criticism. 'Had Donne always written in this style', he says, 'he would not rank much higher than Marino.' I think that, because of his lack of suitable definition or perhaps, because of his belief in an unfortunate one – Professor Praz is failing to see wood for the leaves. Everywhere in Donne there is much that is not metaphysical – that is connected with his activity as a satirist or as a mere wit, or that adheres to him from commerce with his age. In the *Anniversaries*, perhaps, there is a greater proportion of it than elsewhere. Read without due preparation they seem perhaps only bags of ingenious tricks. Read, however, with an adequate notion of the metaphysical in mind they reveal themselves, I think, as highly serious and tragic, as discussions of the dependence of the human on the divine, and of the chasm between the two. This indeed is what most critics have held them to be.

Four poems, especially when dismissed as curtly as I have dismissed these, are not, I know, sufficient evidence in favour of a new theory. But I do not propose to examine any more: partly because it is something that the reader, if he wishes, may do for himself; partly also, because the definition should serve more purposes than the illumination of individual poems. If it is at all adequate, there should be deducible from it some of the characters of metaphysical poetry in general. The isolation of such characters, if possible, will be very useful; and it will be the most searching test to which the definition could be put. One quality at any rate, is I think deducible from it. This is the notorious one, that metaphysical poetry is one of conceits.

First, however, I must make a distinction. The term 'conceit' is freely used to cover any extravagant hyperbole, any far-fetched comparison:

> And, like *Antipodes* in Shoes,
> Have shod their *Heads* in their *Canoos*.
> [Andrew Marvell, *Upon Appleton House*, 771–2.]

> Immortall Maid, who though thou would'st refuse
> The name of Mother, be unto my Muse
> A Father [Donne, *The second Anniversary*, 33–5]

> Shee, whose face, like clouds, turnes the day to night,
> Who, mightier then the sea, makes Moores seem white.
> [*Elegie II*, 45–6]

This is not the sort of conceit whose presence in metaphysical poetry I am anxious to establish. I do not think it need occur in such poetry, or that poetry in which it occurs need be – though it sometimes is – metaphysical. I wish to distinguish it sharply from another type of conceit which, for convenience sake, I will call the 'metaphysical conceit'. (I hope the name will not give the impression that I am moving in a circle: it will, I believe, reveal itself as appropriate, but for the time being should be taken as no more than a conventional mark.) Examples of this type are Marvell's 'green thought in a green shade', or the lines from *The Second Anniversary*:

> her pure, and eloquent blood
> Spoke in her cheekes, and so distinctly wrought,
> That one might almost say, her body thought,

Or, from *The Sun Rising*:

> She is all States, and all Princes, I,
> Nothing else is,

and the apostrophe to the sun, later in the same stanza:

> Shine here to us, and thou art every where;
> This bed thy center is, these walls thy spheare.

From *The Canonization*:

> You...
> Who did the whole worlds soul contract, and drove
>   Into the glasses of your eyes
>   (So made such mirrors and such spies
> That they did all to you epitomize,)
> Countries, Townes, Courts

From *A nocturnall upon S. Lucies day*:

> But I am by her death (which word wrongs her)
> Of the first nothing, the Elixer grown.

Or from *A Feaver*:

> O wrangling schooles, that search what fire
>   Shall burne this world, had none the wit
> Unto this knowledge to aspire,
>   That this her feaver might be it?

Let us take the simplest of them, Marvell's 'green thought'. This is a metaphor, whose two elements are thought and exten-

sion; one of them is substituted for the other, so that thought,
instead of extension, becomes the ground of colour. They have
been held to be contradictorily opposed – all things falling
either under extension or under thought, but none under both –
so that the metaphor is more than usually startling. So too is
that by which Elizabeth Drury's body thinks, or her blood is
eloquent or works as does an artificer; or that by which a lady's
fever consumes the universe; or that by which a bed becomes the
world, and the walls enclosing it the solar sphere. Within them
all there is high strain or tension, due to the sharpness with
which their elements are opposed. So however is there within
the conceits of the first group I quoted. That Antipodes should
shoe their heads, or that a spotless virgin should become of all
things a father, is not less but, if anything, more startling than
that a thought should be green. I imagine this is why all conceits
are usually spoken of as of a kind: their strangeness, so to speak,
dazzles the eye to any other qualities they may possess. But,
putting together the lines in which Elizabeth Drury's body is
said to think, and those in which she is invited to become a
father, it is surely impossible not to become aware of an
important difference between the two. The first image, like the
second, is startling; but also it is plausible, satisfying, natural
or – the contradiction forces itself upon me and should perhaps
not be resisted – *not* startling. I mean this: that while the elements of the second figure, female virginity and fatherhood,
come together only for a moment, at that moment cause surprise
and perhaps pleasure, and then immediately fly apart; body and
thought, coming together, remain together. Once made, the
figure does not disintegrate: it offers something unified and
'solid' for our contemplation which, the longer we contemplate,
only grows the more solid. Similarly, I think, the mind accepts
and dwells on with pleasure the conceit of a 'green thought', or
any other that I listed along with it; while it rejects immediately
the Antipodes who walk with their heads. And this also should
be noticed: the mind's usual way of accepting metaphors is to
kill them. Language is richly stocked with metaphors taken
over for daily use, which are now stone dead. If, even under such
use, they do not disintegrate, that is because within them, there
is no longer any tension which might cause them to do so.
Within the metaphysical conceit, however, even when it is being

dwelt on by the mind, tension between the elements continues. That is the most striking thing about it. As I said, it is at the same time starting and not startling. I do not like to use language of this kind; but, for the purpose of describing the metaphysical conceit, I do not see that any other could be used.

Some explanation obviously must be found. It might be suggested that, in these conceits, Donne once again, and this time Marvell with him, is 'working by abstraction': that they remove from the two elements they wish to unite, all associations that might embarass the union, which therefore endures. I do not think such an explanation will do. It does not account for the initial possibility of the union; nor does it bear in mind all the evidence. A bed, for example, has many and varied associations, yet Donne does not hesitate to link it with the universe; and, on the other hand, deprive fatherhood of all associations which might embarass, and no conceit at all remains in the three lines on Elizabeth Drury. That an immortal maid should beget a poem in the sense of inspiring it is no metaphor; or, at least, is one that has been long dead. So far as I can see, a satisfactory explanation can rest only upon the nature of the elements of the conceit. These must be such that they can enter into a solid union and, at the same time, maintain their separate and warring identity. Are such things to be found? Only if reality is of a peculiar kind. But metaphysics suggests it is of this kind; for metaphysical problems rise out of pairs of opposites that behave almost exactly as do the elements of a metaphysical conceit. Take the multiplicity and unity of reality, for example: the multiplicity submits to the unity for its coherence, and at the same time preserves itself as multiplicity; while the unity, without ceasing to be unity, receives from multiplicity its significance. The two support and complete, and at the same time deny, each other. Consider now 'her body thought'. Here body accepts the attribute of thought, without ceasing to be body; and thought, persisting as such, immerses itself in body. And both gain thereby: for they appear no longer as abstractions, but as a reality that requires nothing further for its completion. Elizabeth Drury seems to us a moment of our own experience. Similarly, the green of Marvell's garden inheres in an unwonted substrate, thought; his thought acquires a hitherto unaccustomed quality: in consequence, his experience in that garden is with us in all its fulness and freshness. If any conceit is taken, of the kind I have called metaphysical, I think it will be found that its elements are either a pair of opposites long known to metaphysics, or reducible to such a pair. In the few which I quoted there occurred, in *The Garden*, extension and thought; in *The Anniversary*, body and spirit; in *The Sun Rising* and *The Canonization*, the individual and the universe; in *The Nocturnal*, privation and actuality. If that is so, the quality of the metaphysical conceit which, at the close of the last paragraph, gave us pause, need no longer appear strange; or rather, it need no longer appear unique in its strangeness. Such strangeness as it has is only that of the world in which it is embedded. And that it should behave as it does is but to be expected from the nature of its parts. It is no association of things on account of a similarity due to an accident, as that a canoe for a moment rested upon a head; but of things that, though hostile, in reality cry out for association with each other.

If this then is the metaphysical conceit, its connection with metaphysical poetry as I defined it is obvious. The two are built up out of the same materials. However, it is not yet fully obvious that metaphysical poetry must deal with these materials as does the conceit; that, to deal with them all, it must have recourse to the conceit. But that becomes obvious, I think, once the method of metaphysicians themselves is considered. These abhor metaphor, for their one aim is to make reality as transparent to the intellect as possible, and metaphor is opaque to the intellect. Nevertheless, dealing with the materials with which the metaphysical poet deals, they cannot escape metaphor as their ultimate resource. That they do so is a commonplace of the history of philosophy: it is the accusation that Aristotle made against Plato, and that has been made against Aristotle many times since. It is the reproach that Thomas sought to avoid by that 'elusiveness' of which I spoke, weaving web after subtle web of propositions to veil a contradiction he inherited from Aristotle, but never quite succeeding. That metaphors employed by the metaphysicians must be metaphysical conceits needs, I think, only to be mentioned to be established. For they must have the character of such a conceit: within them, that is, there must be tension, while at the same time they satisfy in the unity they set up. There must be the tension, if distinctions painfully elaborated in other parts of the system are to be preserved. They must be satisfying, for the sole reason of their invention is that they should satisfy. If then, the metaphysician, in spite of his prejudices in favour of the intellect, cannot avoid the conceit, no more can the metaphysical poet. As a matter of fact, the conceit is what he seizes on straight away, for his sole purpose is to grasp reality, and intellect or sense is indifferent to him. As I said earlier of Donne, it is possible to be a metaphysical poet, and to have nothing or very little to do with metaphysical propositions.

From this point it would be profitable to go on and show how, with the aid of the metaphysical conceit, metaphysical poetry can be distinguished from the other types of poetry that have, at various times, been confused with it. Baroque poetry, for example, or the poetry which Johnson called 'metaphysical', has merely the baroque conceit: which, like Marvell's figure of the Antipodes, tends to fall apart like trumpery. Neither has it any function in its poem other than that of mere ornamentation; whereas the metaphysical conceit, stating impartially and at the same time solving the problem of its context, controls and unifies that context. Or Romantic poetry: in this, the sharp opposition necessary for the metaphysical conceit is rarely attained or, if attained, soon blunted. Opposites, if mentioned, are not united in a conceit, but hastily identified one with another; as in Shelley where, 'by a law divine all things mix and mingle'. Reality, losing its complexity, gives place to a dream. The Elizabethans start with an opposition between the intellect and the senses, fail to keep a balance between them, and come down heavily on the side of the senses. Hence they tend to exuberance or to a stolid quality; whereas metaphysical poetry is always alert, and is rarely exuberant, but rather elegiac. Contrast, for example, the wooing in *The Duchess of Malfi* with that in the *Extasy*. But all these distinctions are in themselves subjects for papers; and I prefer to devote what little remains of this one to the group from a discussion of which it started. I mean Dante and Lucretius, with whom (for many purposes) I class Chapman. These, I said, wrote metaphysics in poetry, rather than metaphysical poetry. The statement can do with a little clarification.

Dante, Lucretius and Chapman are disciples rather than meta-physicians themselves; that is, they make no independent approach to reality, but only through another man's work. This work has impressed them because it seemed to provide them with certainty; but it could do so, only because in their enthusiasm they overlooked such caution as it contained. The final metaphor, for example, which expressed at once the master's failure and the peculiar nature of his triumph – this they ignore. Or rather, they ignore it in so far as it is a metaphor: for, as needs must they take over the words in which it is couched. But the words for them have become a simple statement – astonishing perhaps, but still not to be questioned. The metaphor is dead. The statement they believe like any other in the system, if for no better reason, then *quia impossibile*. To Dante, for example,

> Chiaro mi fu allor com'ogni dove
> In cielo è Paradiso.   [*Paradiso*, III, 88–9]

It is clear to him, or rather was so in Heaven; and he is unconscious of a similar problem facing him in this life, on earth. At the centre of his universe, there is a conflation of substances and accidents. This is a mere conflation: neither substance nor accident puts up a fight for its continued existence as such. But perhaps what I am trying to say is best made clear by putting side by side passages from Dante and from Donne, in which they both touch upon the same difficulty. Dante, speaking of his and Beatrice's instantaneous ascent from star to star, says:

> del salire
> non m'accors'io, se non com'uom s'accorge
> anzi il primo pensier, del suo venire.
> E Beatrice quella che sì scorge
> di bene in meglio, sì subitamente
> che l'atto suo per tempo non si sporge.
>   [*Paradiso*, x, 34–9]

Donne, on the other hand, says of the flight of Elizabeth Drury's soul to heaven:

> And as these starres were but so many beads
> Strung on one string, speed undistinguish'd leads
> Her through those Spheares, as through the beads, a string,
> Whose quick succession makes it still one thing.

Dante presents us with the *fait accompli*: he and Beatrice are at the end of their mystic journey, and it does not trouble him how. Donne, on the other hand, tries to follow Elizabeth Drury point

277

by point: the problem of how the journey was possible interests him at least as much as the fact that it was made. In short, there is in Donne, there is not in Dante, the metaphysical conceit.

Metaphysical poetry, springing from a concern with problems with which the universe must always present mankind, is not confined to either one age or country. Yet the conditions in which it can be produced are by their nature somewhat rare in occurrence. Metaphysical distinctions must have been made; further, these distinctions must be so familiar that they are no longer felt merely as a challenge to the intellect. They must rouse an altogether different emotional reaction, tinged, perhaps, with a certain scepticism. It appears therefore, only at high points of civilization; perhaps only when that civilization is halting for a moment, or is beginning to decay. I find traces of it, I think, in Virgil; in Tasso of the *Aminta*, not of the *Gerusalemme*; but most of all, outside England, in the Spain of the Philips. There metaphysics was to be breathed in at the nostrils. In consequence, in some of the plays of Calderón, not the language merely, but the action is a metaphysical conceit: it is at once fleshly and spiritual, and the one, it seems, because the other. In his *autos* he developed a form of allegory – if that name indeed is appropriate – which would well repay examination. For in them it is not, for example, a beautiful woman who dies, nor is it Beauty that ceases to manifest itself on the earth; but Beauty itself, incredible as it seems, that dies. I mention this, because it appears to me that, in his approach to allegory, Calderón has much in common with Herbert. Herbert, Marvell and Donne, I would say, are the three English metaphysical poets.

9

WORDSWORTH:
A PRELIMINARY SURVEY

I

Wordsworth's poetry is not only an extensive, it is a difficult country; and therefore, before attempting to cross it, I have thought it worth while to summarize what I imagine I know about it. Much of this may be legend, and I put it forward without any confidence that it is anything more; but a summary of legend is useful if, by internal confusion or apparent improbability, it brings home the amount of labour necessary to attain the truth.

II

And first of the traps or pitfalls with which Wordsworth's poetry abounds. One of these is I think its mere amount, by which we should not allow ourselves to be unduly impressed. This may seem a slight temptation, but I am not sure that it is easy to avoid. Staying-power is a comparatively rare thing, and even the appearance of it moves at times to admiration. With Wordsworth it is an important question, how much of it is mere appearance; and an answer can be given only after going through a poem line by line, inquiring into the significance of each. It is not sufficient to listen for the general effect of a passage, which may be a sonorous cadence with a buzzing of meaning in the background. Wordsworth was skilled in sounding cadences, and with him as with any other poet meaning should be either more or less than a buzz.

From the *Prelude* and the Preface to the *Lyrical Ballads* it is I think at least probable that he looked on poetry as a sort of natural product, like fruit and flowers; brought into being by nature rather than by man, or by man only as nature works in him. Thus from one point of view he might be said to shift responsibility for composition from his own shoulders on to nature; from another, to arrogate to himself the privilege of unrestrained fertility. As nature a hundred daisies for a single oak, so he throws up a hundred insignificant verses for one of substance. But towards them all, as towards the daisies and the oak, he feels the sort of reverence due to the manifestations of a higher power. He receives them into his collected works, and arranges them in a cunning order to ensure that all shall be read; and in that way he at least dissuades, if he does not intimidate his critic from the task of discrimination.

III

Secondly we must take care not to be dazzled by his rhetorical skill – 'rhetorical' is a word with a number of senses, but I use it, I believe, in the best. It would be difficult to exaggerate this skill in Wordsworth, and the danger which results from it.

Nature, he seems to have thought, produces only the bare essence of poetry, to which man must fit an outer garment of words and metre; therefore a poet, if he would not be mute, must set himself to acquire the knack of metre, as he would any other accomplishment. Wordsworth laboured early and long for this end. 'I have bestowed great care upon my style', he said, 'and yield to none in the love of my art.' From his use of the terms elsewhere, it seems probable that by 'art' and 'style' he meant the power simultaneously to observe the rules for lucid and grammatical English, and for any verse-form in which he happened to be working. He practised and attained proficiency in a great many: in the sonnet, and in the forms of Spenser, Milton, Pope, Hamilton, Burns and Scott.

The sort of merit which he thus brought within his reach, and which it is important to recognize and name lest, remarkable as it is, it be mistaken for something yet more remarkable, is fairly clearly illustrated by his poem *Yew Trees*. This is familiar, if for no other reason, for being often quoted as an example of the grand style outside Milton. It may be so; but I do not think we can call it anything more than an exercise in Miltonics.

> those fraternal four of Borrowdale,
> Joined in one solemn and capacious grove;
> Huge trunks! and each particular trunk a growth
> Of intertwisted fibres serpentine
> Up-coiling, and inveterately convolved;
> Nor uninformed with Phantasy.

A brilliant exercise, but only brilliant. On re-reading I am sometimes halted by the line in which Time the Shadow, Death the Skeleton and the rest are said to 'meet at noontide'; there seems promise here of a complication of ideas; but if there is, it is soon untied. The ghostly company meet only for the unexpected purpose of united worship, or for the incongruous one of listening to the flood on Glaramara. The yew-trees themselves lack depth, and might as well be figures in tapestry. Wordsworth, I should say, is not much interested in his images or his ideas, except as they serve to support certain rhythms; it is these which claim the greater part of his attention, and which, as with a sterile art, he exploits for their own sake.

Mastery over metre qualifies him to be a conversational poet – the sort of poet, that is, who flourished in a number of countries during the Renaissance, and in England in the early eighteenth century. At these places and periods a firm tradition of poetic performance permitted the treatment of an unusually wide variety of subjects at least as efficiently in verse as in prose, and often with the urgency and vividness of verse. A number of passages in *The Prelude*, like the description of his dame at Hawkshead or of the sights of London, reach a high level of excellence in this way. One of them, on the Terror, suggests that he might have maintained himself fairly consistently at the highest level, if he had been secure of an audience; for poetry of this kind, to persist, depends on a society whose members continually stimulate and restrain. But the audience was lacking, and for various reasons he gradually withdrew into a more and more remote exile. In consequence, some of his later verse, which has been praised for its technical perfection, is no more than scholarly; it is directed, that is, at a distant, almost a disembodied audience. And some of the rest suffers from a lack of focus, as though it were directed at two widely differing audiences at once. This is the fault of the didactic part of *The Prelude*, where Wordsworth seems unable to convince himself that what he has to say is of itself such as to interest the reader. Therefore by means of orotundity and ornament he seeks to provide an elegant diversion, to combine, as it were, the roles of Lucretius and of Dyer in *The Fleece*. The result is a compromise which I find intensely irritating, though it has been praised. But *The Prelude*, because of a multitude of ingredients, deserves more than one paper to itself.

IV

A third kind of trap can be described in Wordsworth's own words. Readers of 'moral and religious inclinations', he says, 'attaching so much importance to the truths which interest them ...are prone to overrate the Authors by whom those truths are expressed and enforced. They come prepared to impart so much passion to the Poet's language that they remain unconscious how little, in fact, they receive from it.' The vocabulary is that of intellectualism; but what it expresses might serve as the basis for a distinction between more and less valuable responses to poetry.

Wordsworth often wrote, not only about joy in widest commonality spread, but about common joys. His subjects in themselves, and apart from any treatment he may give, are such as to evoke memories or aspirations in which it is pleasant, if not always profitable or proper, to indulge. If the opportunity for indulgence were offered alone, it might be immediately rejected; but its nature is masked – and this is the greatest danger; perhaps the last two kinds of traps, which I have taken separately, should be considered together – its nature is masked by the accompanying rhetoric. It is easy to be affected by the subject and by the style or metre of one of Wordsworth's poems, as by two separate things: the one appearing to dignify the other, because of their accidental association; but neither modifying the other – neither the metre imposing itself upon and ordering the subject, nor the subject filling out the cavities of the metre. And at the same time it is easy to assume that the poem as a whole is effective when the truth may be that as an integrated whole the poem does not exist. The point is a difficult and, I think, an important one, which will justify one or two illustrations.

Arnold's selection contains a number of not very striking poems; but the one of least merit is possibly that which begins:

> Pansies, lilies, kingcups, daisies,
> Let them live upon their praises;
> Long as there's a sun that sets,
> Primroses will have their glory;
> Long as there are violets,
> They will have a place in story:
> There's a flower that shall be mine,
> 'Tis the little Celandine.

The lilt, the tone, is that of a music-hall ditty; it is difficult to imagine how anyone with an ear sensitive to rhythm, with a feeling for more than the surfaces of words can have written it. As Wordsworth had both, the explanation may be the abdication of responsibility to which I have already referred. But how has the poem come to be approved? For it figures in other anthologies besides Arnold's – for example, in the *Oxford Book of Regency Verse*. In the first place the language is clear, the metre gives no occasion for stumbling; it has at least the negative virtues. And secondly the subject, or a large part of the subject, is humility, which is a popular quality; it inculcates the popular opinion that to be humble is to be happy, even to be merry; and finally, it harmonizes with the absentee or vacation cult of nature which was a force in English society and in English poetry from the middle of last century onwards. There was nothing that, in his better moments, Wordsworth despised more than he did this cult; there was nothing about which he wrote more lamely – or rather, when he can be taken to be writing about it, he is always at his lamest. Yet his choice of subjects is such, and his unfailing rhetorical skill, that he has imposed himself upon the cult, and figured as its canonized poet. In a similar way he has been the canonized poet of English and of Anglican institutions; and as recently as 1915, with the publication of Professor Dicey's *Statesmanship of Wordsworth*, he was hailed with renewed conviction as the poet of patriotism. His sentiments on that topic are of course unexceptionable; and he dresses them out in a language which the percipient can take to be that of inner compulsion, of inspiration. Yet some of these patriotic effusions, as Mr Leavis has said, are no more than claptrap; the best probably should not rank as high as what I have called his conversational successes. It seems that patriotism, like religion, is not a safe theme for poetry; and that, for the reason quoted from Wordsworth, it is at least as difficult to read as to compose.

The isolated appeal of the subject in passages like the above is no doubt too obvious for it nowadays to form a trap. But it was on account of their obviousness I chose them; it seemed to me they might help in a further discussion, of which the conclusion is not obvious at all. To what extent are we justified in acknowledging Wordsworth as a mystical poet, as is often done?

Are we being deceived somewhat in the manner described – that is, are we responding to the subject by itself, and to certain tricks of style by themselves, rather than to a poem in which both are in alliance and unison? By 'mystical poet' I do not mean one who has intense experiences on the occasion of natural phenomena, nor one who is convinced of the importance of spirit in the life of man and in the affairs of this world. This is perhaps not an unusual meaning for the term, but I employ it in a narrower and I hope more helpful sense. I mean by it a poet who has the sort of experience Wordsworth claims in one or two passages of *The Prelude* – that of a communion or a community with something outside and above the world, with a divine soul or with the highest truth.

The possibility that in these passages the subject may make an isolated appeal arises from the flattering nature of the belief that such communion is possible to a fellow-man; and from certain comfortable consequences which seem to follow. Wordsworth may play upon these rather than convey the experience upon which, if the belief is true, it must ultimately be based.

I take as an example the passage in which he seeks to tell what happened to him when, writing an account of his experiences, he realized that once he had crossed the Alps.

> And now recovering, to my soul I say
> I recognise thy glory; in such strength
> Of usurpation, in such visitings
> Of awful promise, when the light of sense
> Goes out in flashes that have shewn to us
> The invisible world, doth Greatness make abode,
> There harbours whether we be young or old.
> Our destiny, our nature and our home
> Is with infinitude, and only there;
> With hope it is, hope that can never die,
> Efforts, and expectation, and desire
> And something evermore about to be.

Let me first note about this passage the ample warrant it provides for all that has been said about Wordsworth's skill in rhetoric. Like Milton, he knows how to draw out the sense variously from verse to verse; or, as he put it to Klopstock, to secure 'an apt arrangement of pauses and cadences, and the sweep of whole paragraphs'. Secondly, the occasion seems not unsuitable for the display of such skill: an attempt, it seems, is to be made to communicate something by its nature difficult, if not incapable of communication, upon which therefore only a number of sallies can be made. If each is doomed to be ineffectual, all of them together, and the variety of their points of departure and return, may be not wholly without 'effect. 'Strength of usurpation' and 'visitings of awful promise' corroborate each other; and if it is not clear exactly how, inevitable lack of clarity is part of what is to be conveyed. The figure of an invisible world made visible by a flash of light which thereby extinguishes itself, as though by a supreme effort, recommends for acceptance a difficulty for which, even when accepted, there can be no hope of a solution. And as the passage goes on, a solution begins to appear less and less necessary: the metre becomes more regular, the difficulty is not at all impossible, it is even exhilarating to live with. The line, 'With hope it is, hope that can never die' encourages to aspiration; 'Efforts and expectation and desire' suggests an unremitting eagerness in the soul. The last line, 'And something evermore about to be' is the most regular of all.

The trouble is that it is too regular – too regular to be smooth. There is no peace about it, but a merciless beat; and with infinitude there surely should be peace. When we have reached this line the suspicion arises, I think, that Wordsworth is not in fact where a mystic should be – with infinitude, outside or above the world; but rather, well within it. And if so some of the preceding lines need to be reconsidered, and our opinion on them to be revised. Aspiration can be unreservedly welcome only where, as with infinitude, there is certainty that it will be fulfilled; elsewhere 'hope that can never die' is but a euphemism for hope that has never lived. And elsewhere than with infinitude efforts and expectation and desire are grim companions: that eagerness is unremitting is no guarantee that, in this world, it will not be baffled. If we turn our attention from the sound to the sense of the last line we see it to have the minimum of meaning: there is nothing in the future to which it will not apply. So far as we can talk of a future in eternity it is of a piece with the present and prophecy cannot arouse mistrust; but to a creature in time the mere idea of futurity cannot bring consolation, and confidence based upon it and nothing more is a poor thing. Loudly to proclaim such a confidence is a still poorer thing.

If we read over the passage with these and similar reflections in mind we discover I think that the rhetoric is not only skilful, it is too obviously skilful: it has no natural movement which, if we admire, we admire as concrete in the substance which moves; but rather a mechanical, to admire which we must abstract and even oppose it to the substance. 'How subtle the play of the levers!' we say, and all the time are thinking of the unexpectedness of such subtlety in dead matter. The poem is not alive, but an extremely cleverly constructed simulacrum; a robot put together no doubt for high purposes; but still not a poem.

It is sometimes said that, to judge with any security of a mystical verse, one should be a mystic oneself. That would however reduce the number of judges to such an extent, that it is hardly likely to be true. It may be suggested that the questions whether Wordsworth succeeded in conveying a mystical experience, and whether he had it, are two different questions, the one falling under biography, the other under criticism; and that the answers to them are not necessarily identical. Not that biography is irrelevant to criticism, to which it can give valuable if extra-technical aid: and the biographical question it is true might profitably be raised here. But it would require much time and space: to analyse (among other things) the biographical element in *The Prelude*, to compare it with the similar element in *Tintern Abbey* (from which it seems to differ in not unimportant ways; as though Wordsworth altered his views about his own experiences as he grew older), and finally to compare that biography, according to whatever view prove more acceptable, with the history of a mystic or mystics who are fairly widely acknowledged to be such.

In default of such aid, it is perhaps advisable to consider somewhat closely a second passage. I will choose the lines about the Simplon Pass, as the most difficult ones I know to criticize satisfactorily. If, as is only too likely, I cannot make clear my point about them and their kind, perhaps I can at least make the difficulty clear; and that is a sufficiently important matter.

The lines are as follows:

> the brook and road
> Were fellow-travellers in this gloomy Pass,
> And with them did we journey several hours
> At a slow step. The immeasurable height
> Of woods decaying, never to be decayed,
> The stationary blasts of water-falls,

And everywhere along the hollow rent
Winds thwarting winds, bewilder'd and forlorn,
The torrents shooting from the clear blue sky,
The rocks that mutter'd close upon our ears,
Black drizzling crags that spake by the way-side
As if a voice were in them, the sick sight
And giddy prospect of the raving stream,
The unfetter'd clouds, and region of the Heavens,
Tumult and peace, the darkness and the light
Were all like workings of one mind, the features
Of the same race, blossoms upon one tree,
Characters of the great Apocalypse,
The types and symbols of Eternity,
Of first and last, and midst, and without end.

[*Excursion*, vi (1805), 553–572]

I had better say at once, to prevent misunderstanding as far as I am able, that I think the greater part of this passage is very impressive indeed. I think it so impressive that I am disappointed perhaps more than I should be with the rest; but this I think distracts and divides the attention, although it is short. It may also influence unfavourably the style of the whole.

In these lines Wordsworth, it seems to me, is trying to do not one thing but two; or rather, having done one thing and done it well, he goes on to another which perhaps by its nature cannot be so well done. Down to the last three lines he is concerned to express a feeling of surprise, almost vexation: like the thwarting winds he is bewildered and forlorn; while the woods, the water-falls and the rocks about him threaten ruin and decay, they seem fixed for ever. They threaten destruction to one another, and even to the spectator – there are sick sights and giddy prospects – nevertheless there is and there will be no annihilation, only persistence. He finds escape from his bewilderment by, so to speak, living into the phenomena by which it is caused: in all of them he finds the working of a 'single mind', with which he can identify himself, or of which he can become a part. And then he sees that the stresses which they exert upon one another and upon himself, all of which he experiences in himself, serve only for their mutual support. This notion of immobility resulting where action and change might be expected occurs elsewhere in Wordsworth's best poetry, of some of which it is almost a mark; but in such work he rests in the notion as the only satis-faction which the circumstances can afford. Here however he takes a step further, and seeks a satisfaction which so far from springing from the circumstances seems only to discount them. The bewilderment yields to, or is transformed into, a revelation, an apocalypse, and the ground for it is removed by degrading the woods, the waterfalls and the rocks from being themselves eternal into types and symbols of eternity. And this eternity, rather than charged with a greater significance than what are said to be its symbols, seems empty of everything: it is dismissed in flat pentameter, the only content of which is the highest common factor of the many associations hanging about a scrap from the liturgy. In other words Wordsworth (I think) finally adopts an answer which has no particular relevance to, and is therefore an escape from, his immediate problem; which, as it might answer any problem, answers none, and is provided for him rather by talk about mysticism than by mysticism itself – by religiosity rather than religion: at least by a deadening, not a vivifying force.

Perhaps I exaggerate: but I think it is a danger that these last few lines, connected with their predecessors by the sweep of the metre, and offering the reader an alternative against which, in the context, he is least on his guard, may hinder him from entering into the full and difficult meaning of that context; and they may do so, even when the alternative is rejected. How Wordsworth came to write in this mixed and broken way, if, as I think, he did do so, is obviously a serious problem; it would almost seem that acute perception was something of which he had learnt to be afraid. Elsewhere there are traces of a similar fear; of which, of course, it would be a gross impertinence to speak in any tone of censure, not of regret. Perhaps also the phenomenon may be not unconnected with what has already been described as an abdication of responsibility in composition.

v

From a summary account of what may be the traps – the marshly lowlands, the hidden gulfs – in Wordsworth's poetry, I pass to an account which must be yet more summary of what seem to be its highlands. From a distance it is no less possible to be mistaken about these than about the former; and as they are of wider significance, I speak with greater diffidence.

It is I think a useful question to ask how Wordsworth first came to believe that he was a poet; a man, that is, in whom nature works so as to produce poetry. As he thought that nature, instead of repeating herself, provides for a development of the spirit or a gradual revelation of truth, it must have been because he felt he had something new within him.

Part of it was a peculiar sensibility to nature, or a novel intimacy with her and her manifestations. When he was fourteen, he says, he became conscious 'of the infinite variety of natural appearances which had been unnoticed by poets of any age and country', and resolved 'to supply in some degree the deficiency'. But he was more than an observer: the other childhood experience must be remembered, that he sometimes felt himself slipping into 'an abyss of idealism'. He was part of what he saw, or what he saw was part of him. And as early as the *Descriptive Sketches* he speaks of 'abandoning the cold rules of painting' to consult both 'nature and his feelings'. From that date onwards he gives no mere lists of natural appearances, but groupings of them as they served to prompt a dominant emotion.

As long as what he calls the idealism persisted, or whenever it reasserted itself, this emotion was some degree of joy; for there was nothing other than himself by which he might be thwarted. It marks various well-known passages in *The Prelude*:

> The sea was laughing at a distance; all
> The solid mountains were as bright as clouds,
> Grain-tinctured, drench'd in empyrean light;
> And in the meadows and the lower grounds,
> Was all the sweetness of a common dawn,
> Dews, vapours and the melody of birds,
> And Labourers going forth into the fields.

It is at its most exuberant in the spring poems of the *Lyrical Ballads*:

> Love, now a universal birth
> From heart to heart is stealing,
> From earth to man, from man to earth;
> – It is the hour of feeling.
>
> One moment now may give us more
> Than years of toiling reason:
> Our minds shall drink at every pore
> The spirit of the season.

But exaggerations of this kind are themselves a criticism of the mood: as by its nature it is fleeting, it can be maintained for any length of time only by self-deception, to which one means is a loud boasting.

Already in his childhood Wordsworth had made such a criticism: 'idealism' he had recognized as an 'abyss', and to save himself had put out his hand. In doing so he was not repeating the Johnsonian experiment: his intention was not to refute a metaphysic, but to repeat a type of experience, that of being resisted, which for a time he had forgotten. Resistance, thwarting, comes from things outside himself, other than himself: and the second new thing about his poetry is I think its preoccupation with *other things as other*. In various ways they threaten his equanimity, disturb his peace.

In his early years there seems to have been a rapid oscillation between the sense of joyous union, and one of divorce from the external world; the latter giving rise to unhappiness, and at times to fear. A mountain pursued him 'with measured motion, like a living thing'; and 'after he had seen that spectacle' – these are his words:

> for many days my brain
> Work'd with a dim and undetermin'd sense
> Of unknown modes of being; in my thoughts
> There was a darkness, call it solitude
> Or blank desertion, no familiar shapes
> Of hourly objects...
> But huge and mighty Forms that do not live
> Like living men mov'd slowly through the mind
> By day and were the trouble to my dreams.

From time to time he returns to this notion of opposition, of enmity – not only between himself, but between other people and the external world; and at times, as in the Simplon Pass, between the external occupants of the world. But it does not long remain the centre of his interest. Conceived of as enemies, other things are in a measure like himself, and in that measure reconciliation with them might be possible; it is in the measure in which they are unlike himself, in which they are other, that the fascination they exert is unescapable.

Are they real? he seems compelled to ask. They are so different, that there is no quality however abstract he might split off from himself – not even the bare quality of being – in which they might partake. Either they exist exactly as he does, and are himself – but that is impossible; or they do not exist at all – but they obviously do. And as though to convince himself of the latter fact in a subtler manner than by clutching at a wall, he considers repeatedly in his verse the sort of realities which maintain themselves under apparently impossible conditions.

> the lifeless arch of stones in air
> Suspended, the cerulean firmament
> And what it is; the River that flows on
> Perpetually, whence comes it, whither tends,
> Going and never gone; the fish that moves
> And lives as in an element of death.

A rainbow he saw near Coniston, 'the substance thin as dreams', nevertheless stood unmoved through the uproar of a storm,

> Sustain'd itself through many minutes' space,
> As if it were pinn'd down by adamant.

And reflections in water occupy his attention either because of the instability of the element on which they are traced – like that of Peele Castle, which 'trembled, but it never passed away'; or because of their apparent identity with the object reflected, from which nevertheless they are other. Mr de Selincourt quotes an early version of some lines in the *Excursion*:

> Once coming to a bridge that overlook'd
> A mountain torrent, where it was becalm'd
> By a flat meadow, at a glance I saw
> A twofold image; on the grassy bank
> A snow-white ram, and in the peaceful flood
> Another and the same; most beautiful
> The breathing creature; nor less beautiful
> Beneath him, was his shadowy counterpart:
> Each had his glowing mountains, each his sky,
> And each seemed centre of his own fair world.
> A stray temptation seized me to dissolve
> The vision – but I could not.[1]

He had picked up a pebble, but dropped it unthrown. The passage has many defects, but I quote it for one or two phrases – 'another and the same', 'each had his glowing mountains' – and for the conclusion. This suggests that the habit of contemplating things which exist when and in a way in which existence

---

[1] See *The Prelude* (Oxford, 1928), pp. 562-3. (E.M.W.)

seems impossible has led to a respect for them which is almost superstitious. When other things are fleeting they are capable of being destroyed; but that they are fleeting is a vindication of their reality as other, and this forbids destruction like a desecration.

Reflections in water retain form and colour; and carrying analysis as far as it can go, Wordsworth seeks to know what they have which makes them to be other than their objects. What are the principles, which render possible a multiplicity of things? which separate him from the external world, as objects in the external world are separated from one another? The ultimate answer he gives is time and place, duration and extension: it is because the reflection of the ram is elsewhere than the ram itself that, apparently identical in all other respects, it is yet obviously different from the ram. And it is upon duration and extension which, highly abstract as they are, yet seem the soil and sap of other reality, that the superstitious respect just noted finally bears. However confused his account of the experience when he realized that he had crossed the Alps, the experience was of an impressive kind; and, stripping the account of its reference to eternal destiny, we see the experience to have consisted merely in the realization that, whereas he had been on one side of the Alps, he was now on the other. Or we might say that, as he does not contrast the two sides in respect of any of their qualities – their orientation, their contour or their covering – he realized there is diversity of place. It is this, and this alone, that 'wrapt him in a cloud'. That a mountain barrier rose between two particular places – that they were the *sides* of a mountain – was not his concern, for there rose between them another barrier which, if more ideal, is more impassable. It was erected by the very notion of space, of which the parts are by definition external one to another; each, for the rest, an *other*. The experience is perhaps more easily discerned behind a second passage from *The Prelude*, which describes an entry into London. At the time Wordsworth was not occupied by any ideas of the capital as a storehouse of tradition or magnificence, and his immediate surroundings did not invite attention – there were 'vulgar men' about him, and 'mean shapes on every side'. His senses and his memory were unheeded or asleep. But he was awake to the notion of the boundary, the imaginary line which sets up place against place, and by crossing which, from having been without London, he would find himself within.

> The very moment that I seem'd to know
> The threshold now is overpass'd...
> A weight of Ages did at once descend
> Upon my heart.

By a sort of intellectual vision he saw himself as having been *there* and now being *here*, and this was sufficient to move him deeply.

Duration is marked and made manifest by events; and there are passages in some of Wordsworth's poems which are perhaps only too well known, in which the sole purpose seems to be to record that something, no matter what, has happened. Throughout a number of stanzas the metre is supported by little more than expletives, repetitions and tautologies; our attention is claimed, it seems, only that it may be cheated of an object – for the stanzas contain neither narration nor description, and very little reflection. The reader is exacerbated or wearied, though Wordsworth, presumably, is full of excitement: so that when something finally happens, if only the prevarication of a child or an old man's tears, it is hailed with relief.

Passages of this kind are little more than biographical or psychological curiosities: in them, Wordsworth is so fully occupied with abstractions that he forgets the concrete business of living. But when he returns he is the better qualified to face its problems, having a keener eye for their elements. The external world, for example, he sees quite clearly is not to be subdued or placated like an enemy; in so far as it is external, it is there while we are here, then while we are now: it is irreducibly *other* than ourselves, so that to stand in any relations to it, to affect it, even to be aware of it, seems to imply a contradiction. If we wish to give any account of it, we can employ only adjectives which are the opposites of those which we apply to ourselves: if we are active then it is immobile, if we are alive then it is dead, as points in space are dead. Yet it is in such a world that he finds himself, and with which he must come to terms, on pain of a sense of desertion blanker than that to which he was first summoned by the pursuing mountain.

His solution seems to be something like the following. He imagines – but imagine is a weak word; he creates and it is part of his own experience – a kind of being in which both the external world and himself can share. It combines the characters of both: internally it is active and striving, as he is, but looked at from outside it is immobile like the world. While for himself, that is, he renounces the possibility of action upon other things, he need not on that account feel cut off from them. They and he are united by the common possession of a hidden activity, in the knowledge of which he can feel, while among them, at home and at peace. If his spirit is sealed, so is that of the dead Lucy, so are rocks and stones and trees; and with dead things he has a sort of sympathy. The universe as thus apprehended has no very remote resemblance to the Simplon Pass: if it cannot quite properly be spoken of as a balance of stresses, it yet contains a number of stresses which, though they are active, produce no alteration. At these moments of apprehension Wordsworth describes himself as 'seeing into the life of things', or elsewhere, as seeing 'the very pulse of the machine'. The word 'machine' is important, for it gives that sense of change within stability which I am trying to suggest. And the pulse is conveyed in verses, some of which are among the best he wrote, which describe ambiguous creatures like the horse

> that stood
> Alone upon a little breast of ground
> With a clear silver moonlight sky behind.
> With one leg from the ground the creature stood
> Insensible and still, – breath, motion gone,
> Hairs, colour, all but shape and substance gone,
> Mane, ears and tail, as lifeless as the trunk
> That had no stir of breath; we paused awhile
> In pleasure of the sight, and left him there
> With all his functions silently sealed up,
> Like an amphibious work of Nature's hand,
> A Borderer dwelling betwixt life and death.[1]

The horse has one foot off the ground, and that it is clear he might move is one of the reasons for the pleasure which he gives; the other reason is that he is restrained from moving, or that he restrains himself. Similar to the horse in this way are the solitary beings whom Wordsworth met at night, or in almost permanently lonely places: like the discharged soldier, who remained 'fix'd to his place'; 'at his feet His shadow lay, and

[1] See *The Prelude* (Oxford, 1928), pp. 601–2. (E. M. W.)

moved not'. 'I wish'd to see him move', exclaims Wordsworth,
that he might be assured of the reality of the soldier; but when at
last the soldier did so

> I beheld
> With ill-suppress'd astonishment his tall
> And ghastly figure moving at my side.

Most carefully drawn of them all is the Leech-gatherer, who is
compared both to a 'huge stone', and to a 'sea-beast' – that is,
he is capable of locomotion, but will not engage upon it. He is

> Motionless as a cloud...
> That heareth not the loud winds when they call

– he does not hear, not in the sense that he is deaf, but that he
will not obey –

> And moveth all together, if it move at all.

I do not know whether Wordsworth was acquainted with the
doctrine of the school that all motion is by parts; whether or no,
something of the kind has a share in the effect which is intended
here. 'The cloud must move all together' – that is it cannot be
imagined to move, for if it did one part would be seen to take
precedence of another; and yet it may move, for otherwise it
would not have a share in being, in reality.

VI

So far as I know Wordsworth was quite new, and has remained
unique, in concerning himself in this way with 'being as such':
the old phrase is convenient, in spite or because of its habit of
bearing now the minimum, now the maximum of meaning. He
explored the significance, or examined the experience, of being
for other things, and this modified the experience of being for
himself. It would be a mistake, I think, to see in this any
influence of contemporary German thought: there is a difficulty
about the dates. Wordsworth was not sympathetic to German
thinkers, and the whole course of his dealing with the problem
suggests that it was posed for him by what he lived through,
rather than by what he read or what he heard in Coleridgean
conversation. And as the achievement in this matter was his
own, he used it as the starting-point for a new enterprise.

The problem of suffering, if he awoke to it later than to that of the external world, came in early manhood to occupy him no less continually. The notion of being at which he arrived seemed to offer promise of a solution. For if suffering arises from thwarted effort, either to affect other things or to avoid being affected by them, it is a consequence of a creature's desire to operate beyond itself. And if this is renounced, as Wordsworth conceived it might and should be, suffering as the occasion of rebellion or complaint will cease. But is it humanly possible to carry renunciation to the point which may be necessary? It is conceivable that other things should close in to such an extent upon a creature that, if he yields to them, any inner activity left is too insignificant to be called human. There are three poems which are perhaps especially important by the answers they return to this question.

They are *The Leech-gatherer*, *The Lesser Celandine*, and *Michael*. It will be possible to notice them only briefly.

When he comes across the leech-gatherer Wordsworth is a man of moods, and he generalizes from himself to the human race:

> As high as we have mounted in delight,
> In our dejection do we sink as low.

But the leech-gatherer, like the stone to which he is compared, knows no moods; he has few hopes, and such disappointments as come his way do not disturb him. Though the stock of leeches has dwindled, and they are to be found only by wandering alone about the weary moors,

> Yet still I persevere, and find them where I may.

He preserves a courteous and cheerful demeanour, even 'stately in the main'. Wordsworth marvels there should be 'in that decrepit man so firm a mind'; and contrasting the firmness with his own levity, which is at the mercy of other things, he accepts the implied rebuke.

The Lesser Celandine usually closes its petals against the foul weather:

> But lately, one rough day, this Flower I passed
> And recognised it, though an altered form,
> Now standing forth an offering to the blast,
> And buffeted at will by rain and storm.

> I stopped, and said with inly-muttered voice,
> 'It doth not love the shower, nor seek the cold:
> This neither is its courage nor its choice,
> But its necessity in being old.
>
> The sunshine may not cheer it, nor the dew;
> It cannot help itself in its decay.'

Other things have compelled the Celandine to forfeit the last scrap of independence and dignity; therefore it can administer no rebuke – it cannot be admired, but only deplored.

Nevertheless it has had what might be considered its due of glory: if it falls a victim, it is only to the forces of time and senility about which, as nothing escapes them, there seems something equitable. In *Michael* the shepherd and his family are involved in a similar fate while still in their prime – for the old man is 'strong and hale' – and although they have taken every measure to avoid it. Like the leech-gatherer they make few claims on life:

> Our lot is a hard lot; the sun himself
> Has scarcely been more diligent than I;

they are 'neither gay perhaps, nor cheerful'; and if they have objects and hopes, it is for 'a life of eager industry', for the continued performance of the tasks which their ancestors performed before them. Their only pleasure is 'the pleasure which there is in life itself', that which is necessary to the pulse and implied in the spark of consciousness. They are submissive to the natural course of things, of which their tasks are almost a part; and, had circumstances permitted, it might have been said of them as of their ancestors, that when

> At length their time was come, they were not loth
> To give their bodies to the family mould.

They seek to preserve a submissiveness even to their abnormal afflictions; and the hopes and fears which these cannot but provoke, if wild, are immediately curbed. Each watches the other for signs of strain:

> the Old Man paused,
> And Isabel sat silent...
> ...her face brightened. The Old Man was glad.

At night Isabel

> Heard him, how he was troubled in his sleep;
> And when they rose at morning she could see
> That all his hopes were gone.

Here it is the ready confidence of the son which redresses the balance:

> She said to Luke, while they two by themselves
> Were sitting at the door, 'Thou must not go...
> For if thou leave thy Father he will die.'
> The youth made answer with a jocund voice;
> And Isabel, when she had told her fears,
> Recovered heart.

But Luke too has his misgivings; and when setting on his journey he reaches the public way he finds it necessary to 'put on a bold face'. All is in vain; Luke is driven into exile, and Michael survives hardly as a man but as an animal – by his brute strength.

> His bodily frame had been from youth to age
> Of an unusual strength.

is the first thing we are told about him, and almost the last. He is moreover a sick animal, able to perform some but not all of his instinctive tasks. When he visits the site of the projected sheepfold,

> He never lifted up a single stone.

The verse of the poem is a delicate thing. It has almost ceased to beat, and seems maintained only by the flutter of tenuous hopes and sickening fears.

> the unlooked-for claim
> At the first hearing, for a moment took
> More hope out of his life than he supposed
> That any old man ever could have lost.

Wordsworth, who was so often an imitator, here speaks with his own voice; and the verse is the contribution he makes to prosody. He uses it rarely – elsewhere than in *Michael* only, I think, in *Margaret* and occasionally in *The Brothers*; but it should be taken as a measure of his work. Against it the verse of the *Simplon Pass*, though very different in intention, reveals itself forced and harsh. As I believe I suggested, what is noble in the *Simplon Pass* is in a measure debased by the immediate context.

VII

From *Michael* it appeared that the extinction of suffering is the extinction of humanity. To be sure of this lesson, it had been necessary for Wordsworth to experience suffering in an exquisite form, unadulterated in any way – as for example with the satisfaction of playing either to himself or to an audience. There is no audience in *Michael*, except shepherds too close to the hero to do anything but 'feel pity in their heart'.

I do not know that any other poet has done quite the same thing; I do not think that Wordsworth did it either before or since. It is as though he exposed a nerve which, as it was too sensitive for the impressions it could not but receive, must immediately be deadened.

The conclusions of both *The Leech-gatherer* and *The Lesser Celandine* suggest that something like this happened. Though both are less intense than *Michael*, neither maintains such intensity as it possesses to the end: suddenly both run down with a sickening whir – or, to change the metaphor, the music in both poems is broken by a discord. After the discovery of firmness in the leech-gatherer, Wordsworth does not prepare himself for any rigorous self-discipline: he 'laughs himself to scorn':

> 'God', said I, 'be my help and stay secure;
> I'll think of the Leech-gatherer on the lonely moor!'

In this jauntiness there is no relevance to his circumstances. It is as though he had become oblivious of these; as though they were now presented to the deadened nerve: and the jauntiness had opportunity to supervene from a disconnected part of his consciousness. In *The Lesser Celandine* the break is even more noticeable. It happens in the last line of a stanza:

> The sunshine may not cheer it, nor the dew;
> It cannot help itself in its decay;
> Stiff in its members, withered, changed of hue.
> And, in my spleen, I smiled that it was gray.
>
> To be a Prodigal's Favourite – then, worse truth,
> A Miser's Pensioner – behold our lot!
> O Man, that from thy fair and shining youth
> Age might but take the things Youth needed not!

The word 'spleen' has a multitude of meanings, one of which might be suitable to the poem; but there is no reason, other than a complete abandonment of seriousness, why Wordsworth should smile. And this would explain the final stanza, which is the sort of platitude with which we dismiss an argument when we have not solved it, and when it has come to weary us; or the copybook maxim with which we hand over a vexing problem of conduct to chance for its decision. Wordsworth's maxim is not so much irrelevant to his problem as a denial of the conditions which it presupposes. The Celandine 'cannot help itself in its decay' – 'if only it could!' observes the final stanza.

But, as though foreseeing the outcome of the solution attempted in *Michael*, already in *Margaret* Wordsworth had prepared for another way of dealing with suffering. Unlike *Michael*, *Margaret* plays to an audience, who are the author and the Wanderer; and like all spectators of tragedy, in so far as mere spectators, they are in the role of *tertius gaudens*. Evil to the actor is good to them. Some of the better poems of the middle years – up to *Peele Castle* and beyond – are devoted in part at least to affirming the belief that evil is in addition and in some way good. The belief may be true, or may be necessary; but as, without revelation or an augmentation of the faculties, it cannot be comprehended without at least partly neglecting evil, the poems, if they can be looked down on from no mean height, can certainly be looked down on from *Michael*. Others of Wordsworth's occupations were, with the help of the optimistic Hartley, refashioning his memories of the past so that they might support the belief (and hence *The Prelude*, in passages like the two we have examined, is of the nature of a palimpsest); or indicting scholarly poems and less disinterested ones on behalf of patriotism, Anglicanism and the like. Some of these have already received summary notice.

But an exploratory paper is no occasion to draw the lower contours of Wordsworth's poetry. It is enough to indicate the high peaks; for even about these – I hope I may be forgiven this last repetition – a distant observer is likely to be mistaken.

10

BAUDELAIRE

I

Baudelaire is in many ways so remote from us – we do not like his age, nor his more obvious reactions against the age – that we need, I think, to be specially careful when we study him. It is easy to mistake his word and gesture.

For example, it is sometimes assumed that, because he frequently mentions the devil, he was not only a Christian, but a sort of Christian ascetic; or, to use the humbler and more appropriate term, a Puritan. A number of well-known poems can be taken to imply this; and there are notorious phrases from the *Journals*, such as: 'Faire l'amour, c'est faire le mal.' But it will be suggested in this paper that the poems, if they are not to be largely emptied of their meaning, cannot be read in this way; and as for the *Journals*, it may be doubted whether they can be appropriately discussed by a critic at all. They are rather matter for the psychologist or the biographer. Baudelaire had not that habit of systematic reflection, at least on moral subjects, which alone makes *obiter dicta* immediately instructive: in his case they tend to be accompanied by sound and smell, rather than by light. They are explosions, provoked by a momentary joy or pain. It is they which need to be interpreted with the aid of considered utterances such as the poems, rather than the other way round.

If we read the poems closely, we see that Baudelaire does not always talk about the same kind of devil. One he describes as above all cunning – 'rusé', 'savant' – and his sole business is to deceive; another can spare himself this labour, for he has the power of a despot over slaves; while yet a third is a sort of honest merchant, the excellent quality of whose wares secures him clients. The importance of these distinctions is that whereas the first devil is a part of Christian tradition, which has satisfied centuries of thinking men; the second and third are drawn – ultimately perhaps from the Manichees, – but immediately from the Satanist or diabolist poets, who have satisfied few men but themselves.

Accordingly, the quality of Baudelaire's poetry making mention of the devil varies considerably. At times he does not much differ from Swinburne, at least in the paradoxical mood.

> O Satan, prends pitié de ma longue misère!
> Toi dont la large main cache les précipices
> Au somnambule errant au bord des édifices...
> Toi qui, magiquement, assouplis les vieux os
> De l'ivrogne attardé foulé par les chevaux...
> Toi qui, pour consoler l'homme frêle qui souffre
> Nous appris à mêler le salpêtre et le soufre

and so on. There is no clear reason why such benefits as the above should be attributed to Satan; nor why – if they exist, if the sleep-walker has a special immunity from precipitation, or the senile drunkard from pounding under horses' feet – they should be singled out for praise. It is true that gunpowder may console, but that is not its obvious purpose. In such verses as these Baudelaire is not only intending to astonish, he is content with doing so; he is irresponsible in his writing; he cannot therefore be taken seriously.

There are however other verses about the devil which are highly serious; and yet others which, while not ostentatiously trivial like the above, do not carry conviction. Perhaps it is best to call them, simply, poor: and if they are poor, Baudelaire's skill being what it is, it must be that he is dishonest – either with himself or with the reader. These two kinds of verses can, I think, be illustrated from the introductory poem to the *Fleurs du Mal*, where they are somewhat curiously juxtaposed.

The opening stanzas I would call highly serious. The adjectives trim their nouns to the exact shape required, and at times to a pin point; the images not only arrest, but retain and satisfy the attention. The subject, human levity, is one with which we are well acquainted.

> La sottise, l'erreur, le péché, la lésine,
> Occupent nos esprits et travaillent nos corps,
> Et nous alimentons nos aimables remords
> Comme les mendiants nourrissent leur vermine.
>
> Nos péchés sont têtus, nos repentirs sont lâches,
> Nous nous faisons payer grassement nos aveux,
> Et nous rentrons gaiement dans le chemin bourbeux,
> Croyant par de vils pleurs laver toutes nos taches.

Man's folly and ignorance are mentioned first, because they alone explain the facility of his remorse, and the vanity of his pursuits. Rather than solid and durable goods, he chooses those which are unsubstantial and fleeting; his energies are therefore dissipated, and his will enfeebled. And in this he is encouraged by the devil, who maintains the supply of unsubstantial goods.

> Sur l'oreiller du mal c'est Satan Trismégiste
> Qui berce longuement notre esprit enchanté,
> Et le riche métal de notre volonté
> Est tout vaporisé par ce savant chimiste.

In these lines, the devil is the devil of Christianity. But it is not necessary to be a Christian to see in human experience a succession of problems, subtle enough to be worthy of a malign intelligence; and serious enough for a wrong answer to ruin the nature of man.

In the first line of the next stanza, however, the devil is transformed into the despot of the diabolists:

> C'est le Diable qui tient les fils qui nous remuent!

Moral problems would thus seem to vanish from experience, and responsibility for action be lifted from human shoulders. But, lest man should appear blameless, Baudelaire hastens to accuse him of another failing. He is no longer frivolous, but perverse. He is not only forced on evil, but, says Baudelaire, he also chooses it and longs for it as such. Precise attention to the meaning of 'choose' and of 'evil' would show this to be impossible, were not precision the last thing with which Baudelaire is now concerned.

> Ainsi qu'un débauché pauvre qui baise et mange
> Le sein martyrisé d'une antique catin,
> Nous volons au passage un plaisir clandestin
> Que nous pressons bien fort comme une vieille orange.

The adjectives no longer sharpen but, if anything, blunt their nouns. That a debauchee should be poor serves to lighten, rather than deepen any horror inspired by his partner; that an orange is old is an obvious reason why – if no other fruit can be obtained – it should be well squeezed. A few lines earlier the reader was informed that men take the path to hell 'sans horreur': it is not therefore clear why the pleasures which they snatch should be clandestine. An increasing disorder in the poet's ideas becomes apparent through lines like

> Et, quand nous respirons, la Mort dans nos poumons
> Descend, fleuve invisible, avec de sourdes plaintes

– which are not only obscure in themselves, but irrelevant to the context – and the Swinburnian exuberance of the following:

> Mais parmi les chacals, les panthères, les lices,
> Les singes, les scorpions, les vautours, les serpents,
> Les monstres glapissants, hurlants, grognants, rampants
> Dans la ménagerie infâme de nos vices,
> Il en est un plus laid, plus méchant, plus immonde!

Obviously the intention is to arouse disgust. But, it seems necessary to ask, why cannot Baudelaire fulfil this intention, except by heaping together nouns and adjectives? This defeats its own end; and if he really felt disgust, it may be assumed from the rest of his work that he would communicate it forcibly and concisely. Perhaps then, in spite of his protestations, he is not unduly disturbed at the prospect of vice; perhaps, as was suggested above, he is not altogether sincere. And if so he has adopted not only a devil from the diabolists, but their manner of thinking and writing too. Under cover of reproaching Satan, these poets not infrequently express a private satisfaction with their lot; they acquiesce in a way of life, which conscience or convention allows them to acknowledge only if they brand it as evil. But the branding is no painful operation, their iron is cold.

Some such diagnosis as this would seem to be confirmed when the vice, to which Baudelaire reserved pre-eminence in the lines last quoted, is finally introduced. It is ennui: not accidie, the most terrible of the soul's maladies, which renders all action impossible; but boredom, such as afflicts the soul when an infinite variety of actions seems possible. To none is it compelled or attracted in a distinguishable degree; it craves therefore (like Nero) an unheard-of excitement:

> Il ferait volontiers de la terre un débris
> Et dans un bâillement il avalerait le monde.

Compared with this vice there is none other, the text implies, which may not be condoned; it is a sufficient excuse for 'le viol', 'le poison', 'le poignard', 'l'incendie' that they were undertaken to stifle a yawn.

This is levity very similar to that with which the poem started: but the poem is no longer about levity, it is light and frivolous itself. The last line

> Hypocrite lecteur, – mon semblable, – mon frère!

reads in its original context somewhat differently from the passage in which it is quoted in *The Waste Land*. It is not yet a cry for sympathy in pains, but a hint of partnership in pleasures. These are not such as to be creditable, and one knowing fellow gives another knowing fellow a dig in the ribs.

II

Before basing any general conclusion about Baudelaire's poetry on his statements about the devil, it would thus be necessary to classify these statements into groups; for they are by no means of a kind, either in what they say, or how they say it. And when this labour is over it might appear that none of these groups is large enough to support a general statement. That at any rate is what I fear.

I do so largely because I feel that the striking character of Baudelaire's verse is the way it deals, not with supernatural but with natural existences. Baudelaire is I think remarkable, not so much for the converse he may have had with spirits, fallen or erect; but for the closeness with which he observed, and the care with which he analysed, his converse with men and things of this earth. And if he was a Christian, I would say it was because this observation and analysis convinced him that Christianity was true. At any rate, in reading Baudelaire I have found it useful to have in my mind, not doctors of the supernatural to whom he is frequently compared – Dante or Tertullian, for example – but rather the Anglican Bishop Butler: who in his *Sermons* studies the natural world, and especially human nature, in the endeavour to propagate his faith.

In particular, in preparing this paper, two doctrines of Butler's have frequently occurred to me. They are, first, that human nature is not 'one simple, uniform thing'; and secondly, that for its happiness and misery, indeed for its very existence, it is dependent on an external world. It is not simple because, says Butler, it consists of 'appetites, particular passions and affections'; and it is dependent, because each of these passions and affections is directed, not upon the self, but upon external objects. A hungry man, in so far as he is hungry, cannot be satisfied with anything within himself, but only with food; a thirsty man craves a potable liquid; ambition will rest only in the esteem or respect of others, benevolence only in their well-being – and these, if not material, are none the less external to the ambitious or benevolent person. Human nature, in other words, is necessarily engaged in commerce with an outside world; and, by the first doctrine, this commerce is multifarious, conducted not by a single agent but by many. Each agent pursues a different kind of object – some physical, some immaterial and spiritual; but in human life each plays a necessary, and may play a proper, part. To see that each plays this part and no other, Butler would say, is virtue and happiness; while vice and misery result from disorder. But this is not immediately relevant to my purpose.

If we take the second of the above doctrines, it might I think be illustrated from Baudelaire, or used to illustrate him, in some such ways as the following.

The external world is of the greatest importance in his poetry. Not only do sense-impressions so crowd his lines as at times almost to embarrass the reader –

La nuit s'épaississait ainsi comme une cloison –

they do so because they are of significance for his moral life. He recognizes that it is by their occasion his life will be either maimed or perfected. They announce the presence of objects, for which the desire may be untimely or tempestuous; in that case temptation will need to be resisted:

Et son bras et sa jambe, et sa cuisse et ses reins,
Polis comme de l'huile, onduleux comme un cygne,
Passaient devant mes yeux clairvoyants et sereins;
Et son ventre et ses seins, ces grappes de ma vigne,

S'avançaient plus câlins que les anges du mal,
Pour troubler le repos où mon âme était mise,
Et pour la déranger du rocher de cristal,
Où calme et solitaire elle s'était assise.

Or they may foretell the thwarting of a desire by the decay of

an object; therefore, by meditation on this event, the desire is
to be moderated:

> Les mouches bourdonnaient sur ce ventre putride,
>   D'où sortaient de noirs bataillons
> De larves, qui coulaient comme un épais liquide
>   Le long de ces vivants haillons.
> Tout cela descendait, montait comme une vague...
> Et pourtant vous serez semblable à cette ordure,
>   A cette horrible infection,
> Etoile de mes yeux, soleil de ma nature,
>   Vous, mon ange et ma passion!

Passages of this kind, covering all the senses and a wide gamut
in every sense, are so frequent as to make his work appear a sort
of inventory or catalogue: drawn up, it might be said, to guard
against surprise from the external world. He wishes to be
prepared for any action which, as he is inevitably in commerce
with that world, it may be proper for him to take. He may not
always, and indeed often does not take it, but at least he is aware
that he should do so.

The main virtue of a catalogue is its exactness; and Baudelaire's
can I think be allowed to be exact in a very high degree. In his
poetry the external world is as in real life; it is neutral and public,
and not in any way coloured or deformed by his desires. Our
desires might have business in it too. If he enumerates more
detail than we have observed, that is because his senses are more
acute and more alert, not because they are less reliable than ours.
Were we not immediately convinced of this as we read, we
could not perhaps resist the temptation, which is strong, to
dismiss at least some of his adventures as nightmares. They are
such consequences of the failure to take proper action as it
requires fortitude to contemplate. But we see they have occurred
under the conditions with which we are acquainted when awake;
we must therefore gather fortitude whence we may.

If we read carefully, we shall do so from the poetry, which is
too great merely to disturb. Baudelaire, when he is fully himself,
is of an heroic fortitude. And the source of this, once again,
would seem to be the external world. The commerce which is
natural to us is our opportunity of happiness; and it must remain
so, however much through our mismanagement it has yielded
misery in the past. The proper action may have become difficult
to take, and still more difficult to find, because of previous errors;

yet the external world by its mere existence is a guarantee that the proper action may be taken. In this existence therefore – in the external world as external, before he has attempted profitable commerce with it or after he has attempted and failed – Baudelaire finds a consolation: a promise of happiness which, however conditional, is sufficient to ward off despair.

If the consolation appears small, that is the measure of what I called Baudelaire's heroism. He can be compared to those peasants whom Wordsworth describes as reduced by poverty to

> The pleasure which there is in life itself;

reduced, that is, to finding a pleasure in mere existence, to that flicker of interest and of hope without which any life is inconceivable. Yet whether because of conscience or mere healthy instinct – whatever the name, the thing is wholly admirable – they do not 'wish not to be'. Nor does Baudelaire, reduced by spiritual rather than physical deprivation to a similar state; he clings firmly to what little life is left.

Hence what has been described as his catalogue of the external world is not merely a catalogue; or rather it is not such a catalogue as is drawn up by a dealer, interested merely in the use of objects, or in what they will produce. The author is someone for whom the things in themselves, and even before they have benefited him, possess importance and a value; if they were pictures we should call him an amateur, if books a scholar. Baudelaire eagerly scans the horizon, like his own sentinel

> Qui guette nuit et jour brick, tartane ou frégate
> Dont les formes au loin frissonnent dans l'azur:

but with this difference: the *frissonnement* itself, as an appearance in and part of the external world, has a value for him, apart from what it may signify for his immediate future. It arrests his attention, and he transfers it to his verse. In the following lines, the rain is a symbol of all that excludes him from happiness:

> Quand la pluie étalant ses immenses trainées
> D'une vaste prison imite les barreaux...

but it too is part of the external world, and as such can detain him a moment from his melancholy. Before he returns to this there is a felt pause, and the melancholy becomes deeper for the contrast.

If this latter distinction is thought over-subtle, it should be compared with that drawn by Baudelaire himself in the stanzas already quoted from *Les Bijoux*. The contemplation of his mistress threatens to plunge him into lust which he recognizes as wasteful; nevertheless he does not on that account desist from the contemplation, or shut his eyes to his mistress. To do so would be to endeavour to exclude from the external what is and must remain a part of it; and what as such, however near it is bringing misery, may yet be a source of happiness.

But here, it is true, a new factor has come into play. The external world contains objects for the sense which are in themselves either pleasant or repulsive. When he encounters one of the former, such as his mistress, Baudelaire lingers over it as long as possible; for as both pleasant in itself and as external, it is doubly important: 'J'aime avec fureur', he says,

> Les choses où le son se mêle à la lumière.

But even intrinsically unpleasant things, by their character as external, can induce him to linger long enough to comprehend them fully:

> Les yeux étaient deux trous, et du ventre effondré
> Les intestins pesants lui coulaient sur les cuisses,
> Et ses bourreaux, gorgés de hideuses délices,
> L'avaient à coups de bec absolument châtré.

Because these lines and others of their kind are obviously dictated by something more than disgust, they have sometimes been made the ground for a charge of morbidity, or *morosa delectatio*. To disprove this, it is sufficient to refer to the lines about the vices quoted from the introductory poem; where, if anything, moroseness dominates. But the present lines give no hint of a secret pleasure, or of a pleasure which masks itself behind vituperation: all that they contain is frank and open.

The last few paragraphs, I am afraid, have not been at all clear; the transcription of an experience in reading poetry is very difficult. Perhaps I may be allowed a further attempt to illustrate my meaning, from the *Rêve Parisien*. Baudelaire recounts a dream in which he has inhabited a world containing only

> L'enivrante monotonie
> Du métal, du marbre et de l'eau.

Babel d'escaliers et d'arcades,
C'était un palais infini,
Plein de bassins et de cascades,
Tombant dans l'or mat ou bruni;

Et des cataractes pesantes,
Comme des rideaux de cristal,
Se suspendaient, éblouissantes,
A des murailles de métal.

This is often taken as a sort of *Kubla Khan* landscape, and indulgence of the fancy for its own sake. But Baudelaire the mere fantast would be as negligible as Baudelaire the devil-worshipper; and the truth would seem rather to be that he is recreating himself in the original, not in the modern sense of the term. He is imagining a world in which that minimum life to which, as has been said, he is at times reduced, is of itself a fully satisfying life. It is so in the first place because no other life is possible: time, and the stars that measure time, have ceased, and with them action:

Nul astre d'ailleurs, nuls vestiges
De soleil, même au bas du ciel;

so too has the pursuit of truth, for there is no reasoning, no speech:

Et sur ces mouvantes merveilles
Planait (terrible nouveauté!
Tout pour l'oeil, rien pour les oreilles!)
Un silence d'éternité!

And in the second place all that is offered to the senses is intrinsically pleasant: there is no motion, and therefore no disorder; no animals nor plants, and therefore no decay. Finally, the external objects in the vision are

ces prodiges
Qui brillaient d'un feu personnel;

which I take to imply that they are not, as are objects in the real world, mere dead material by means of which a satisfying life is yet to be achieved; they themselves lead such a life, in which it is possible to share by mere contemplation. The vision however is no more than a vision:

En rouvrant mes yeux pleins de flamme
J'ai vu l'horreur de mon taudis,
Et senti, rentrant dans mon âme,
La pointe des soucis maudits;

La pendule aux accents funèbres
Sonnait brutalement midi,
Et le ciel versait des ténèbres
Sur ce triste monde engourdi.

To quote Butler: 'We cannot remove from this earth, or change our general business in it;...neither can we alter our real nature.' Baudelaire is the last person to pretend otherwise, and immediately on waking he brushes aside the vision as a

terrible paysage
Tel que jamais mortel n'en vit.

It has served, not as refuge to slacken his efforts in this world, but rather as an ideal by which to intensify them: it is here, if anywhere, that he must achieve the fully satisfying life, in spite of and because of repulsive sights, and the difficulties of right reasoning and right action.

The second of Butler's doctrines has occupied us somewhat too long. The first, it will be remembered, was that human nature is a bundle of, among other things, 'appetites, particular passions and affections'. Butler had already been anticipated in holding this by a number of expressions of common speech; and these Baudelaire takes over with marked approval. 'L'esprit humain regorge de passions' he says in *Les Paradis artificiels*; 'il en a à *revendre*, pour me servir d'une autre locution triviale.' Further, his poems contain lines such as

vers toi mes désirs partent en caravane.

That is, he recognizes not only the multiplicity of human passions but what Butler calls their disinterested quality: though they are part of the self they are by no means directed upon it, and therefore for the self's sake may need to be controlled and to be denied. When nevertheless they insist upon satisfaction Baudelaire has other terms for them: they are 'un peuple de démons', or 'un choeur de vermisseaux'. But a discussion of these terms would be one of the pains of the soul; and this needs to be preceded by a discussion of its pleasures.

III

The Infinite Being who created us has, says Butler, provided objects for the satisfaction of all our desires. None of these therefore is in itself evil, and its satisfaction is not only compatible with, but a condition of, perfect happiness. Paradise is a place where we find 'a supply to all the capacities of our natures'. A desire becomes evil only by insisting on more than its due satisfaction; and then, thwarting other desires, it needs itself to be thwarted. But this thwarting is a character of the disordered, and not of the healthy life. Similarly Baudelaire is – it is not too much to say – haunted by the notion of an existence that shall be as rich and as harmonious as possible; of 'cet état charmant et singulier, où toutes les forces s'équilibrent'.

He finds a symbol of it in the 'admirable et lumineuse promptitude des enfants'; and in youth –

> la sainte jeunesse, à l'air simple, au doux front,
> A l'oeil limpide et clair ainsi qu'une eau courante,
> Et qui va répandant sur tout, insouciante
> Comme l'azur du ciel, les oiseaux et les fleurs,
> Ses parfums, ses chansons, et ses douces chaleurs!

The youthful races of the world, he thinks, enjoyed the same privilege. And once or twice, if only for a moment, it has been his own.

'Il est des jours', he writes, 'où l'homme s'éveille avec un génie jeune et vigoureux. Ses paupières à peine déchargées du sommeil qui les scellait, le monde extérieur s'offre à lui avec un relief puissant, une netteté de contours, une richesse de couleurs admirables.' That is, part at least of the *Rêve Parisien* is a reality. But there is more, which did not enter into the dream: 'Le monde moral ouvre ses vastes perspectives, pleines de clartés nouvelles. L'homme, gratifié de cette béatitude, malheureusement rare et passagère, se sent à la fois plus artiste et plus juste, plus noble, pour tout dire en un mot.' This account in prose may be supplemented by the following in verse, in which Baudelaire addresses his soul as Hopkins did the windhover:

> Au-dessus des étangs, au-dessus des vallées,
> Des montagnes, des bois, des nuages, des mers,
> Par delà le soleil, par delà les éthers,
> Par delà les confins des sphères étoilées,
>
> Mon esprit, tu te meus avec agilité,
> Et, comme un bon nageur qui se pâme dans l'onde,
> Tu sillonnes gaiement l'immensité profonde
> Avec une indicible et mâle volupté.

This striving is not to an end, for a full and properly ordered activity is an end in itself. In the final stanza therefore the soul is compared to things which rest in themselves, things immobile and mute; and, to play their part in the figure, they in turn are endowed with the striving of consciousness:

> Heureux celui qui peut d'une aile vigoureuse
> S'élancer vers les champs lumineux et sereins!

> Celui dont les pensers, comme des alouettes,
> Vers les cieux le matin prennent un libre essor,
> – Qui plane sur la vie, et comprend sans effort
> Le langage des fleurs et des choses muettes!

Baudelaire, says Mr Eliot, is a *poète des départs*. But he is also, and it is perhaps more important, a *poète des arrivées*. He is not one of those whom he ironically describes as 'les vrais voyageurs',

> coeurs légers, semblables aux ballons...
> [Qui] sans savoir pourquoi, disent toujours: Allons!

Except in the address to Death at the conclusion of this poem (where the ironical intention still continues) he is always fully aware where he wishes to go. It is to the paradise in which a life like the above is lived: 'un vrai pays de Cocagne, où tout est beau, riche, tranquille, honnête; où le luxe a plaisir à se mirer dans l'ordre'. There 'la cuisine elle-même est poétique... comme une belle conscience'. All human needs being satisfied in their proper order, the most diverse can be ranked together, as here. If this is felt to be incongruous, it is no more than a device common in mystical poets widely acknowledged to be serious. They transfer to paradise, as to its natural place, the earthly pleasure which at the moment occupies them; and they claim from paradise the satisfaction of an immediate earthly want. Between such poets and Baudelaire there are some fairly close parallels to be drawn. Herbert, returning from Salisbury, heard cathedral choirs about heaven's gate; Baudelaire, who delighted in the plastic arts as Herbert in music, saw within that gate

> Des meubles luisants
> Polis par les ans.

Again, Herbert in a moment of exhaustion looked forward to death as 'a chair'; to Baudelaire it is

> l'auberge fameuse inscrite sur le livre,
> Où l'on pourra manger, et dormir, et s'asseoir.

IV

Baudelaire is thus not of the Puritans, if these, as I assume
they do, set apart and prohibit as necessarily evil an object or
objects of enjoyment. And in the same way (in addition to all
other ways) he is to be distinguished from the Satanists, who
are inverted Puritans. They claim to prohibit as evil what they
nevertheless enjoy. By definition their enjoyments are dis-
orderly; Baudelaire's always depend upon the possibility of order.

Nevertheless it might be thought that Swinburne for example
is not without a notion of a 'pays de Cocagne'. He writes of a
garden of Proserpine, where the weary may slumber; and of a
noble, nude and antique world, where the eyes may be refreshed.
These are, however, merely refuges, where life may be avoided
rather than organized to the full; places of diversion or relaxation
between which Swinburne may choose, and which he may or not
visit as he fancies. The 'pays de Cocagne' on the other hand is
Baudelaire's good, which he cannot but try to reach; and if he
fails, there is nowhere else for him to turn – he is condemned
to evil and misery. Hence there is a note of urgency in his
writing about paradise unlike anything in Swinburne; who is
never in the least reminiscent of Herbert.

This note deepens to tragedy, as the barriers between Baudelaire and paradise seem to increase. It is heard most clearly
perhaps in *Un Voyage à Cythère*; which also provides the sharpest
contrast to Swinburne.

The poem opens with an image with which we are now
familiar:

> Mon coeur, comme un oiseau, voltigeait tout joyeux
> Et planait librement à l'entour des cordages;
> Le navire roulait sous un ciel sans nuages,
> Comme un ange enivré d'un soleil radieux.

It seems that the paradisal state has already been achieved, in
the delights of which the physical universe, and even the ship
itself, have a share. But the delights are interrupted by a brief
question:

> Quelle est cette île triste et noire?

The answer comes in an off-hand tone, as though to deprecate
alarm:

> C'est Cythère,
> Nous dit-on, un pays fameux dans les chansons,
> Eldorado banal de tous les vieux garçons.

The suggestion is that no one on board can be concerned with the doings on the island.

Here it may perhaps be noted that, in this poem, changes of tone are of the utmost importance. It consists entirely of speeches, and is now dialogue, now monologue; there are no stage-directions, and even the number of speakers is not clear. It is only by a careful observation of tone, therefore, that the speeches can be fitted into their proper relations. Written in this way, the poem gains remarkably in economy and strength; but also, the degree of that strength is not immediately apparent.

At least one passenger is not wholly reassured, and needs to confirm with his eyes the report which he has heard:

> Regardez, après tout, c'est une pauvre terre.

The phrase 'après tout' suggests that the report was not wholly disingenuous; and as if to confirm this, someone on board breaks into what, by contrast with the lines which precede and follow, can only be called a hymn:

> Belle île aux myrtes verts, pleine de fleurs écloses,
> Vénérée à jamais par toute nation,
> Où les soupirs des coeurs en adoration
> Roulent comme l'encens sur un jardin de roses
>
> Ou le roucoulement éternel d'un ramier!

To what island is this addressed? If to that in prospect, it would seem, in spite of all reports, well deserving of attention. But this idea is no sooner conceived, than it is extinguished by the curt lines:

> — Cythère n'était plus qu'un terrain des plus maigres,
> Un désert rocailleux troublé par des cris aigres.

The two islands, that in prospect and that of the hymn, have nothing whatever in common; the ship's company may continue in their aloofness.

The off-hand tone is resumed:

> J'entrevoyais pourtant un objet singulier!

A traveller is about to describe what entertained his idle curiosity for a moment. He begins with a mocking reference to the hymn he has just heard:

> Ce n'était pas un temple aux ombres bocagères

then gives a few causal details:

> voilà qu'en rasant la côte d'assez près
> Pour troubler les oiseaux avec nos voiles blanches

and finally the object itself is described. It is a gibbeted corpse, surrounded by birds and beasts of prey. The lines have already been quoted as an example of Baudelaire's writing at its least casual, and when he is alert to every stimulus of the sense. Accordingly from this point on the poem becomes more and more deeply charged with emotion. The spectacle is first assimilated to one of human justice:

> Une plus grande bête au milieu s'agitait
> Comme un exécuteur entouré de ses aides,

then to one of divine. The corpse is seen to be alive, and suffers the pains of purgatory or hell:

> Habitant de Cythère, enfant d'un ciel si beau,
> Silencieusement tu souffrais ces insultes
> En expiation de tes infâmes cultes.

The speaker's sympathies are already warm; soon he identifies himself with the victim:

> Ridicule pendu, tes douleurs sont les miennes!

All trace of aloofness has now disappeared.

The physical universe remains as at the beginning of the poem:

> Le ciel était charmant, la mer était unie;
> Pour moi tout était noir et sanglant désormais –

but the ship's company find it impossible to return to the bliss which they thought they enjoyed. This was not the paradisal, which endures; but only make-believe. As such it crumbled, either before self-examination or before the mere course of events. The company sought to keep all rumours of Cythère from their ship, and to persuade themselves they were made of different stuff from the men of Cythère. But their stuff is the same, and so their lot will be: either they will achieve paradise in the island, and in that case it will blossom as in the hymn; or they must endure the island in its present state, and finally hang in chains. It is not possible to sail away to a Swinburnian refuge.

In the last two lines:

> Ah! Seigneur! donnez-moi la force et le courage
> De contempler mon coeur and mon corps sans dégoût!

the accent falls on 'contempler' rather than on 'dégoût'. They are not a repudiation of the flesh so much as a recognition that the flesh and the desires with which it fills the heart cannot be repudiated. Baudelaire fears that his is too much ravaged to be healed but he faces the situation as best he may.

V

By their frequent satisfaction desires are strengthened, and it is only too easy for them to become strong enough to destroy the equilibrium of our nature, and therefore the possibility of happiness. A desire, says Butler, should not be pursued beyond a certain degree; for otherwise it 'is always attended with more inconvenience than advantage...and of ten with extreme misery'.

In some cases this degree is imposed by the nature of the object upon which the desire is directed. If it belongs to this world, where 'rien...n'est certain...tout craque', a too insistent desire is exposed to the danger of a shock so grievous as to maim it. Then it will be impossible to look at a human body without seeing behind it a corpse, or to read in the eyes of others friendship or affection, but only a 'secrète horreur du dévouement'.

Again, desires in themselves, and apart from their objects, differ in the esteem in which we hold them. Conscience cannot, for it is a form of the reason, say that any should be wholly neglected; but some it says are to be cherished more than others. 'There are some, the having of which implies the love of them, when they are reflected upon. This cannot be said of all...It were ridiculous to assert that a man upon reflection hath the same kind of approbation of the appetite of hunger, or the passion of fear, as he hath of goodwill to his fellow-creatures.'

Substitute for the appetite of hunger that of the flesh; and for the goodwill of men the comfort that is to be found in God; and this quotation becomes immediately applicable to Baudelaire. That men have a need of God, as much and more than of any-

317

thing else external to themselves, is clear to both Baudelaire and Butler from self-observation, and from the observation of others. 'It is plain that there is a capacity in the nature of man, which neither riches nor honours nor sensual gratifications, nor anything in this world, can perfectly fill up, or satisfy: there is a deeper and more essential want.' And this only the Infinite Being Himself can supply. Baudelaire speaks of an infinite within us, needing the infinite which is outside; and whose demands we can never escape. 'Fuyez l'infini que vous portez en vous', he calls in scorn to the women of Lesbos; knowing that they cannot, and that this is their punishment.

This desire for God is the desire of which conscience and the reason most strongly approve; therefore for complete happiness, says Butler, its satisfaction must be preferred to that of all others. But in the Baudelaire of the poems other desires are already far too strong to admit of being postponed, for whatever reason. They demand satisfaction here and now, or will secure it by guile.

They can do so because every satisfaction has a moment in which it appears infinite; and accordingly the inexperienced return for it a 'gratitude infinie et sublime'. But, unless it corresponds to the desire of an ordered soul, it brings, not boundless riches, but only a pittance; it provides, instead of a true infinity to bear up the soul on every side, only a vacuity through which the soul plunges headlong. Baudelaire learns to be on his guard against these gulfs; but they threaten him at every moment, so that the mere thought of them fills with horror.

> Hélas! tout est abîme, – action, désir, rêve,
> Parole! et sur mon poil qui tout droit se relève
> Mainte fois de la Peur je sens passer le vent.

This is the beginning of the pains of the disordered soul, which take on a thousand forms. His one-time care for the desires now standing between him and God turns to hate: they are not caravans setting out for merchandise, but a chorus of worms launching itself upon a corpse. Hysterically, as in calmer moments he admits, he vituperates the objects of these desires as not only the cause of evil to him in his present circumstances, but as necessarily such a cause at all times to everybody. It is as such a vituperation that 'faire l'amour, c'est faire le mal' is to be interpreted, and all similar passages in the poems. Then he finds that the desires themselves, not being properly subordinated to the supremely valuable desire, are maimed: he 'eats without hunger, and drinks without thirst'; finally the desires weaken to such an extent that he falls into accidie. He can do nothing but contemplate, helplessly, his own forlorn state; he would prefer insensibility –

> Je jalouse le sort des plus vils animaux
> Qui peuvent se plonger dans un sommeil stupide,
> Tant l'écheveau du temps lentement se dévide!

Rescuing himself with an effort he seeks an escape in pride, in the scorn of his fate. But for him to do this, he soon sees, is ludicrous:

> Qui fait le dégoûté montre qu'il se croit beau.

The only possible escape is to face the evil of his situation, secure what little good remains, and endeavour slowly to increase it. He has sufficient fortitude for this; and he was preparing for it, for example, at the end of *Un Voyage à Cythère*.

VI

In a brief paper it is impossible to discuss Baudelaire's poems in technical detail; an Englishman would in any case find it difficult to do so. But technical excellence, as an aspect of precise statement, depends at least partly upon width of experience and clarity of view; and an effort has been made to indicate these.

They will be found to lie behind any of Baudelaire's poems which make more than a temporary impression on the reader. To refer to a section of his work which has so far received only passing mention, they give force to his satire: to *Un Voyage* for instance, directed against those who, finding comfort in travel, see spiritual significance in the achievement of a Columbus:

> Ce matelot ivrogne, inventeur d'Amériques.

Or to *Femmes Damnées*, which is a double satire, at once against those who would limit human happiness to the flesh, and those who, unconscious of limiting themselves thereby, seek to equate the two. They are 'des rêveurs inutiles', who wish

> Aux choses de l'amour mêler l'honnêteté!

Whereas, if earthly love may be part of the good life, the good life is not part of earthly love. With some satisfaction, Baudelaire reflects that these dreamers are ignorant (the mind flies to many English poets who were contemporary), not only of what might be the rest of life, but of the flesh itself.

> Celui qui veut unir dans un accord mystique
> L'ombre avec la chaleur, la nuit avec le jour,
> Ne chauffera jamais son corps paralytique
> A ce rouge soleil que l'on nomme l'amour!

He himself is acquainted with both; but as he is unable properly to order his life, what might have been a constituent pleasure in paradise is only a torment in hell:

> Et, comme le soleil dans son enfer polaire,
> Mon coeur ne sera plus qu'un bloc rouge et glacé.

The word 'fortitude', which has been used so often, again suggests itself to describe the clarity of this view of his own experience.

Another comparison with an English poet may serve to define this fortitude a little more closely. As has already been stated, Hopkins and Baudelaire have much of their spiritual experience in common; it is deep and wide in both. But there is a point at which it diverges. After a day of struggle, Hopkins finds it possible to rest:

> Here! creep,
> Wretch, under a comfort serves in a whirlwind: all
> Life death does end and each day dies with sleep.

It is as though a supernatural power restored to him, at least for the moment, the innocence and confidence of childhood: no harm will come from any source, and he may sleep. But to Baudelaire, who waits as anxiously for it, nightfall brings not the opportunity for sleep but only the duty of watching. He receives no supernatural aid, and must himself prepare for the struggle of the morrow. He does so by shrinking into the life of the senses; and conceived as parts of the external world, even his spiritual failures can bring comfort:

> Vois se pencher les défuntes Années
> Sur les balcons du ciel, en robes surannées;
> Surgir du fond des eaux le Regret souriant;
> Le Soleil moribond s'endormir sous une arche,
> Et, comme un long linceul traînant à l'Orient,
> Entends, ma chère, entends la douce Nuit qui marche.

According to Christianity, there is a sense in which the child is spiritually richer than the man, who needs to abase himself before he can rise to his full dignity. This must be taken account of, in estimating the amount of Christianity in Baudelaire (no doubt he has now separated from Butler); but to many readers the opening lines of the sonnet just quoted will seem wholly satisfying, both in what they admit and what they deny of human weakness:

> Sois sage, ô ma Douleur, et tiens-toi plus tranquille,
> Tu réclamais le Soir; il descend, le voici.

To judge with confidence between Hopkins and Baudelaire would however require a depth of spiritual experience approximating to that of either; and perhaps this is an occasion when, if ever, one should be content to talk of technical perfection.

11

CROCE*

Really hard workers in the intellectual line are very impressive, for they are so few. There are still fewer who, neither blinded by the dust of their labours nor exhausted by the fatigue, can give concise and readable accounts of what they consider to be their results. I do not by any means believe that Croce always works hard when he writes – indeed, I think that in his 'philosophical' productions he is doing not much work at all – but at times he does. And that, I think, is one of the more reputable reasons for the reverence which, from 1915 or thereabouts, has attached itself vaguely to him. Whatever you think of the rest of the essay on Corneille, you must be impressed by the opening chapter: a rapid, but by no means confusing, review of all the critics of importance who have ever written on Corneille. In a note to another essay, Croce says: 'I believe I have examined all, or nearly all, of the literature of erudition and criticism, old and new, which is connected with Ariosto: this will not escape the expert reader.'[1] As far as I can see the statement is true; to an expert reader it must be little short of amazing. Add to this, that Croce is historian, not of literary reputations alone, but of aesthetics, philology and logic. Add too that, when he is not writing on metaphysical and logical matters, his style is easy and even sparkling. A certain amount of reverence cannot be withheld. Nor can the question: 'How does the man do it? What is the source of his energy, and in virtue of what principles does he feel himself the master of so much matter?' To this

---

* I have had to prepare the above paper in the most barbarous of the provinces, where books are difficult to come by. I have been able to consult only four works in the original Italian, namely: the *Estetica*, the *Problemi di Estetica*, the *Nuovi Saggi di Estetica* and the *Saggio sullo Hegel* (all published by Laterza, of Bari). The translations from these works are my own, and references to them in the notes are to the Italian edition.

References to other works are to the translations published by Mr Douglas Ainslie. In quoting from them in my text I have of necessity followed his version; but, for reasons which all his readers will appreciate, I have had no scruple in altering that version from time to time.

[1] *Ariosto, Shakespeare and Corneille*, p. 3, n. 1.

question, which has presented itself to me many times, I can find only one answer. If it is true it should be sufficient, for it is Hegel.

'Hegel', says Mr Eliot, 'if not perhaps the first, was certainly the most prodigious exponent of emotional systematization.' For him, things became words, and words, uncontrolled by things, became 'indefinite emotions': a soft material he could mould as he wished, and thence proceed, with the lack of scruple which is born of confidence and the courage of success, to the solution of such problems as remained. Croce follows closely the same practice. 'No one', continues Mr Eliot, 'who was not witness of the event could imagine the conviction in the tone of Professor Eucken as he pounded the table and exclaimed *Was ist Geist? Geist ist...*' Similarly, no one who has not laboured through the *Logic* or the *New Essays in Aesthetic* can represent to himself the emotional atmosphere in which passages such as will often be quoted in this article appear appropriate, or even – given a fair amount of sympathy with the author – informative. Perhaps at the outset I should do what I can to display this atmosphere; but perhaps again that is best achieved by a rapid outline of Crocean doctrine. Such an outline is at any rate indispensable for an estimation of the *Aesthetic*.

Croce is no blind admirer of Hegel.[1] He is as little impressed as anyone by the discovery of dialectical moments in the poles of the magnet, the emergence of the Prussian monarchy, or the topography of the globe. Further, he realizes that, by the operation of the dialectic, all things threaten to be swallowed up into the sea of the Absolute, and he is as inexpert as most of us in the navigation of that sea. He says, therefore, that such navigation is unnecessary: that there are, rising up in the sea, rocks or islands on which any man can take his rest. They are the concepts. For Croce the concept has three marks: it is expressive, universal, and above all concrete. If concrete, it is fully real; if real, it must be permanent: that is, it cannot be at one moment, and cease from being the next. Hence while abstractions – as for example the bad, the ugly, and being and not-being themselves – are drawn into the vortex of the dialectic, to emerge, if at all, only in a metamorphosis – the dialectic

---

[1] Croce gives an admirable summary of his attitude in the *Saggio sullo Hegel*.

passes the concepts by.[1] Art, which is a concept, will always remain art: it need not fear the dissolution prophesied for it by Hegel,[2] that on the voyage to the Absolute it would be absorbed into religion or philosophy.

Art has a second name, intuition; and, as intuition, groups itself naturally with three other concepts: those of logic, of economic, and of moral action. These together with intuition make up the four activities of the mind, in which the mind exhausts itself: there is no fifth activity. They form two groups: intuition and logic are both theoretic – that is, they are concerned only with knowledge and are knowledge; the economic and moral activities are practical – that is, they are actions. We must be careful not to consider any of them as in any way psychological; as we shall see later, psychology, along with the other natural sciences, is for Croce completely alien to philosophy – and to adopt the psychological approach to his intuition is to play the part of Bishop Barnes towards an aesthetic eucharist. To know what intuition is, all we can do is to think ourselves back into the moment when we first awakened to theoretic life. Our mind was filled with images, and with nothing but images; we did not ask whether they were real, or indeed what they were. We just accepted them, as it were sank into them. We *were* the images. Then we were being active intuitively. And we must be active in an exactly similar way whenever we wish to enjoy a work of art. We must surrender ourselves completely to it, and have no part of our mind left over to ask questions. Thus Croce establishes, as the first step in his aesthetic, the independence of art, and its complete distinction from those functions of the mind which we should normally call truth-seeking or truth-enjoying. At a blow he rids himself of problems like that of the role of belief in poetry, by saying that such problems cannot arise. Whether he is justified in doing so, we are as yet hardly sufficiently advanced in his system to say; but we may note in passing that the effects on his applied criticism do not seem too fortunate. He seems, we should normally say, to be emptying works of art of their significance. Because of his isolation of poetry from philosophy he feels himself entitled to dismiss the *Divine Comedy* as a collection of lyrics, embedded in wholly

[1] *Logic*, pp. 102–3, 224.
[2] At least that Croce says he prophesied. I am aware that the view is contested.

alien matter. Because of the autonomy of art, he is bold enough
to dismiss all allegory. He may of course mean nothing more than
that *romans à clef* and their like are reprehensible, in which case
he is probably right; but, appealing to his essay on Dante once
again, it is difficult not to feel that at his hands the figures of
the *Divine Comedy* suffer a degradation. After reading that essay
I for one am compelled to doubt whether he could read an *auto*
by Calderón with adequate understanding.

But to proceed with the system. If concepts, according to
Croce, escape the dialectic, they do not remain inviolate long.
Upon them there operates a principle which, to all except a
disciple, must appear equally mortal. He calls it *synthesis a
priori*.[1] All concepts, though distinct one from the other, and
permanent in that distinction, are, by their own nature and the
nature of the mind, at the same time identical one with another.
The word 'identical' is strong, but I do not think it exaggerates:
I wish, if possible, to get main outlines clear. Let Croce speak
for himself: 'What is thought is never *a* concept, but always *the*
concept, the system of concepts.'[2] 'The concept is...all distinct
concepts. But each one of them is, as it were, distinct in that
union...the thinker, when thinking reality, can think it only in
its distinct aspects, and in this way only he thinks it in its
unity.'[3] Perhaps an illustration may help. Art, as we have seen,
will not die into philosophy – is at the present moment, and
always will remain, *toto caelo* distinct from it (let me note that
for Croce, philosophy is the same thing as logic); nevertheless
art is philosophy, and philosophy is art. How does that come
about? Something in this way: art, being the first activity of the
mind, is logically conceivable apart from philosophy – we do
not need to philosophize first, to become artists. But philosophy
or logic, being the second activity, demands art as a necessary
condition of its existence. Philosophy brings concepts, but
concepts are real only as manifested in intuitions; and intuitions
are already the products of art. What is philosophy must there-
for also be art. But the converse is true as well: for it is only
'logically' – that is, abstractly – that art exists apart from
philosophy; reality has nothing to do with abstractions. We shall

---

[1] On this see the *Logic*, and especially the *Saggio sullo Hegel*. Croce takes the name
from Kant; and, he says, the process too. On its importance for his thought, cf.
Logic, p. 220: 'Mind, considered universally, is nothing but *a priori* synthesis.'
[2] *Logic*, p. 268.   [3] *Ibid.*, p. 81.

see later that the adjective 'first', applied to the activity of intuition, has no real meaning. The mind, in any manifestation of itself, manifests the whole of itself: what is art, being a product of the mind, must therefore be philosophy as well – for philosophy, no less than art, is part of the mind. The *Divine Comedy*, therefore, is both art and philosophy; but we must add – remembering Croce's judgment on the *Divine Comedy*, which we have just read; remembering also that concepts in their *a priori* union are yet distinct – that as art it is not philosophy, and as philosophy not art. I despair of making this thing clear: perhaps however clarity is not what I should aim at. Let me return to the image of rocks in the sea, which I used of the concepts. This can be made more exact. The concepts do not stand as rocks in the sea: rather the sea, at any and every moment, congeals itself – the whole of itself – into any one of the rocks. This rock is thus all the rest of the rocks. The image has been stretched to the point of absurdity; but that is not wholly a defect.

When Croce, in the name of the independence of art, expelled from it consideration of truth, it seemed perhaps that the price of independence, inanity, was to be a heavy one. But now the tables are completely turned. Art, being merely art, is at the same time the whole cosmos. Further, art itself is an abstraction: what is real and what only is real is an individual work of art. Each work of art, then, contains the cosmos. In it, says Croce,[1] 'there breathes the life of the whole, and the whole within the life of the individual; every pure work of art is itself the universe... In the poet's every tone, in every creature of his imagination, lies all that human destiny contains – all hopes, all illusions, all joys and all sorrows, the splendours of man and his humiliations.' This conclusion, which might seem paradoxical to some, Croce hails as a confirmation of his theory. The character of 'totality' belonging to a work of art is, he says, the reality of which many critics have caught a glimpse when they have said that art is 'universal'. Which is, of course, possible; but must be left to the critics themselves to decide.

For a second character of the synthesis interests us much more than its totality: namely, its unity. 'Art one and indivisible' is an old cry, but it can never have been raised with such vigour as by Croce. In the first place, art for him is identical with its

---

[1] *Nuovi Saggi*, p. 126.

expression: we cannot ask what a poet meant to say, and judge whether or not he said it well – what he meant to say was what he said, and we must leave it at that. Here Croce makes a shrewd bid for popularity: for nothing more impresses the poetic public than the truism that, if a series of words is altered, it is no longer the same. Why a series of words should be pitched upon, by both Croce and the public, as the expression with which a poem is identical, is difficult to say. This series, says Croce, is itself a unity: not a succession of words, but a word. A poem is not divisible into cantos, stanzas and verses, an essay into paragraphs and sentences, a drama into acts and scenes, not even – in spite of Aristotle – into beginning, middle and end. A picture cannot be analysed into planes or forms or colours; nor a building, *qua* architecture, into masses. If we wish to consider a volume of prose, then we must consider the whole of it, and at once: 'the whole book or the whole discourse, from the first word to the last, including all that in it may seem accidental or superficial, including even the accent, the warmth, the emphasis, the gestures of the living word, the notes, the parentheses, the full stops and commas of the written'.[1] Literature we may not divide into *genres* – the lyric, the epic, the drama and so forth: if we do so, we commit what, according to Croce, is the 'rhetorical heresy' of criticism. If we consider separately the inspiration of a poem, finding this in contemporary conditions or events, then we follow the 'sociological' heresy; if we find it in the poet's biography, then we follow the 'psychological'. Nay more, we are forbidden to divide art itself into the arts. There is no such thing as music, apart from poetry, sculpture, painting and architecture: they are all one. Art, manifesting itself only in individual works of art, has the unity of these individuals: not to be broken down, even temporarily, with the aid of any critical instrument whatever. These, says Croce, are as useless for their supposed purpose, as is a knife for the disruption of a syllogism.[2]

The question whether criticism is possible immediately arises; and it is, I think, a grave one – perhaps the touchstone of Croce's system. But we must postpone it for a while, until we have considered his theory of criticism. This is part of his theory of the judgment, the product or manifestation of the second or

---

[1] *Logic*, p. 118. Croce is speaking of definition, but the words can quite as well be applied to our context.　　[2] *Problemi*, p. 251.

logical activity of the mind. Upon intuition, entirely contempla-
tive and allowing of no questions, there usually follows a state of
mind which both allows and answers them. This is one of
Croce's accounts of the process: 'I am for example in such a
condition as prompts me to sing or to versify, and thus to make
myself objective to myself; but I am objective and known only to
the imagination, so much so, that at the moment of poetical or
musical expression I should not be able to say what was really
happening to me: whether I was awake or dreamt, whether I saw
clearly or caught glimpses, or saw wrongly. When from the
variety of the multitude of representations which preceded and
which follow it I pass on to inquire the truth of them all (that is
to say, the reality which does not pass), and rise to the concept,
those representations must be revised in the light of the concept,
but no longer with the same eyes as formerly – they must not be
looked at, but *thought*. My state of mind then becomes determinate,
and I say, for example: "What have I experienced (and sung and
made poetry of) was an absurd desire, a clash of different ten-
dencies that needed to be overcome and arranged, it was
remorse or a pious desire", and so on. Thus, by means of the
concept is formed a judgment of the representation.'[1] The
quotation shows the role Croce intends the judgment should
fulfil in the life of the mind; its terms are however too general
to show the mechanism of judgment. This is once more – and I
am afraid a second intrusion cannot be avoided – synthesis *a
priori*. In every judgment an intuition as subject is synthesized
with a concept as predicate; every judgment, being such a
synthesis, is, like a work of art, an indivisible unity. Really
therefore neither subject is distinct from predicate, nor predicate
from subject. In so far as its subject is individual, the judgment
might be called singular; but in so far as this subject is the same
as the predicate, it must be called universal. Further, in so far as
subject and predicate are the same, all judgments are of identity.
Finally, in so far as the concept exists only in the judgment –
each judgment being unique – all judgments are definitions, and
they are verbal definitions. Again, we are faced with a conclusion
before which we might expect Croce to recoil; once again, however, he accepts it without flinching. It is just because definitions
are verbal, he says, that they are real.

[1] *Logic*, p. 150.

To apply this to criticism. Judgments of criticism have, naturally, intuitions as their subjects; and they have one common predicate, the concept art. Their common form, Croce says more than once,[1] is: A is (or is not) a work of art. Now, 'work of art' is itself an abstraction, and in any actual judgment it must disappear, to be replaced by a reality. If the work of art A is being judged, this reality can be no other than A itself. The judgment will then be, either *A*, or, if this seem not sufficiently articulate, *A is A*. It can certainly be no more than this. And as a matter of fact we do occasionally find in Croce's essays judgments of this type. The grand conclusion of the essay on Ariosto, for instance, is that Ariosto is a 'poet of harmony', certainly – 'but also of something else, of harmony developed in a peculiar world of sentiments...in fact, the harmony to which Ariosto attains is not harmony in general, but an altogether Ariostesque harmony'.[2] Of the *Divine Comedy* Croce says: 'The final synthetic image, which sums up all the impressions made by the poem in its different parts...is, in short, the image of Dante himself.' Romantic critics Croce condemns as being largely concerned with history and sociology. Their work, however, contains an aesthetic element. As they were not merely historians and sociologists, but also artists, they had the following valuable experience: 'When they began to discuss poets and their works in particular, Dante was revealed to them as mediaeval and at the same time not mediaeval, Cervantes as one who satirized chivalry but at the same time yearned for it, Shakespeare as the poet of the universe. In short, Dante was revealed to them as Dante, Cervantes as Cervantes, and Shakespeare as Shakespeare.'[3] It might be thought that these are mere rhetorical flourishes, not altogether inappropriate in a 'literary' exercise; I will therefore give one more quotation from a serious context, where the theme is that critical judgments and historical judgments are the same. To judge a work of art is at the same time to judge the 'historical complex' of which it is an integral part. Then, says Croce, giving an example of a critical judgment, 'To say that a thing is the fact which we call the *Divine Comedy* is to say what its value is, and so to criticize it.'[4] That is, apparently, by

---

[1] *Problemi*, p. 56; *Nuovi Saggi*, p. 83.
[2] *Ariosto, Shakespeare and Corneille*, p. 94.
[3] *Nuovi Saggi*, p. 174.   [4] *Logic*, p. 294.

pronouncing a formula of baptism we summarize no small portion of the development of the Western World.

Croce can claim, and must be allowed, credit for a kind of consistency: one does not need however to be of a very distrustful nature to question whether it is more than terminological. Did Croce know only one judgment containing the term '*Divine Comedy*', that judgment could hardly be so enlightening to him as he says it is. We have found in his essays some examples of tautological judgments; but if they contained nothing else beside they would hardly arouse either so much criticism or so much applause. Enthusiasts may revere as gospel something that says nothing, and founds its claim to reverence upon its saying nothing; but a protevangel which says something is first necessary to seduce them into enthusiasm. I assume therefore that somewhere Croce is inconsistent with his doctrine, and I propose to return to the beginning of his system to discover, if I can, where.

It is, I believe, at the very beginning; in fact, where the *a priori* synthesis enters. This principle identified or confused all concepts one with another: claiming it is true to keep them distinct in that identification, but offering not the slightest proof that this is possible. Now if all concepts are one concept, it is difficult to see what can result but immediate aphasia. In a universe consisting entirely of cats, when all cats are grey, there is, or there should be, complete darkness on the subject of their complexion. Or we may put it another way: each one of Croce's concepts – and later, because of the doctrine of judgment, each one of his intuitions – can as it were deputize for the universe. It can therefore be considered only as an indivisible whole. Of indivisible wholes there is no discursive knowledge: if there is any knowledge at all, then it can resemble only that of the Aristotelian God, which is an eternal contemplation. The Aristotelian God does not engage in conversation – but he is not so circumstanced that one expects it of him. Croce however is; and no ingenuous person, surveying the pile of books that have come from his pen, would judge that he has fallen short of that expectation. Here is our inconsistency; if we can, let us explain it.

I think it is to be explained by an error or oversight or trick which, for the moment, seems to put Croce on a level with Spinoza. Croce and Spinoza have this in common, that they seek to establish a monism, the one over against Descartes, the other over against the eighteenth-century tradition in philosophy. Spinoza endeavoured to do so by sinking thought or knowledge among the infinity of attributes possessed by substance. It was, he said, merely one amongst such an infinity; correlated with each of them of course, for all attributes are correlated one with another: but not setting itself up over against the rest, as knowing them all. Yet in practice the rest of the attributes were revealed – one of them actually, the others potentially – only in thought or knowledge, and so the old dualism was restored. In an almost exactly similar way, Croce endeavours to sink his knowledge or 'expression' among the multitude of the concepts. If we confine ourselves for the moment to the concepts of the activities of the mind, only one of these, he says, namely the first, is 'expression'. Only one, that is, is expressive; as for him the form and the matter of expression are identical, only one for him is 'expressible'. As a matter of fact, he says in so many words that the concept or second activity, 'abstractly considered' – that is, considered as not yet synthesized with intuition – is 'in-expressible'.[1] Either then we know nothing about it; or we know about it, and dualism is restored. 'Inexpressibles' and 'ineffables' are the sign of a dualism, or at least of an uneasy, self-conscious one. And, indeed, dualism reasserts itself in the very sanctum of the Crocean system, in the intuition itself: it is at least doubtful whether this indivisible thing, of wholly monistic intent, is itself known. The question was raised by Aliotta, who is no unsympathetic critic; Croce's answer, for what it is worth, can be found at the end of the *Problemi di Estetica*.[2]

On an all-important point however Croce makes an advance on Spinoza, who quite happily persisted in employing the word 'idea' to denote, now the object, now the subject of knowledge. Croce sees the confusion threatening, and meets it – how? The remedy is drastic but, if it can be swallowed, effective. Whenever he finds himself face to face with an 'ineffable' or 'inexpressible' thing, the recognition of which as known would reveal him a dualist, he recognizes it indeed; talks about it, seeks to persuade us of its existence, of its 'ineffable' nature – but, he says, he does not *know* it. He discusses it – his lips move, his pen flies across the paper: but behind these movements there is no

[1] *Estetica*, p. 48.   [2] *Problemi*, p. 481ff.

knowledge, no thought. What is behind them? As the mind has only two kinds of activities, theoretic and practical; as the mind, when not knowing, can only be acting: behind the movements on these occasions there is, he says, only the practical activity. Though he appears to be doing so, he is not making judgments; though he appears to be using concepts he is not, but using only pseudo-concepts. These are not a form of concept, or concepts in process of elaboration; they are something altogether different. They are not part of knowledge but, in the fullest sense of the word, actions. They are not, for example, concepts 'directed to action but are themselves actions. Their practical character is not extrinsic, but constitutive.'[1] By means of them we are enabled to do a great many things, to 'manipulate and classify', for example, and even the 'products of the theoretic spirit'; but we do so 'without knowing any one of them'.[2] In short, pseudo-concepts and all that is built upon them – the natural sciences, for example, and protreptic such as Croce writes – may be persuasive; but they are persuasive not as is a logical proof – for Croce such proof is at once impossible and unnecessary – but as are, we must suppose, the third-degree methods of the American policeman; or as were those of the Athenian orator, when he paraded beautiful women or weeping children before the court.

It may be objected that, after all, we are dealing only with names: that it does not much matter what Croce says he is doing, if only what he does is useful. The reply is that names are above all the things that Croce takes seriously. He does not rebaptize parts of his doctrine merely that they may appear consistent with the rest – as, in the old story, the priest rebaptized the beef a capon, so that he might eat it in Lent. Croce resembles much more closely a priest who, having performed this ceremony, should on the strength of it refuse to foot the butcher's bill. From the principle that in his criticism and other writing he is engaged, not in thought but in action, he draws the momentous conclusion that he is wholly free from supervision by thought. Thought and action are as distinct as any two concepts, and the one cannot encroach upon the other. Pseudo-concepts are elaborated and are useful, but how or why it is impossible to inquire. 'The formation of pseudo-concepts', he says, 'is outside theory.'[3] 'The empirical or natural sciences', being founded on pseudo-concepts,

---

[1] *Logic*, p. 332.   [2] *Ibid.*, p. 343.   [3] *Ibid.*, p. 248.

'are indestructible by philosophy, as philosophy is indestructible by them'.[1] The upshot of all this is that, having arrogated to himself an omniscience of which, like the divine, evidence neither can nor need be given, Croce claims, when in combat with his critics, a divine invulnerability. It is impossible to attack him anywhere. Or we may say that, in a very useful sense, he has improved on the Hegelian Absolute. In my opening paragraph I compared this to a sea; Mr Schiller, less politely, once called it a rag-bag, into which the philosopher may drop anything furnished by the universe, which embarasses him. In the practical activity Croce has a rag-bag which is always to his hand; into which he can drop anything which impedes him, out of which too he can fish up anything of which he feels the need, without having to explain its nature or provenance; into which, further, it is his duty to dip. For the practical, no less than the logical, is an activity of the mind; to have recourse to it is therefore no sign of weakness, but rather of fullness or completeness of the mind.

Hence the light-heartedness in which Croce bestrews his pages with phrases like: 'for the convenience of exposition let us posit...',[2] 'ordinary discourse demands...'.[3] 'the necessities of life impose'.[4] Hence his repeated warnings that what he says must not be taken too seriously: 'the use of all forms of language for the purpose of dissertation...is accompanied by the danger of misunderstanding'.[5] Hence his drawing of distinctions which later he asserts to be 'philosophically valueless',[6] and still later uses once again. Hence the difficulty of expounding his system: I have had to explain that concepts are distinct and yet are not so; that intuition is and is not the first activity of the mind; that judgments being singular are also universal, that being tautologies they are also informative; that criticism saying nothing yet says all. Hence, finally, Croce's unhesitating use in criticism of all the heresies which, in other critics, he roundly condemns. If he is to be articulate, he is forced to recognize a distinction between poetry, painting and sculpture; between beginnings, middles and ends; between expression and what is expressed;

[1] *Ibid.*, p. 361.
[2] Cf. *Estetica*, p. 14. The matter of expression is 'postulato per comodo di esposizione, ma effettivamente inesistente'. [3] Cf. *Logic*, p. 72.
[4] *Ibid.*, p. 252. Distinctions between philosopher, artist, butcher, baker, jeweller, etc., are 'imposed by the necessities of life, but have no philosophical value at all'. [5] *Ibid.*, pp. 79, 100. [6] Cf. note 4 above.

between form and matter. He even looks upon such recognitions as his duty: 'No philosophy of language or art...can eliminate the classifications of artists and of literary kinds, and those of the arts according to what are called means of expression.'[1] 'Among the difficulties of literary criticism...it is impossible that there should not be introduced, along with concepts that are scientifically (*i.e.* philosophically) exact, others which are not so... These are expedients, no doubt, and somewhat dangerous; but they cannot be dispensed with.'[2]

Again, perhaps the question may be raised whether we are not attaching too much importance to names. Croce's applied criticism may give his theory the lie; but what of that if the application is good? And again I must stress the reply that names are very important for Croce. Having rejected that of 'thought', he feels himself licensed to caprice: to fish up from the rag-bag, as it were, whatever he imagines will be most convincing at the moment. At one time he says[3] that the critic's office is that of the museum-guide, who takes us to the spot from where, he knows from previous experience, the picture can best be seen; at other times he spurns this comparison,[4] and claims as critic to be expressing the ineffable individual,[5] or to be thinking out its internal dialectic.[6] He wavers much more in matters of detail; these are, perhaps, of most importance in aesthetics, and I shall devote my last paragraphs to his treatment of them.

Take his dictum, 'Art is expression.' As I said, this has been most effective in drawing thousands to his banner: it seems so comprehensive, so simple, and to get rid of so many vexing problems. But if examined carefully, it is found to raise as many problems more. If we ask, 'What is expression?' we receive as answer (expression for Croce having no external reference or, as we should say in normal language, 'expressing nothing') that 'expression is art'. The two terms are empty synonyms, and neither can shed light on the other.[7] To procure light, Croce is

---

[1] *Logic*, p. 369.   [2] *Problemi di Estetica*, p. 163; cf. *Nuovi Saggi*, pp. 290–2.
[3] *Nuovi Saggi*, p. 229.   [4] *Ibid.*, pp. 77–8.
[5] Cf. *Estetica*, p. 41.   [6] *Nuovi Saggi*, pp. 181, 261, 272.
[7] 'When language is despoiled of its full capacity for significance, in order to equate it, or level it with expression in general, the manoeuvre is self-destructive. Language has become a gesture or a tune, and to compare a tune or gesture to language is now to compare a thing to itself.' – The late Prof. Bosanquet, in *Croce's Æsthetic* (Proceedings of the British Academy, IX (1919), 261–8).

compelled to define further; and this he can do only arbitrarily.
First he excludes[1] from expression what he calls the physical
consequence of emotion: the yowl of pain, for instance, which a
man gives when someone kicks him in the stomach. Behind this
yowl, he says, there is nothing theoretic, no 'vision': that is, it
is excluded from expression because it 'says nothing', although
we were told that this was a common character of expression.
What would Croce do, it is interesting to ask, if faced by an
exclamation in a language totally unknown to him? Would he
dismiss it as a yowl, or accept it as one of those sighs which, we
saw, contain within themselves 'the joys and the sorrows of
human destiny'? Probably he would dip into the rag-bag, and so
escape our pursuit.[2] But to continue: a second thing from which
Croce distinguishes[3] expression is what he calls the 'externalization' of art. This is the transference of the artist's vision from
the mind to the marble or to the canvas. Expression is over, he
says, before either chisel or brush is raised: it is over once the
'vision' is over, and it is for the practical activity to decide
whether this vision shall be followed or not by externalization.
So far, so good: it would be obviously absurd to maintain that
painters and sculptors do not need to develop a technique.
However, Croce says that expression is not over when a poet
has 'seen' what he wishes to write: in his case it is not over until
the words themselves are formed, and the words themselves
are the expression. It is difficult not to see caprice – or worse –
here. If it is true that, as Croce says, a poet is not sure of what he
wishes to write until he has written it: is not the same true of
painters and sculptors, that not until they have painted or
carved they are sure of their vision? Externalization in the case
of literature is reduced, according to Croce, to proof-reading.
We can therefore chide a painter for being unhandy with the
brush; but a poet – not for solecisms, or redundancy, or
cacophony – only for negligent reading of proofs. Solecisms,
indeed, find Croce in a difficult position. He holds that all
language is expression; or rather, all utterances (apart from
yowls) – for language is an abstraction, and what is real is only

[1] *Estetica*, p. 104.
[2] As a matter of fact, this is what he does. 'Se un'opera letteraria ci stesse innanzi
come un'iscrizione etrusca; se non ne intendessimo la lingua, tutta la condi-
zionalità storica, nella quale fu prodotta; non potrebbe sorgere nessun giudizio
estetico.' – *Problemi*, p. 167.   [3] *Estetica*, ch. 15.

the utterance, wherever and whenever made. Being unique, incommensurable and so on, there is no reason why it should be classed as Italian rather than as Chinese; and there is no possibility of our being taught to make it. How then, asked[1] one of Croce's compatriots, are we to behave in the elementary schools? If a boy uses a dialect word, are we to pass it? Are we never to correct any prose? Croce, recoiling no doubt from an obvious absurdity, said yes; but, he said, no general rules for correction, that is, no rules of grammar or of spelling, can be given; and the case of the dialect word must be decided on its own merits. One can only pity the teachers of Italian, who look up and are not fed. But most of all, I think, Croce reveals his instability on the subject of prose. In the *Aesthetic*[2] all prose, he said, was art – with this proviso, that it should be well written. It would be well written if well thought out: there were no such things as books sound in their doctrines, but badly written. Reflection on the case of philosophers like Schopenhauer and Kant perhaps gave Croce pause; at any rate, in the *New Essays*[3] he is to be found distinguishing between prose as expression and prose as a sign. As an expression, it is art; as a sign also it is art – but in addition a sign of thought. It has therefore two sides or aspects: an aesthetic and a logical, and Schopenhauer may quite easily be a wretched thinker and at the same time a good writer. But in this way is there no prejudice done to the much vaunted indivisibility of a work of art? Perhaps Croce himself thinks so; for, uneasy about his concession to commonsense, he goes on[4] to warn us that we must not be too ready to criticize the prose of philosophers. They should know how to write on their subject, he says; at any rate, they are not to be lectured on the art of writing by men of the world, men, that is, who have not lived through 'their mental drama'. The would-be critic of prose is given about as much help as the Italian schoolmaster.

Transferring his attention from form to matter, Croce is equally capricious. A general rule is enunciated and this time is obviously merely empty words; free play is thus given to Croce's moral and intellectual prejudices. To be articulate a

---

[1] *Problemi*, p. 217.   [2] *Estetica*, p. 28.
[3] *Nuovi Saggi*, p. 140; cf. *Logic*, pp. 111, 148.
[4] *Nuovi Saggi*, p. 150; cf. *Problemi*, p. 127.

critic must, as we know, have recourse to history and biography; he must not however take into consideration either the whole of a historical period or the whole of a biography. These are not the matter of a poem: but only that portion of the background, of the biography, which – *is* its matter. 'Those elements of fact which a critic must keep before him are those, and those only, which in fact enter into the construction of the work of art he is criticizing ...those which are indispensable for the solution of the critical problem he sets himself.'[1] Anyone familiar with the literary essays will know how this works out: Croce condemns as matterless, and therefore mere *simulacra* of art, works which do not believe as he does that a woman's place is in the home; that are tainted with 'morbidity' or 'decadence'; that are not 'spontaneous' or 'lyrical' or 'warm with passion'; or that have pessimism as their theme. This last, he says, is logically impossible; and so reduces Leopardi to the rank of a love poet. But I need not labour this aspect of his work for English readers: they have the essay on Shakespeare, in many ways a commendable production, but surely the most irresponsible that ever issued on such a subject from so renowned a pen.

In this last-mentioned essay, Croce somewhere[2] speaks of Shakespeare and of Vico as two 'mighty spirits...apt frequently to overlook details and to make slight mistakes...convinced "that diligence must lose itself in arguments which have anything of greatness in them, because it is a minute, and because minute, a tardy virtue"'. 'Vico', he says, 'thus openly vindicated the right of rising to the level of heroic fury, which will not brook delay from small and secondary matters.' Of the uneasy fury in Croce's philosophical works there can be no doubt: they avoid details – which cannot *en masse* be dismissed as secondary – they make a parade of unrelieved greatness, they are largely repetitive. At first they are impressive by their number, but then it is seen that there is no reason why they should not be twice as many, or indeed twice as few. As I suggested at the beginning, we may be grateful to them for setting Croce free for labour that few of us would care to undertake, and fewer still would carry through. But I do not think there is any pressing need for us to be grateful to them for any other reason.

[1] *Problemi*, p. 44.   [2] *Ariosto, Shakespeare and Corneille*, p. 290.

ON WILLIAM EMPSON'S
'SEVEN TYPES OF AMBIGUITY'

An ambiguity, according to Mr Empson, is 'any consequence of language which adds some nuance to the direct statement of prose'; and his first type is 'a word or syntax effective in several ways at once'. This covers, he says, 'almost everything of literary importance': that is, it covers the six following types, to which we can proceed. The second type occurs when 'two or more meanings all add to the single meaning of the author'. Examples of this Mr Empson finds in Shakespeare, in the Augustans, and, among the moderns, in Mr Eliot. He analyses very impressively, let us note, a passage from *The Waste Land*, and is able to give convincing demonstration of what he calls 'the interpenetrating and fluid unity' of the *Sonnets*. In the third type, 'two ideas...connected only by both being relevant in the context', are 'given in one word simultaneously'. This is the pun, which Mr Empson traces from Milton, through Marvell, Dryden and the Augustans, down to its inglorious end – but it is not always inglorious, Mr Empson shows – in the early nineteenth century. There is a variant of the third type in which a comparison 'is not merely using one thing to illustrate another', but 'makes them illustrate one another mutually'. Here Mr Empson finds, I think quite rightly, the secret of pastoralism, of the true greatness of Pope, and of Herbert's peculiar use of allegory. In the fourth type, 'two or more statements do not agree, but combine to make clear a more complicated state of mind in the author': here the great figure is Donne. We have the fifth type when 'a simile applies to nothing exactly, but lies halfway between two things', because the author, not holding all his idea in mind at once, is moving from the one thing to the other. This type tends towards decadence, and is to be found chiefly in the later nineteenth-century style: in which the reader must take his cue from conceits that have been subdued, from metaphors that, owing to false delicacy, have been admitted not as active, but as sleeping partners of the poet. 'This delicacy can reasonably be called decadent, because its effects depended on a tradition that its example was destroying.' When a statement 'says nothing, by tautology, by contradiction, or by irrelevant statements', it falls under the sixth type. Examples of this Mr Empson finds chiefly in situations of the drama; but he has a very good example from Herbert, and is again able to refer to the nineteenth century. The seventh and last type occurs when 'two meanings...are the opposite meanings defined by the context, so that the total effect is to show a fundamental division in the author's mind'. The examples are once again from the drama: those from Herbert and from Keats I do not find convincing, and those from Crashaw are hardly of aesthetic importance.

That Mr Empson's first type is redundant, that the rest are not sharply defined but blend one into the other, is perhaps not of too great concern. In these matters we do not expect mathematical precision. But I think we can regret that Mr Empson's method of statement, though it must necessarily be vague, is quite as vague as it is. To take his definition of ambiguity: where are we to find the 'direct statement of prose', acquaintance with which it assumes? And would it usually be said that a nuance added to direct statement (if such there be) produces ambiguity? Towards the end of his book, Mr Empson speaks of the weakness of nineteenth-century verse as due to a 'decay of ambiguity': would it not usually be said that nineteenth-century verse is highly ambiguous? And again, we do not ordinarily accuse a pun, or the better kind of conceit, of being ambiguous because it manages to say two things at once: its essence would seem to be conciseness, rather than ambiguity. Mr Empson has, of course, the right to define his own terms; and a wide definition has this advantage, that it brings within his reference anything he desires to discuss. If, however, this reference is of importance, it should not be made nugatory; there is danger in using words in a sense widely different from the usual; and there is, finally, a great danger in overlooking distinctions that long experience would have us consider well founded. I am not quite sure that Mr Empson has recognized this.

He does not, for example, seem always clear about the nature of his scale, what it is supposed to measure. In one passage, I believe, he suggests it measures something which is peculiar to verse, peculiar even to English verse. Nevertheless, he frequently draws examples from the situations of drama, he frequently refers beyond the ambiguities of drama to those of life itself. That life is two-faced, *gratissima poma cum fugiunt, pueritiae maximus in exitu decor*, is a truism as old, at least, as Seneca: there needs no psychologist back from the unconscious to tell us that. What, however, is its relevance, here, if we are dealing with a phenomenon of English verse? The relevance can be only very slight. And I think it will be found that, the further Mr Empson descends his scale, the further he is lured from poetry. We have already noted that the examples for the last two types are drawn largely from the situations of the drama. Even here Mr Empson finds his scale a help, for he is able to say almost as many good things about drama as he says about poetry. But it is, I think, a pity that scales for two purposes, for the appraisement of drama and for the appraisement of poetry, should be lumped together and presented as one.

For the effect of the dramatic upon the poetic scale is almost sure to be unfortunate. The first business of the student of drama, in so far as he is concerned with ambiguity, is, I imagine, historical: he records that situations are treacherous, that men are consciously or unconsciously hypocritical, to such or such a degree. The student of poetry, on the other hand, has as his first business the passing of a judgment of value. It is not his main, or even his immediate, concern that a word can be interpreted, that a sentence can be construed, in a large number of ways: if he make it his immediate concern, there is a danger that, in the enumeration of these ways, judgments of values will be forgotten. And, unless they are put in at the beginning of an analysis, they do not of their own account emerge at the end. Quite a number of Mr Empson's analyses seem to have no properly critical conclusion: they are interesting only as revelations of the contents of the poet's, or of Mr Empson's, highly ingenious mind. Further, some of Mr Empson's analyses deal, not with words and sentences, but with complexes and conflicts supposed to have raged within the author when he wrote. Here, it seems to me, he has very probably left poetry completely behind. Though the day may come when, with the aid of psychoanalysis, we shall be able to assess the value of poetry scientifically – I do not believe it ever will, nor perhaps does Mr Empson, who shows a robust contempt for the adverb – though this day may come, it surely is not arrived.

There are then a number of irrelevancies in Mr Empson's book; and, as in a measure they derive from, so probably in a measure they increase, his vagueness about the nature and scope of ambiguity. Discovering this everywhere in the drama, in our social experience, in the fabric of our minds, he is led to assume it must be everywhere discoverable in great poetry. I doubt whether the reader who remembers his Sappho, his Dante, or the Matthew poems of Wordsworth is even prepared to be convinced of this: but if he were, he could not be so until Mr Empson had made his position much clearer. Is the ambiguity referred to that of life – is it a bundle of diverse forces, bound together only by their co-existence? Or is it that of a literary device – of the allusion, conceit or pun, in one of their more or less conscious forms? If the first, Mr Empson's thesis is wholly mistaken: for a poem is not a mere fragment of life, it is a fragment that has been detached, considered and judged by a mind. A poem is a noumenon rather than a phenomenon. If the second, then at least we can say that Mr Empson's thesis is exaggerated.

It is, of course, partly true; and the determination of this part will be the determination of the value of the substance of Mr Empson's book. I do not think his attempt to discover the pun on a large scale in English poetry written before the sixteenth century is successful; though it may be that I am less sensitive to Chaucerian English than Mr Empson. No doubt, however, the Elizabethans had their 'fluid unity', which Mr Empson's critical instrument is peculiarly able to detect and to display. His work on Shakespeare, both the *Sonnets* and the plays – though at times he may exaggerate about the *Sonnets* – is quite notable. His history of the pun and of the conceit is valuable, not only for the seventeenth and eighteenth centuries, but also for the nineteenth. His study of nineteenth-century verse in the light of its predecessors breaks new ground, and is at once sympathetic and judicious.

I have confined myself to the substance or skeleton of Mr Empson's book, because it was what seemed to me (Mr Empson rides with all the impedimenta of the White Knight, and in choice of attack shows the ardour of Don Quixote) most likely to escape the consideration of the reader. But it would be unfair to close without a reference to the accidental riches the book contains. Mr Empson's judgments upon a poet or a period; his remarks upon the principles and workings of literary *genres* other than poetry; his discussions, not only of ambiguity, but of rhythm and prolixity in verse – these are unusually brilliant and sound.

JAMES SMITH (1904–1972)

James Smith was born at Batley near Leeds on 17 June 1904. His father was a schoolmaster. Though his great-grand-father had been Parish Clerk of Batley, his descendants were brought up Congregationalists. James attended the Grammar School at Batley, and from there he won an open scholarship to Trinity College, Cambridge, a county-major and a state scholarship, as well as another open scholarship in 1922.

He had rooms in *I* staircase of the Great Court at Trinity. He showed some talent – and made some powerful enemies – in the reviews he composed for *The Granta*; later he became dramatic critic of *The Gownsman*, in which he castigated the more bizarre productions of the Cambridge Festival Theatre. His academic successes were considerable: he received the Pemberton prize and a senior scholarship at Trinity in 1923; he won the Charles Oldham Shakespeare Scholarship and obtained a first class with distinction in the English Tripos in 1924; and the following year another first in the Modern and Medieval Languages Tripos (French and German) and a Goldsmiths' award which enabled him to engage in postgraduate research. He then began to investigate the borders between literary criticism and philosophy, but he failed in his efforts to win a research fellowship at Trinity. This was the greatest disappointment of his life.

He was awarded the Jane Eliza Procter visiting fellowship to Princeton University (New Jersey) in 1928; it was renewed for the year 1929–30. During the summer vacation of 1929 he travelled through the American West and South. He returned to England in the summer of 1930, when he found himself without a job and short of money. He taught first at what is now the Percival Whitley College of Further Education at Halifax. He then found a more satisfying post teaching German, French and Spanish at the King Edward VII School at Sheffield; he was appointed there from mid-September 1931, and he left in July 1933. In the following October he told me that he was then working in London at the Board of Education. On 1 January

1934 he became one of His Majesty's Inspectors of Schools. In this capacity he visited Brazil, Argentina and Chile; he already knew Spanish well and had spent some weeks with me in Burgos and Madrid in the autumn of 1931. Private reasons and bad health compelled him to resign from the inspectorate in the autumn of 1937.

In the summer of 1931 his review of William Empson's *Seven Types of Ambiguity* had appeared in *The Criterion*. In the following year he met Dr F. R. Leavis, and he then began to contribute with some regularity to *Scrutiny*. Before the end of 1937 the following studies had appeared in that journal: 'Croce' (1933); 'On metaphysical poetry' (1933); 'Alfred North Whitehead' (1934); 'George Chapman' (1935). Not surprisingly he decided to return to Cambridge, where – after some search – he found a house in which he and his father's sister, Miss Hannah Smith, settled in spring 1938. The house was opposite that in which Dr and Mrs Leavis lived, and his friendship with them was strengthened thereby. When his father retired some time later his parents shared the house with James and his aunt.

James Smith rapidly succeeded in finding work as an examiner for the Cambridge Local Examinations Syndicate (for his linguistic ability was great) and some supervision for the English Tripos. He also gave evening classes in neighbouring villages. I was able to introduce him to some Spaniards who had literary interests and to Mr (later Professor) Alexander A. Parker, then a research fellow at Gonville and Caius College, who, like myself, was working on Calderón. For many years Smith had found congenial the system of St Thomas Aquinas, and it had already, perhaps, exercised some influence on his thought and expression. The sudden death of a younger acquaintance, coupled with an analysis (which he saw in typescript) by Mr Parker of Calderón's sacramental allegory of Belshazzar's feast (*La cena de Baltasar*), precipitated a spiritual crisis, which was resolved by his conversion to Roman Catholicism in 1938–9. During the years in Cambridge the following articles by him appeared in *Scrutiny*: 'Wordsworth – a preliminary survey', 'Baudelaire', 'Mr Chase on words', 'Mallarmé – Life and art' in 1938; 'Marlowe's *Dr Faustus*', 'The tragedy of blood' in 1939; '*As you like it*' in 1940.

James Smith (1904–1972)

The War took him to Venezuela. Under the auspices of the British Council he was appointed Lecturer in English at the Instituto Pedagógico at Caracas in September 1940; in the October of the following year he became Director of the British–Venezuelan Cultural Centre in that capital. He did much good work there to help Venezuelan scholars to investigate their own past as well as to provide them with lectures and other help with different aspects of our own civilization. There he published in Spanish some articles in a review issued by the Cultural Centre; unfortunately I cannot give their titles. His main object was triumphantly attained, but he was impatient with some officials whose interference with his duties he resented. The result was that his very success told against him after his return to Cambridge on 1 January 1946. He resigned from Council service in August of that year.

For some months after his return he carried on useless negotiations with the British Council. The proposed book on Shakespeare's comedies, however, seemed gradually to be taking shape. At William Empson's request I sent him the draft preface to the second edition of *Seven Types of Ambiguity*, in which the author replied to some of the criticisms made in the review in *The Criterion* in 1931; Smith read, but did not comment, on it. On 6 April he told me that his essay on *Much ado about nothing* was to appear in the next number of *Scrutiny* (i.e. of spring 1946); in it too appeared a review of Mr Parker's book, *The allegorical theatre of Calderón*. During this time he was again examining and supervising, chiefly, I think, for Downing and for Christ's Colleges.

Various possibilities seemed open after he resigned from the Council: a research-assistantship at the Foreign Office (which came to nothing), a lectureship at Leeds, and the Chair of English at the (then) Roman Catholic University of Fribourg, Switzerland. The interview at Leeds was disastrous, but he heard that he had been unofficially appointed to Fribourg in May 1947. He left for that country on 29 September and eventually obtained accommodation in the religious house called Salesianum, where he resided until February 1963, when he moved into a flat in the Grand' Rue. He sometimes returned to Cambridge for Christmas and very often during the summer vacations.

Fribourg, though he liked the city, brought him little happiness. He found himself overworked and had difficulty, at first, in lecturing. Cambridge supervisions had of course kept him in close touch with large ranges of English authors, but he was not at first prepared to lecture on set courses several times a week. He found that he was alone responsible for all the literary teaching in an under-staffed department. He tackled these problems with extreme conscientiousness but at an enormous cost of time and effort. He wrote out in long-hand all his lectures; he had also to supervise numerous doctoral dissertations. Administration and meetings caused him exhaustion and – of course – loss of time. Before he went to Switzerland he had hoped that he would have leisure to write; he was disappointed. His only free time came during his vacation stays in Cambridge, and even then he often found much of it taken up in reading for new courses of lectures. More than one of his pupils told me afterwards how good his lectures and classes were, how well he had directed their particular studies. We, however, can only regret that he took his duties so seriously and that he was unable to publish more than an occasional review during those years.

He returned to England in the summer of 1968 and became very seriously ill. He was taken to Addenbrookes Hospital in October and remained there until after Christmas. There he had time for reflection. The Vatican Council and the reforms of John XXIII made him uncomfortable from the first; the Church had, he thought, taken a wrong turning. ('I joined the Church of Pius IX', he once said to me.) Other things perhaps added to his disillusion, but the main arguments he used were based on what he thought of as innovations. What he had been told when he was under instruction from a learned Dominican was now considered false; if the Church were now untrue to herself, she could never have been true. He stopped going to Mass and left instructions with his executor that no religious rites should be held at his funeral. He parted with some books after he left Fribourg; among them was the edition of the *Works* of Sir Thomas More of 1557 which before he had greatly prized.

He returned to Fribourg after Easter 1969 and retired at the end of that term. His cousin, Mrs Miriam Vary Haigh went out to Switzerland and drove him back in her car. Then he went back to live with his aunt and his mother in Chesterton Road, Cambridge. (His father had died some years earlier, and the family had left the larger house for a smaller one.) The disposal of books brought back from Fribourg took up time and energy. Then, despite illness and the infirmities of his old relatives he began to read again and to write. Through the good offices of Dr Leavis he received an invitation to lecture at Bristol; the result was the essay 'Chaucer, Boethius and recent trends in criticism', printed in *Essays in Criticism*, xxii (1972), 4–32. Later he received another invitation from the English departments of the University of Wales – and this lecture, 'Notes on the criticism of T. S. Eliot' also appeared, though posthumously, in the same journal, xxii (1972), 333–61. His last winter was much saddened by the death of his aunt on 21 November 1971, followed by that of his mother in the following January. He stayed on in the old house, and, after the legal consequences of the bereavements had been settled, began to work again. He then decided to submit his publications to the Cambridge University Press.

He began to plan two books: one devoted exclusively to his interpretations of Shakespeare's comedies, the other a series of essays designed to establish an English literary tradition going back to *Beowulf*. He intended to start with T. S. Eliot and to work back through Henry James, Tennyson, Wordsworth, the metaphysicals, Chaucer, *Sir Gawain* and finally *Beowulf*. (The study of Beowulf, as yet unpublished, exists; it dates from about 1957, for in the summer of that year he showed a draft of it to Professor Bruce Dickins.) The volume we now publish disregards the second project, except for the republication of the articles from *Scrutiny* on the metaphysicals and on Wordsworth. He worked hard on Shakespeare's comedies during the few months left to him. He was found dead on the morning of 1 August 1972. Copies of the Arden editions of *Measure for measure* and of *All's well that ends well* lay open on his table.

It might be supposed that in so varied a life as James Smith's the character of his writings would have changed sharply in accordance with the changes in his situation or, still more, of his religious beliefs. There were a few changes, chiefly in his estimations of some authors, but violent contrasts in attitude were remarkably absent. There is throughout his work an

underlying consistency in approach, style and thought, whether
he was writing a book-review or gradually polishing a long-
meditated essay. The Aristotelian (even Thomist) temper of
his mind remained consistent from the time he returned from
the United States in 1930 until his death in 1972: his sensitivity
to the resources of the English language was constant; his acute
literary judgment, undiminished – whether he was writing about
Wordsworth, *The Merchant of Venice* or *Beowulf*. Perhaps the
isolation he felt at Fribourg and the suppressed protests that
he could not make during those years may account for some
inequalities in the recent Chaucer lecture and for the polemical
tone of the 'Notes on the criticism of T. S. Eliot.'

The works in this volume are of two kinds: some published in
the 1930s and 1940s in *The Criterion* and in *Scrutiny*; others
edited by me since his death from a profusion of typescripts and
manuscripts. After the critique of William Empson's *Seven
Types* in *The Criterion* the articles selected from *Scrutiny* came
out in the following order: 'Croce', 'On metaphysical poetry',
'Wordsworth: a preliminary survey', 'Baudelaire', '*As you
like it*', '*Much ado about nothing.*' And I think that the order of
publication corresponds with the order of composition. How
much preparation these essays received is hard to determine.
That on the metaphysical poets was probably the result of years
of meditation; from his letters to me I can say with certainty that
he began to work on Wordsworth in October 1935 and was still
discussing some of the poems with me in March 1938. The
hitherto unedited works on Shakespeare's comedies were
composed, emended and revised, some of them at least, over a
very long period.

His plan for the Shakespeare book was formed before the War.
The essay on *As you like it* was printed in 1940. On 17 March
1946 he referred to his work on *As you like it* (presumably the
finished essay), *Much ado about nothing* (completed), *The Merry
Wives of Windsor* (which I never heard him refer to afterwards –
presumably he disliked it and destroyed it), *The Merchant of
Venice* and an almost completed essay on *Twelfth Night*. Three
weeks later he wrote to tell me that he had completed his study
of *The Merchant of Venice*, that that on *Much ado* had been
accepted by *Scrutiny* and that that on *All's well* was now
'cleared up'. He had, however, made little progress with

Twelfth Night. Later on he sent me the essay on *All's well that ends well,* and – as I was then teaching at King's College, London – I showed it to John Crow and to C. L. Wrenn, both of whom admired its quality but thought it too long to appear in a journal. Crow later suggested that he might edit this play in the New Arden series, but the project came to nothing. In May 1947 some undergraduates at Cambridge asked him for a pre-examination lecture on one of the Shakespeare prescribed texts; 'I knocked together a paper on *The Winter's Tale* which seems to have been extraordinarily well received', he wrote to me afterwards. In the same letter he told me of the bad interview at Leeds, so the success of the lecture probably came at a good time. In the late spring of 1947, then, he had completed and published essays on *As you like it* and on *Much ado*; there were drafts of essays on *Twelfth Night* and *The Merry Wives* (both of them now lost), *The Merchant of Venice, All's well* and *The Winter's Tale.* He did not at that time mention either *Measure for measure* or *The Tempest.* He read a paper on *The Merchant* at a congress that I have been unable to identify, sometime in the late 1950s: it remained unpublished.

In June 1954 he asked me about some Spanish attitudes towards the American Indians, which, he thought, might be relevant to *The Tempest.* A reply to my answer, though too long to quote here, shows that he was thinking along the lines of the long chapter printed in this book. When he was next in England I showed him the *Noches de invierno* of Antonio de Eslava in a rare early edition in the Emmanuel College library, and a year or two later I acquired a reprint of it, which I lent to him. Readers of Smith's essay on *The Tempest* will see that he said in it that the Eslava novel had not been reprinted and he relied instead on the full summary given by Marcelino Menéndez y Pelayo in the second volume of the *Orígenes de la Novela* (Madrid, 1907), pp. cxxiff; we can therefore assume that he did not revise this long essay after about 1956 or 1957.

The whole essay on *The Winter's Tale* was revised carefully by him early in 1972. The text printed here is the revised text; earlier versions have not been taken into account. Though he left notes on *Measure for measure,* which dealt with other scenes in the play, only the pages he wrote in June–July 1972 are included here; the last acts of the play were much in his mind at this time, and such earlier views as he once held he had then discarded. I read the pages of this fragment in July about three weeks before he died.

In editing the unpublished essays I found that I had often to collate differently emended carbon-copies of the same essay. I tried to find what seemed to be the most recent version (sometimes the most corrected one) to go to press; the corrections nearly always made for clarity and elegance. In some places the handwriting was indecipherable or doubtful; in such cases I have put a conjecture in square brackets. The most important of the manuscript corrections are the first dozen or so pages of the chapter on *All's well*, rewritten in long-hand during the last weeks of his life, and the long note in the essay on *The Tempest*.

Here, then, are the approximate dates of the Shakespeare chapters:

As you like it: published in Scrutiny, 1940. Reprinted.

Much ado about nothing: published in *Scrutiny*, 1946. Reprinted.

The Merry Wives of Windsor and *Twelfth Night*: lost.

The Merchant of Venice: begun in 1946–7. Formed the basis of a contribution to a congress, probably in the late 1950s. Two different versions of the essay exist in typescript; the one printed here appears to be the later one.

All's well that ends well: begun in 1946 or perhaps earlier; the essay completed in that year. The first section of the published chapter was probably written in July 1972. The rest is the early text, with perhaps a very few later revisions.

The Winter's Tale: drafted in May 1947, completely revised in the spring of 1972.

Measure for measure: an uncompleted fragment written in June–July 1972.

The Tempest: the complete text was probably written by 1954. Apparently it was not revised afterwards.

How much he would have revised these chapters must remain conjectural. There might have been substantial alterations in order and in phrasing; but when early in 1972 he dug out the early drafts, he was not disappointed in them. I can think of two passages where his change of religious views might have made him alter what is printed here: in *All's well* he might possibly have softened the analogy he made between Bertram's humiliation and the confessional and removed the quotation from Joyce; in the essay on *The Tempest* the references to the doctors of Salamanca and to the Inquisition would, I hope, have been modified. In any case readers will find in the unrevised portions of these essays the workings of an acute, highly sensitive, critical mind and of a master of English prose.

I have already alluded to the method of editing I have used with the hitherto unpublished material. In all the essays I have tried to verify the quotations from the authors dealt with, by reference to reliable editions that James Smith probably, or could have, used. In one or two cases I have not been successful. Readers may notice that in the two already published essays he quoted from an old-spelling edition (but with the modern use of 'u' and 'v') whereas in the unpublished ones he probably used the Arden or New Cambridge editions. I have allowed this anomaly to remain.

I am grateful to the following persons who gave me facts and dates about James Smith's life: his first cousin Mr Leslie A. Haigh and Mr Haigh's daughter-in-law Mrs Miriam Vary Haigh; Mr J. B. Fallows, the Headmaster of the Grammar School at Batley; Mr A. Jackson, Deputy Headmaster of King Edward VII's School, Sheffield; Mr J. H. Coe of the Establishments Personnel Division of the Department of Education and Science; Miss G. Andrews of the Personnel Department of the Overseas Section for the British Council. Professor T. A. Birrell of the University of Nijmegen, Professor Kenneth Muir, F.B.A. of the University of Liverpool and Mr P. G. Thomas of the Percival Whitley College at Halifax courteously replied to questions which they were unable to answer. I must also thank Dr P. Rickard of Emmanuel College for his help with the proofs of chapter 10.

EDWARD M. WILSON